ROBERT BRIEN

THY KINGDOM COME

A systematic study into God's revelation of His purposes for mankind

ROBERT BRIEN

THY KINGDOM COME

A systematic study into God's revelation of His purposes for mankind

MEREO
Cirencester

Dedicated to all those who 'look for new Heavens and a new Earth where righteousness dwells'.

2 Peter 3:13

CONTENTS

	Preface: a kaleidoscope of images	P. I
	Introductions	P. XI
■	A Disconnected World	P.1
■	Why was the Revelation Written?	P.11
■	Tis Jesus the First and the Last	P.28
■	The Testimony of Jesus is the Spirit of Prophecy	P.38

Section One
	God is Working His Purpose Out	P.49
	Preface to Section One	P.50
■	The Right Character	P.56
■	The Right Pedigree	P.65
■	A Calling to Account	P.74
■	A Deafening Silence	P.91
■	A Spectacular Phenomenon	P.101
■	The Imminent Marriage	P.114
■	The Perfect Marriage	P.123

Section Two
	The Significant Issues and Affairs	P.138
	Preface to Section Two	P.139
■	The Age of Duplicity and Doubt	P.143
■	The Four Living Creatures within the Throne	P.150
■	The Supremacy of the Lamb	P.162
■	A Fanfare of Trumpets	P.177
■	The Majesty of God and His Mission	P.193
■	The Sinister Beast	P.202
■	'666'	P.215
■	The Return of the King	P.228

Section Three

The Spectacular Realisation of God's Purposes	P.237
Preface to Section Three	P.238

- The End of an Era — P.243
- Where Are We all Going? — P.257
- The Irresistible Presence — P.273
- Broken Promises — P.289
- Mankind's Last Chance — P.296
- The Die is Cast — P.318

Section Four

The consummation of all history	P.331
Preface to Section Four	P.332

- Parables of the Kingdom — P.336
- The Kingdom of God within Us — P.355
- The heavenly Life within Us — P.366
- Christ in Us the Hope of Glory — P.379
- If anyone is in Christ He is a new Creation — P.387
- Spiritual Maturity — P.397
- The Kingdom of our Lord — P.412
- Spiritual Adultery — P.422
- Seven Hills and Seven Kingdoms — P.438
- Seven Hills: A Spiritual Allegory — P.451
- The New Heaven and Earth — P.464
- The Foundations of the Holy City — P.482
- Paradise Restored — P.508

Postscript: the end of the visual imagery

Epilogue

- 1. The Day of the Lord   P.526
- 2. The Purpose of History   P.541
- 3. Moral Responsibility   P.554

Appendices

- An Outline of the Consecutive and Recurrent Themes   P.558
- How the two Sequences of Themes Intersect   P.560
- A Summary of the Gospel Discourse and the Four Main Sections of the Revelation   P.561
- Symbolic Meanings   P.562
- The Seven Letters to the Churches   P.568
- The Seals Trumpets and Bowls compared   P.569
- A Summary of the Historical Significance of the Seven Heads of the 'Beast' to Israel   P.570
- A General Index of Cross References   P.571
- A General Index of Ancillary Themes   P.587

Credits   P.593

PREFACE

A kaleidoscope of images

The Thematic Structure of This Study

One thing is very apparent if we read through the Book of the Revelation: that it is about a series of visions or scenes, some set in Heaven, some on Earth. Some it would seem are historical while others are contemporary or refer to a future time; some are naturalistic, some seem quite surrealistic. Many are clearly written in picturesque language while others have a simple, direct message. The purpose of this study is to look at how these different scenes or visions relate to each other and to see the themes that appear to run through the whole Book.

Most of the book of Revelation cannot be seen to happen consecutively in time as it is multi layered, about eternal issues, spiritual, moral and judicial mostly. However, those scenes in this book that relate to God's dealing directly with mankind on Earth, such as the seals, trumpets and bowls of wrath, probably do happen successively as mankind is a temporal creature. There is then a partly temporal basis for this book though for the most part it is a sequence of overlapping themes rather than events in time.

Four of these themes are consecutive through the Book, covering several chapters at a time, each one developing towards the climax of the effect on Earth of the coming of Christ. Another theme that runs parallel to these can also be traced through our Lord's own earthly account of how His second coming will bring about the fulfilment of the Kingdom of God on Earth, recorded for us in three of the four gospels. These themes or settings are existential in quality and can be broadly described as:

- God's purposes for mankind, revealed in and through the person of Jesus Christ.

- The character of the settings, or arenas, of their implementation.

- The removal of everything of the old natural order that prevents the reign of Christ at present.

- The Kingdom of God on Earth; the new state of Divine order.

There are also five sub-themes however that are recurrent, that is repeated, ideas that appear sequentially through each of those gospel accounts, particularly Matthew's, and also through each of the four consecutive themes or 'theses' of the Revelation. Each of the recurrent sub themes running through each of the sequential passages are spiritual in nature or consequence, relating broadly to a particular aspect of God's purposes for mankind, and how He is revealed and made real to us in salvation. They show how these themes all work towards a climax in a particular aspect of the revelation of Christ. Broadly these themes or settings define five aspects of each theme or stage of the bringing in of God's kingdom in the Revelation of Jesus Christ.

- The temporal or physical perspective.
- The heavenly or spiritual perspective.
- The moral perspective or the standard of perfection that God requires.
- The judicial perspective manifesting all that is evil and separating us from God, yet also the contrasting perspective of graciousness or the mercy of God, calling for repentance while offering forgiveness and protection.
- 'The New Divine World Order'; the final realisation of God's purposes.

This study seeks to concentrate on the deeper spiritual meaning of each of these scenes or settings as described recurrently in the gospels and the Book of the Revelation and show how they complement each other. The arrangement of this study will follow those spiritual themes as they would seem to be presented in the scripture. These spiritual themes as delineated are clearly expressed throughout scripture and are not just a fanciful reinterpretation of particular scriptures to fit modern viewpoints or popular ideas from any other places or era.

Think of the layout of this study as a chess board with columns of squares running vertically down and rows of squares across. The narrative of the Revelation runs down the first column of the chess board, each square representing a new vision or group of visions. The last square in each column is one aspect of the complete revealing of Jesus Christ, and all the other squares in that column lead up to that conclusion. The narrative then continues in the next column, concluding with another aspect of the coming of Christ. This continues down four columns in all, there being five 'squares' in each column. Each column has a particular theme building up to a conclusion. How this works in practice you can see from appendix 2 to see which chapters and parts of this study come in each 'square'. The Book of the Revelation then is different consecutive accounts of the coming of Christ.

Each section of this study however is represented by a row horizontally across the chess board, each part or sequence of parts is represented by each square in that row with each row also having a particular theme to it. However the squares in each 'row' will be a sequence of themes that are the same in each row; these are the themes of the columns referred to above, suggesting there is a matrix of themes running through the Revelation both sequentially and recurrently.

The Texts or Passages

In our Lord's discourse, as recorded in Matthew Gospel chapter 21:28 – 25:46, our Lord adds considerably to the subject of the 'Day of the Lord' as it is referred to in the Old

Testament by describing what God has purposed for mankind, particularly His chosen people Israel, and how He will bring about the setting up of His Kingdom on Earth, despite the fact that His plans see no outward sign of fulfilment at the present.

Jesus said to His disciples in John 15:15:

> A servant does not know what his master is doing,
> But I have called you friends,
> For all things that I have heard from My Father
> I have made known to you.

This is in fact also why the Book of the Revelation was written, to show us how God's Will and character will be fully implemented through the revealing of Himself in Jesus Christ. There are four main aspects of God that are revealed sequentially in this way, each following a similar recurrent pattern; see items 2-5 in the table below. These four great attributes of God that are revealed to all mankind can be traced through the Book, showing in relevant detail how each is revealed.

The Revelation does not just reveal to us what events on Earth will surround the coming of Christ to establish His Kingdom throughout the world, however, as does our Lord's Olivet discourse, auspicious as they will be; rather this great vision that was given to St. John reveals to us just who God is in all His majesty and how He is both working to bring about a tremendous blessing for the whole of His creation and also the nature of that blessing.

Each of the consecutive themes then are five great theses that can be summarised as follows:

1. Matthew Chapter 21:28 Chapter 25	A Temporal Perspective: Our Lord's parables in Matthew's Gospel chapters 21 - 23 and the Olivet Discourse as recorded in chapter 24 and 25; this is God's plan for mankind, the events on Earth that will indicate salient features and signs and how this will be implemented practically.
	The Revelation however is about altogether more spiritual issues.
2. Chapters 1-7	A heavenly Perspective: A spiritual viewpoint displaying how the Mercy of God is revealed in salvation
3. Chapters 8-11	A Moral Perspective: Declaring the righteousness of God on a global stage and man's responsibility to God
4. Chapters 12-18	The graciousness of God in mercy but also the justice of God is realized in the elimination of evil from the world
5. Chapters 19-22	The Establishment of the Divine Order: When the glory and love of God are fully manifested

Through each of these four sections we are presented with a particular aspect of the Almighty through the revelation of Christ to the world, a facet that we can comprehend and enter into in a full understanding of and extending to a personal and special relationship with Him.

The Spiritual Themes Running Through Each Passage

As already intimated, however, there is a sequence of sub themes or a pattern that emerges through each of these topics that is common to each; each of the first four theses described above building to a climax in the return of Christ. The final thesis in Revelation chapters 19-22 climaxes with an exposition of what the new Heaven and Earth will be like after all God's purposes in this world have been fulfilled. This last episode starts with the culmination of what God is doing at this present time, through the coming of Christ as King over all the Earth, and then the judgements and eventually the New Heavens and Earth where only peace and righteousness are present; where everything and everyone that offends those principles is excluded.

Each of these five precipitous scenarios themselves then have an order of development, a pattern that can be traced through each of the four recurrent themes referred to above. They are in fact an outline, not just of what we can know subjectively yet experientially about God, but rather the way that God reveals and will reveal Himself to us in each of these five facets. Thus the whole Book of the Revelation is relevant to each one of us. Each and every part identifies with an area of our lives that is allied to our salvation and relationship with our Lord. Each section is a stage in our spiritual progress in that relationship.

The layout of this study then follows these four recurrent spiritual themes that run through each thesis grouped together in sections 1 to 4. This analysis may seem complicated and difficult to grasp, but a study of the 'The Recurrent and Consecutive Themes' in the appendix will illustrate the layout.

Introductions	These are general introductions to different aspects of the whole study.
Section 1	God's intentions manifested: His method in establishing His purposes for all creation.
Section 2	The significant issues and affairs: that give warning of the imminent termination of all that prevents the attaining of these objectives.
Section 3	Their spectacular realisation: God's course of action in establishing His purposes.
Section 4	The consummation of history: the fulfilment of God's Plans in Salvation.

Looking at it this way gives the Book of the Revelation a beautiful symmetry, as each section of this study is in a sense complete in itself, just as the five theses or passages of scripture referred to above are complementary to each other.

The Gospels answer the disciples' questions as to when Christ would return (as the master of His vineyard) and what would be the sign of the end of the age; two very practical questions that receive a direct and positive reply from our Lord. The corresponding sections of The Revelation then develop what our Lord taught in His Olivet discourse, to acquaint us with a full understanding of God as He is revealed in Jesus Christ.

There are many bible references indicated throughout the book. They either illustrate the text, giving biblical evidence for statements, or are there merely to illustrate the symbolic use of word meanings within the whole of scripture, which are regarded to be wholly consistent throughout all of it, if properly understood.

There are also many references to the 'Church' in this study as there are many references to it in these scriptures. The word itself, however, in scripture can mean different things. It can mean a local community of Christians, as it can today. In scripture, however, it more often has a much deeper meaning, that of the body of Christ, His 'Bride', His 'Brethren' or His followers. All these ideas do not give it an exclusive identity, however, but a particular character, a deeply spiritual character as those that seek to do the will of God as revealed by Him, those that love honour and serve Him. As we will see in this study, Christ taught that it was not those that belonged to some exclusive group that would inherit the Kingdom of God but those that showed true compassion and mercy to 'his brethren'. The 'Church' is not an exclusive group but an inclusive group.

INTRODUCTIONS

'Blessed is he who reads
And those that hear the words of this prophecy
And keep those things that are written in it.'

This book is a reflective study into the Revelation of Jesus Christ and associated scriptures. To read the Revelation, understand and assimilate it is to come to a greater knowledge of Him and to walk more closely with Him.

INTRODUCTION ONE

A Disconnected World

The Need for a New World Order

Mankind is fundamentally self-centred. We are all driven by a basic initiative to fulfil vital survival needs, for security, food, water, sex and ambition to exploit, to assert ourselves and our agendas and to dominate our environment to our own advantage, both physically and socially. These different characteristics may vary in intensity between individuals, for different psychological reasons, though fundamentally in this respect we are basically no different from the rest of creation. This is the natural spirit that is common to us all, an inherent survival necessity, to state the matter from a scientific perspective.

We are instinctively driven then towards self-preservation, which informs all our thinking and feelings and attitudes, and is hard wired into our DNA. Our reputation, rights, security and comfort for example are all things that we spontaneously protect; we can moderate, even suppress our response when these things are threatened, but we cannot be free of them or even think entirely independently of them.

However, we may also aspire to an idealistic world of universal peace, comfort, harmony and freedom; a state that is good for ourselves but also good for all, though it is an ideal to which we can aspire but seem never able to deliver. This aspiration itself is what we may desire primarily for our own contentment and comfort, but the aspiration of mankind to control and exploit the world and people around directly conflict with this, and this creates disappointment and inconvenience for others.

Mankind may be fundamentally self-serving, but we are also social creatures. From a Neo-Darwinian perspective this may also be necessary for our survival and security, but it does not at heart change the way we are. Cooperation is essential for our survival at least and certainly for our contentment, though inevitably this often conflicts with the first premise, our most basic instinct for self-survival. Cooperation ultimately works to our individual advantage, though that is not to deny that our inclination to collaborate and connect with others is also innate. Hence are present within us conflicting emotions, the desire to unite and live in peace and the more dominant selfish emotions that drive our thinking and outlook on life to survive and dominate. Thus, despite millennia of civilisation, experimenting, developing and honing the way we interact, this has failed to deliver the peace and happiness that we desire, individually and corporately. We are however intelligent creatures, which potentially enables us to resolve the dilemma.

Mankind, as intelligent, rational beings, can see a fundamental principle of cause and effect operating throughout the whole world, indeed the universe. It therefore becomes intuitive to assume that every effect has a cause, although we may not always be able to sense that cause directly, but only infer it from the effect.

We are also a self-conscious species, one that appreciates that as we ourselves can be the cause, we can have an effect on our environment and that this has consequences for other people and other creatures. Coupled therefore with our inclination to collaborate, there comes a sense of personal and social conscience, of altruistic inclinations and empathetic consideration. Still this has not been sufficient to provide a single society that is entirely fair, ordered and content. The best that we can manage is a precarious compromise that is tolerated by the majority of individuals and imposed to varying degrees upon the rest.

From a humanistic perspective the world in ancient times was very dangerous and unpredictable and so, because mankind appreciated the principle of cause and effect, it was logical for them to infer that unseen forces acted on their lives and for them to fear those assumed forces or agents. Likewise the actions of those around them were a potential threat to their wellbeing and so the concept of moral principles became imperative, if mankind was to cooperate in living and working together for the good of all. Thus a common belief system of mutual behaviour was intrinsic to civilisation and quickly learned, if not intuitive.

Common interests then emerged, the mutual fulfilment of basic needs and desires, not the least of these being survival and protection from dangers seen and from unseen agents and forces in the world, actual or otherwise.

Thus we can see the rise of simple superstition within groups of individuals and how it became a cohesive influence within and in defining society; then as these were discussed and speculated upon more complex folklore and belief systems developed. Thus religion is intuitive for us all, with an instinctive belief in forces or unseen beings that influence our lives, together with the adopted practice, personal and collective, that emanates from that belief.

This does not though entirely account for the intuitive regard that mankind has shown for the sacred since antiquity. Placation of inferred supernatural beings, supplication to and worship of them may be a spontaneous response to a fear or awe of the unknown, just as we may have such a fear of sensed physical threats and dangers, but it does not fully explain that non-rational appreciation of the Divine, of higher morality and of a deeper meaning to life that we have as expressed eloquently and symbolically in art, philosophy and social ritual. This instinctive understanding has been seen in the most primitive tribes and expressed in mythological belief systems and superstitious practice throughout millennia. It is something that is inherent in the social identity of tribes, largely forming the adhesion of that society to form a common outlook, identity and understanding of the world. Primarily though, it is an inner conviction that is very individual and something that is incompatible with a purely materialistic explanation for the physical world that we see around us.

Such convictions then produced another, more powerful inclination for individuals to combine to integrate and cooperate, though this gave each group an exclusive identity and thereby created divisions and distinctions between different social groups. However, such powerful emotions fostered and cherished by the members of each group were insufficient to even control the tendency towards the assertion of individual self-interest, let alone lay it to rest.

This was typically seen in the ancient Roman Empire. Life in ancient Rome was controlled by the belief in their gods. Nothing of any consequence was done without consulting them first, and to disown them was to invite their anger and retribution and the suspicion of the other citizens.

The religion of ancient Rome was therefore closely fused with its political power, the one giving meaning to the other for the citizens. This autocratic political and religious power was concentrated in the high priest of Rome, the 'Pontifex Maximus', particularly when that position was to become adopted by the Emperor himself under Augustus, 53 BC - 14 AD

It was in this environment that Christianity first came into being and flourished, a short while after Christ died, rose again and ascended into Heaven. At first this new sect was persecuted by the Jews, who hated the Christians as much as they had Christ Himself. Later it was to suffer severe persecution by the Romans, who were becoming fearful of this new sect that was pervading the whole of the Roman Empire. By the beginning of the fourth century though, Christianity began to be adopted as the official religion of the Roman Empire, giving Christianity political and religious power throughout the Empire, a supremacy that it was largely to retain in Europe even after the demise of Rome as an empire, in the west and eventually in the east. Thus Christianity changed from a simple religion based on personal faith in a benevolent God to one that defined and controlled the social and national lives of its citizens, exerting considerable political influence.

Before Christianity emerged however, before even the mighty Roman Empire gained the ascendancy in the civilised world, there was another force that was beginning to gain influence amongst the intellectuals of the dominant Greek Empire and influence it politically. This was not a military force or religious persuasion but rational argument; mathematics, logic and scientific analysis.

Politically this had begun with Plato in about the beginning of the 4th century BC with his ideas of a republic with philosopher rulers and compliant citizens. After Plato, Aristotle published his ideas as regards logic and science. Both these thinkers had an influence on later thinkers, particularly on a fourth century Christian, Bishop Augustine of Hippo, later known as Saint Augustine. It was about this time that Christianity had become acceptable in the Roman Empire and started its process of becoming the official state religion.

Philosophy then became in the west, largely synonymous with Christian theology, a school of thought known as scholasticism; this persisted throughout the dark ages until the time of the Protestant Reformation in Europe in the 16th century.

Philosophy though, as a distinct intellectual discipline, did not emerge again to flourish independently until the Renaissance with the advent of Descartes and his sceptical thinking. His technique was to distinguish between what we can know for certain and what we believe without sound intelligent foundation.

Thus was born modern secular thought which has directed the development of science and philosophy ever since. Scepticism, materialism and liberalism have continued to fashion all reformed intellectual and popular thought to this day. We have now arrived, in the West, at post-modernism where all is relative to context, whether it is personal and social moral responsibility or our concept of truth and religion. It is the new 'religion' that replaces speculation and folklore with science and scientific theory to explain the operation of the world we live in. Humanism replaces Divine accountability; personal gain and satisfaction replace dependence on and the worship of a Divine being or beings for our continued wellbeing. Mankind puts himself in control of his own destiny and denies any responsibility to a higher order. Thus self-consideration is promoted to the detriment of more benevolent ideals.

Where then has this Relativism led to? Has it made us more secure, content and confident? Has increased knowledge and the technology that has flowed from it benefited mankind? To be sure it has benefited those that have been the recipients of its produce but what of our quality of life? We are also the more restless, fearful and inward-looking than we have ever been. The world as a whole has become a more dangerous and polluted place. 'Relativism' has merely lead to mediocrity and exacerbation of the status quo, subjectively and socially at heart we remain entirely motivated by self-interest. Progress has not led us to the goals of security and personal fulfilment that we long for.

Are God and the religious imperative therefore dead, as the philosopher Friedrich Nietzsche maintained, something that the world ever since, from conviction or convenience, has increasingly believed? Has Hegel's dialectic thought delivered mankind from unremitting self-serving?

What is the hope for mankind and for this world, ravished and exploited as it increasingly is by an incorrigibly rapacious creature?

And is there any solution? Can mankind ever escape from the seemingly fundamental drive of its basic human nature? Can our superior intelligence ever rescue us from overwhelming self-interest in the way that we conduct our lives? Is an absolute moral purity a fantasy, a mental projection? Is a perfect society, as Plato, Marx and others have imagined, possible for us to create?

The fact that we can give it real parameters shows that it is a theoretical possibility to exist even if it is not possible to deliver.

Is it even in our powers though to achieve personally, as Pallagius asserted? Experience so far has shown us that the best we can achieve is a poor compromise, not even an approximation to what we really aspire to. There is one person though that has offered a solution, a solution that has not been tried yet, beyond a few individual and parochial examples, and one that ultimately guarantees to deliver.

Christ never preached Christianity. In fact what He did have to say about established social religion was very little. Even about personal religious practice He said relatively little; what He did teach and preach about widely though was the advent and character of the Kingdom of Heaven. A

Kingdom based on absolutes, absolute personal goodness, purity and truth. It was from this basis that the Kingdom of Heaven that Christ taught could establish a universal kingdom where absolute and comprehensive peace and righteousness would prevail.

Christianity though, the religion that developed in the early centuries after the early church of Jesus' disciples, has singularly failed to deliver Christ's Kingdom of Heaven on Earth. Over two millennia it has become too eclectic in its belief and practice to deliver what Christ taught, except at a personal and esoteric level.

Christ had presented this solution to mankind's dilemma from a new and completely different perspective, not one that disregarded the problem of self-interest. This, the Kingdom of Heaven, was a completely new order, not like Plato's republic or communism for example, which was dependant on mankind to deliver, but one that could and would only be delivered by God alone. Not an absolute remedy that we can just aspire to, but one that God alone can and will deliver. A kingdom that is here now, one that is developing within us, one that we may personally achieve now if we are willing to accept it, see Luke 17:20-21; one that God alone will deliver Himself, one that will be universal though and total in its effect.

This is what the Book of the Revelation is all about; it brings together all that is contained in the whole of the Bible regarding God's final plans for mankind, what they are and how God will implement them. It is all about what is prophesied in the OT, revealed in the NT and made real and relevant personally to us through faith alone. This will be the definitive solution to the problem of mankind's inherent self-absorption, that predominantly self-interested view of the world. Thus God will change and is changing the status quo, now in the hearts of individuals but in a future age throughout the whole of the natural world. It is this ongoing establishment of this new Divine world order that this Book of the Revelation is all about.

INTRODUCTION TWO

Why was the Revelation Written?

Who the 'Revelation' is Addressed to and Why

Our Lord's instruction given to John at the beginning of the Book was to write down what he saw and send it to all seven churches in Asia Minor. These seven local churches typically represent the whole Church for the whole of the church age; every experience of John throughout this revelation was expressly intended as much for the whole Church as for John himself. He is not relating the drama as a mere commentary though, but throughout as a powerful experience in which he is intrinsically involved, either dynamically or receptively, and as understanding important details regarding our responsibilities and involvement in the purposes of God, both now and in the future. This had such a powerful effect on him on several occasions, eg verse 17, chapter 1: 'When I saw Him I fell at His feet as dead'.

Likewise for ourselves, if we are to grasp the real significance of these passages, if we are to be open to what God would say to us through these extraordinary verses, if we are to be open to Christ and to 'be in His Spirit' (v.10) regarding what He has to say, then it will have a similar effect on us; powerful, dramatic and life changing.

'Blessed, (favoured, endowed), is he who:

1. Reads and
2. Those who hear the words of this prophesy, and
3. Keep those things which are written in it.'
   Chapter 1, verse three.

It is clear from this that we are all instructed to be closely involved ourselves.

Apart from these words which imply the powerful effect that the experience had on John, there are many references where John makes very specific reference to scenes where he and/or the church are intrinsically involved in the Divine manifestation. Jesus Himself says to John, right at the end of the Book, 'I Jesus ... testify unto you these things in the Churches', which reinforces how directly the Church is involved and how specifically the prophecy is directed to the Church. Earlier in the Book we read that 'Round the throne were twenty-four elders' which implies the immediate presence of the Church itself, represented by its elders, as they were an image that the early churches particularly would have understood as being typical in the constitution of their individual church localities.

They sang a new song:

> 'Thou hast redeemed us out of every kindred and tongue and people and nation and hast made us unto our God kings and priests;
> and we shall reign on the Earth.'

This theme was introduced in verses five and six of chapter 1 to leave us in no doubt as to who the enthroned elders refer to in chapters four and five. Their role as recorded in subsequent chapter exemplifies this and also shows what an important and dignified role they occupy in a heavenly capacity. Throughout the book they:

- Sanction the judgement of God, as seen from a spiritual perspective.
- They worship in full adoration.
- They appreciate intelligently and welcome the coming reign of Christ.

These elders then are clearly identified, not to just label them but to identify them by their spiritual characteristics:

1. As the redeemed – identifies them firstly as specifically those from among mankind that have been saved and sanctified by Grace.
2. The concept of elder – One who is mature in the faith, by virtue of their experience, having authority, wisdom and understanding
3. As kings and priests; this signifies the specific role of the

elders. In the Old Testament it was Israel that had that special function; Exodus 19:6 'And ye shall be unto me a kingdom of priests, and an holy nation.' In the new Testament it is the Church that is spoken of as having these qualities, suggesting these elders are the redeemed of Israel, or the Church in its fully perfected or mature state, or both

4. They surround, literally encircle, the Throne, implying they:

i. Are intimately associated with it, the Almighty, the Lamb and the four living creatures.

ii Totally identify with it.

iii Are fully expressing and testifying to it.

5. They are clothed, that is revealing only their assigned identity and function.

i. Clothed: that is having the character and qualities attributed to them.

ii In white, signifying purity of purpose and function.

6. They have crowns of Gold on their heads

i. Crowns, signifying authority and glory.

ii Of gold, signifying what is eternal and incorruptible; what is Divine in character.

7. They are twenty-four in number, identifying them with the 24 courses of priesthood in the temple order (see 1 Chronicles chapter 24). This implies that it is associated with the priestly function of those that are assigned by God from among mankind to fulfil that purpose. Under the Old Covenant it was solely male persons of a certain

age from one particularly tribe of Israel, a very exclusive group indeed. Under the New Covenant it typifies the role of all the redeemed, as far as they are qualified as being 'Elders'.

There are many references throughout scripture that support the thesis that these qualities are examples of the characteristics of those that have been redeemed from mankind to serve the Living God. It is the particular spiritual qualities that identify them, it is not just superficially some particular individuals or group as we tend naturally to identify people. As we consider the function of the elders throughout this study, this should be exemplified.

The Nature of Priesthood

In verse three of chapter 8 it is the prayers of the saints that come into view. Here then it is not the very public, albeit heavenly role that the elders occupy that is of significance, but the very private and intimate prayer-relationship with God Himself through the sacrifice of Christ. A role that precipitates the trumpets announcing to Earth, and its inhabitants, the terrible calamities that will befall the Earth and those that will not turn from their pernicious ways.

It is then in chapter 21 that we are finally introduced to the final object of God's purposes - the Holy City, the New Jerusalem - and given insight into the special part that the Church will play in that holy plan of God. It is the Church as represented by the twelve apostles that form the foundations of that place. All that God is realising in His saints on Earth during this present time, all the spiritual characteristics that are created in us through the work of the Holy Spirit as symbolised by the precious stones of the foundations, will form the basis of that heavenly building. What a joy, what an encouragement to a suffering Church to endure, to remain faithful to the end; what a strength to the 'over-comer' to look ahead to the crown that awaits him. This shows clearly that the heavenly city, New Jerusalem, is not just a physical entity, though it may be that as well incidentally, but the significant thing about the heavenly City is its character, its spiritual substance.

When we look at the world as it is today, there seems little to even give us hope or encouragement regarding the future, let alone to give us confidence and real contentment, even less a state of real joy. Seven times though in this book, even at times when what is being described seems absolutely horrific, we hear in stark contrast the announcement, 'blessed are' or 'blessed is he'. What a special privilege of grace is promised in these pages. Not just a blessing on the Church but also a sevenfold blessing awaits all those that are fully involved in its teaching and directives. When we consider each one of the sevenfold blessings that are given, we realise how extensive our involvement is in the expanse of this prophecy, and how completely it encompasses our individual being and experience. The first three blessings relate particularly to those who are still in this sphere of trial and suffering for Christ's sake; it is an encouragement to all the Church to remain faithful. The first is a blessing awaiting us for just reading the book, as we have considered earlier. It does not presuppose any experience or knowledge as a disciple of Christ; the only call is for faith and an open mind; all that is necessary for all the blessings.

One of the most prominent characters in the Revelation is the 'Beast' that is introduced at the beginning of chapter 13. A lot of detail is given to us in chapters 13 and 17 so we understand the influence this formidable creature commands. The most succinct detail that we are given though is at the end of chapter 13; it is his name, or the number that represents his name, that is symbolically his character or what he means to the world. It is in fact the amalgam of three numbers that give us the meaning, six hundred, sixty and six. Sinister as it sounds, it is what these numbers symbolically represent, as we can glean from scripture, that indicates to us his true spiritual significance in the judgment of God, as we shall see in a later chapter. Six, sixty and six hundred probably represent in this context what mankind is capable of in every way, or perhaps more closely to a direct interpretation of the symbolism, man's natural effort or ambition, his innate capacity for it and the totality of his performance. The three numbers 600, 60 and 6 together then would signify the end of man's time, of his working or the allotted span of his management of the Earth. It is the end of the days of grace and the execution of wrath and the deliverance of God's people. A fuller examination of this symbolism will be expounded in section two.

It is this particularly characteristic of the 'Beast' that the Church is called to be cognisant of, as joint heirs and governors with Christ; it is important particularly to us now as its influence is extant in the world now, as John tells us in two of his letters. It is knowing its meaning now that can give us wisdom to show others of its significance and its sinister outcome. It was as John stood on the sand of the seashore that he saw the beast emerge from the sea, the restless sea, symbolising a restless threat, probably the heaving masses of the surrounding pagan nations as the scriptures often convey the 'sea' to represent. He takes the position of Israel in taking cognisance of the creature as a person, as physically it is to Israel that it will have the greatest significance. This is particularly emphasised because it follows on immediately from chapter 12, the chapter that gives a brief history of Israel from the point of view of its relationship to its Messiah, that is Christ, and the fate that will befall Israel in the later days.

The Encouragement of Promised Blessings

The first, as has been mentioned, is a special blessing promised to those who read the Book of the Revelation of Jesus Christ. In contrast there are also curses given to those that add or take anything away from it. Reading means to heed, to take note of and act upon, not just to casually or critically peruse. How indeed though could reading what seems at first such a horrific account be a blessing to anyone, least of all those whose hearts are filled with the love of Christ? This is a question that can only be answered individually and personally as we read the scriptures with faith and an open mind. It is then that we begin to understand the true nature of God, an absolute, Holy God who cannot accommodate anything that is contrary to pure peace, happiness and righteousness.

The next blessing is in chapter 14, a blessing for those that are experiencing the pain and trials of this life, for now and also during the time when this miscreant, pictured as 'The Beast', imposes such mayhem on the world:

> 'Blessed are the dead that die in the Lord,
> for their works do follow them'

This can only be telling us that whatever we go through for Christ's sake, whatever pain and sorrow, even death, it will be for our ultimate blessing. If we consider this in the context of verse eleven, it compares this with the anticipated end of those that worship the beast or his image, and so emphasises the dramatic contrast between the hope and end of those that love Christ and those that reject Him.

The third blessing is not only an encouragement to faith; it is an encouragement to patience and fortitude:

> 'Blessed is he that watches and keeps his garments'

Watching and waiting patiently and meekly for our blessed Lord's return and being clothed in the beauty of life that the Holy Spirit lives within us is what is encapsulated here for us. It is in the context here of the impending horror of Armageddon, that which indicates the end of all and everything that rejects Christ. For those that love Him, however, it is the moment in time that will usher in the perfect reign of Christ upon the Earth.

The next blessing is also an encouragement, but not only an encouragement to faith but also to hope and anticipation to the life that awaits us with the one we love. Heaven, as a deeply personal experience, is just to be with Christ; it can be no more, it is no less. It is a blessing to those that are called to the marriage of the Lamb:

> 'For His wife hath made herself ready'

This blessing is actually for the guests, those with whom the bridegroom and the bride have a special relationship, for a time of mutual rejoicing and celebration. There has been some confusion in the past as who these guests might be, though if we compare this passage with our Lord's parables of the wedding feast in chapters twenty-two and twenty-five of Matthew's Gospel, the context is explained. We begin then to get a clear idea that on each occasion, what is being referred to is that particular special relationship that Christ has with all His saints. The emphasis of the parable is on the nature of the relationship, not to identify different groups; this will be discussed in a later chapter.

The fifth blessing is for all those that are resurrected just after Christ returns to reign on the Earth, in chapter 20, verse 6:

> 'Blessed and holy is he who has part in
> the first resurrection'

This is said in the context of the judgement by the elders that we see sitting on the thrones, those thrones that surrounded the throne of the Almighty and so by implication receiving their authority to rule from Him. It was Jesus Himself that had said to His disciples:

'He... shall sit on the throne of His glory, you also shall sit upon twelve thrones,
Judging the twelve tribes of Israel', Matthew 19:28'

Again this confirms the special place of the Church in relation to He who has received 'all authority and power' from His father. It also portrays the Church's function in its heavenly role. Particularly we see here the special place of government delegated to the Church, yet also one of welcome to the saved of a different time, one of sharing the position of being priests of God and also of having a joint reign with Christ for the period of a thousand years. It is as it were the Church being in spirit with their brothers during their time of tremendous suffering, in a time of 'Great Tribulation'. The idea of government here, though real in its normal sense, is not one of control or domination as rule implies in most societies today, but the rule of love, joy, peace etc, the Spirit of God Himself, that character that pervades and indwells all that love Him.

In chapter 22 we come to another special message given directly and primarily to the Church. The context there is where the Church is involved in the government or administration of the Holy City New Jerusalem.

In verse seven of chapter 22 we are given the sixth blessing; it is the same as the first one at the beginning of chapter 1:

> 'Blessed is he who keeps the words of the
> prophesy of this book'

A blessing to those that keep, that is to say live by, the sayings of this book. How important to understand and hold firmly to all its precious truth, that we do not miss any of its great import. To see it merely as an objective scenario that will be physically played out without understanding the spiritual language will be to miss most of its meaning.

In verse 14, the last blessing is promised:

> 'Blessed are those that do His commandments
> that they might have the right to the tree of life'

That is the commandments of the 'Alpha and Omega', His commandments being all His teaching in here at least and also elsewhere in scripture. He that is the beginning and end of everything and has all things at His command. Here it becomes clear, not only what that blessing might be, but also that it applies to all saved of all spheres and ages throughout history; they will have access to the tree of life and to the Holy City, that spiritual domain of which the Church itself is the foundation; Revelation 21:14. What insight this gives to the Church, now in this age, to the tremendous privilege and responsibilities it is destined for; what great joys and glory in serving our Lord now and in what ways we will serve Him and all those that are saved from sin and corruption.

As if that is not enough to comprehend, as well as to realise why we have been given this glorious piece of scripture, there are also the many lessons that these texts teach us that give us further insight. To understand will not just be to realise why we have been given this book, but also of the paramount importance to study it and fully understand what important things it has to teach us, both in this life and in preparation for the next.

Our Time Left on Earth, How We Should Conduct Ourselves

No less poignant then than the many blessings promised in this remarkable book are the many lessons that we can glean from its pages; also those warnings that are expressly made to us throughout its chapters and to the other issues that our attention is prominently drawn to, from the sinister warnings of chapter 13 of the penalty for imposing our selfish will or sanction on others or of limiting their freedom, to the rewards for those that are the overcomers of their own selfish will. Then from the warnings in chapter 14 of being conformed to this world, to the glorious delight of that city the New Jerusalem, that is all of God's chosen people. This is represented, at least in part, by the bride of Christ in her final state as we see in chapter 21.

It is in verses 9-10 of Chapter 13 that we find the warning: 'He that leads into captivity shall go into captivity etc.' Here we have an illustration of something that pertains particularly to the Day of the Lord but also something that illustrates a principal that is relevant for all time. This is another reason then that the prophesied events of this time are revealed to the Church of every age, not that all or even any of us will be faced with the particular trial of those events, but that typically its teaching is applicable to every era, just as the trials of that era are typical of the tribulation we suffer in every age.

Hence it is also brought to our attention that 'here is the patience of the saints,' that they should find freedom, that God-given right to mankind, true freedom, that is spiritual freedom, not just an absence of physical constraint. It is a freedom from all compulsion of the world or of self-interest, freedom to follow only God's own law and commandments but also by implication a freedom to choose to do so or not as well. This is what the Ark in the Old Testament represents, telling us 'He that doeth these things shall live'. This was God's covenant with mankind that God made with the Children of Israel in Leviticus 18:4-5 and Deuteronomy 8:1, 30:6. If then we live by the indwelling of the Holy Spirit we will do these things by default. If we live according to our natural desires, we will not.

It was our precious Lord Himself, now in His supreme position and Divine glory, that condescends to explain to John, and through him to ourselves, the meaning of the angels and the candlesticks, in that awesome vision of the glorious omnipotent Jesus, in chapter 1. In chapter 17 though it is the sight of the prostitute that was riding the beast that also caused John to wonder. This time though it was not because he was amazed at the sight of his Lord whom he did recognise, but rather here he did not recognise the woman or the symbolism implied at all. Hence the rest of the chapter is devoted to the angel's explanation of the sinister character that the woman represented and the beast on which she was carried – Chapter 17:1-3.

'Come hither, I will show thee the great whore'

This, as we shall see in a later chapter, is all that displaces Christ in our affections, all that would draw away our faith and loyalty to Christ as Lord and cause us to live according to our natural desires.

It is then in the following chapter, once we realise that the great whore and the beast that she rides represent different aspects of our present evil world, that environment in which we all exist. This emphasises our need to be constantly and actively separated from all that distracts our attention from following our Lord, we see the need for an unqualified dedication and devotion to Him, turning our backs on anything that gives an inkling of this world system. No wonder in chapter 18 the words echo from the page:

'Come out of her, my people, least you share in her sins and least you receive of her plagues.

Thus when she finally meets her demise in chapter 18, verse 20 we are instructed

'Rejoice over her O Heaven, and you holy apostles and prophets;

for God hath avenged you on her.'

It is then with a similar imperative that the words at the end of the book warn us of the importance of the prophecy and the dire consequences of adding or taking from its meaning. The book is not just significant to the church; it is of vital importance. It is not something for our curiosity about what is to come at the end of the age; it is something we need to be concerned with at this present time. It is not just some warning to flee from the wrath of God when Satan's power is unchecked upon the Earth; it is a warning now to disentangle ourselves from the very elements of antichrist that prevail even at this present time and ask ourselves how we should conduct ourselves then in this present evil age.

Not only are there many blessings, not only are there many warnings in this book; not only are there many references that show intrinsically that the church is involved in the issues raised in its chapters, there are also important and specific instructions recorded for the church of Christ to take heed of and that are paramount to comply with.

When Christ begins to explain to John the meanings of those things he has seen, he no doubt recognised that voice of Jesus with its grace and authority. When Christ says 'what you see, write in a book' he implies the enduring significance of those words. Here are matters of eternal consequence that are to be unveiled to him, words of the Lord of Glory Himself, of things that God Himself would reveal about His Son and His Divine manifestation to the world. He that is the 'First and the Last', He in whom we have absolute faith that He that promised these things is also able to bring those things to pass.

John was told to write. Later he was told also to take a little book, to eat the book and then to measure the temple with the reed he was given. These were not just words to attract his attention but instructions to him to get directly involved in the revelation. To reinforce this at the end of the book John is reminded to make the prophecy public, because it was soon to come to pass.

He was told to play an active role in making known the truth, but also a restricted one. The angel told him to worship God only and in so doing emphasising unequivocally the divinity of Christ, Christ being given worship in chapter 5 for example. He was told also to seal up the things that the seven thunders said to affirm that not all was to be revealed yet, for some aspects of the mystery must remain a mystery until their completion, although there was a specific reason and mandate for their consequence. The purpose of this book then is as its title states 'The revelation of Christ,' not just to make known the future. It is a declaration by God of how His eternal will and purpose will be universally established by Christ alone, and that all that would purport to stand in opposition will be removed and destroyed; but all that embrace what is revealed and embrace it on His terms will have a place within His kingdom.

INTRODUCTION THREE

'Tis Jesus the First and the Last

What, or Rather Who, this Book is About, and How it Should be Read

The book of the Revelation is possibly the most misunderstood book of the Bible. It is a book that has been little read over the centuries, in fact it was even excluded from the canon of scripture on occasions during the history of the Church, yet with events reported daily in the world news today that seem to have such an 'apocalyptic' quality, Christians and non-Christians alike are turning to its pages as they see a certain concurrence of those events with the things prophesied in this book.

It is perhaps a good idea though to state first what the Book of the Revelation is not before attempting any exposition of this scripture.

It is often understood by non-Christian people to be a

macabre description of how the world will end, a cataclysmic vision of events that will bring mankind to an end. It is read as a consecutive narrative of events that all seem rather unrealistic and therefore it is dismissed as a bizarre form of pre- medieval science fiction.

Others regard its message as valid with a relevant warning to mankind for today, but believe that it was written using abstract metaphors and fables that have to be deciphered by one's own imagination or relative to one's own views and experiences. What is then understood is profoundly personal or esoteric and would seem to have little objective value, cp 2 Pet. 1:20. What emerges from this understanding is what we find sometimes dramatically portrayed in modern 'end-of-the-world' fiction.

Some liberally-minded Christians consider that some of the Book is 'Christian' though much of it contradicts the idea that God is love, and therefore it is then disregarded. They then 'cherry pick' what seems relevant to them and ignore what doesn't seem acceptable or consistent with their view of God and the world. The objection to this view is of course is that if God is Love, absolutely and not in just some popular sentimental way, then He is also just, as love cannot preside over a world of lawlessness. He must then not only be benevolent and merciful but also a holy judge.

The Book was written by the apostle John in AD95 during his imprisonment on the Isle of Patmos, under the persecution of Domitian, and written down probably a year after on his release (hence the statement at the beginning 'I was on the Isle' etc.) Scholastic analysis though questions the identity of the author and therefore by implication calls into doubt its full apostolic authority and in consequence, its

Divine authority. Its authenticity though is secured through faith, as is all spiritual truth. Much controversy exists as to its scholarship, but this is unhelpful in finding assurance. If this is the word of God, then its secular history may be interesting, but is not what is authenticating or invalidating of its Divine inspiration. Obedience is always the first step of faith and the first step to knowing the Truth of God.

Many Christians accept that it is the inspired word of God, but are confused by the number of interpretations 'on offer' by different exponents. Some say that the whole book refers to events in the first century AD, written in allegorical form; others that it is the 'history of the church' written in advance and see the events described as typical of events that have occurred during the past two millennia. Others see its descriptions as all predictive and yet to be fulfilled. A further exposition is that its message is entirely spiritual and relevant to every age and dispensation in a general sort of way. This is just to briefly summarise the broad schools of interpretation; there are many sub-schools of thought within each of these groups.

All this does not affect the fact of the Divine inspiration of the Book though, but it does call into question the authority of the different interpretations. This is of course a subject in itself, too large to develop here. Suffice to say that they could all be true, to a point at least, within the context of the suppositions and perspective of the various points of view.

There are many books already available reviewing these different views, so they will not be considered here. It is however worth undertaking a study, disregarding all contentious ideas that surround the interpretation of this book, to see just what all the other scriptures have to say regarding its subject matter. This will involve carefully considering the meaning of individual words in the language that they were originally written in and what images the writers of other scriptures intended to convey. Above all we have to search our own hearts to individually see what the Holy Spirit will say to each one of us.

Anyone picking up this, yet another book on the subject, is going to be suspicious about another exposition that purports to offer further understanding and insight into this Book, so it is this doubt that we shall deal with first.

> In interpreting this book, no assumptions are made except the following:

- It is the inspired word of God and therefore of instruction to all members of Christ's Church, to whom it was written, of every age. It is a prophecy explaining about the past, the things that are (extant at the time of writing, including perhaps the present time) and the things that shall be hereafter. It is about events, meanings and matters of importance, particularly if not exclusively of spiritual significance.

- Above all, what the Book is about is as defined in the first verse: 'The Revelation of Jesus Christ', who He is, what He is, to whom He will be revealed and how. It is also about the significance of this to Christ's church, to Israel, to all who trust in Him and also to all that refuse to acknowledge Him. It is far more than just an account of how the world will end, though the end of this present age is implicated in its revelations.

- Much of it is written in symbolic language, as indeed is the Book of Daniel and parts of several other Old Testament prophets such as Zechariah and Isaiah and Jesus' parables. To these scriptures many references are made or inferred, and also to other scriptures such as some of Our Lord's doctrine and other more direct teaching. The fact of its symbolism is largely apparent, being preposterous if taken prosaically and literally, especially as it is then also usually incongruous with other scripture.

- The interpretations, particularly of symbolic features, are consistent with the rest of scripture, and therefore any assumptions outside of this are probably irrelevant or at least to be regarded cautiously.

- Many of the images in the 'Revelation' are allusions to writings in the Old Testament Prophets and for the most part at least refer to actual events that have been fulfilled or will yet be fulfilled. Sometimes these events have been fulfilled or partly fulfilled in the past, yet still are highly significant for the future; for example, consider Matthew 24 verse 15. Maybe also all the other images in the 'Revelation' are actual prophesied events; though essentially the Book is primarily providing deep and important spiritual truth and instruction that is entirely consistent with the teaching of the rest of scripture. Throughout this exposition there are many quotations from the scripture, and other references to it, to endeavour to keep within the overall message of the scriptures.

- This interpretation will take as a starting point our Lord's own discourse of 'The Day of the Lord' and His

Second Coming as related in Matthew 23-25, Mark12-13 and Luke 20-22. A large part of the Old and New Testament is devoted to this subject and this will be crossed referenced, though by no means exhaustively. There are several good study bibles that follow the theme through the scriptures and these are recommended as a good means of further study.

- The verification of the Revelation's Divine inspiration and therefore authority is threefold, but taken together:
  - Its complete consistency with the rest of scripture in its spiritual teaching. The most significant of these will be in Paul's epistles, as well as from Old Testament prophecies and from our Lord's own teaching.
  - When prophesied events come to pass that is proof of their Divine origin Matt. 24:25.
  - The inward knowledge of the power of the Holy Spirit of truth, which the fully committed believer will experience by virtue of their faith, to 'test the spirits whether they are of God' 1 - John 4:1.

The important themes of the Book, which become apparent, are the complementary ones of justice and mercy, cp Romans 9, and the absolute wisdom, authority and glory of God and of Jesus Christ

From a superficial reading of the Book it becomes apparent that the mood, character and presentation change often, which can make it all rather confusing at first to understand. A deeper study reveals themes and similarities that hold it together and link it with other scriptures that give it its real meaning. The style of literature in which it is written is as a spiritual allegory; images are clearly not intended to be visual as they would often be incongruous and therefore meaningless. Reference to the Book of Daniel in particular show that meaning is to be taken as moral or spiritual, depending on the context, though some of it referring also to future times. Some or most of the images may have a literal fulfilment eventually, though it is in its spiritual significance that it is relevant to the church of every age.

It is clear that many animals, numbers, precious and semi-precious stones and natural phenomena such as mountains and trees have a symbolic meaning and the symbolism is consistent throughout the Bible, maybe throughout Hebrew culture as a whole, though this meaning is not always clear-cut or specific and needs to be understood carefully within its context where it is not explained in the text.

As already intimated, any meaning that may be drawn that is not consistent with the scriptures is regarded as invalid. There is a danger with all scripture in making assumptions or reading into it what is not intended, perhaps unwittingly because we tend to add new ideas to what we already believe, assume or have been taught. That is why always when studying the scriptures we have to approach them with an open mind, which involves being entirely honest with ourselves and having a healthy self-criticism and re-estimation of what we already think and believe.

This all means that below the surface of what, if taken literally, seems rather bizarre, is a wealth of deep spiritual meaning that will educate and encourage anyone who has a living faith in their Lord and is watching for His coming; they will find that it will fill them with worship and adoration of their Lord.

The Book is expressly not all about the church. Chapter 1, verse one, for example states that it is given by God, concerning Jesus Christ in His full majesty, as Lord of His Church, as King of Israel, as benefactor of the nations and as redeemer and Judge of all mankind. It was given to John to send to, inform and encourage the local Churches in particular but by extension to the whole church since and throughout the present age.

Reference has already been made to the fact that the Book might refer to a certain time scale. This is an assumption in itself. The symbolism is usually metaphysical and is 'spiritually discerned' 1 Cor.2:13-15. Thus it is primarily about eternal issues and principles, as is the rest of scripture, though clearly times or epochs are implied, expressly and alluded to as in Daniel's visions. They may be about actual physical events that have or will occur, but even so they are always about much more than that, they are about the significance of these things and their relevance to us all.

Jesus foretold the cataclysmic events that would come upon the world at the end of time, ratifying prophesies that were made in the Old Testament and also events that are expounded upon in the book of the Revelation. What though is 'this World' as it is referred to in the scriptures?

John tells us in the second chapter of his first epistle, 'be not conformed to this world but be transformed by the renewing of your minds'. This is a message that Christ

Himself taught when He said, 'Love not the world, neither the things in the world'. The only problem then is what is the world, to what does it refer to in totality and does each reference, direct and symbolic, imply the full gambit of meaning found in scripture?

First then, what is the world from a biblical perspective? As one may well at first envisage it covers a vast subject; the following give just some of the individual descriptions that are included by the term as is enlarged upon in a later chapter.

1. The whole Earth and our natural environment.
2. Mankind with our empires, our citizenship and societies.
3. National powers and authorities.
4. Its history, its philosophy, its values and outlook.
5. Its riches, materialism and the love of money.
6. Its entertainment, its diversions and pleasures.

In The 'Revelation' there are various images used to symbolically describe the world or an aspect of it. As a commercial entity it is described as 'Babylon'. It is also referred to as a whore in respect of its character. As a political entity, it, or its ruler depending on the context, is referred to as the 'Beast'. Other images are also used to describe aspects of 'the world' and the quality of life of its inhabitants.

To focus first on just one or a few aspects of the world, for example the political aspect of this world; this was represented in Daniel so graphically as the image that Nebuchadnezzar saw in a dream. This vision was interpreted as representing the empires that would arise throughout the history of this age, much of which has already transpired with the Babylonian, Persian, Greek and Roman Empires with just the fulfilment of the final brief world empire yet to come that will attempt to control all the countries of the world just before our Lord comes to establish His Kingdom. Even this is clearly not a simple account of the passage of history as large epochs don't appear within the currency of these empires. That is not say that its message is not relevant or only partially relevant to the whole of the time since it was written at least.

The danger of looking at scripture in just this way is evident. It is that we are seeing the scriptures solely in the light of current events; we are seeing what is written in spiritual language in the context of the physical and so form a rationalised scenario based on our own perception, hampering the enlightenment of the Holy Spirit. The result is then that we get a distorted view of the precious Word of God, one based on our own understanding. This then makes our understanding and beliefs subject to stage-management by Satan. We then lose our way in understanding the scriptures as a whole on the subject and in the context of our Lord's coming and overlook the significance of dangers that we are warned against in this setting; things that are so relevant to our spiritual growth and stature. Perhaps it is that because the subject is such a minefield that many Christians avoid the subject altogether, an attitude that is encouraged by Satan in view of the importance of the issue to our sanctification.

INTRODUCTION FOUR

The Testimony of Jesus is the Spirit of Prophecy

The Deeper Inner Meaning of Prophecy

A paramount aspect of biblical prophecy is that it is not just of temporal substance. Even when it relates specifically to some occurrence that will happen within a time frame, as indeed do most prophecies, such as the return of Jesus Christ to this Earth, the prophecy itself relates to what is eternally significant and not just to the temporal elements. In fact, aspects such as dates and time spans are specifically omitted for the most part. God does not just want us to know what and when affairs will happen, quite the opposite - He wants us to trust Him implicitly for and in everything. He tells us through prophecy just what is of eternal significance, that which affects and builds us spiritually in faith for now and eternity; that we should ever grow in grace and the knowledge of our Lord Jesus Christ. Thus when we are given passages of scripture such as Daniel chapter 9 we have to study it carefully and prayerfully as it does not just give us a sequel of events according to our calendar as would at first appear. To read it simply as that means that we both fall into fundamental errors and also miss the deeper meaning that God's Holy Spirit wishes us to understand. Likewise the parallel passage, Revelation chapter 17, has a wealth of meaning of essential issues that are relevant to our spiritual growth in Christ and our understanding of our place in God's plan of salvation for mankind.

This is well illustrated in Acts 15:14-16 where a prophecy in Amos 9:11, made in respect of the future restoration of Israel, is applied to the salvation of the gentiles. Clearly what Peter is saying in Acts in his address to the church at Jerusalem (a church that was troubled with a doctrine that had arisen that gentile converts should be circumcised) was that it was the eternal essence of the prophecy that was its real significance and therefore was relevant to the then present establishment of the church as it will yet be to the re-establishment of Israel.

The ordinary meaning of 'prophecy' in today's language is simply the prediction of the future, that is, prognostication; with dubious or no authority it often carries little credibility and is invariably superficial and unreliable. However, the primary meaning of a 'prophet' has meant something rather different until recently; it is 'One who speaks for God (or any other deity) as the inspired revealer or interpreter of His will'; this is the main definition given in the OED. This is significantly different, though the anomaly is sometimes not even appreciated by Christians, even less so those of no faith. This OED definition is the meaning that is intended throughout the Bible; in fact the implications of prophecy as given by God throughout the Bible make it even more specific. It is not something written just for our curiosity about the future but a message to learn from and to obey; ie 'blessed is he that keeps the prophecies of this book', Revelation 1:3, 22:7. It not someone who just peruses these prophecies or even anyone who is enthusiastic about and revels in them but blessed is he that complies with and conforms to their teaching

It is not written in some enigmatic code either that only a few can understand. It is straightforward in its presentation, although often written in symbolic language. This though is a language that has spiritual meaning and is a language that is common throughout the whole of the Bible, a message that is profound and yet universal in its scope. It is not just history written in advance either, but again it is about eternal issues; not about future events only, but more significantly to let all of mankind know the omnipotence and glory of God and what His plan and will is for mankind. It is given so that mankind should know that not only does God know the end from the beginning, but also that He has predestined what is to be and that He will also bring it to pass. It is about what we are at heart, our characters, our life and our relationship with our Lord and Master. This is what is spirit or what is spiritual.

What then is the meaning and indeed the purpose of prophecy in the Bible, why has God made know His will and purposes to us, how can we trust it as being His Word and how should we read it?

As history has unfolded the prophecies of the Bible have also come to pass, authenticating the writings and showing to mankind God's reason for telling him what must still come to pass, why and what He must do about it.

The Bible, Old and New Testament, is full of prophecy, much of which has been fulfilled, some of which has not yet been. For example, the fulfilment of many prophecies relating to judgements meted out to certain cities, such as Tyre in Ezekiel chapter 26, in the Old Testament have all come to pass, as indeed have all the prophecies relating to Christ's first coming as the Redeemer of mankind. This in itself authenticates the scriptures, as Deuteronomy 18:21-22 points out. Most of this prophecy is direct in its language and unmistakable and simple in meaning, unlike most apocalyptic prophecy that is symbolic in presentation but no less unequivocal in meaning.

As history has unfolded, God has revealed more of His Holy will and plans for mankind.

From the fall of man in the garden of Eden God made known the first prophesies; to man He cursed the ground that in future he would have to toil to be able to eat from it, and to the devil that had deceived them, He foretold of his eventual defeat and the sufferings that He would inflict on 'the woman's seed', even the One that would defeat him in due time at Calvary.

The book of Genesis continues with the stories of Noah, Lot, and Abraham to show that God will bless the righteous and destroy the wicked; albeit in His grace He will first give the opportunity to all mankind to repent and be saved. After this Moses spoke to Pharaoh telling him to let his people go to worship in the desert as they had once done, but when Pharaoh refused, the plagues were meted out on his people until he finally relented. The prophetic message from the early chapters of the Bible is quite clear to all mankind. A life of sin, disobedience or of independence from God is on a course for judgement and destruction. It was a message preached to the people of Nineveh by Jonah, whom we know repented of their evil and they were spared the consequences. It was a message that was preached repeatedly to Israel, for example in the days of Samuel, when they repented of their idolatry, they were restored to favour with God and their cities captured by the Philistines were restored to them, 1 Samuel 7:14. Subsequently on different occasions when they ignored the call to repentance by the Prophets of God, they were taken into captivity, first into Babylon and later, the tribe of Judah which was restored again 70 years after their captivity, was again taken captive, to be dispersed among the nations. This state of affairs persists now, with Israel as a whole still largely scattered throughout the world, and will chiefly remain so until the end of this present age.

As history has unfolded, God has made it plain that there is an integrated connection and plan in all that He reveals. It shows us that He will implement what He says, even when mankind in foolishness, chooses to ignore God, or it believes Him to be a god of their own invention and then to continue in a life of self-determination, refusing to recognise or honour Him. God in His mercy, not willing that any should perish, has declared though, through His authenticated Word, not only His demands as a righteous God, but also His way of salvation and plan for mankind.

God then has revealed Himself, who He is and also what He has planned for mankind; namely:

- Mankind's responsibility towards his God and the need for him to keep His moral law.
- His justice in that He will recompense every man and woman according to the respect he has given to God's law:
- Through the natural consequences of breaking His law in this life.
- In the Final Judgement at the end of time.
- That the course of mankind is on a downward spiral of destruction.
- His plan of redemption to restore mankind that is lost in sin and so alienated from Him.
- That He has special plans and instructions for His chosen people Israel.
- That He has special plans and instructions for the Church of Christ.
- His promise that Christ will return for His Church.
- His promise that Christ will return to Israel as their Messiah and King.
- His plan to bring in His perfect kingdom of righteousness and peace on Earth.

If then the Bible is a spiritual book about who and what God is and what we are, it is written in spiritual language. It is concerned about eternal issues; temporal issues are subservient to eternal issues. It is about matters of eternal destiny, it is about eternal precepts, it is about complete fulfilment, for the outcome for individuals and for the benefit of all the world; it is about absolutes.

When therefore we read 'we also have a more sure word of prophecy', 2 Peter 1:19 KJV, we should not consider it to be merely about matters of physical change, however dramatic the expected events. This is a mere secular view, just seeing things from a natural perspective. That is not to say that prophecy does not have a temporal framework, it does by implication; the importance is to keep it within its eternal perspective and dimension. When metaphorical language is used it is a spiritual issue that is being brought into view. To interpret literally or merely tangibly or prosaically is to completely trivialize the passage and fall into error. Where symbolic language is used in scripture in respect of an isolated occasion or thing, the meaning is specifically and simply given, eg Revelation 17:18.

Interpreting 'spiritually' is not the same as 'spiritualising' either. The first is using wisdom and enlightenment by the Holy Spirit alone, see 1 Corinthians 2:14, it is to spiritually appraise, judge closely.

To 'spiritualise', as the word is usually used, in a derogatory way, is merely to downgrade prophecy to a matter of general metaphors or similarities or reducing it to merely an aesthetic; to see it expressing merely a recurrent idea or theme or to imprecisely 'read into' a prophecy certain events of history, or to use it to reinforce preconceived ideas. This use of the word 'spiritualise' in this way is in fact a misnomer; the word 'generalisation' or 're-construction' would be more appropriate.

To see prophecy as merely predicting the future is to be merely taking a secular view of a spiritual matter and is therefore wrong in principle and probably wrong in understanding. To see prophecy simply as a commentary on history when it happens is also seeing prophecy as the world sees it, as a matter of speculation and wonder. To see the things of God and the person of Christ, how He will become all in all, is what lies in prophecy and is only something that can be understood with the illumination of the Holy Spirit; see Revelation 19:10:'The testimony of Jesus is the spirit of prophecy'.

When we read in God's word that He will gather His people back into the land of Israel just before Christ shall come to reign, that is after being scattered amongst all the nations as they are now, and when we see that has already started in living memory, something that is so remarkable in that it is unprecedented and naturally unlikely, it is no wonder that God's people are filled with anticipation at Christ's imminent return. This though is not 'reading' prophecy into the events of history in a generalised way; it is seeing the real fulfilment of the Word, albeit partial as yet, as fulfilling God's purpose and bringing His glory to our view.

It is quite plain then that prophecy calls for an active and heartfelt response from us all, as it does involve us all. What then should be our response to prophecy? Clearly that will depend on the nature of the prophecy itself.

- Our initial response to having ours eyes opened to the scripture, that is when we truly appreciate God's grace and the awesome greatness of His power and authority and His love towards us, must be one of awe and reverence. When we see the wisdom of His holy law and the necessity for man to keep it for his own benefit and happiness, our hearts will then turn towards Him in honour and acceptance of His will, unconditionally.

- When we see the promises made and fulfilled to the saints in past ages, our response to God is one of hope and trust in His faithfulness for His promises made to us.

- We are not just excited by the prospect of coming events, things that we can know will come to pass, but rather our response is to be exercised towards a Heavenward outlook, in holiness and anticipation of seeing the Blessed Lord we love and know in our hearts. It causes us to be filled with all the fullness of God.

- When we understand God's plans in bringing about His Divine rule over all things, we appreciate His Divine wisdom and His grace that He should make it known to us.

- We understand what will be the end of all things in this life and how that should affect our outlook and attachment to the cares of this life now. This fine-tunes our sense of responsibility towards ourselves and to the world, but above all to our God, who becomes such a real and joyful presence within us.

- It teaches us of the unfathomable grace of God that not only will He regard us as His servants, but also more than servants, to regard us as friends, because we are allowed to appreciate His Divine counsels. It then follows that we learn to adopt and follow His Divine values, by conviction at first, then instinctively.

- We appreciate the Holiness of God and worship Him spontaneously and praise Him with heartfelt awe. It then deepens our devotion to our Lord and maintains our perspective as to our goal in life, even to those objectives that were of our Lord Himself; to obey the will of His Father and our Father, His God and our God.

- We do not just learn about these things but rather we become fully devoted to Him, His life in us purifying and sanctifying, qualifying us for the role as priests to Him and as witnesses of His grace in us. It then becomes clearer that we are also being tutored for the role of Kings and Priests to our God in a future age.

- Prophecy is a spiritual guide to keep us focused on the issues of life that are the most significant. It is because these matters don't appear to us naturally that we need them to be revealed to us.

'So we come full circle to the conundrum we started with; how can mankind who is fundamentally self-orientated live in a perfect society without corrupting it and likewise how can a perfect society exist of individuals programmed to act out of self-interest? The two ideas are mutually exclusive. If then there will be a future age of perfect peace and happiness, one that is guaranteed by an almighty God and not just a fanciful projection, it is the fundamental nature of mankind that must change. It is only the nature of Christ, how He reflected perfectly the nature of God and sought to fulfil only God's will and never His own, that can exist in such a culture, a nature that must be characteristic of every single citizen within that society.

Our nature then must change completely. We must

either live to serve our own interests and disqualify ourselves from God's Kingdom or live to serve God in His Kingdom, we cannot compromise, that will merely change our behaviour and thinking as well perhaps, but not change us fundamentally.

It was Christ that said, 'We cannot serve two masters, either we will love the one and hate the other or he will hold to the one and despise the other. We cannot serve God and Mammon'. There is no half way or compromise position possible, morally or rationally.

How then do we do the impossible and radically change our whole nature? The answer is simple – we can't. However this study is all about how God can and will do just that, now in the lives of individuals who will accept that total reformation. Then about how God will effect this on a global scale, how all the failure of mankind will be removed first is what the Book of the Revelation is all about. This of course begs the question of why God, if He is a totally good and loving God should allow evil in the world in the first place. This question will also be addressed in this study.

SECTION ONE

**God is Working His Purpose Out;
God's Purposes for Mankind**

PREFACE TO SECTION ONE

'God is Working His Purpose Out'

The 'apocalyptic' revelations that our Lord conveys to us in the synoptic gospels and in the Book of the Revelation are telling us from a general viewpoint what God is doing to complete His purposes for mankind, indeed for all creation, on a global scale. However they are also addressed to each one of us individually as members of Christ's Church and so are intimately relevant to our personal lives and destinies. Our consideration and response to these things are therefore paramount.

Each of the five parts of this section follow the themes of what those purposes are, firstly in Matthews Gospel and then from four more angles in the Revelation. As mentioned in the introduction: they follow the spiritual themes or perspectives in sequence, temporal, heavenly, moral, judicial and the Divine objective.

In this first section of this study we will consider what God's practical objectives for mankind are as revealed in Matthew's gospel chapters 21:28 to chapter 23:39, in The Revelation chapters 1 – 3 and in chapters 8, 12 and 19 respectively. The topic that connects these five passages is essentially spiritual, albeit in a temporal context, as it is as much about what God is doing in the hearts and lives of mankind as what He is doing for all mankind.

In the first part of this section, from the gospels, our Lord shows us what it is that God expects of us, in the words of the parables, that we should bear fruit to God, that is to live for His service by the indwelling of His nature within us. As His servants, that is our purpose and calling during our lives here, we should daily become more like our Lord as we are transformed into His likeness, see Romans 12:2. This is the essence of our Christian duty, our intelligent and reverent service; or worship as one translation renders it.

The second part of this section is from the early chapters of the Revelation. This shows in much more detail that our lives are under the constant scrutiny of our Lord, guiding us, commending us for those aspects of our lives that show God's glory, but also exposing those areas of our lives that fall short of the standard that is necessary to attain to serving Him fully. Here we see that although it is the work of God alone, transforming our lives into the image of His Son, it involves our active acquiescence and co-operation, accepting in faith the illumination of His Spirit within us. We live in an environment that is not only contrary to God's nature; it is entirely alien and antagonistic to it. It pleased

God to place us in such a setting so that our faith can be constantly strengthened, tested and purified. This we see more clearly at the end of the Revelation when we consider the foundation stones of the Holy City, what it is that God is developing within each of us now, if we will live according to His will.

In the third part of this section we are shown not what the purposes of God are in us, but rather what His purpose is for us, as actively involved in the carrying out of His particular objectives. This however is not something different from our assimilation of His nature as in the previous passage, but rather it is intrinsically linked to our communion with Him as His life is imparted to us. All true prayer echoes the words of the archetype Our Lord Himself taught us, 'Thy kingdom come' etc, in whatever day-to-day context that request may pertain to. In chapter 8 of the Revelation it is in the context of the breaking of the 7th seal that the answer to all these prayers can finally be answered on a global scale. It is the very breaking of the final seal that releases the final hindrance to the authority of Christ to be made fully known and implemented.

The immediate effect of this happening, the scroll of Christ's authority lying open and now fully functional, is for silence to descend in Heaven. The worship and praise that has ensued up to that point now ceases, as it were; the powers of Heaven go into abeyance. Mankind is allowed a brief period to continue unchecked and without further restraint or warning as he is allowed to display all that he is capable of.

It is then that the prayers of all the saints are offered on the golden altar. The answer is symbolised in the casting of that golden censer to Earth, suggesting that the fire of that censer begins the time of judgement on Earth that will cleanse it from everything that stands contrary to God's will. The prayer of the saints down the ages, 'Thy Kingdom Come' is at last to be answered; it is about to come in and on a global scale. Thus it is our very communion with our Lord and Saviour that pleads daily for His will to be done in our lives, in the lives of those that also know and love our Lord, indeed as we plead this for all mankind, we are intimately and spiritually involved with the implementation of that supreme purpose of God for His world. Our earnest prayer and longing for the deliverance from evil and for the reign of Christ everywhere, starting with ourselves and to be completed everywhere at the breaking of the seventh seal.

The establishment of God's Kingdom on Earth however requires more than the development of His will on Earth, both personally and socially. Part of that process has been for us to learn to overcome evil at a personal level. The next, or fourth, stage though of God realising His objectives on Earth is for evil to be removed entirely from the Earth. This is what the most dramatic images of the Revelation are about, firstly the effect of the seven seals, trumpets and bowls of wrath, signifying the complete removal of all comfort, pleasure and complacency in our material lives. Secondly comes the destruction of the world system with all its wealth, attraction and power, in the fall of Babylon.

Thirdly must come the end of the world political system of government, with its philosophy and principles of self-promotion. Once this world has been rendered devoid of all that would oppose the reign of Christ, then He will return and subdue the world under His benevolent but absolute sway.

Having established His Spirit within the hearts of individuals, having then made known to the world what His will is for mankind and for all creation; having then removed everything that can obstruct God's perfect plan for mankind, the final stage of God's purposes is to establish His new world order throughout the world.

The imagery used to convey how God will set up His Kingdom is described in the Revelation as a marriage feast to which all of the world that accept Him are invited. Details of this marriage feast, as a description of how God's Kingdom will function, are given by our Lord in His parable in Matthew chapter 25. In the Revelation though it is just mentioned in the context of our Lord's return and the bringing in of His Kingdom. This will be a time of removal of all the defunct elements of the old world order and the establishment of the new.

This will be the time spoken of by the prophet when 'the Earth will be filled with the knowledge of the Glory of the Lord as the waters cover the sea.' This will be a new age that will last typically or literally for a thousand years when the 'lion will lie down with the lamb'. Mankind will then be led by the Spirit of God alone; everything that is impure, selfish or corrupting will no longer find expression. This is something that we can experience personally within ourselves now, though then it will be universal, no longer tested and in conflict with a world at present under the rule of 'The prince of this world'.

SECTION 1: PART 1

The Right Character

Matthew chapter 21:11 – 22:46
It is What We Are, not Who We Are, that Decides our Suitability to Enter the Kingdom of God

What anger the religious leaders must have felt when Christ preached the parable of the wicked husbandmen to His crowd of listeners. They would have quickly realised who Jesus was referring to, just as would have His disciples and the rest of the people listening. How horrified they would have been as He went on to say that the 'Vineyard' was to be taken from them and given to others. What did He mean? Was God going to take away His 'chosen people' status from the Jews? Jesus was saying to them in effect, 'Do you not realise that God's promise to Abraham was given for a purpose and that that purpose was to involve their active participation? Jesus was making it quite clear that Israel was not just chosen to become a great nation, but to 'bear fruit' to God through bringing those blessings that they enjoyed to the nations. Instead they had regarded themselves as an elite, as inheritors of God's Divine Law, which the religious leaders in particular had jealously regarded themselves as the keepers and up-holders thereof.

In Genesis 12:3 God had promised to Abraham that in him would all the nations of the Earth be blest. This promise was reiterated to his grandson, Jacob, after God had appeared to him in a dream at Bethel. It was added as well to Jacob that his descendants would become a great nation, Genesis 28:14. This the Jews, the tribe of Israel that still dwelt in the land at the time of Christ, assumed was the status quo that they would continue to enjoy until their long-promised Messiah came and then they would be the superior nation ruling over all the Earth.

Jesus makes it quite plain to them though that not only had they failed to give to God what was expected of them and bring Him true worship and service, but as a nation they had murdered His messengers sent to call them to change their ways. On top of this Jesus exposed their motives that would lead them to kill their own Messiah, so that they could maintain their existing reputation, and control God's own kingdom to suit their own interests.

The Jews were hoping at that time for their Messiah to appear, but what they were wanting and expecting was a great military leader who would lead them to victory over the Roman tyranny. It was plain though from Jesus' parable that the coming of Messiah was to be the coming of their Lord in the form of His own Son. This was to be a time of reckoning, a time of giving account, not one of glory and exaltation.

Jesus then goes on to tell two further parables that would further challenge their self-esteem and anger them even more. First He likens the state of Israel to a building, though only Judah and a half tribe of Benjamin had existed by now as a state for about seven hundred years. What the religious leaders would have conceived that building to be can only be imagined, though Jesus is now plainly talking of Himself as the stone rejected by the builders. It would have angered them though to be told that He was the one on whom that building would be formed, He was the one part that would hold this building all together. This 'building' is of course the Kingdom of Heaven, a spiritual 'building', or administration, not a physical one or even just an outwardly religious institution. This implied that their religious works were not acceptable to God as the foundation for His Kingdom and that just as they rejected and would kill the one whom God had chosen, so too would God destroy them, individually and collectively.

Jesus then goes on to tell the parable of the guests that spurned the invitation to the wedding feast. The inference as to the Jews being the guests that will be excluded from God's blessings and that those people that they despised as becoming the guests that do enjoy His blessing is too obvious for them to miss. Their intuitive assumption perhaps would have been for them to imagine themselves as the bride in the story in any event, considering scriptures like Hosea 2:19-20, which likened Israel as to a 'bride' of Jehovah. Jesus though clearly intimates that rather than being a favoured people, their disobedience would cause them to be excluded from blessing and be destroyed instead. Anger is beginning to turn to fury, especially when He goes on to condemn the

Pharisees and teachers in plain language for their hypocrisy and the burdens that they were imposing on the people of Israel, bringing them into religious 'slavery' rather than bringing them the blessings that God would give them; which is what they would have done if they had truly honoured and obeyed the law of God.

Looking at things objectively though, it may have seemed that God had failed in His plan to bring all nations to blessing through Israel as He had said He would to Abraham. God forbid; rather that through man's failure God had shown that mankind was incapable of administering those blessings themselves.

Christ Himself has given us a clue already of quite the opposite, that God had not failed, rather it is now God alone that would fulfil that promise; He tells us how in the following parable, in is His metaphor of the rejected stone of the builders.

God Himself had planned before the world was created as to how mankind would be redeemed and that was not through religious observance, or of Israel's own ideas of keeping of God's Holy Law. It certainly was not through the distorted religion that Judaism had become. It was indeed through the One who would come from the tribe of Judah as prophesied in the Law and the Prophets. It was God's own Son, Israel's Messiah, who would be the only one who ever fulfilled the law completely and would then lead His people in living as God intended.

The verse of scripture from Psalm 118:22 that our Lord quoted to the Pharisees was, 'The stone which the builders rejected has become the chief cornerstone'. At first this doesn't seem to fit in with what Christ has just been saying.

On the face of it, it would seem that He had just offered this scripture in reply to the Jew's answer that the vineyard would be given to new husbandmen. Indeed in verse 43 He confirms that this is exactly what He means, but why had He made this quotation first in reply to them. We can imagine His audience quizzically curious about what He saying; then Christ goes on to say by way of explanation, but in a way to make them think, in verse 44 'Whoever falls on this stone shall be broken...' but then adds ominously, 'But on whomever it falls, it will grind him to powder'.

It is the very fact of His rejection that has qualified Him to become the head of all God's creation, see Philippians 2:5-11; as He said Himself, 'All authority is given to me in Heaven and on Earth' Matthew 28:18.

It then follows that those who 'fall' on Him, who are broken by His rejection and death, who in repentance and contrition share His meekness and humility, will find restoration in Him; As the Apostle Paul describes the character of those that fall on Him: 'For we are to God the fragrance of Christ,' 2 Corinthians 2:15, and 'An offering and a sacrifice to God for a sweet smelling aroma,' Ephesians 5:2.

The metaphor in these parables of what God is doing has moved on from a vineyard to a building, an analogy in connection with the spiritual building that we now know to be His Church, from (Acts 4:11) and (1 Peter 2:7), though the vineyard and the building are different aspects of the same thing, as indeed is the third metaphor of the wedding in the next parable that Jesus tells. The key 'character' changes from 'The Son' in the first parable to the 'chief corner stone' in the second, then back to 'The Son' in the third metaphor. The 'building' then has a purpose, to bear fruit to God, to bear His character and so be suitable to occupy and enjoy the 'feast' of His heavenly presence.

In each we have something that God has planned and brought into being for a specific purpose. That purpose in each is the inheritance of Christ, built around Christ or for His glory. If as a vineyard it is the place that God receives spiritual 'fruit', Ephesians 2:19-22 develops the picture for us to explain it as a building in its nature, construction, function and purpose, where God dwells within us as the nature of Christ is manifested in our lives:

'The household of God,
having been built on the foundation of the apostles and prophets,
Jesus Christ Himself being the chief cornerstone,
in whom the whole building, being fitted together,
grows into a holy temple in the Lord,
in whom you also are being built together
for a dwelling place of God in the Spirit.'

It is this whole 'household' who bear the 'fruit'. This building though is still in construction at present. At the end of the book of Revelation though we see this building as the Holy City New Jerusalem, 'coming down from Heaven adorned as a bride for her husband', complete in every detail, some things of which are not yet in view here, but this is something to look forward to at the end of the Book.

To return to Matthew 21 though, here Jesus just wants to develop the issue of the fact that Israel, and the Jews in particular to whom He was talking, had failed to live up to what God required, where He likens the Kingdom of Heaven to a royal marriage. Israel had not only failed to bear fruit through honouring God in keeping His law and rejected the one in whom this could and would be fulfilled, they had also spurned their God who wanted to fill them with every spiritual blessing as David expressed in Psalm 23. They had though consistently pursued other gods instead, flouting the very first commandment, (cp Psalm 81:9-12) they had also pursued their own interests turning to their own standard of living and to business. They had then despised and persecuted the messengers of God who had come to tell them of His blessings so freely available to them by returning to their true God.

So follows the counterpart to the previous parable, the nation to whom the vineyard was to be given to, to bear the fruit in their place; that comes in the next parable at the beginning of chapter 22. This group is now depicted as those that were the most disreputable and ignoble in society, the ones that were to inherit what the Jews had regarded as their unalienable right. It would not be lost on the leaders at least that what He was implying was that the blessings and privileges of God would be taken from them and given to those that they despised the most, outcasts and gentiles.

There then follows an extra episode to this story, one that sounds rather inconsistent at face value until we realize the implications. The man, taken off the streets, a complete stranger, poor, rough and vulgar, was brought not only to the King's palace but also to such a prestigious event.

He wasn't dressed though for the occasion. The custom in the Jewish culture at that time was for the marriage supper to be held at the bridegroom's home and the wedding garments for the guests to be provided by the bridegroom's father. The metaphor here then is clear, the 'garment' that the guests must wear at this celebration in the Kingdom of God must be provided by God Himself. We cannot come 'dressed' in our own fitness; cp Revelation 19:7-8:

> 'Let us be glad and rejoice and give Him glory,
>
> for the marriage of the Lamb has come, and His wife has made herself ready.
>
> And to her it was granted to be arrayed in fine linen, clean and bright,
>
> for the fine linen is the righteous acts of the saints.'

Christ though was making a profound spiritual point here. No one can come as they are into the presence of God; no one can receive the blessings of God except on His terms, no one is good enough to come as they are without being clothed in the garments of the 'Kingdom'. Luke 15:22 has the same idea in Jesus' parable of the prodigal son. It was the son's returning to his father and having faith in his mercy that caused him to receive the 'robe' of blessing and acceptance. The Jews at the time had their own interpretation of what made them acceptable to God. They were the biological descendants of Abraham and Isaac and that they thought would qualify them. Jesus is saying, no, not what you are by nature but only as being clothed by the standard that God requires can you come into His presence and into His Kingdom. This episode in the story just gives us another aspect of the truth that Jesus was explaining in His previous parables. It is the son that did the will of his Father, it is those that bear the fruit that God requires, it is those that are built on the chief cornerstone that are acceptable and only those that are clothed in an acceptable character that are approved to inhabit that spiritual sphere.

The scene then changes as the Jews respond by trying to discredit Jesus by catching Him in His answers to their questions. This, as we might expect of course, they fail to do and Jesus instead confounds the teachers, showing their weakness up to the crowds. Jesus continues then to warn the crowd of the error they are being led into by the Pharisees and Sadducees. His disciples though are still waiting for the opportunity to ask their master something. They point out to Jesus something that seems to them inconsistent with what He had been teaching in His parables. The Temple buildings still stood strongly as a testimony to the Jews and God's dealings with them. If God was going to give His blessings to 'another nation', how could this be?

Our Lord then in chapter 24 of Matthew's Gospel goes on to answer His disciples' question about how these things could happen, when all these things should take place and what the sign of His return to Earth would be. This we will go on to look at in the next section of in this book.

Jesus' warning then is both salutary and sinister. It is God Himself 'built' within us individually and together that qualifies us for the Kingdom of God, not what we do of ourselves, however enthusiastic and outwardly religious that maybe. Also we cannot experience the state of joy and pleasure of 'Being in Christ' without being clothed with His righteousness, His nature of love, humility and obedience.

SECTION 1: PART 2

The Right Pedigree

Revelation Chapters 1-3
Christ Alone is Worthy to Bring in the New Order

Man was first created by God to govern over His creation. This man has done but not to care for and promote it as he should have, but rather he has simply refused to accept his accountability and exploited it for his own ends, to the point that today it is fast being destroyed. Likewise when God made a covenant with Israel that would give them success and happiness, a blessing that they were then to extend to all nations, they turned their backs on it or distorted its tenets to create a religion that was elitist and selfish. Throughout their history they had singularly failed to be faithful to the principles of God's Law, so now they must step aside while a new community could be established, one taken from among all the nations, to administer the blessings of the Kingdom of God. It is as Lord of that new community, His Church, that Christ is first revealed in the Revelation. He it is that is encouraging that people to become the society that will be of that disposition that God requires, a people indwelt by His own nature, a people reformed from what is natural and carnal into what is gracious and Divine; the image of Christ.

The Book begins with the affirmation that it is God Himself that is the authority, both on the way that Christ would be revealed and to whom it would be made known. This is conveyed in the first place to the apostle John, the one specifically that bore witness to Christ, His testimony and the things that he saw Him do. How then are we sure that all this is absolutely authentic? It is through the medium of faith alone, not by reason or logic:

- First by reading it, that is carefully considering the prophecy.

- Then hearing it, that is accepting it.

- Then believing its message and also keeping it, that is living according to its tenets and implications.

The confirmation that we get then is directly from God Himself, the assurance of its truth and the hope in God that it brings about to us; something that then becomes true knowledge as we experience its reality in our lives.

The reason for taking such notice is given 'because the time is near', that is at hand, very close. It is something that is repeated in the last chapter of the Revelation. That though was nearly two thousand years ago, so what is meant by 'near'? It means primarily that its message is particularly relevant now because the times we are living in specifically precede its fulfilment. It is not about the length of time but its bearing on the present time.

John then sends greeting to those to whom the Revelation is addressed, that is, God's servants (v.1). 'To the seven local churches that are in Asia Minor'; according to Young this was where the earliest Christian churches were planted. The implication here is then it is addressed to every section of the Church in its various conditions and localities, historically and successively. It is pertinent to all the Church, to every member in every generation.

To emphasise, this it is not only addressed to all those that can know the grace of God and the power of His sevenfold Spirit; more specifically it is for those that do know Christ personally, His faithfulness and the power of His resurrection. Then it is also addressed to those that have known personally His love and cleansing power and the place of privilege and prerogative that we can know in Him. It is specifically addressed then to all those that belong to Christ. Each letter then is relevant to each of us individually; it is not that different letters pertain only to different persons, groups or eras. The seven letters were sent to all the churches.

John then finishes his preamble to introduce the one of whom the Book is all about, His coming and His pre-eminence. Firstly then, the dramatic event of His coming itself; Christ is coming, not just to a select few but to everyone in the world, not just to those that love Him but to those also that reject and hate Him. For them it will be a time of regret and sorrow. Right from the beginning of time though Christ has been God's original and ultimate purpose for His world. The whole course of human history has been to establish His character and prerogative throughout the whole world. It is He that is the Almighty, it is His grace, humility and gentleness that will be completely ascendant in His coming Kingdom. It is He that is the First and the Last in all God's purposes.

Verse 10 then begins the vision, or rather sequence of visions, with Christ Himself speaking to John. Turning, the first thing he sees is the symbolic representations of the local churches, though central to them all is the glorious figure of Christ Himself. His appearance and dress identify His Divine character, being and might. It is He that is central in all things to the Church, that is His people. It is He that has total authority, command and glory. The effect on us to really see Christ as He truly is in this way is like it was to John, to utterly prostrate ourselves before Him, totally inert and amenable to Him. His response then is gentle and reassuring, before giving John his commission and the meaning to the things he had seen.

What he is told to write seems at first somewhat enigmatic. First each letter is not addressed to the individual churches but to 'their angels', though what the angels are is perhaps not immediately obvious. Next, the content of the letters addresses the state of those churches though the rewards are promised to individuals. Thirdly the messages are also addressed as a private message to each specified church, though John's instructions are to 'Send it in a book to all the churches' (ch. 1:11).

We are told that the 'angels' are represented as stars, so perhaps we can start with that. The symbolic use of a star is common in our own language as well as in the Bible, though we can fall into error if we put our own or a familiar meaning to things. The scripture itself defines the meaning and gives us ample understanding of these mystical words if we study them. For example, in Daniel 12:3 we have: '...Those who turn many to righteousness shall shine like the stars forever and ever'. Paul, in 1 Corinthians 15:41 says, '...One star differs from another star in glory'.

We have then in these two verses alone the concepts of 'light, brightness and glory', that is their spiritual radiance and expression or the honour and dignity they display, in a word the testimony they radiate. If this is the character then of the churches that is being focused on, that is being addressed at the churches, how though are they 'angels' as well?

We usually think of an angel as simply a glorious heavenly being, a messenger or servant of Jehovah and most usually this is what is meant by 'an angel', though it's significance is as a spiritual being, not necessarily physical, even if a supernatural one. We can get the best understanding from scripture itself: 'Who makes His angels spirits; His ministers a flame of fire'- Psalm 104:1-4. Hebrews 1:14 asks us the rhetorical question, 'Are they not all ministering spirits, sent forth to minister?'

Sometimes though it can simply mean 'messenger' (as the Greek word 'angelos' maybe translated), either as an animate being as in 2 Corinthians 11:14, 'Satan himself transforms himself into an angel of light', or as an inanimate or abstract being as in 2 Corinthians 12:7, 'a thorn in the flesh... a messenger of Satan to buffet me'.

The angel in Revelation 22:9 identifies himself with John as his 'fellow-servant', which broadens our understanding of angels as spiritual beings and messengers and servants of God, a spiritual image that the corporate Church also shares. The meaning then of 'angel' then is spiritual; their manifestation though may vary.

These angels in our passage then are messengers of the respective local churches and therefore are the ministry of those churches themselves as an entity; that is in what they give to God in service and worship, and in their testimony and witness, both actively and passively to all His creation. The message then is addressed directly to the churches' testimony that they radiate; the spiritual essence of each Church.

The angels are clearly a function of the churches themselves and the individual members of them in their particular ministries, in identifying their individual character and Christian responsibility. As 'stars' they are held in His right hand, which reminds us not only of our Lord's leadership of our service but also of course the security we have in the service that we are called to do. Also from our point of view it reminds us of the necessity of our obedience to Him as Lord, and our responsibility to His calling; primarily in our mystical representation of His holiness that our lives display as a witness to Him.

Christ then is to be revealed to the whole world as absolute Lord Master and Judge. This Book though starts with His manifestation to the Church, when it was only a few decades old, but one that has already developed the failings and problems that will be a feature of the Church throughout its history. In chapter 2 He appears now not as Saviour and upholder of His Church as we had in chapter 1, but now He holds sway as Lord and overseer of His

Church. He now is revealed in us rather than just to us in the 'the things that are', an ongoing process of being manifest in the lives of each and every believer. This is what Christ meant in Luke 17:21, 'The Kingdom of God is within you'. Christ is being revealed through the process of sanctification in the hearts of all that love Him. In these chapters therefore we see the process still in the state of being realized at this present time in each successive generation. When that process will be complete our heavenly Father alone knows.

Each individual locality or church has its own set of assets and in most cases failings, and our Lord represents Himself to each one as having the particular quality that is relevant to their situation. Not only does He censure the assemblies but He first commends what is good and profitable, not only make warnings regarding what is deficient, He also makes promises to those that amend and do well. The work of creating the life of Christ in each believer is the work of God alone. We cannot even begin to conceive what that work is of ourselves; it is God alone that reveals that work in us throughout our lives. It is not just a passive process though, where we just get on with our lives and leave our sanctification to God. It is a process that we need to be actively, continuously and thoroughly involved with and cooperating with in every aspect of life. This is shown quite clearly in these chapters; first our Lord reveals to each of us what is lacking in us, that is if we are seeking diligently to follow Him. It is then if we repent, honestly seeking to turn our short fallings around, that God empowers us to do so. This is being an 'Overcomer', one that overcomes through the Blood of the Lamb, cp chapter 12:11.

It is a process of self-renunciation and sacrifice in identification with Him; letting His Lamb like spirit permeate our own hearts and souls.

At the beginning of each letter, Christ starts by saying to the church, 'I know your works', that is, what is significant to Him as His servants. Israel was ordained to be God's servant (Isaiah 49:3) but as we have seen, singularly failed to do so as the Mosaic Law was not in itself sufficient to produce the faithfulness and works of grace that are necessary. Now Christ not only recognises the progress that the churches are making, but also recognises the problems that have arisen in the discharge of their responsibilities as servants. It is in serving Him that we glorify Him as His glory is displayed, that is revealed, in us. We do not serve Him as we do earthly masters in that what we achieve is of our own strength and personal qualification, but rather we serve Him through the out-working of what God has achieved in us. We serve Him as His Glory is displayed in our lives; this is what true witness is.

Thus we do well to consider the failings recognised in each of the seven churches, failings to which we are all vulnerable and then open our hearts before God to see what our needs are. These are highlighted in these chapters; religious formality, idolatry, fornication, heresy, hypocrisy, worldly compromise, deadness, materialism and pride. All these things are very subtle and insidious and things we all naturally tend towards and lack insight into. A heart that is receptive though will hear the voice of their Lord speaking to them.

However to each church He does not talk first of their failings but of those 'works' that they do excel in, patient continuance in suffering, faithfulness, diligence, virtue, loyalty and compassion. As an encouragement to continue therein and as an incentive to overcome their failings He paints a picture of the life that is and will be experienced by those that do fully and sincerely love Him. What they will know is a deeper and fuller identification with Him and a more profound familiarity with His Divine Life.

SECTION 1: PART 3

A Calling to Account

Revelation Chapters 1-3
'Because Lawlessness Shall Abound The Love of Many will Grow Cold': Matthew 24:12

After about 60 years of Church history it is our Lord Himself that calls His Church to account, to review their progress with them, to see what might be going wrong and to bring things back on track. He may be the 'owner of the vineyard who has gone away to a far country', but that does not mean that He is not watching closely over the progress of us all and also keeping in contact with all His Church. What we can glean from these letters, to advance our own spiritual growth to a deeper and more fulfilling relationship with Him, cannot be overestimated; what we will consider here is just some insight as to how profound these letters are and important to each one of us.

To start with, let us look at a summary of the rewards promised in these seven letters to the churches just to see what it is that Christ is looking to do in and for each of us. This is a brief summary of where our potential in Christ lies, one that can show us the fullness of what God has for those that overcome our natural weaknesses; one that shows us the unique spiritual nature of every blessing that is promised:

- For those whose love for Christ is paramount and constant, they will experience the life of paradise.

- For those that maintain their witness in persecution, they will never ever suffer the pain of separation from their God; these are those that are the faithful, that are resurrected on Christ's return to Earth to reign.

- For those that resist the temptation to compromise with the values of this world, they will know an especially intimate relationship with Him, and find true and satisfying nourishment in Him.

- For those that stay faithful to Him, resisting the desires of our instinctive nature, ruling over their own fleshly desires and propensities, will rule with Him on Earth and in the meantime be given that confident expectation of His coming to sustain us. (The morning star in our hearts, see below)

- For those whose faith and principles remains pure and uncorrupted by other motives and interests will attain to be like Christ Himself, clothed in His righteousness.

- For those, albeit weak, having remained true to His

word and testimony will be the strength and upholder of His Church; He will keep them from further tribulation and deception and publicly identify them as His own.

- Lastly to those that relinquish the security of materialism, self-satisfaction and worldly wisdom to adopt heavenly ways will rule with Him in that heavenly city for all eternity.

The pathway to these blessings though is fraught with many dangers and difficulties; the Christian life is a constant battle against evil, in the world, in our own nature and against the devil. It is necessary however to travel this path if we are to attain to those blessings. As Paul said in Romans 8:18:

> 'I reckon that the sufferings of this present time
> are not worthy to be compared
> with the glory that shall be revealed in us.'

In Ephesus Christ is seen as 'holding 7 stars in His right hand and walking amidst the 7 lampstands'. He is the 'chief executive' of the Church, to use a modern term, and watching over this fledgling congregation He sees immediately where they are beginning to fail; they have lost none of their patience, virtue, wisdom and enthusiasm, but they have lost the very thing that should underpin all that, their simple and un-compromised love for their Lord.

They had lost that fundamental link with their master, the very life of His Spirit flowing through them and around them. This was not a human love that was dependant on fickle whims and passions but something far greater, something that had been the very 'ground of their being,' changing their whole life perspective, attitude and direction.

So why had they lost it? Had other affections or interests come in to displace them from their once glorious position? Had they become judgmental in their attitudes? Were they now just obsessive in their enthusiasm or elitist in their outlook? We don't know is the simple answer, we are not told; it could have been all or any of those things. To fall away from that Rock, to lose that spiritual bond with their Lord, meant that whatever they did then was in their own strength and therefore was of no consequence, a formal outward expression of religion, albeit worthy in form but one that had lost that undercurrent of Divine love. The remedy though was not to try a little harder, patch things up and try and love the Lord more. There was nothing they could do, practically, intellectually or emotionally but simply repent, that is turn around entirely, turn back to Christ in simple obedience and penitence, asking for forgiveness and restoration. As they waited thus on Him, He would do the rest and restore them to their state of grace and devotion.

Why though would the lampstand soon be removed if nothing were done? How was their continuing status dependant on their ongoing, unconditional love for their Lord? We have to remember what the imagery is here. What John saw in his vision was seven golden lampstands or a seven-branched candlestick. It is the lampstands that hold the candles. Christ said twice in Luke's Gospel, in chapter 8:16 and 11:33 that no man lights a candle and then hides it under a bed or jug. It is put on a lampstand for all to see. The function of the lampstand is simply to display the light of the candle. Likewise our only function is to display the light of Christ. If we cannot do that, we become redundant and useless. Here the lampstand is specifically the local church; that would cease to exist, at least as a proprietor of the light of Christ. To move the analogy a little, it depends on what our treasure is; Christ and His graces or our own good works. As Christ said in Matthew 6:20-23:

> 'Lay up for yourselves treasure in Heaven
> where neither moth nor rust destroys
> and thieves do not break in and steal,
> for where your treasure is, there your heart will be also.
> The lamp of the body is the eye;
> if therefore your eye is good, your whole body will be full of light.
> But if your eye is bad, your whole body will be full of darkness.
> If therefore the light that is within you is darkness
> how great is that darkness!'

> 'He who has an ear, let him hear what the Spirit says to the churches.
> To him who overcomes I will give to eat from the tree of life,
> which is in the midst of the Paradise of God.'

The next church, at Smyrna, was a materially poor, weak, troubled flock that had been infiltrated by false brethren and teaching. The Lord though presents Himself to them as the one that was dead but now is alive. It was through His weakness and suffering that He had conquered and now so would this little church in Him. We no doubt, would have seen Ephesus as the strong, dynamic church that was doing well and Smyrna as the small weak one that might succumb to the pressures upon it. The Lord though does not look upon the outward appearance but upon the heart. Ephesus had lost its heart; religion had become formal, albeit sound in practice. Smyrna, though weak and vulnerable, had its heart in the right place; their faith was founded upon a rock, their love for their Lord was living and vibrant. Their works, that is their deeds, their inward grace and outward love was noticed by their Lord; that was all that mattered. All our Lord has to say to them is by way of encouragement and reassurance that He would sustain and reward them. What else could we ask for?

> 'Be faithful until death, and I will give you
> the crown of life.
>
> He who has an ear, let him hear what the Spirit
> says to the churches.
>
> He who overcomes shall not be hurt by
> the second death.'

The next Church, Pergamos, had already been through the trial that still faced Smyrna, they had held fast through evil surroundings and persecution; even to the point where one of them had been martyred. They had though come to the next impediment in the Christian life. After having overcome persecution, we can fall prey to false teaching. Such ideas can be so insidious, credible and seemingly reasonable that not realising our own vulnerability at the time we are so easily led astray. Our Lord here though portrays Himself as the one with the double-edged sword, the sword that divides between the thoughts and intents of the heart, Hebrews 4:12. The Lord knew their spiritual condition though, their progress inwardly and outwardly that they had remained faithful even in a satanic environment. They had however fallen prey to subtle but perfidious ideas.

2 Peter 2:10-15 summarises the error of Balaam, recorded in the Old Testament in Numbers 22-24. Balaam was a soothsayer who led Israel into idolatry and adultery so that they would be cursed and defeated. So easily are we tempted into seemingly innocuous activities and interests that lead our hearts away from following the Lord single-mindedly. Such is the implication of idolatry and adultery in scripture. It was something that Israel was reminded to guard against several times after Balaam, over the years, by the prophets; it is a perennial threat. It is important here to note that it was not the practice of these things that was the problem in Pergamos, but that they were tolerating those there that believed that it was acceptable to eat meat offered to idols and to indulge in sexual immorality. As Paul said; Galatians 5:9, 'A little leaven leavens the whole lump', false ideas and inappropriate behaviour soon permeate through the whole company.

Turn this situation around immediately says Christ, or I will have to come and personally intervene through my word, battling with you until the matter is resolved.

'He who has an ear, let him hear what the Spirit

says to the churches.

To him who overcomes I will give some of the hidden manna to eat.

And I will give him a white stone,

and on the stone a new name written

which no one knows except him who receives it.'

In Thyatira the church seems wonderful, the people's relationship with their Lord was sound, they were loving faithful, patient and serving their Lord and community. They were also growing in grace and knowledge of their Lord; what more could you ask for?

The problem here was that the ethical standards that were tolerated at Pergamos had not been dealt with at Thyatira, although these believers were more developed spiritually in other ways. They had not rooted out the leaven and now the lax moral outlook had developed into toleration of an outwardly corrupt person, a person compared here to the evil wife of King Ahab, who wreaked such havoc in Israel; see 1 Kings 18-21 and 2 Kings 9. This later 'Jezebel' was corrupting the hearts, lives and practice of some of the members of that church. Idolatry and adultery can take so many subtle forms in practice, from sexual craving to the love of money and material things. Our Lord though understands that we cannot defend against these things by ourselves sufficiently, however devout and spiritually mature we are.

Christ though presents Himself to this church as one with eyes as flames of fire and feet as fine brass. His penetrating vision will shine into our hearts and consciences, convincing us and teaching us, consuming what is debauched. He will teach us His walk, one worthy of Himself in radiant strength, to exercise restraint and rule our hearts with power and steadfastness.

> 'And he who overcomes, and keeps My works until the end,
>
> to him I will give power over the nations—
>
> He shall rule them with a rod of iron;
> they shall be dashed to pieces like the potter's vessels'.
>
> As I also have received from My Father;
>
> and I will give him the morning star.
>
> He who has an ear, let him hear what the Spirit says to the churches.'

To read through these letters suggests that they are collectively a spiritual journey, enlightening us as to the dangers and problems that we can expect to meet on our way. When we come to the next congregation at Sardis there is little said to describe their status, but what is said is sufficient. Their outward appearance was of a lively, thriving community, they were no doubt loving, caring, enthusiastic and outwardly devout. Christ though presents Himself here as the one that has the seven spirits of God, cp Isaiah 11:2-3.

- 'The Spirit of wisdom
- and understanding,
- The Spirit of counsel
- and might

- The Spirit of knowledge
- and of the fear of the Lord.
- Finally, his delight is in the fear of the Lord,'

Christ knows though that the true spirit that inspires that church is not His own, to Him they are dead in many ways, that is dissociated from His love and communion; religiously perfect, culturally above reproach but without His Spirit inspiring and guiding them.

It seems strange perhaps that such a mature church, one that seemed to be thriving outwardly could be so severely sanctioned by the Lord, so what had gone wrong? The clue comes in verse 3, they were not looking for or living in the expectancy of His return, something that had been promised to be given as a spiritual gift to the church at Thyatira.

Now the morning star is a beautiful picture that we find in 2 Peter 1:19. Speaking in the general context of Peter's letter which is the second coming of Christ, this verse comes from his introduction, where he is concerned that the believers to whom he was writing should be settled and strong in their faith. This he says we are encouraged in our faith by considering the reliable words of prophecy in scripture, all that which is yet to be fulfilled; Christ's coming again. This he says:

> 'The more sure word of prophecy to which you do well to heed,
>
> as a light that shines in a dark place,
>
> until the day dawns and the morning star rises in your hearts.'

The morning star is that which shines just before the sunrise, typically Christ's actual coming; in the meantime you will have that promise of its immediacy shining in and illuminating your hearts.

Christ gives us another eloquent picture, yet a poignant warning of how we should be living faithfully with regards His return in Matthew 24:42-48. It is those that carry on faithfully doing the work that we have been appointed to do, in the hope that He will return any moment, always longing to see Him; that will be rewarded.

Our Lord presents Himself in this situation though also as having the seven stars, that is, messengers or ministry of the church; note that it is Christ that has that, not ourselves. These seven stars are not the doctrine that we might hold dear and preach but the light that the Holy Spirit alone gives to our hearts and radiates in witness from our lives. What they had been taught, what they believed and the doctrine that they held was true, but it had ceased to be relevant to their lives, and what they believed was just theoretical. They must return to their former state where what they believed was the foundation for an active, vibrant faith and real trust. Their way of life was imperfect it was inspired by the wrong motives, there was little left of thought, feeling or action that was motivated by a deep love for the Lord. There were those however who had not become tainted by that outlook even with the apostasy of some; they are those that are encouraged and commended. There were others though that were genuine but had become spoiled by the influence of those that had relapsed. They were called to return to their former state.

There were those there also though that had relapsed entirely, their profession was just a complete sham; Romans 8:8-9 tells us their status:

'Those who are in the flesh cannot please God...
Now if anyone does not have the Spirit of Christ he is not His.'

Those that are in Christ, even if their faith is weak and inadequate, He will continue to encourage to the end; what He has saved however cannot be lost, 1 Corinthians 3:12-15. What can be lost though is the prize for faithfulness. Those that had remained pure or had repented would walk with Him in purity, be one with Him in mind and heart, this was the prize here to attain to.

'He who overcomes shall be clothed in white garments, and I will not blot out his name from the Book of Life;
but I will confess his name before My Father and before His angels.
He who has an ear, let him hear what the Spirit says to the churches.'

Philadelphia is the next stage of our journey through the Christian life, or as characterised here the state of a whole local community. Our Lord says to them as to each of the churches, 'I know your works'; He knows everything about them, their essential spiritual state and what fruit that had born. They pass, full marks, there is no criticism here. As in Smyrna they were weak and faced difficulty and danger, but our Lord just has encouragement and reassurance. They had made the grade; as with Paul they had 'fought the good fight, they had finished the race, they had kept the faith,' 2 Timothy 4:7. They would be spared any further tribulation that was coming on the rest of mankind, to test and purify them. Like Paul they just had a crown of life to look forward to and the particular three-fold prize that they would receive.

They were weak but had kept faith, outwardly poor and seemingly taciturn perhaps and ineffectual but at heart they were loyal. It is they that will be the upholders and character of the future heavenly administration, not the just outwardly religious however enthusiastic they maybe, cp Matthew 21:31. They had suffered persecution but had borne it patiently, they were now promised an 'open door', and nothing could now stand in their way of reaching their prize; there is just a caveat to remain vigilant lest they be distracted from the path. They were now in sight of the heavenly city as Pilgrim in Pilgrim's Progress.

> 'He who overcomes, I will make him a pillar in the temple of My God,
>
> and he shall go out no more.
>
> I will write on him the name of My God and the name of the city of My God,
>
> The New Jerusalem, which comes down out of Heaven from My God.
>
> And I will write on him My new name.
>
> He who has an ear, let him hear what the Spirit says to the churches.'

Our Lord's harshest words though are reserved for the last of the seven Churches. The contrast here between Philadelphia and Laodicea couldn't be more dramatic. Philadelphia, that is the church of 'brotherly love', its heart was right and it was progressing well. Laodicea may also have been like this once, but serves as a reminder that although we may be progressing well we are still vulnerable in this life to fail. This was why Philadelphia was warned, 'hold fast what you have, that no man take your crown'. We can easily be deceived or drift into apathy and contentment; this had happened at Laodicea. Christ though doesn't threaten to reject or disown them; rather He encourages and cajoles them to restore them to a state of grace.

'I am the Amen,' He says to them, that is the steadfast one, 'the Faithful and True Witness.' In effect He is saying:

'I always remain totally true and faithful; it is you that have become barren and insipid.

'I am the beginning of the creation of God:' everything in all creation started with me, it was I that chose you and drew you to me, but you have drifted away from Me.

I know the workings of your heart, you are not dead and completely indifferent to me as some of those at Sardis, on the other hand you are not fervent either as those at Philadelphia or Smyrna. I could wish you were either indifferent or fervent. If you were one or the other that might be as expected or sympathised with. Those that are not mine will ever stand as a witness to the righteousness of God and the mercy He has shown to others. Those that fail out of weakness I have compassion for. Of my own people they will one day be perfect, my bride for all eternity.

Some convenient accommodation in between apathy and fervency though is repulsive to me; I cannot accommodate it. You, because you are lukewarm, are neither cold nor hot.' (Christ reiterates this for the third time to give it paramount emphasis, to show how significant the matter is) 'I cannot contain you, I have no fellowship with you.'

The reason why they had drifted into that twilight relationship with their Lord was because they thought, 'I am rich, I have become wealthy, and have need of nothing.' They had equated material blessings with spiritual blessings. All the other Churches had had difficulties, persecutions and anxieties, life was difficult often because of their faithfulness to Christ. At Laodicea however things were quite different. They were comfortable, they had all the modern conveniences of life, were well-fed and materially secure. Their religion had become a routine, their faith wasn't relevant to their day-to-day lives; they still acknowledged Christ as Saviour but He had ceased to be truly Lord and Master. Their love for Him had become part time and mediocre. Our Lord though is understanding and just wants to show them the way back. In effect He is saying,

'You do not realise that what I see is your spiritual state, your physical status is incidental; it is your heart that I see, holiness, virtue and understanding is what I expect to see, but I see none of that'.

'What you need is resources that you get directly from me, gold, that which is everlasting, my steadfastness, faithfulness and truth. It is my Spirit that you need and white garments, that you may be clothed. It is my righteousness with which you need to be clothed; at the moment you have neither; you are 'wretched, miserable, poor, blind, and naked. You should be embarrassed at your shame; then anoint your eyes with eye salve so that you can see the truth.'

What though is this eye salve and how do we apply it? The word here is 'collyrium', an ointment or poultice to heal the eyes. It implies then that we need to be healed as does the context, our sight needs to be restored. The ointment though we apply ourselves, the clue to what this is in the way that He introduces Himself to this congregation as 'the beginning of the creation of God'.

John 3:3 'unless one is born again he cannot see (ie appreciate) the Kingdom of God', he has no comprehension of it. The Kingdom is what has to be continually born in us in every area of our being and throughout this life. This ointment then that we apply is His healing balm, His precious Spirit recreating in us. This does though require our due diligence and putting into effect by casting ourselves on Him. Philippians 2:12.

'That you may see;' says Christ, that is see your real state; letting the Holy Spirit guide you into all truth, convincing you of your fault, of what is the right way and giving you the power to correct the matter. cp John 16:8

He says in effect 'My love for you hasn't changed, it is yours that has waned; I only want you to accept me as truly Lord and that means that I must scold and discipline you. So be fervent, be 'hot', turn back from the direction you have been going, return to the place where you left the straight and narrow path and focus your eyes alone on me in future. I died for you that you might live alone for me and in me. He that forfeits his own comfortable, convenient self-life for my sake and the gospel shall find it, the true, lasting, meaningful, victorious life found in Christ alone.

'Behold, I stand at the door and knock.

If anyone hears My voice and opens the door,

I will come in to him and dine with him, and he with Me.

To him who overcomes I will grant to sit with
Me on My throne,

as I also overcame and sat down with My Father
on His throne.'

'He who has an ear, let him hear what the Spirit
says to the churches.'

SECTION 1: PART 4

A Deafening Silence

Revelation Chapter 8:1-6

'Because Lawlessness Shall Abound The Love of Many will Grow Cold': Matthew 24:12

At this present time quite clearly, with all the distress, evil and corruption in the world, the reign of God's kingdom throughout the world has not yet materialized. In this prophetic scene though, all that is about to change; the seventh seal is about to be broken and then that heavenly scroll of authority, that mandate to rule the world, will be open in the hand of the Lamb, the only one in Heaven and Earth found worthy to possess such an auspicious distinction. Now it is open it is fully effective and apparent to all. The worship and acclaim that had greeted Christ as He was given the scroll though now fades to silence, an ominous hush of expectation descends: 'When He opened the

7th seal there was silence'. All the acclamation of the glory, majesty and power of God and His anointed one are now withheld. The silence though is just in Heaven, Heaven being the dwelling place of God, where His will alone prevails and where all is pure and Holy. It is on Earth though that the witness to God's power and authority is imparted, it was this that the breaking of the first six seals had proclaimed, the imperative that man must forfeit his self-rule to God and His anointed one, making it clear that this world can no longer continue to be governed by the sin and self-interest of man and a new order must be ushered in.

What is the significance of this silence that follows the breaking of the 7th seal and why is it specifically for half an hour? Such pronouncements are not just incidental or for dramatic effect, they are there for a significant and poignant reason.

Now an hour in scripture signifies the time of a specific occasion, see for example Revelation 3:10, 14:7 and Matthew 25:13, or it can refer to a specific length of time as in Matthew 26:40. A half of that hour signifies a dividing of that time into two sections.

The opening verses of this chapter give us a perfect understanding of God's principle in calling men to repentance in whatever age. In His position of absolute judgement and justice, His mercy and patience, are also perfectly exemplified. The half hour is the period, the space of non-restraint that is for the specific purpose of allowing mankind to repent (cp Acts 19:8 and 10). It is the first part of God's plan to restore His people Israel and innumerable people of the nations into blessing. This precedes the second half of that hour when the seven angels will announce to the world the sevenfold judgement that will bring mankind to their senses.

We have in a nutshell, in these verses, the whole of the final period of history, particularly here in the context of God's final dealings with and restoration of Israel before Christ's return. It is synonymous with the 'hour' of judgement in chapter 14:7, though in the context there of the demise of 'Babylon'. Here though it is in relation to God's work in salvation.

Time actually is something that is relevant just to Earth. In Heaven eternity prevails, the laws and principles on which all truth, government and substance are founded, so time in any event is used here symbolically in Heaven's relationship with Earth. Here the implication of the silence is that Divine government is suspended on Earth while man is allowed to go his own way unchecked, to let him discover the folly of his ways and come to his senses. Luke chapter 15 is the perfect example of this Divine principle, in the prodigal son, where his father not only lets him go, but gives him the facilities to find his own way to discover for himself that sin and selfishness inevitably end in self destruction. He ever though watches for his return in repentance; in this way God shows His infinite love and mercy, waiting for man to come to Him of his own free will. It is a period of liberation for the son to immerse himself in excess and self-fulfilment, but then later comes the time of testing. God never imposes His will on anyone during this time of grace, but ever gently entreats us if we will listen to Him, calling us back to Himself when we wander from Him. At first then there is silence in Heaven but then comes the golden altar that will show God's justice in the time of trouble that is to follow; this is the other half of that hour.

The seventh and final seal then is the quiet before the storm. The breaking of the seven seals involved letting it become apparent all that man could and would attain to, once the restraining influence of God's Blessed Holy Spirit was removed from the Earth; the period of silence in Heaven. Man had been shown what degradation lives of independence from God had led to in the first six seals. The seventh seal is then broken; the book is now open for all to see, if they only will; Heaven itself in all its power and authority is waiting before the final announcements of judgement are made. Heaven itself, the elders, the four creatures, all the saints and the angels stay silent, waiting; waiting for the most momentous event in all history to take place. A short space, not so as to delay the bringing in of that glorious kingdom, but just sufficient space for man to repent, and reveal just how far he would stray from God once 'all the brakes were removed'. An ominous silence that focuses on and portends the warnings to come; this is the last appeal to man to take notice of where he is actually going. Events on Earth had declared man's need to repent in the first six seals, now Heaven waited for a response. It was going to be man's last chance to take notice and be saved from the judgement that would soon befall the followers of the 'Beast'. There would be only two options and they would be plainly clear to all, follow God and His Laws and live, which many will, chapter 7:9+14, or to follow all that are opposed to God and suffer His wrath.

> 'And I saw the 7 angels that stand before God and to them was given 7 trumpets.'

As God's messengers the angels stand ready to carry out God's will in announcing to mankind His sevenfold warning of the judgement of God that is to fall on the Earth. Mankind will be reminded of his failure to fulfil God's first commission to man to replenish the Earth and subdue it (Genesis 1:28). He had not replenished it but exploited it for his own ends, had not subdued and tamed it but had destroyed it. Mankind had offended against God and His Holy Law; God had commanded men to repent of their sin but they only ignored Him. Men had brought such suffering on themselves and the rest of God's creation, but God is going to give them yet another opportunity to amend their ways and to act responsibly. First of all though there is another scene that must be realised. A glorious scene that explains what is acceptable and pleasing to God and therefore why His judgement must befall on all that is contrary to His holy nature.

> 'Then another angel, having a golden censer, came and stood at the altar.
>
> He was given much incense that he should offer it with the prayers of all the saints
>
> upon the golden altar which was before the throne,
>
> and the smoke of the incense, with the prayers of the saints
>
> ascended before God from the angel's hand.

Then the angel took the censor, filled it with fire from the altar,

and threw it to the Earth.

And there were noises, thunderings, lightnings and an earthquake.

So the 7 angels who had the 7 trumpets prepared themselves to sound.'

Heaven itself is waiting, the court of Divine government pauses in expectation, hushed, for a divided period of time, a division between waiting and action, grace and judgement, a waiting until all is ready. In Matthew 21 it was as the proprietor's son and heir of all things that He was murdered, as the 'stone rejected,' that He suffered and died to redeem mankind from the sin and degradation that they had fallen into. It was this sacrifice that is now such a sweet savour to God. It was this that qualified Him to be 'firstborn among many brethren' (Romans 8:29). It is then the prayers of these brethren that have been made in His name (John 14:13 and 15:16), that is, are made by them in the same spirit of humility and sacrifice that was in Christ Jesus (Philippians 2:5). These prayers are such a sweet savour to God; it is indeed why they are called brethren, a special people (1Peter 2:5-9), because they are of one mind and character with their Lord.

The Altar of Gold

This is where we see Christ as at His most precious. This is where we see that great mystery of God that the greatest in the Kingdom of Heaven is he that is the least (Matthew 23:11-12). Christ fulfilled this more than any; 'He humbled Himself and became obedient unto death, even the death of the cross (Philippians 2:8). This altar is the sacrifice of Christ, the very mind of Christ that 'made Himself of no reputation'. The altar of the burnt offering in Leviticus chapter 4 symbolises perfectly the cross of Christ and His death to put away sin. The golden altar of incense then is its counterpart, representing that same sacrifice but in its pleasantness to God Himself, symbolised in the incense that is burned for a sweet smelling savour, cp Exodus 30:1+3.

The Angel at the Altar has a special function. Angels are messengers, (cp. Hebrews 1:14), though they have other functions in Scripture such as the seraphim that surround the Throne of God in Isaiah 6:1-4 and as ministers to Christ after His temptation in the wilderness, Matthew 4:11. He is not performing the High Priestly function of Christ here though, but presenting to God Himself something that was uniquely pleasing about Christ and of those 'brethren' filled with His Spirit.

The Incense, the Sweet Fragrance of Heaven

The incense itself is something very precious and absolutely spiritual. It expresses the manner in which Christ Himself in His graciousness and humility only pleased His Father. The incense signifies that spirit as a sweet smelling savour to His Father. As 'brethren' of Christ, the only way that we can please God, indeed and to know the joy of His Holy presence with us at all, is to have that same Spirit in complete control of our hearts. It is not the prayers of His saints themselves that are pictured here, that are offered with the incense; it is just the savour of those prayers. It is 'the smoke of the incense' which came with those prayers;' it is the fact that they are made in His precious name of humility and obedience. The substance of the prayers is something different. It is only the fact that they are 'asked in His name', of humility and submission to the will of God that they are acceptable and pleasing to Him.

Even so the substance of those prayers is very relevant here. For millennia Christians have been praying fervently, 'Thy Kingdom come, Thy will be done', and this prayer is about to come to pass in all that follows.

It is important to note that incense gains its especial value to God only when it is burned in the censer, for that is when it releases its sweet savour, for that we need fire!

The Golden Censer

The censer here is typical of the golden censer in which the high priest of the Aaronic order took fire from the altar of sacrifice and carried it to burn incense on the golden altar and is symbolic of the blessed obedience and submission of Christ to the Holy will of His Father. The 'censer' is what carried the 'fire' of God's judgement against sin on the cross. It was that obedience and meekness that led Christ to say in the garden of Gethsemane, 'not my will but Thine be done'. That submission to His Father's will that bore all the derision cast upon Him by the Jews and the Roman soldiers. That complete self-denial that carried the pain and anguish of the cross. That sacrifice that led to such humility that was such a sweet savour to His Father. It is in this way that the censor represents the spirit of Christ Himself, that meekness of spirit that 'contained ' the incense. It was in this way that Christ was perfected as a High priest for all His saints (Hebrews 2:10-17). It is in this way that He not only is our perfect example but the only one that can provide the way, who indeed is the only way for us to personally know God the Father and for our prayers to be acceptable to Him. It is only through our meek obedience in our lives and hearts that we can approach His Holy Presence in communion with Him, to offer our worship and make our petitions to Him.

It is by considering the perfect example of Christ's humility, meekness, obedience and self-denial that we see the full nature of Divine Love in human form, in all its beauty. How far it transcends beyond just the emotion of human love. Here we see the full motivation that carried the fire of God's judgement for sin. It is the same sanctifying fire that indwells everyone that is born of the Holy Spirit of Christ. This is the complete meaning of the symbolism in the golden censer. How much then should our own 'brazen censers' (cp. Numbers 16:39) be a reflection of that perfect love? This is the 'agape' love that we have so much of in the first and second letters of John.

In contrast, it was the disobedience of Nadab and Abihu in Leviticus 10:1-2 in wanting to assume the priesthood that was appointed by God alone, that caused them to be consumed; their fire was not of God; typically it was not the sanctifying fire of the Holy Spirit that we have in Acts 2:3-4. It was pretence, an assumed position of priesthood, and a hypocritical stance. See also Numbers 16:18-38

- **At the casting of the censer to Earth:**

Voices thundering, lightning and an earthquake ensue. This is the chaos and insecurity that prefigures the trumpet calls, this is the disturbance to man's environment that will alert him to be receptive to God's voice. It is the golden censer that is cast down, that very obedient love of our Lord that bore our judgement for sin is now cast down as a testimony to all mankind to see. God's two witnesses in chapter 11 had preached that very love and shown it in stark contrast to all that still reject and hate Him. Mankind must now sit up and take notice because that censer is now filled again with fire, not only against sin in judgement now, but against the very world of sin; a fire that will soon consume all that is contrary to God's Holy Will. Now the world is sitting up and listening, the trumpets will soon speak…

- **Prepare Trumpets!**

What an ominous picture, laying bare the imminence of the warnings. The trumpets are prepared ready to sound; the angels are holding those instruments to their lips to sound God's message to Earth. This, this is the beginning of the end and the coming again of Christ to reign…

SECTION 1: PART 5

A Spectacular Phenomenon

**Revelation Chapter 12:
How Israel Features in the Revelation**

'Now a Great Sign Appeared in Heaven: A Woman Clothed with the Sun, With the Moon Under Her Feet and On Her Head a Garland of Twelve Stars'. v 1

We now move to another majestic scene, and what a beautiful image it is! It is perhaps here better than anywhere that it becomes apparent that this book is so full of symbolic language. These are word images though, not visual images, that are intended; otherwise all becomes preposterous or surrealistic. We do not need to guess the symbolic meaning though, that is just to imprint our own ideas on the text; we can find the allegorical meaning of the imagery elsewhere in the scriptures. 'A woman', clothed with the sun, speaks of her presence and charisma; clothed with glory and established, see Psalm 89:37; or clothed in brightness, see Job 31:26; or endurance, see Psalm 72:7.

If then the crown of twelve stars – or sons of Israel, Genesis 37:9 - does not identify her as being the nation of Israel itself, then surely verse five identifies her as the one who gives birth to Christ Himself. This is unequivocal; the child can be none other than Israel's Messiah! See Psalm 2.

The significance of the twelve stars as a crown will become apparent from chapter 7 of the Revelation, which is considered in section four of this study. The fact that it is a crown conveys the impression of fulfilment and glory.

We are also told that she had the moon at her feet. Now the significance of the moon is that it gives light - Isaiah 30:26, it controls the hours of darkness. - Psalm 136:9, having glory – 1 Corinthians 15:41 and endurance Psalm 89:37. All that mankind rightly aspires to in life, confidence, understanding, security and true honour are 'at her feet', she is in full control and possession of them.

God Himself ordained that it should be through Israel that all the nations of the Earth should be blessed - Genesis 26:4. This of course was fulfilled perfectly through Christ and His vicarious work - Galatians 3:16. The Old Testament prophets though also foretold that Israel as a nation would be restored and blessed and that it would become a strong nation - Micah 4:6-8. The Northern Tribes of Israel though had been cut off and taken captive into Syria a few years before this prophecy was made in the 8th century BC and then later dispersed and their identity lost. The Southern Tribes were then also scattered following the destruction of Jerusalem in AD 70. In Jeremiah 32:36-41 God promises however that He will bring all Israel back into His favour and into their land. Paul uses the metaphor of 'Grafting Israel back into the Vine' in Romans 11:23. Hosea uses an even more graphic example to show how Israel will be restored after what has been now many centuries. This he did poignantly by marrying a prostitute but divorcing her afterwards for adultery. He then takes her back again in latter days, quite clearly portraying not only Israel's shame and the reason why they were cut off as a nation, but also signifying that they would be reinstated when God had accomplished His time of discipline with them. See Hosea chapter 1 et seq.

Throughout her history until the time of Hezekiah, Israel had suffered under first one nation and then another until the time of Christ, then, after the ten tribes had been scattered, to 'be sifted like grain' among the nations - Amos 9:9, the tribes of Judah and Benjamin, the two remaining tribes, had suffered persecution under first one subjugator and then another. These indeed were the birth pangs spoken of in this scripture - cp Micah 5:2-3, as God brought one judgement then another on Israel to get them to turn from the false material gods of the nations to follow after the one true invisible God of Abraham and Isaac, their national 'fathers'. At the time that the Revelation was written even the remnant of Israel, the Jews would soon be dispersed and the nation of Israel would cease to exist altogether. Paul however explains the spiritual principle behind such trauma that Israel has suffered; it was a sign of God's love and care for His own that He allowed these things to happen, so that mankind would return to Himself, their only one possible source of true happiness and security– Romans 11:26-27.

We quite clearly though have a villain of the piece, a red dragon. We are told in verse nine who the identity of this monster is, though we are called to consider first his nature by perceiving his dramatic representation. It is difficult or even impossible to create a coherent visual image of this creature, though as a word image it makes a lot of sense and describes most graphically its historical and political connotations in relation to Israel. Chapter 13 sees another beast arise out of the sea having a similar description, quite specifically obtaining that character from the red dragon. We shall see in later sections how this description, particularly the seven heads, is specific to the empires that dominated Israel up to the time of the end and how they act, or here are symbolically 'minded' to bring to birth the Israel that God has purposed. Micah 5:3

It is the power of the dragon though that is in focus here, which through those dominions, have wreaked such havoc on the children of Israel, by his persecution of God's holy nation through the centuries since the time of Joseph until recent history. Looking at things historically at present, we might consider that God has failed to bring to pass that which He intended, but that would be to consider things out of context. God has not forsaken Israel. In our own time, indeed from the end of the First World War and especially since 1947 we have seen the nation of Israel begin to emerge again with the return of the Jews (the tribe of Judah and the half tribe of Benjamin only) returning to the land of Israel after nearly two thousand years of dispersion; a most remarkable, unlikely and unprecedented event. Cp Joel 3:1 and Jeremiah chapter 30-33

Genesis 15:5, 22:17, 26:4, and Exodus 32:13 promise to Abraham and then to Isaac and Jacob that their seed shall be like the stars of Heaven in number. We also have another analogy here though, Genesis 1:16 describes the stars as lights in the Heaven, ie giving light to the whole Earth. Genesis 22:18 tells us of God's promise to Abraham that 'in him shall all the nations of the Earth be blessed.' The sons of Israel (Jacob) are also signified in Genesis 37:9 as heavenly bodies, secondary to the 'sun' and 'moon'. The implication in these scriptures then is that Israel as a nation, as the stars, will bring light to all nations.

In verse 4 a third of the stars are drawn to Earth, the very place that Satan himself and his angels had been thrown to when he was cast out of Heaven, v.9. Compare Luke 10:18. This is the sphere of man, his natural place of being. A third of the stars lose their heavenly function and become Earthbound in their outlook. This is not a third section of the stars though in number, but a third part of their function as we have at the sounding of the first four trumpets for instance in chapters eight, where they lose a third part of their purpose, influence or value and beauty.

This monster had stood in front of the woman in a position of direct confrontation, diametrically opposed to all that the child stood for and would achieve and was intent on devouring Him, for example:

Satan entered into Herod in an attempt to have the child slain before He could achieve God' work.

He faces Christ directly in the wilderness to tempt Him to depart from His total devotion to His Father's will, and so disqualify Him as Israel's Messiah and as redeemer of mankind.

He entered into the Scribes and Pharisees to catch Him in His speech and to put pressure on Pilate to condemn Him to death.

He entered into Judas to have Him betrayed.

He entered into the Jewish authorities and the crowd to clamour for His execution.

This same Devil, now cast out of Heaven, having finally lost any position in that glorious sphere of eternal principle and government is conclusively relegated to the sphere of death and decay, and that only for a short time.

Our Lord makes reference to Satan in Luke 10:18 where He says that He saw Satan fall from Heaven like lightning. The reason for this we find in two places in the Old Testament, in Isaiah 14:12-15 and Ezekiel 28:12-15 where the kings of Babylon, verse 4, and Tyre respectively are likened to him. Here though he only lost his status as an illustrious angel, the 'shining one', Lucifer. After this his place is as a fallen angel on Earth, represented as the serpent in the Garden of Eden for example, yet also as the accuser of mankind before God in Job chapter 1. This is an activity he continues until the death of Christ, when he is defeated and excluded from Heaven altogether, cp Hebrews 2:14-15, though see below regarding the victory of the saints over Satan. All the imagery here seems highly mythological and obscured by metaphors, until we realise that it is spiritual beings and spiritual issues that are at stake here, not temporal or spatial, and it is something that we can directly relate to in our own consciousness.

He now appears again, having lost that province and all heavenly influence, he is now only personified in his earthly role as the dragon, inspiring the destruction of God's people, filled with fury against the woman, God's chosen nation on Earth. He had ultimately failed to curtail the Divine work of Christ in securing salvation for His people, he had failed to prevent the victory of His saints over him through Christ's sanctifying work in their lives, now he has but a short time to try and thwart the ultimate salvation of Israel and the nations.

In verses one to six we can clearly see where God is working with Israel alone. There is however a very obvious gap chronologically between verses five and six, when Christ is caught up to Heaven and when Israel faces the years of tribulation after they become a nation again.

Verses 7 – 12 of this chapter are now an interlude. We know from Romans 11 that this gap is the 'Time of the Gentiles,' spoken of also by our Lord, in which God has been calling out for Himself a people from both Jewish and Gentile nations, something that to this day is still hidden from Israel; to them the Church of the present time is simply a heresy.

This process however is entirely separate from God's dealings with Israel; as Israel's recognition is only being held in abeyance until the time of the Gentiles is fulfilled; Luke 21:24. Paul speaks of this time in Ephesians 3:9 where he says that this time is a 'Mystery, which from the beginning of the ages has been hidden in God'. Again in Colossians 1:24 he speaks of 'Christ's ... body, which is the Church,' and in verse 26 that this is 'the mystery that has been hidden from ages and generations, but has now been revealed to His saints.'

Throughout the New Testament we have what God is achieving spiritually in the Church through the work of

Christ, transforming its members into the image of Christ, building His Kingdom in their hearts. Prior to this God was working in and through Israel to achieve His purposes under the Old Covenant. The New Covenant and the Church of Christ that was to emerge from it was concealed before Christ came; Ephesians 3:9. Later in chapter 21 of the Revelation we finally see how all of God's purposes under the first and second covenants are brought together in one.

The beginning of chapter 8 of the Revelation, we saw, focuses on what God is doing through the obedience of Christ and of the prayers of His saints, in their efficacy in this hour of Israel's judgement, specifically the first half; of Israel's time of re-instatement as a God-fearing nation. There we saw Christ's saints, not from an earthly perspective but a heavenly, spiritual, one. Again we see His saints in view here in chapter 12 from a heavenly perspective in their being morally effective in casting Satan from Heaven by their overcoming through the blood of the Lamb, verse 11; that is overcoming the world, human nature and the devil as is outlined in chapters 2 and 3 of the Revelation and in 1 John 5:4-5. Michael and the angels, as God's own agents, carry out Satan's complete removal, suggesting perhaps that the overcoming work of the saints at this present time is then finished and therefore they are no longer effective in this present sphere of testing in which Satan could still accuse them before God. cp 1 Thessalonians 1:10.

Satan, he that embodies and indwells all that is evil, is defeated first by Christ - Hebrews 2:14, then by the overcomers of His Church. There now remains one final respect in which Satan must be destroyed. Israel is now brought back into focus with a complete resumption of all that God intended for Israel; also showing how He is bringing that about. Satan is allowed his final leave to create such chaos on Earth that mankind will finally reject the works of darkness and turn unequivocally to the God of peace and goodness.

World War Three!

Isaiah 28:14-18 foretells of the time when God Himself shall re-establish Israel after they have drifted away from Him completely, having made a covenant with death. They will be rescued from the effects of that state that they have created for themselves but only after passing through an 'overflowing scourge'.

> 'Therefore hear the word of the Lord, you scornful men,
> who rule this people who are in Jerusalem;
> because you have said, 'We have made a covenant with death,
> And with Sheol we are in agreement.
> When the overflowing scourge passes through,
> it will not come to us,
> for we have made lies our refuge,
> and under falsehood we have hidden ourselves.'
>
>
> Therefore thus says the Lord God:
> 'Behold, I lay in Zion a stone for a foundation,
> a tried stone, a precious cornerstone, a sure foundation;

whoever believes will not act hastily, (ie be anxious).

> Also I will make justice the measuring line,
> and righteousness the plummet;
> the hail will sweep away the refuge of lies,
> and the waters will overflow the hiding place.
> Your covenant with death will be annulled,
> and your agreement with Sheol will not stand;
> when the overflowing scourge passes through,
> then you will be trampled down by it.'

Daniel then over 200 years later had a vision from God of what would happen to his people at the end of the age before God would re-establish Israel, when their Messiah would come to rule the whole Earth. This would be for a period of seven years (an explanation of this is covered in more detail in section 3). This will be when they make this covenant with death that Isaiah first mentioned; Daniel adds further detail to that in Daniel 9:27, speaking of the 'Prince that will come'.

> 'Then he shall confirm a covenant with many (Israel)
> for one week;
> but in the middle of the week
> he shall bring an end to sacrifice and offering.
> And on the wing of abominations shall be one who makes desolate,
> even until the consummation, which is determined,
> is poured out on the desolate.'

A 'week' here is literally a 'seven', meaning a sabbatical year or seven years, which is explained in more detail in epilogue 2.

Not only will it be for a period of seven years but also in the middle of that period the one with whom this covenant is made reneges on it. Just as Isaiah prophesied; there follows a time of great trouble for God's people for the remaining three and a half years. It is something that Daniel refers to again in chapter 7:25 of his prophecy, describing it there as a time and times and half a time, indicating then not only that it would be for a specific period but also that it would occur at a time that was especially appointed. The seven here is significant from a spiritual perspective; it may be literally so, as well, but to focus just on that we miss what the scripture is really teaching us.

In verse 14 of Revelation 12 this expression is again used, in the context that God will protect His people during that appointed time, revealing also that this time will be a satanically inspired persecution of Israel.

The agent of this fury instigated against Israel is Satan. It is Satan that is really behind the political system and leadership that has overwhelming control throughout the world at this time, the one with whom Israel has made this covenant of protection.

This period however is spoken in respect of this time earlier in verse 6, though there it is spoken of as being 1260 days, which is three and a half years by the calendars of the day. The number of days suggests that the Divine protection here will embrace all of God's people, it will be especially sufficient and bring the woman, Israel, through to full maturity as His people during the time of desolation. (See appendix 4, 'symbolic meanings', regarding the scriptural symbolism of numbers)

This is a great principle to learn when we go through

times of trouble that although it may be our own weakness that leads us into the time of testing, God allows these things for our sanctification, yet He provides for and sustains us during those times.

Though at first Israel seems to rise above this onslaught, on 'eagles' wings' it takes them into the desert, a state of spiritual and probably political barrenness. This doesn't thwart the Devil though, he inspires, ie out of his mouth, by what he 'says', arouses an overwhelming flood, perhaps an outpouring of anti-Semitism against the Jews for example, in an attempt to concentrate all forces to finally annihilate God's chosen people. This is the time of Jacob's trouble – cp Jeremiah 30:7 and Daniel 12:1. God however is still in control, Satan cannot achieve more than God will allow. It is through the general inhabitants of Earth however that the effect of this onslaught is nullified. They speak out against such an onslaught. Perhaps the atrocities of World War Two are still fresh enough in people's minds to stop this wave of uncivilised aggression in its tracts. Israel however remains in the wilderness, literally or metaphorically, as still the war against them continues. It will do so until their true King comes to finally deliver them.

It is a Divine and general principle that God will not allow any of us to be tested beyond what we can sustain, see 1 Corinthians 10:13.

Every person is born with a free will, to follow God and His principles for their lives, or follow his or her own objectives and ideas. It is through the events of life however that we learn the futility and ultimate failure of going our own way. It is by trials and temptations that arise from going the 'way of the world' that we learn to turn back. For

Israel it will be no different; God will allow them to suffer a greater time of trouble than they ever have before, until they turn again to their God in complete dependence on Him alone; then they will all be gathered together again as a nation. They will turn unequivocally to God and be filled with His spirit. See Joel 2:28-29

There is however a finale to this chapter; the dragon persecutes the offspring of the 'woman', Israel. Perhaps Galatians 3:7 is the answer to the question that this begs, as to who this offspring refers to: 'Only those who are of faith are sons of Abraham'. It is not asserting a physical relationship but rather a spiritual relationship and a general principle of salvation that it is through faith alone that we are 'Sons of Abraham', whether it is with regards to Israel, the Church or those in any other part of God's purposes and blessings for mankind. It is this faith that is the secret of the 'Overcomer' – 1 John 5:4-5, overcoming the adversity that is in the world, a world of chance, danger and cruelty, a place of pain, disappointment and disillusion. It is through this adversity that our faith is perfected, our love for God is forged and our own rejection of all that is contrary to Him is realised, whether it be all that is in the world or what is in our own hearts and lives. It is in this way that all those of faith become true sons of God, pure and holy, filled with the Spirit of God alone, for time and eternity.

SECTION 1: PART 6

The Imminent Marriage

Revelation Chapter 19: 1-10
The Glorious New Age

As we considered earlier, the Jews must have been incensed when Christ preached His parable of the marriage feast in chapter 22 of Matthew. It is glaringly patent what Jesus was saying to them; the die is cast. 'You have consistently ignored the prophets who have told you to prepare for the Kingdom of Heaven; you have only been concerned with your own interests,' He says effectively, 'because now you have also rejected the Kingdom of Heaven', Symbolised here as the marriage supper, 'You will also be killed and the whole city of Jerusalem razed to the ground'. The Pharisees typically being portrayed as the ones that mistreat and kill God's second delegation of servants, that is John the Baptist and Christ.

They had not repented but closed their minds to John

the Baptist and to Christ as they preached the Kingdom of Heaven.

The Pharisees particularly were looking for a king who would shake off the Roman yoke and so promote their own prestige to one of world importance. They could only envisage the Messiah as a conquering hero and one that would sanction and maintain or even enhance their own status quo. They could not, they would not, see otherwise. Christ's message was unequivocal; they were completely wrong, malicious and needed to repent. Their whole way of life was one of reinforcing the (self) righteousness of their own culture of religious tradition. Their response was like that to Stephen later when they could only 'stop their ears' and rush in and silence him permanently. Their hatred of Christ was only exacerbated by His teaching, adding to their determination to silence him permanently.

The model of the parable in Matthew however is perfect as a model of the Kingdom that God has planned and will bring to pass, though only the details relevant to the context in chapter 22 are mentioned at this point. The existence of a bride is only in chapter 22 by implication of there being a marriage feast. The calling out of Christ's Church, His bride, from among Jews and gentiles, would actually occur between verses seven and eight of that chapter; though that is not mentioned here because the fact of the Church was still hidden from all but the disciples until after Christ had ascended into Heaven. God however had chosen the bride of Christ 'before the foundation of the world,' Ephesians 1:4.

Paul builds on the theme of Christ's Kingdom very little in his epistles, as his doctrine mainly concerns the calling out of Christ's Church (bride) from both the Jews and the gentiles during the present time. Christ said in Luke 17:21 that the Kingdom of God is within us, not here or there as being a position or situation, but it is that individual, spiritual character that is the subject of Paul's letters. In places like Ephesians chapter 5:22-32, in explaining his reason for practical doctrine regarding Christian marriage relationships, he makes it quite plain that the reason for this doctrine is that this should be a model of the relationship between Christ and His Church (verse32). See also Isaiah 62:5, Matthew 9:15 – also in Mark and Luke - John3:29, 2 Corinthians 11:2 and Colossians 1:18.

Thus the 'Kingdom' at this present time is the building of the relationship that culminates in the wedding feast, that metaphor for the real character of the Kingdom and how it will function.

When we come to Revelation 19, we find that the bride is now all ready for the marriage supper. The guests are anticipated. Babylon and all that had seduced the world and persecuted God's servants has finally been destroyed. Now The Lord God's reign of supremacy is in view, the thousand years of rejoicing and reign of Christ can begin. We can now see clearly the ultimate purpose that God has for mankind through and for Christ, after one more epic event that we come to in section 2. We can begin to see how His purpose is going to be effected, expressed first to Abraham, that all the nations of the Earth would be blessed in Him. No wonder that once the marriage supper can happen, Christ and all God's people of all ages will be together 'in complete control', so that then all creation will stop groaning and breathe a sigh of relief, Romans 8:22. It is when we come to the end of the Revelation however, that we see the final order in place for complete eternal peace to be realised, that is after the marriage supper is complete, cp 1 Corinthians 15:28.

It might seem at first sight that in using the metaphor of a marriage supper for the Kingdom of God, several different individuals and groups would be implicated in the Kingdom of Heaven. There are three places in the New Testament where this analogy is used, in Matthew chapters 22 and 25 and in our passage here in Revelation 19. In Matthew 22 however the only parties mentioned in the parable are the King, his son, his servants and the guests. In Matthew 25 it is only the bridegroom and the bridesmaids or virgins that are mentioned. In Revelation 19 it is the Lamb, His wife and the invited guests are the only ones mentioned. On each occasion only those persons that are relevant to the point of the parable or spiritual picture are mentioned, so it would be wrong to read other parties into the accounts. In Matthew 22 the parable tells the Jews that they have neglected God's invitation to the Kingdom so that the offer will now be made to those they regard as unworthy. In Matthew 25 it is a different point that is being made, though still in the context of the Kingdom being likened to a marriage celebration; here it is a matter of having to have the right spirit and character to enter into the Kingdom. In the Revelation account the emphasis is put on the marriage itself and the significance that that has for all of Heaven, that spiritual realm that will be the life of all that dwell on Earth in that Kingdom; that is why those that are invited are called blessed. Only in this last account do we have two clearly defined parties, apart from Christ, that can be identified as human, the bride and the guests. In the penultimate chapter of this book we see most clearly that this relates to the different spiritual functions that they have within the Kingdom, not primarily to any temporal distinction now though as we might think in terms of.

Chapter 19 starts with what seems just the finale to the previous chapter, the 'voice of much people' in Heaven rejoicing in the destruction of the great whore. Looking more closely however we see that primarily what the great company in Heaven are so happy about is that salvation and glory to God have now emerged because of the demise of the whore and the corruption and martyrdom that she was responsible for. They then respond to the voice from the throne with anticipation of the reign of the 'Lord God omnipotent'. By the beginning of the next chapter we have the thousand-year reign of Jesus on Earth beginning; this is what they are anticipating. In between however we have mentioned the marriage supper, also about to happen. This would seem incidental, a parenthesis, until we realise that the marriage supper and the millennium are just different aspects of the same thing. To the saved, it is a time of unprecedented happiness and joy. To the Earth, the whole of creation and the nations that are alive, it is just a time of complete peace, righteousness and prosperity.

The chapter begins however with rejoicing for a different reason. The language here now is entirely heavenly. This is all about the role of Heaven and its spiritual significance and character.

'After these things I heard a loud voice of a great multitude in Heaven...' Heaven itself now speaks, that is bears witness; this is not a physical voice but an affirmation of those that reside there by virtue of who reigns there. The voice is loud by virtue of its imperative, while the great multitude alluded to are not defined, though who they represent is inferred by what they say, 'Alleluia! Salvation and glory and honour and power belong to the Lord our God!'

It is those that have a personal relationship with their God as their saviour, that is, His saints.

'For true and righteous are His judgments, because He has judged the great harlot who corrupted the Earth with her fornication.'

The term the 'great harlot' defines what she is rather than who she is and that is what we are called to consider. She is the antithesis of the Church, idolatry and self-indulgence in all its insidious forms both religious and secular; that which corrupted and persecuted those that belonged to Christ, but in so doing defined and purified the true Church.

'He has avenged on her the blood of His servants shed by her.'

Her destruction has given full justice; this is what 'avenge' means here as in chapter 6:10. That which corrupts, pollutes and destroys must be revoked and removed if everlasting goodness is to thrive and rule without impairment.

'Again they said, Alleluia! Her smoke rises up forever and ever!'

She is now judged and removed and yet she remains a contrast and a witness to the purity of Christ's Church forever and that any such institution that would stand against or independent from God in His purity and holiness must forever be entirely separated from Him.

> 'And the twenty-four elders and the four living creatures
> fell down and worshipped God who sat on the throne,
> saying, Amen! Alleluia!'

They are the heavenly priesthood; the saints in their priestly function as understanding God's Divine purposes. To appreciate the truth and significance of this is paramount to our sanctification. The saints in their role of co-regents with and through Christ understand and also reflect the absolute holiness and character of God, as is also testified by the four living creatures. It is these living creatures that from the throne testify as to the Holiness and the everlasting nature of the throne; they also substantiate the testimony of the creation. In the next section of this study we look at who or what these creatures represent.

Now all that stood in the way of that glorious kingdom of God, for which the Church has prayed for the last two millennia, will finally be realised. God has not delayed its implementation but has in mercy been building His Kingdom first in the hearts of His saints, the Church, the bride of Christ, before His Kingdom could be established throughout the whole world.

> Then a voice came from the throne, saying,
> 'Praise our God, all you His servants
> and those who fear Him, both small and great!'

The throne itself now 'speaks', that is witnesses to the glory, virtue and power of almighty God. This calls forth praise from all of mankind, of every culture and creed, all those that honour and respect Him and welcome His supreme government.

> 'And I heard, as it were, the voice of a great multitude, as the sound of many waters and as the sound of mighty thunderings.'

John is made instinctively aware of the sentiments of the many people and nations in their heavenly identity and their praise to God, also rejoicing in triumph and expressing their approval, saying, 'Alleluia! For the Lord God Omnipotent reigns!'

They then continue:

> 'Let us be glad and rejoice and give Him glory,
> for the marriage of the Lamb has come,
> and His wife has made herself ready.'

Salvation is the work of God alone, there is nothing we can do to add to it. To think that we can do anything, to fulfil one commandment of God in our own strength will be of the wrong character and be abortive. The bride however has made herself ready. Making use of the endowment of salvation however is something that does involve our active affiliation; Philippians 2:12-13,

> 'Work out your own salvation with fear and trembling,
> for it is God who works in you both to will and to do for His good pleasure'.

When we acquiesce in and allow that work by His Spirit

then we are blessed, we are dressed in His righteousness:

> 'And so to her it was granted to be arrayed in
> fine linen, clean and bright,
> For the fine linen is the righteous acts of the saints.
> Then He said to me, 'Write:
> 'Blessed are those who are called to the marriage
> supper of the Lamb!"

This principle has now been established; all those that serve and fear God are called to His Kingdom, that is all that will submit wholly to His reign.

> 'And he said to me, these are the true sayings of God.'
> 'And I fell at his feet to worship him.
> But he said to me, see that you do not do that!
> I am your fellow servant, and of your brethren who have
> the testimony of Jesus.
> Worship God! For the testimony of Jesus is the spirit of
> prophecy.'

SECTION 1: PART 7

The Perfect Marriage

Revelation Chapter 19:1-10
The Glorious New Age

Chapter 19 of Revelation tells us nothing about the character of marriage itself; in fact it seems just to put the marriage feast here into its consequential and thematic context and little more. It does not tell us more here of course than is relevant to the passage, although the bride of Christ and their relationship is a theme that pervades the Holy Scriptures from Genesis to Revelation and therefore all that doctrine and character of that affiliation spoken of can be recalled here; the theme of the passage is to show us the context in which the marriage feast will occur, though to consider the nature of marriage in scripture will inform us of the character of the reign of Christ on Earth, and that is very relevant to the book as a whole.

Marriage is an institution that we first see in Genesis

when God establishes it in the Garden of Eden. God made Eve from out of Adam, to be a suitable companion for him in his commission from God to have dominion over all the Earth; something that is carefully recorded for us in Genesis chapter 2; something that Paul takes up in 1 Corinthians chapter 11 to show us the spiritual significance of this.

It soon becomes quite clear as we read through the Old Testament that the human institution of marriage was more than just a social convenience for mankind. The Old Testament prophets, Jeremiah, Isaiah and Hosea for instance, all refer to Israel's relationship with God as one of being married to Him. As we come to the New Testament though Paul uses the same language in Romans chapter 7 to describe the relationship between Christ and each believer in Him as being a marriage relationship. There is however a fundamental difference here in which we begin to see that marriage far from being a convenient analogy that is used in scripture to describe a more spiritual relationship that we can have with God, it suggests that it is a fundamental principle of creation. The relationship that Israel had with God was a marriage relationship, not merely like one, one that was made under the covenant of the Mosaic Law. In Romans however we have to die to that Law before we are morally free to become married to Christ.

Our relationship with Christ however, that Paul goes on to develop in chapter 8 of Romans, was one that was established by God before the Foundation of the World. Not only then is our marriage to Christ something that is based on a principle of creation, more than that, it is an eternal principle. Perhaps we can think of nothing that can be more profound than that, however there is more.

As we read on through the scriptures, we come next to 1 Corinthians. In chapter 11, Paul refers to the marriage relationship between men and women in the context of that between mankind and Christ, but also that that same sort of relationship exists between Christ and God Himself. What is being referred to here is not just the institution of marriage but also the fundamental basis of that relationship, one of fidelity and dependence, not just something that we can define for ourselves or out of political convenience. Not only is it a principle of creation, not only is it an eternal principle but it is a Divine principle centred in the very Godhead.

It is not surprising therefore that marriage is such an important subject in the New Testament in relation to our individual union with Christ; in respect to Christian marriage and particularly with regard the local church congregations on Earth. Paul returns to different aspects or contexts of marriage in 1 Timothy chapter 2, Colossians chapter 2, Ephesians chapter 5 and three times in 1 Corinthians. This is not to mention the many times that marriages are mentioned in the Gospels and other letters in the New Testament, each giving us further insight into the significance of marriage as a concept in itself. Also of course in the Old Testament there is the Song of Songs and the story of Ruth, which are more beautiful accounts of what married love can be.

Christian marriages are not just typical of Christ and His Church; they are of the same fundamental character. Just as the closer our individual union with Christ is, the closer we will be to each other and to Christ in our relationship. The more perfect a Christian marriage is, the more it will represent our experience of Christ in His Church and with His Church. The wife is an example to her husband in this respect, the husband is an example to his wife and both are witnesses in and to all the Church. Paul in fact puts it more powerfully than this in chapter 11 of 1 Corinthians; the wife is sanctified by the husband and the husband is sanctified by the wife, that is made holy. The relationship itself however is described quite simply, though the implications are profound. The husband is the head and his wife has the place of submission and meekness, just as Christ is head of the Church and all in it occupy a place of complete subordination and obedience. This puts very great responsibilities on both partners, each in the sanctification of the other; the husband loving his wife in the same way and to the same degree of selflessness as Christ loved us – Ephesians 5:28. This seems a commission that is above any man, as indeed it is impossible to even begin, except through the power of the Holy Spirit. His wife then showing the same submissiveness to Him, by the same Spirit, as we all show to Christ as Lord of our lives:

> 'Which is very precious in the sight of God' ...
>
> 'As Sarah obeyed Abraham, calling him lord, whose daughters you are'.
>
> 1 Peter 3:4+6

The idea that women should take an inferior, subservient role in marriage and that men should be aloof and overbearing, as is popularly assumed, is as far removed from the New Testament model as could be. Men should be as

Christ, representing Him to his spouse, meek, gentle, kind and compassionate, seeking the welfare of his wife above all things. In being meek, self-effacing, obedient and deferential she is demonstrating the spirit that we all need to be if we are truly to know the fullness of Christ in our hearts and lives. This is the model ordained by God.

Peter however then continues the theme in verse seven to include the husbands in that they should give due honour to their wives: 'As heirs together of the grace of life, that your prayers may not be hindered'. This shows us the mutual benefit and great refinement in our own lives of living according the spirit that God would have us do.

If then the marriage relationship is so important in the Christian life it is not surprising that it should affect our behaviour, particularly in the way we present ourselves to each other, and together before the world. This is the first point Paul seeks to establish in chapter 11 of 1 Corinthians after asserting the hierarchy of headship from the woman up to God Himself.

The head of Christ is God; that is, the mind and purpose of God are entirely those also of Christ. He is in complete subjection to His Father, of one mind with Him to do only His purpose and therefore represents God so fully that He could say, 'he that has seen Me has seen the Father'. Likewise the husband is called to have the mind of Christ, to be in full submission to Him, seeking to be like Him alone in character. In the same way then again marriage should reflect the same model, the husband displaying the mind of God no less in all his love and mercy towards his wife, who reciprocate in the same way that we all must relate to Christ, in complete faith and in submission to Him.

Thus are both parties filled with the Spirit of Christ, the husband with the same spirit that Christ has, as head of His Church, one of utmost goodwill, caring for and supporting his wife in the grace and mercy that he learns of God, and the wife having the spirit that Christ has towards His Father, one of perfect submission and contentment in that setting. Thus as a perfect marriage it is only realised as a bilateral relationship, though it is necessary for us individually to seek to be so filled with the Spirit of God.

A man showing himself in public to be praying or expounding his faith with his head covered shames his head, ie Christ. Christ is our head, master and Lord; He is not submissive to us and our desires but we to Him and His Kingdom. A woman however showing herself in public to be praying or expounding her faith with her head uncovered puts her head, ie her husband, to shame. She then represents herself symbolically as having authority vis à vis her husband and therefore Christ.

Clearly this is practical symbolism and a matter of witness, firstly to the angels Paul says, that we should observe the correct order of things within the marriage relationship and Church protocol. The angels in 1 Corinthians 11 may refer to spiritual beings, messengers of God, or in an abstract sense the 'message' that is conveyed, that is the testimony, or both.

For example, for the wife it indicates publicly and to her husband her attitude of modesty and submissiveness, concealing her devotion and teaching modesty in the situation she finds herself, though by the witness she makes in this way demonstrating it succinctly. Within the church itself an even more rigorous protocol will be observed to maintain the true relationship between the church members and their Lord; chapter 14 of 1 Corinthians.

Paul then goes on to appeal to the natural, created order of things, as apparent throughout the civilised world, as evidence that to ignore this mode of public display is to go against an intuitive mode of conduct. To disregard this is to be in opposition to God's precept for His established created order within human society; long hair a natural covering promoting and suggesting modesty and diffidence. For a woman this is her beauty; for a man, as typifying Christ in the context of the relationship, it is inappropriate. Paul is teaching a spiritual principle, as in the previous paragraph, so therefore it is relevant to the church.

However, western culture today is based largely on post-modernist ideals, promoting an individualistic approach in all areas of life, teaching that there is no absolute authority in matters such as religion, that all beliefs are relative and that we can make our own choices in everything, including what we believe. Individualism is more however than just a modern philosophy; it is endemic throughout society, influencing theological debate and in turn interpretation of scriptural doctrine. Women for example in the past fifty years have for the most part become independent, career minded and seeking the same rights as men in society and in marriage. Men accordingly have become dominated and emasculated as a direct result. The reasons can be argued as inevitable in a modern industrial society; they can also be argued as sound from a humanistic perspective, but this later point of view has certain dubious preconceptions.

The effect that modern society has had on the ancient religious societal model of marriage then is to suppress it, as it militates against the values that society is promoting towards the idealistic culture it is trying to create. The child of God however is no less immune to this pressure than any other person in society of whatever political or religious persuasion. It does however spell danger for the depth and comprehensiveness of their faith, the quality and integrity of their marriage and indeed the whole character of the local church that they identify with. It was liberalism towards these very issues that the apostle Paul had to confront in about AD 60 when he wrote to the Corinthians, setting out for them the basic constitution that will characterise each local church assembly if it is to reflect, indeed to be truly a part of, the body of Christ, His Bride, the Church.

It is evident in chapter 11 of his first letter that he had to face up to these very issues about marriage and its significance within the body of Christ itself; issues that the church again faces today. This may have been due to a confusion as to the teaching of Christ and His apostles that in Christ there is no difference between male and female. This indeed is absolutely true, both men and women have the same status in their relationship with Christ. The practical role that we represent in the Church and in marriage however is complementary.

What the scriptures have to say on the subject of marriage and church etiquette is something that is very controversial in today's society and indeed in the churches. What is paramount to bear in mind though when considering the matter is that what the scriptures say is sacrosanct. The scriptures however are not referring to outward forms of religious observances primarily, but to what is spiritual. The whole subject is about the basis of our relationship with Christ. That cannot be modified or compromised without considerable harm to our relationship with God, which will also become compromised and therefore distorted and weakened.

The outward signs are as a testimony, first to ourselves, then our spouses, to others of the household of faith and also to the angels or our public witness. In New Testament times for example, women having their heads covered would have meant the wearing of a veil, all the time, in public at least. With this they would cover their faces when in public or speaking to anyone outside the family. Whatever the cultural implications were then, they would not be appreciated or relevant in our culture today; but to simply to say that the doctrines of scripture are out of date or are now irrelevant or to ignore what the scriptures have to say is a grave error. Whatever the outward signs that are used as a testimony, it is the inward state of the heart that is paramount. The biblical picture of the veil is stronger even than we might realise in our modern society.

What is important is that it is these spiritual characteristics that are observed by all that belong to Christ, both men and women. The way that we present ourselves to each other is then a matter of testimony to encourage each other and enhance the bond that we have with each other in Christ. The outward signs or forms that are used are significant, but only insofar as they are a true representation of our state of heart and a realistic demonstration of our heart-felt attitude.

How then can we live lives of holiness in this present

evil world according to God's holy model for us; given the insidious force that our modern culture has on our lives and hence in the life of the church as well?

> 'Do not be conformed to this world, but be transformed by the renewing of your mind', Romans 12:2

This identifies not only the root of the problem from our individual perspective but also points us directly to the answer of the problem.

Note that the ideal that Paul outlines in this chapter, as in all scripture, is that of God's perfect will and fulfilment. The Church of Christ will perhaps only ever aspire to this, when it is:

> 'Presented to Christ as a glorious Church, not having spot, or wrinkle or any such thing' Ephesians 5:27

'If as husbands we do not represent to our wives the perfect person of Christ it is because Christ is still being formed in us; yet we ever press towards the goal for the 'prize of the upward call of God in Christ Jesus', Philippians 3:14

If as wives we do not present as yet a perfect example of the submission that Christ displayed to His Father, yet we would ever 'Be diligent to present ourselves approved to God', 2 Timothy 2:15

> Still however we are called to be perfect, 'Just as your Father in Heaven is perfect', Matthew 5:48

However it is to this end that we sanctify each other.

It is not what we believe then, it is not what we say that is relevant; what we do and say of ourselves is of little consequence. It is what we are that matters, the working of God, the love of God in our hearts that make us the sanctifying influence on each other and a true witness to the world, see 1 Peter 3:1. It is the fruit of the Holy Spirit in our lives, see Galatians 5:22. It is His grace that overflowing from our lives is the beauty that causes others to praise God, when 'They may see your good works and glorify your Father in Heaven.' - Matthew 5:16

These things are paramount; the outward signs of modest dress, scriptural protocol in the way we behave and present ourselves to each other and the world, can only come from this quiet and gracious spirit, borne out of love and devotion for our Lord, or it is worth nothing. Such things will be considered prayerfully and intelligently according to the society in which we live, if we are to express the right attitude and give the proper witness. The scriptures however stand and can only be disregarded as out of date or inconvenient at our own spiritual loss and the deprivation of those to whom we have such a sacred responsibility. Remember it is our Lord in His Divine wisdom that has given us these teachings to bring us to eternal life; He will guide us to interpret them aright, if we acknowledge Him without compromise. See Proverbs 3:5-6. If though we seek to compromise with worldly attitudes and philosophy, we all suffer loss.

Women were once oppressed in the West as they still are in some countries in the Middle East. They are encouraged now to be assertive, to stand up for themselves rather than take that position that Christ took see Philippians 2:5-8:

> 'Let this mind be in you which was also in Christ Jesus,
>
> Who, being in the form of God, did not consider it robbery to be equal with God,
>
> but made Himself of no reputation, taking the form of a bondservant,
>
> and coming in the likeness of men. And being found in appearance as a man,
>
> He humbled Himself and became obedient to the point of death,
>
> even the death of the cross.'

Now women generally have more freedom, but only the freedom of this world; which is no freedom. It is a different bondage that is worse than the first. (cp. Matthew 12:43-45). For Christian women civilisation has evolved so that they now have more temporal cares competing with the liberty, which is in Christ. This is not to sanction the attitudes and pressures that women faced fifty years ago and more; it is to assert that the greater temptation that women face today to depart from God's ideal can cause their growth in Christ to suffer. Once they were humiliated, now they must learn humility or submit to the loss of those superior spiritual graces of dignity and beauty, those distinctive attributes of humility, meekness and benevolence more often seen in our older saintly women.

Likewise generally men are rarely the gentlemen of past generations; individualism encourages pride, self-centredness and self-assertiveness. For Christian men this generates greater pressure not to bear the image of Christ in the same way; an image that once was respected in society. How much do we all suffer in not coming to Christ and in His words; (here is true freedom):

'Take My yoke upon you and learn from Me;
for I am gentle and lowly in heart.
and you will find rest for your souls' - Matthew 11:29

How then does headship and submission work within a marriage in practice? As with Christ and the believer, the lead comes from the husband as the image of Christ, acting in love.

'Love is patient, love is kind. It does not envy, it does not boast,

it is not proud. It is not rude, it is not self-seeking.

It is not easily angered; it keeps no record of wrongs.

Love does not delight in evil but rejoices in the truth.

It always protects, always trusts, always hopes, always perseveres.

Love never fails:

1 Corinthians 13:4-8 N.I.V.

Simply put, this is living to serve the interests, both temporal and spiritual, of one's wife in Christ. Thus they serve each other, one taking the initiative in mutual encouragement and the other following in like mind. They are one in the Lord as Paul points out in verse twelve of 1 Corinthians chapter 11. When and where this relationship is not perfect, when and where the partners are not of the same mind or spiritual maturity, where they are not of equal commitment, then that ought to be a matter of exercise and prayer, which in itself brings us closer to Christ in subjection and like mindedness to Him.

The world's accepted wisdom is that husband and wife should be allowed to have their own breathing space, to be able to live separate, private lives to some unspecified degree. This is totally alien to the scriptures and is a device of Satan to draw mankind away from God's created order, including, or rather more particularly His saints away from that order and Himself. It is an insidious danger for Christian couples that leads to promoting a life independent of Christ, rather than seeking to 'crucify' that nature, in the words of scripture. It is not a viable option for marriage, as though we can define our own relationship. Such is not a true marriage; it is a compromise, it is lukewarmness, cp. Revelation 3:16; it is to dilute, to contaminate, that is to adulterate, a pure relationship. It becomes weak, superficial and lacking in real joy and power. The same spirit will be prevalent in our relationship with Christ, if we 'keep our private space', our own interests, ie of the flesh and of the world. Our marriage to each other is like our marriage to Christ, it requires 100% commitment; the one spouse feeds off and promotes the other. This is not to be restrictive or possessive in any way, it is to be quite the opposite, to facilitate and share in everything, promoting each other's faith and wellbeing,

This then is the ideal foundational character of each local church. This relationship is to be lived out in each local congregation or church, not just as an example but also inherently so, in its very spirit and constitution. The gathering together in Christ's name means gathering together in His will and character of selfless love, humility and service, not just acknowledging Him as our motive for being there. The women in the assembly as representing the Whole of the Church in its affiliation with Christ, present submissively, obedient, demure in dress and conduct, all as subject to Christ alone who Himself was the perfect servant, submitting completely to the will of His Father. Here it is the women that are the spiritual leaders for men to follow, the example for men to look up to. Then is Christ and His Holy Spirit more perfectly in our midst, a foretaste of that greater time when the whole Church will be gathered together into one, the bride of Christ complete and faultless at that blessed marriage supper, the marriage supper that all others have been but a pale reflection.

SECTION TWO

The Significant Issues and Affairs

The Context in which God's Objectives are Realised

PREFACE TO SECTION TWO

The Significant Setting - in which God's Purposes are Brought About

In section one of this study we considered each of God's purposes for mankind in its specific physical, spiritual, moral and judicial facets, and God's Divine objectives in parts 6-7. In this second section we look at the background that is relevant to the carrying out of those purposes, which are considered later in sections three and four. In this section the scenes are outlined for us particularly in Matthew's gospel, chapters 24:1-14 and in The Revelation, chapters 4, 9-11, 13 and 19; we also make reference to Daniel's and to other prophecies. This section covers the various 'stage sets', or backdrops as it were, where God's intentions in salvation are to be realised. This is important, because the context is relevant to the outworking and fulfilment of those purposes.

Each of the five parts of this section follow the themes

of what those purposes are, firstly in Matthews Gospel and then from four more angles in the Revelation. As mentioned in the introduction: they follow the spiritual themes or perspectives in sequence, temporal, heavenly, moral, judicial and the Divine objective.

In Matthew chapters 21-23 Jesus had explained what God's purposes were for the whole of mankind and how Israel had failed to realise that state of affairs through hypocrisy and unbelief. Now in the first half of chapter 24 He explains how the world will be during this present time that the Kingdom of God is being prepared in the hearts of individuals from all the nations, Israel and gentile alike. He says that it will be a time of testing and proving, but those that win through will be purified and saved by means of the troubles and difficulties. He reassures His disciples that He will be with them to sustain and strengthen them.

Associated with the time that God is preparing His Kingdom on Earth in the lives of individuals, in Revelation chapter 4, Christ is in Heaven taking the scroll that gives Him the authority to rule that Kingdom. It is related because it is the elders that lead the acknowledgement and worship to Christ. Their thrones (representing their governing role) surround the throne of Christ, taking their authority from Him. Thus the elders represent the heavenly or spiritual role that the people of God fulfil, albeit that they are qualified and made ready for that role in an earthly setting of war, persecution and difficulty. This scene is of course also looking back to chapters 1-3 where Christ is revealed as the Lord of His Church in their various states and needs, overseeing the progress that His people are making in qualifying for their heavenly roles. The sequence here however shows how the mercy of God is progressively revealed to mankind. With Matthew chapter 24 the connection with Revelation 4 is a spiritual one, both contexts in which God is working His purposes out. First though in this part we consider the nature of the throne itself, which represents all the authority in Heaven and Earth that is to be delegated in the giving of the scroll.

The next two background scenes stay within the setting of Revelation chapter 4 but consider the way in which the trials on Earth at the present time persuade mankind to face up to their moral accountability and responsibility to their creator. Following this God shows His mercy in making a dramatic appeal to mankind to warn that time is running out. These scenes are recorded in chapters 9-10; in chapter 8 the scene is the golden censor from the altar being thrown to Earth that was considered in the previous section of this study. That scene is what precipitates the warnings of chapters 9-10. Chapter 4 is the spiritual background to why these things take place.

The fourth background scene in this section is more physical in its imagery, though no less spiritual in its subject matter. Here we see how low the world has sunk politically and religiously, but that through this God is protecting His own, yet also warning of the end and of calling all of mankind to account. The purposes of God were outlined in Revelation chapter 12 where the epitome of evil, Satan, is defeated through the victory of the Lamb and through Him the victory of His saints over this world. In these scenes, from Revelation 13-14, it is the political character of the world system that comes up for review and how it will end.

The final setting for the development of God's purposes on Earth is the return of Christ to Earth as King of Kings and Lord of Lords. This looks back to the scene in Revelation chapter 19 of the wedding supper; here Christ's bride, that is all His saints, is now seen as an army coming in support of His mission to establish His Kingdom on Earth. In chapter 13 the vision of Armageddon had been plainly brought before mankind. Those that still refuse to listen must finally face the meek and gentle Lamb of God and His multitude; all that is contrary to Him must first be removed from the earth before He can reign supreme.

SECTION 2: PART 1

The Age of Duplicity and Doubt

Matthew 24: 1-14: The Olivet Discourse

The Events on Earth that Will Feature in This Age as God's Kingdom is Increased

As we might expect, the tone was largely upbeat and optimistic as we considered in section one of this study what God's objectives are in Christ for mankind. The imagery was filled with wonder and scenes of worship setting out what God in His wisdom has planned and how glorious the fulfilment will be. It was not without a sombre introduction as our Lord set the scene initially of the failure of Israel to live up to the standard that was necessary for the bringing in of those plans, but that this in fact is now being fulfilled in the Church through the Lord Jesus Christ Himself.

Now however in section two we have a contrast of different scenes as we consider the spiritually significant background through which God achieves His purposes.

Positive seems to turn to negative, wonder to horror and glory to degradation. It starts with the effect of Israel's rejection of their Messiah and continues with the downward spiral of man's total rejection of God and the chaos and anarchy that this will ultimately lead to.

After mentioning the destruction of the temple, Christ continues immediately with this present age of the church where both Jews and gentiles are being called into God's favour, while Israel is dispersed among the nations for the time being. During the past century though, this situation has changed as we have seen the Jews coming back in their own land as a sovereign nation. God however has not yet continued working with them again in terms of continuing His task of their salvation; they are mostly just a secular nation without a temple at present. They are still under the censure of God for their disobedience, though He has not forgotten His promises to their forefathers, Abraham, Isaac and Jacob.

Deuteronomy 7:8 tells us:

'The Lord loves you, and because He would keep His oath '
(ie Genesis 22:16) 'which He swore to your fathers ...'.
Jeremiah 31:3 is another example:
The Lord has appeared of old to me saying,
'Yes I have loved you with an everlasting love'
and in verse 10,
'He who scattered Israel will gather him and keep him.'

This promise was not conditional as others may have been; God has not given up on Israel forever; God forbid that He should renege on His oath. As the Psalmist says as he asks the rhetorical question, 'Has His mercy ceased forever? Has His promise failed forevermore?' Psalm 77:8.

It is a theme that permeates so much of the Old Testament, the fact that Israel would be removed from the land, as they had been under Nebuchadnezzar BC 483, for the land to have its Sabbath years rest (2 Chronicles 36:21).

In AD 70 however they were not just to be taken captive this time, something that had meant that before they had retained their nation integrity, but this time they were to be separated and dispersed among all the nations, until the full number of the gentiles have come into blessing alongside Israel (Romans 11:25). This was because they had rejected their Messiah; the one promised of God to them to deliver them from their sin and bondage.

So our Lord starts with foretelling the unthinkable happening, from the point of view of the contemporary Jews. Their glorious temple, built for them by Herod, and the evidence to them that they were God's chosen people, would be completely razed to the ground; 'not one stone left upon another' was Jesus' graphic description of its coming destruction. God was finished working with Israel now under the covenant that He made with Abraham, albeit just for an indefinite period. Jesus by His Sacrifice that He was soon to accomplish was to usher in a new constitution, a time of grace towards mankind. The nations had failed to be blessed by the nation of Israel, as God Himself had foretold they would. Their opportunity would now be deferred while the gentile nations would be blessed through the work of Christ alone and His Holy Spirit, and in and through His own saints on Earth, His followers, His church.

Having then foretold the end of the temple as a witness on Earth of God's presence among mankind, our Lord turns to His disciples, on whom the mantle has now fallen to carry the good news of salvation through faith alone to all men. The testimony of the Ark, a symbol of God's Holiness was to be removed. The testimony of His Holiness was now to be displayed in the midst of mankind in 'temples of flesh and blood', that is those men and women who would now be filled with the Spirit of Christ after the Day of Pentecost, once Christ Himself was no longer on this Earth.

This was the band of men that our Lord was speaking to now; not to tell them about a glorious world that was coming, but first to relate the tribulation and 'birth pangs' that the world would suffer before His Kingdom could be ushered in. It was only through the greatest difficulty and opposition that this could and would be fully achieved. False Christs would arise to deceive the whole world. The true Christ had been rejected and murdered. The true Christ, the prince of peace and King of righteousness, had been cast out in favour of a thief and a murderer. Man in his natural state would never choose what was good and holy. That would mean a path of self-denial and embracing one of meekness and humility. That would mean rejecting his own natural inclination of self-preservation, repenting from his rejection of God's Holy law and living no longer to serve himself, but instead to live a life of following Christ in weakness and self-sacrifice. False Christs would offer a more palatable way of life, but one that would lead ultimately to eternal death.

False Christs will offer a path of conquest, a path to utopia through the means of force. Many with the spirit of antichrist would pervade the whole of society, indeed the

Church on Earth also. The spirit of conquest of course leads to conflict and conflict to wars, continuing disharmony among man on Earth. Wars lead to famine, the world no longer sustaining life, physically or spiritually; famine then leads to disease and poverty. Wars rock the very fabric of society, rupture the basis of life itself; the way that 'earthquake' is used symbolically in scripture, emphasising that 'earthquakes in various places' will not only be literal but also become more prevalent figuratively. As the depressing scenario deteriorates however, the social order that opposes God and the reign of Christ will break down into complete chaos and anarchy, but that comes later.

To His disciples a new world was coming. Our Lord had prepared them on several occasions to be ready for their mission after He was taken from them. A new era of persecution had arrived, a time of their rejection because of whom they represented. A world of persecution and martyrdom awaited them, a time of hatred of them because of whom they were living witnesses. Opposition waited from those that saw them as a threat to their status quo; a world where those that saw their testimony of Divine goodness would hate them, a world where they were to suffer treachery, belligerence, harassment and enmity. 'Be not afraid' though our Lord had said to them, 'for I have overcome the world' John 16:33

Not only will they suffer the resentment and antagonism of the world, there would be the enemy within to withstand also. False prophets would bring in false doctrine to undermine the pure truth of Christ. They would seek to draw away the Disciples of Christ after themselves, endeavouring to snatch them from the true 'Light of the

World', corrupting and debasing the virtue of the Gospel, confusing its power so that it would be of no effect. Yet within the true Disciples of Christ, this would only strengthen their faith, purifying and sanctifying their love and devotion for their Lord and increase their power through increasing their dependence on and completeness in Him. The 'fire' of their ordeal and difficulty would serve only to increase a heavenly nature within them. From a human standpoint they would be worn down, but for those that stayed faithful to Christ it would produce purity and endurance; as Christ said so succinctly, 'he who endures to the end shall be saved;' verse13.

Christ however has not only the sanctification of His followers in view, but also their part in the extension of His Kingdom on Earth. Not that He would bring it in instantly, as the disciples expected it at first after His resurrection, but rather after the full number of His Church had been called out from mankind and after the evil empire of 'antichrist' had finally run its course. In the meantime, this empire would not only be a witness against and the instrument of the judgement of God in and on the world, but also the instrument of sanctification of both His Church and finally Israel. During this time the Gospel of the Kingdom would be preached to the entire world first, the Gospel of faith in Jesus Christ and His sacrifice.

So the Gospel will be preached worldwide, as a 'light that shines in a dark place', a counterpoint to evil and error. A gospel that is 'foolishness to those who are perishing' 1 Corinthians 1:18, but a gospel that will continue until the coming of the end of this present age.

These few verses of words from our Lord Himself at the

beginning of chapter 24 down to verse 14, would be a summary of the next 2000 years or more! This is just a succinct summary of the age when the Gospel will be preached by His Church worldwide. What He has to tell His disciples however doesn't end there. There is then a distinct change in theme in our Lord's discourse as He then continues in verse 15 to give a summary of what will happen from the end of the gospel age until He returns to set up His kingdom. He starts with the ominous sign that will occur to begin the time when the prophecy becomes relevant to Israel. This however is where we take up our study of the rest of this chapter in section three.

SECTION 2: PART 2

The Four Living Creatures Within the Throne

Revelation Chapters 4-5
It is God that Confers the Right to the One to Reign Supreme on Earth from His Heavenly Throne

Revelation chapter 4 now takes a new perspective on what God is revealing to mankind concerning His purposes, purposes that extend through the whole of time. The whole of this book is addressed to the church; though only the first three chapters were directly about the church. Chapter 1 presents the Lord of the Church in all His glory as overseer and principal of the church, while chapters 2 and 3 are about the state of the church during this present time, its responsibilities and Christ's expectations for it.

Chapter 4 now leaves this temporal, terrestrial aspect

of God's Divine purposes in the Church to view all His purposes for mankind from a heavenly aspect. We now see a much wider view of His objectives, the establishment of His kingdom on Earth. His objectives in the church is fully revealed, we now see how He will establish His plans for this world through into its final era when,

> 'The Earth will be filled
> with the knowledge of the glory of the Lord,
> as the waters cover the sea.' Habakkuk 2:14

John however had to look, the vision had to be attended to, it is not something that is obvious or can be taken for granted, indeed it is not even something that we can be aware of at all unless we take note of it to understand and assimilate it. What he noted first was a door open into Heaven. Now we can just picture this as in a literal sense, though it must be in a spiritual sense that it will have any relevance. What we 'see' first is that there is a way, a manner in which we can understand a heavenly perspective of God's plans; cp 1 Corinthians 2:14. To view what is revealed in the following chapters from an earthly perspective is simply to see it as describing a vengeful God inflicting havoc and revenge on a creation that hasn't acknowledged Him.

To see things from a Divine, that is, heavenly perspective, we have first to listen for the invitation to be raised to that position where we can see things clearly. John heard; he was receptive to the voice that spoke to him. Unless we are in that spirit of contrite acceptance to what God would say, unless our own ideas and ideals are set aside, unless we are completely open-minded to listening to the voice of God speaking to us, we cannot even hear that voice or begin to conceive or enter into what this Divine perspective will be. The voice was like a trumpet, that is it spoke with all the authority from the place from where it came, Heaven itself. The first thing we are told is that what is to be revealed is what is to happen after all that has been made known in chapters 2 and 3 has been completed. This does not mean necessarily that this will be events that must all take place at a time after this present era, though that may be partially so. Chapter 12 for example clearly includes events on Earth that occurred before the coming of Christ and the beginning of His Church. The question here is a matter of precedence, the order in which things will be effective and the relevance of their context. What are being revealed are eternal plans and principles; that is the nature of what is heavenly.

Then John relates, 'Immediately I was in the Spirit.' We can only comprehend what is spiritual, that is what is heavenly, by being subject to the Spirit of God; this is the spirit of reverent humility, to set aside our own ideas, preconceived notions, prejudice and values to listen to God alone. To use an Old Testament expression, this is 'The Fear of the Lord'.

It is then that John sees the throne set in Heaven. That is the central theme and order for all that is heavenly, that throne, which represents the Divine sovereignty that prevails over all of Heaven and Earth, nothing happens except it is according to the express or permissive will of the One that occupies the throne. It is then in that context that we next see the One that is sitting on that throne, described as being first 'like a jasper... stone in appearance.' The picture given in the scripture here is a brilliant, clear stone with a shining lustre, its beauty inherent in its radiance. The picture being conveyed is one of clarity, purity and radiance, moral transparency and intensity; entirely separate from anything that is of this world order. This is a succinct description of the Holiness of Almighty God Himself. Then as if to emphasise that this is a word picture, not just a visual image, describing the character of Almighty God, He is also described as 'a sardius stone in appearance.' This was probably a bright red stone of slightly cloudy appearance, suggesting a private, passionate sentiment. Here again its interpretation is confined to the appearance of God, but it presents it as an attribute that we can perceive and understand directly. God is first Holy but also, as the scriptures testify often, He is also a passionate and compassionate God, indicating both His love for His creation but also His hatred of all that is contrary to His holy nature. It is in this context then that He rules over His creation, patiently and caringly.

Another feature however of the throne is that there was a rainbow encircling it. Now the rainbow in scripture first appears in Genesis chapter 9, where it represents the mercy of God that He will never again destroy the Earth by flood. Here around the Throne however it was in appearance like an emerald; that presents us with a picture of something that is a rich translucent green, an impression of a deep, rich shining lustre that irradiates an inherent beauty, intimating a congenial harmony of soul by association with an idyllic natural scene. This alludes to the beauty of the glory and radiance of the graciousness of God. This then is a succinct picture of the nature of God and His association with mankind, not of an austere irascible tyrant, but as a benevolent, gracious, merciful and patient ruler, but also one that cannot accommodate anything that is unholy, corrupt or immoral in anyway.

Then around that throne there were twenty-four thrones. This clearly shows that God is not an autocratic dictator; absolute power has not nor cannot corrupt the Almighty, who alone is pure and holy. He delegates His government to twenty-four vice-regencies. These are placed around the central Throne of the Almighty, indicating that they are satellites, gaining their authority from their centre alone.

There has been some speculation as to who the elders are that have this delegated prerogative. The scripture here however doesn't give them labels; rather their relevant attributes are described. These elders reappear however again in chapter 5 where there is more detail given, which is explored in the next piece; six times in all the 24 elders feature in this book. The fact that they were elders indicates that they were spiritually mature and so qualified for an administrative function; they were clothed in white indicating their singleness of purpose and purity of character and the crowns confirm their competence and delegated authority.

The Four Living Creatures within the Throne

What is clear from little more than a cursory reading of these chapters is that little or nothing is said as to the identity of the individuals described, though much is said of their character and function. Even Christ, who is unequivocally the one who takes the scroll, is presented as a sacrificial lamb, identified only by the attribute that qualifies Him to take the authority conferred by the scroll. Likewise the elders are identified by their number, implying their priestly function. The throne however is perhaps the most remarkable in this respect; it is probably the most significant feature of Heaven excepting the Almighty Himself, yet at first sight it tells us nothing about the throne itself, even its character or function. But that is not so if we look at the text carefully. The imagery here is very succinct but also very profound. We are told that within, that is in the middle of the throne contained by the throne itself, and also all around the throne, are four living creatures. These creatures are not given a discrete identity of their own but they form part of the throne itself and its immediate surroundings. It would seem therefore that they are in fact living created or creative qualities of the throne itself. As one would expect, if this were so, that they would feature prominently throughout the whole of the Revelation of Jesus Christ in this book and they do repeatedly.

The whole scene is presented in a way that we can easily visualise, but to get a better understanding we must go beyond a visual image. The creatures are something that is or are within and around the very throne of God Himself; much closer even than the saints. It is a graphic image that tells us what they represent and what they tell us about the glory of God and His throne, to whom all power in Heaven and on Earth is reserved.

It is quite apparent from the outset that they represent that which is intimately connected or acquainted with the throne of God itself and its function, as they testify as to its character and propriety in its portrayal of Divine authority. Now the Throne itself is not some material item but speaks of the rule and omnipotence of Almighty God. It is an attribute of the Almighty, not something with its own discrete identity.

The characteristics of these creatures are similar to many Old Testament images. For example they have similarities to the seraphim of Isaiah 6, but are not identical to them. The creatures of Ezekiel chapter 1 have similarities but also differences, which must suggest that they share characteristics with these images but also represent something unique.

The first creature is like a lion, which speaks of authority and power, a beast that all others regard with respect, apprehension and awe. The second is an ox, a beast of burden that speaks of strength and potency, sufficient to achieve the task set before it. The third has the face of a man, clearly representing the characteristic of the expression of wisdom or intelligence, while the fourth beast is depicted as representing the grace and overseeing position of an eagle in flight.

In summary it is the creatures that testify to the supreme authority, strength, wisdom, graciousness and presidential function of the throne that they encompass.

However the living creatures are also full of eyes, looking into the past and into the future; they have Divine awareness, not overlooking transgression but fully cognisant with all that pertains in Earth and Heaven. They graphically portray then also the omnipotence, omniscience and omnipresence of the Almighty.

The function of a wing in scripture is commonly to

denote that which provides a covering or protection, as when a mother bird covers its young. Clearly therefore the justice and rule of God is something that is to protect man rather than to destroy him, to cover his weakness rather than primarily to convict him. Hence is the grace of God so long suffering, waiting for man to turn to Him that he might obtain that protection.

Even as Lord and judge of all creation, in all His majesty and power, God in Christ is gracious and the protector of all those that come to Him and trust Him. Only those that stubbornly refuse to accept His Lordship, who are determined on their own way of life of self-achievement and satisfaction, exclude themselves from His care.

To summarise these attributes and qualities of the living creatures then:

- Their appearance testifies to the supreme authority, strength, wisdom and graciousness of the Throne.
- They are situated within and around the very throne of God Himself.
- They have six wings, something that is to protect man rather than to destroy him.
- They are intelligent beings or features not just something conceptual.
- Their function is to make known the character of Almighty God.
- They testify in themselves by their presence as to the holiness and the everlasting nature of the throne as they say without ceasing, 'Holy, Holy, Holy, Lord God Almighty, who was and is and is to come'.

- They attribute glory and honour and praise to the Almighty
- They substantiate the testimony of the creation itself regarding its creator in saying simply 'amen' to the praise of its creator that the creation itself is witness to.

Thus we can see that they are of an essentially spiritual constitution, as we would expect given the nature of this book, reflecting the attributes of and the qualities inherent in the throne itself; that is, an eminence that proclaims the authority and justice of God Himself. They witness particularly to the creative and life-giving character of the power and majesty that emanate from the Almighty.

The Functions of the Four Living Creatures

The first function then of these mystical creatures is to represent the creativity, character, wisdom and graciousness of the Almighty Himself in relation to His sovereignty. Also it is very important to note the close relationship that the elders have with these creatures; throughout most of this book where the elders appear, so do these living creatures appear, revealing the influence they have upon the elders. Five times in chapters 4 and 5 the living creatures are mentioned before the elders as praising and glorifying the Almighty. In chapter 14 they come between the throne and the elders when responding to the song of the 144,000 on Mount Zion, suggesting in each case that their status and significance is greater than that of the elders, that the elders are led by the creatures in worshipping the Almighty. However in chapter 7 the elders take the lead, which the creatures follow when the elders acknowledge the shout of the great multitude before the throne praising God for their salvation. This is something that the elders have also experienced and so their acknowledgement is endorsed by the creatures, is not inspired by it. Also in personal integrity they take the lead; it is the elders that lead the praise when it is announced in Heaven that the great harlot has been judged and destroyed, as they were the ones that knew from experience the sin and persecution that she perpetrated.

However when we come to chapter 6, it is each of the creatures that introduce the breaking of the first four seals that fasten the scroll. Again in chapter 15 it is one of the creatures that gives the bowls of wrath of Almighty God to the angels to administer. On these occasions the elders are not mentioned.

From this then we can glean more about these creatures; they inspire the worship of the redeemed, bringing them into full appreciation of the majesty, honour and authority of the Almighty. They inform the redeemed of all the innate qualities of the Almighty that are inherent in His Divine relationship with all His creation. They also institute some of the retribution of God in bringing about His Kingdom on Earth. When it comes to God's work in salvation however, they only echo the wisdom, righteousness and graciousness of God; they are not beings that could ever be independently conscious of the innate beauty and kindness of God.

These remarkable creatures then represent those attributes of the power, wisdom and graciousness of God, in actively proclaiming those traits, approving the glory evident in all creation. They are then purely spiritual representations, of all the truth that we can know about the majesty and power of God from the wonder of nature and all we can know about God from our daily experience of how the world operates according to moral principles. They represent all that we or anyone can know of God apart from what we can only know intimately by faith, which is the joy and peace of salvation and the secret communion that we can have with Him in Christ.

The elders however represent not the revelation of the mystery of God but rather what we are together in Christ. They have a corporate identity, albeit one of spiritual character. They understand who God is from the witness of the creatures and praise Him for it, taking their cue from the 4 creatures. However they worship Him also for His love and favour to them, taking the lead in worship when the great multitude praise God for their salvation and when the great harlot is destroyed.

What the four living creatures are then is the character or likeness in which they are portrayed in verse 7. They are the character of the throne, which is the majesty, glory and supremacy of the Almighty.

The living creatures then are a witness to the disposition of the Almighty in His relationship with His creation and creatures, as is the whole persona of creation itself.

These attributes of God in His administration of His creation are in absolute righteousness, mercy and in intelligence of what transpires.

The 24 elders are the priestly role of the saints in their worshipping and praising God. Their function seems to be in worship, praise and appreciation, not in any representative position.

Their worship is inspired and enlightened by the testimony of the creatures, a testimony that is mediated through a true consideration of the attributes of God, seen in creation and His government in creation and in our lives.

In summary they are mythological, metaphysical and metaphorical characteristics of the power of the Almighty that are evident in creation itself, in the way that it functions and from our own experience of life and in faith; that which testifies to the supreme authority, strength, wisdom, graciousness and presidential function of the throne that they encompass.

SECTION 2: PART 3

The Supremacy of the Lamb

Revelation Chapters 4-5
It is God that Confers the Right to Reign Supreme on Earth to the Only One who is Worthy to Do So

It is Christ that is not only Lord of His church, as portrayed in chapters 1-3, but also now in chapters 4 and 5, the one who alone in all the Heavens and Earth is worthy to take the supreme position of authority to reign and judge the Earth. He alone is worthy to take the scroll from the One who sits on the throne. It is not because of His innate majesty or Divine splendour that qualifies Him either; it is as a 'Lamb as though it had been slain'. It is because of this that He fulfils all the Divine qualifications that enable Him to receive supreme authority and propriety in Heaven and on Earth, next to God, His father. It was His sacrifice, the sacrifice of His own perfect life, the only life of perfection that had ever been, that could count Him worthy to take this position. Throughout this book the implications of this are developed to show that it is this principle alone that must pertain throughout the Kingdom, for us and for everyone in it; the sacrifice of our own self-image and life of self-fulfilment and self-interest. Existentially this is the central principle that must operate perfectly for God's perfect Kingdom to be viable at all.

It is in Genesis, chapter 3:21 that we first have sacrifice, of an animal to clothe Adam and Eve, to cover their shame after they were alienated from God through sin. Abraham sacrificed a lamb when he worshipped God, after he was tested by God to offer his son as a sacrifice. Isaac offered a sacrifice of thanksgiving after he learned that his son Joseph was alive, before he went down into Egypt to meet him. It is a theme that permeates the whole Bible, indeed the very foundation of the Old and the New Covenants of God with mankind, that we can only be reconciled to God, to know His life and offer Him true praise through sacrifice.

It was then, 400 years after Isaac, when Israel had become the great nation, as God had promised Abraham they would, that they were delivered out of the slavery in Egypt. It was of course after the nine plagues that God brought upon the Egyptians that Pharaoh finally let them go, though it was the last plague that was most significant for the Egyptians but more particularly for the Israelites.

The story of the Israelites' deliverance is found in Exodus chapter 12:2, which begins, 'This month shall be your beginning of months'. This was to be the birth of the nation as a great culture. God was about to work a miracle in the land of Egypt that would show the nations the favour that God showed to the nation of Israel for Abraham's sake, as it would be through him would come He who would redeem the world from the enslavement of the fall. More immediately though, He was going to show the Israelites the special deliverance that they would receive through the sacrifice of a lamb. They were to kill the lamb and put its blood on the door lintel so that the angel of death should pass over every family that was covered by the blood of the lamb.

It was then soon after this very occasion that they were to receive, through Moses, the ceremonial law of sacrifice for sin and communion with God. Their culture, their religious identity, indeed their communal identity was to be founded on the Passover lamb, a festival that was to become the most important in the Israelite calendar.

It is then when we come to the New Testament, in Luke 22:15, that Christ links this festival with the sacrifice that He is about to make at Calvary. The whole Old Testament ceremonial law now becomes symbolically identified with the sufferings of Christ and the work that He is about to accomplish on behalf of all mankind. Christ fulfils not only the law of Mount Sinai but also the whole of the ceremonial law that was to follow, which the letter to the Hebrews explains. He is to become the true Passover Lamb, the Lamb that all the lambs sacrificed under the Old Testament law were really symbolic of. Paul therefore says with absolute precision in 1 Corinthians 5:7

'Christ our Passover was sacrificed for us'

Clearly now the symbol of the Passover Lamb is the essence of all that God has achieved in redemption and resurrection through Christ and His sacrifice. This symbolism however is very much the depiction of Christ's work in salvation on Earth.

When we come to chapter 4 of the Book of the Revelation we see things from a purely heavenly perspective; a view that only those of a heavenly disposition can truly appreciate, cp Ephesians 1:3. A door, that which prevents or conceals, is opened to reveal the heavenly scene. This is a very important interpretation to understand as it explains the change of style of the text from chapter 3 to chapter 4, from the simple instruction of our Lord in chapters 2-3 to the pictorial representations of the remaining chapters. Jesus, no longer now a man of sorrows, despised and rejected of men, in chapter 5 is introduced as the Lamb that was slain. Not now just the Passover Lamb, the one that took on Himself the judgement of God for our sin, or the sanctifier His people as in chapter 2 and three of Revelation, but the redeemer, firstly of His Church, represented here by the twenty-four elders, then secondly through the Church, the whole earthly creation that was under the dominion of sin; cp Romans 8:19. He had paid the redemption price of His own blood to redeem mankind's right to the tree of life, to restore the full sovereignty of the world to God and to receive for Himself the Kingdom. The scroll itself refers to the authority that is conferred onto the one who receives it, as is discussed below. The symbol of the giving of a scroll to confer authority is an ancient cultural practice, one that is still performed today, for example in the conferring of degrees in our universities.

Now He is the one who is worshipped and praised above all others, alongside 'The One on the Throne'. The only one in all creation that is worthy to receive the mandate from God Himself, to 'buy back' from the dominion of sin all that had been lost and to judge and rule the Earth. The only one who could take the scroll of supreme authority. All creation blesses the Lamb; the angels worship. The church, as being redeemed out of every tribe and nation, represented in its priestly capacity, understands and worships. Foremost of all are the four creatures that are in and around the throne. They appreciate His merit and say 'amen' to the accolade given by all creation on Earth, endorsing His right. The lightning and thunder of verse five tells us that the throne itself speaks of the awesome 'voice' of God and of judgement, which gives us some indication of what the scroll itself relates to.

The elders are mentioned as sitting on twenty-four thrones, though if we consider carefully, the elders represent not individuals or even a material entity as the Church in itself, per se. That this is the Church that is signified there seems little doubt as they say, chapter 5:9-10:

'And have redeemed us to God by Your blood
out of every tribe and tongue and people and nation.'

What is being depicted is rather more subtle, however. The elders themselves sing a new song:

' And have made us kings and priests to our God;
and we shall reign on the Earth.'

Now the number of twenty-four elders makes allusion to the twenty-four courses of the Aaronic priesthood in 1

Chronicles chapter 24, all with their separate duties within the operation of the priesthood under the Old Covenant.

It is therefore the function of all the church and potentially the special function of each member in particular that is in view here, as priests and also as kings, hence the twenty-four thrones and the crowns of the elders. It is in a priestly capacity that they bring praise and worship in full appreciation of all that God has achieved on their behalf. All these details have a meaning here, to help us understand the spiritual message that is being portrayed.

With the twenty-four elders it is their spiritual characteristics that are mainly in view, the most important features of the church and its particular members. It is not their identity that is significant, but what each one holds that is precious to God. It is not what they have attained, but their individual comprehension of the glory and omnipotence of the 'Lord God Almighty' and what the four creatures give testimony to. It is they that show understanding of the full power of God and the Lamb, offering praise and worship and thanksgiving for their redemption.

This is not to say that what the respective parties 'say' here is just a passive, silent impression rather than a real active expression, that it not the case; it is just to say that it is not just a physical or verbal expression as we would experience in this temporal world, it signifies also what they are and represent. This scene is Heaven, a spiritual, eternal realm and the dwelling place of God. What is being expressed here is that Heaven is alive, resonant with these themes. It is not a material communication but a real expression of eternal truth, situations that occupy that blessed scene, vibrant issues that are an evident outpouring in witness from those groups of creatures. Everything in all creation reverberates with and to the glory of God. It is all about fullness of experience not just outward articulation.

Likewise, to say that the angels 'say', as in a temporal sense as giving verbal expression, is to demean what they are actually communicating. What is significant is their living witness and the testimony they convey as glorious created beings and faithful servants of God. In this way they speak more eloquently of the glory and power of their Creator and of the Lamb who is the centre of all things in Heaven. It is the angels especially that appreciate the riches, wisdom and strength of the power of God and of the Lamb. This then is also fully appreciated by those that inhabit that place, through their testimony.

This then has set the glorious scene that is not only the dwelling place of God and the Lamb, but also the place that reflects and articulates their glory so fully and completely. The focus of attention now centres on the Lamb Himself, a Lamb as it had been slain, who alone in all creation was found worthy to take the book and open its seals. We need to understand what this book represents if we are to understand in full the status and true glory that this confers. The first thing that we are told is that the scroll was given to Him from the right hand of Him that sat upon the throne. The right hand is the executive hand and so signifies the full intention and responsibility of the one that confers it. It was as the Lamb that was slain that He was alone found worthy to take the scroll. As the Lamb that was slain, as the one that was sacrificed for us, He was found worthy, that is, is qualified to take the scroll.

The authority given to Him is recorded in this book, which in scripture means that if it is written it is established permanently, cp Job 19:23 and Isaiah 30:8. It was written on the back, (or 'from behind' the word means), signifying that the authority was established 'from behind', that is previously written down, by the prophets, cp Revelation 4:6 and Matthew 9:20 for broader usage of this word. The scroll was also written from within, that is that His authority was innate, this qualification was also recorded by the prophets, cp Revelation 4:8 and Mark 7:21 for meaning of the word. This is God's mandate of delegated executive power to rule throughout all the kingdoms of the Earth, as we see when we come to Revelation 11:15; that is when the scroll has been fully opened (all the seals broken) and its contents fully declared (that is when the trumpets have all sounded). Jesus Christ, the meek, rejected Son of God, who became the Passover Lamb, that the judgement of God should pass us by, has now become the supreme authority in Heaven and on Earth, subject only to His Father's will. He attained this status because of, not in spite of, His sacrifice.

There is also another aspect of the glory of Christ that is mentioned here. The elders sing that they were redeemed out of every tongue and nation. It is now the blood of Christ, as the redemptive price that was paid for our salvation, that comes into view. Now to redeem simply means to 'buy back, recover by expenditure of effort or by stipulated payment', but how did the expression arise in respect of our salvation from sin?

As 'dead' in trespasses and sins as the scripture describes us, we are in the spiritual state of separation from God. We have no appreciation of Him, no relationship with

Him, no experiential knowledge of Him. God cannot revive our relationship with Him as long as we are in a state of sinfulness, that is, living in a state of separation from but also of selfish indifference to Him.

As a man, in His physical death Christ was also separated from His Father and therefore then in this respect was in the same spiritual state as ourselves in our relationship with God.

For all then who will be associated with Christ must be united with Him in His death, and then to be resurrected with Him to become alive to God, to have our proprietary right reinstated as it were. It is a mystery that still defies our comprehension completely, how Christ can be united with our spirit and give us eternal life by virtue of His moral position, because we are unable to fully comprehend the extent of Divine wisdom and understanding. That is one reason why the doctrine of salvation is:

'Foolishness to those who are perishing,
but to us who are being saved it is the power of God.'
1 Corinthians 1:18

To those that believe it is their intimate experience, in its fullness; of everyone that accepts it as truth and in dependence upon Him. It is then something that we can't fully rationalise, but we can receive and fully experience by faith and experience its effect in our hearts and lives.

There is a beautiful story in the Old Testament, in the book of Ruth, of how a man called Boaz paid the redemption of a piece of land that had belonged to the late husband of Ruth, Elimelech. Under the Mosaic Law he could pay the stipulated redemption money of a property that had been mortgaged so that it could be reinstated to its original owner, if they were unable to pay the cost themselves, but only if he could afford to and if he was a relative.

This is a succinct figure of how the precious sacrifice of Christ reinstated our proprietary relationship with God that had been lost through sin. We were 'sold under sin' to use Paul's words and the penalty under the law is death, eternal separation from God. By His death on Calvary, by the shedding of His blood, He paid the redemptive price for us, that which was stipulated under the law. Under the law He had to be a relative, ie one of mankind, and also able to pay it, so He had to be sinless Himself. Only by being also Divine could He ever fulfil this qualification. Only through death Himself, separation from His Father, could He come to us, where we were spiritually, only there could He be identified with us. Only then by our identification with His death and resurrection can we become alive once more unto God. Only as His death becomes real and active in our hearts and lives can we become one with Him in His resurrection. This makes no sense of course rationally in a material sense, but as a spiritual principle and in terms of relationship, particularly our relationship with God, it makes perfect sense emotionally and experientially. It may however be difficult to grasp even so at first until that relationship grows and is strengthened.

To briefly return to the scroll though, it was sealed with seven impediments to it being opened and its contents becoming effective. The seals are that which hinders its mandate coming to pass, those things which must happen on Earth in their fullness, that which will execute the judgement of God on all that is in opposition to His Holy will and that which will bring to an end all that stands in the way of His glorious kingdom. The Lamb alone is worthy to open the book and release its seven seals. He alone has the seven horns (symbolising authority), 'all the authority that has been given to Him in Heaven and on Earth' Matthew 28:18; He alone has the power to bring about the release of those things that must occur before the contents of the scroll can be revealed.

Next in chapter 5:6 we are told of:

> 'A Lamb as though it had been slain, having seven horns and seven eyes,
>
> which are the seven Spirits of God sent out into all the Earth.'

It is only the sacrificial lamb that has the sevenfold perception, the Divine wisdom, to comprehend the complete rule on Earth of the 'One on the throne', to see what must be realised to bring that glorious rule of Divine majesty and grace to fruition. What it is in practical terms that the seven seals prevent we will come to in the next section. They are seals though in that they prevent us from realising what it is that prevents the reign of the Kingdom of God on Earth. Until this is revealed and judged they cannot be removed.

There are two other relevant details in this section however regarding the spiritually significant background to the achievement of God's purposes that we have passed over, which are introduced at the beginning of the scene in chapter 4 and are relevant to the Divine power and glory of Christ.

First, we have not considered the seven lamps before the throne which we are told are the seven Spirits of God, Revelation 4:5. In Revelation 5:6 the Lamb has seven eyes that also symbolize 'the seven Spirits of God that are sent out into all the Earth'. These are again mentioned in chapter 1, verse four and chapter 3 verse one, so their presence would seem very important. How do we reconcile this however with the one Holy Spirit, the third person of the Godhead?

The seven Spirits of God - the term itself is rather an enigma - are symbolized in these two ways in the Book of the Revelation but in three different contexts. In chapter 5 the Lamb has the seven eyes that are the seven spirits of God. In chapter 1 and chapter 4 they are the seven lamps burning before the throne, but in chapter 3 they are mentioned in context with the church of Sardis, which 'had a name of living but was dead'.

Now the scriptures have many different titles or names in different places to describe the work of the Holy Spirit in the life and souls of His saints. Nowhere however does a single scripture itself give us a definitive list of what the seven represents, but in Isaiah 11:2, spoken prophetically in respect of Messiah, there is a list of seven qualities, referred to in section one of this study, which would seem at least to be relevant:

> 'The Spirit of wisdom and understanding,
> the Spirit of counsel and might,
> the Spirit of knowledge and of the fear of the Lord.
> His delight is in the fear of the Lord.'

In chapter 3 of the Revelation, it is Christ who has the seven Spirits of God and promises the Overcomer to be clothed in a robe of white, which is the righteousness of the saints, Revelation 19:8. It is the names of the Spirits of God in Isaiah 11, (though spoken prophetically of Christ Himself, His servant, specifically), that are the foundation of and lead to that righteousness.

Likewise in chapter 5 the seven Spirits of God are the seven eyes of God sent into all the Earth and are inherent in the Lamb Himself. In this context the seven Spirits of God would refer to cognisance and judgement, so again Isaiah 11:2 is relevant as this leads directly to the judgement and righteousness of God in verses 3 and 4.

The other two references refer to the lamps 'before the throne;' again the context would be one of judgement and righteousness, where all seven of the qualities of Isaiah 11 are appropriate and give insight on how Christ is now sat down on His Father's throne Revelation 3:21.

There are other texts for example that define the work of the Holy Spirit, quoted below, that help put this verse into context of the scriptures as a whole. These are mainly relevant to our particular concern, namely the seven Spirits of God, but are just a sample and by no means exhaustive.

- He is described as the Spirit of Grace in Zechariah 12:10.

- In Galatians 5:22 as producing the nine fruits of the Spirit in the lives of those indwelt by Him.

- In Romans 8:4 it is the righteous fulfilment of the law that the Spirit mediates.

- He is the Spirit of Life and of Holiness in Romans 1:4.
- In John 14:16 Jesus refers to Him as our Helper.
- Romans 8:15 describes Him as the Spirit of Adoption, whereby we know God experientially as 'Father'.
- In 1 Peter 4:14 as the Spirit of Glory.
- In Revelation 19:10 He is the Spirit of Prophesy,
- In John 16:13 the Spirit of Truth.

The second relevant detail not yet mentioned is that before the throne etc there was a sea of glass, verse 6. Now the sea in scripture is simply a mass of something as we use the analogy in English; in scripture often symbolising the restless intrusion of the nations around, the warring tribes that ever threatened the security of Israel, Isaiah 5:30, 2 Corinthians 11:26, James 1:6, Jude 13. It surrounded and in that sense defined the land, which was the place of habitation Psalm 24:1-2. This interpretation however is patently not appropriate here. In contrast this sea, the one that surrounded the throne, was a sea specifically of glass, a state of peace and tranquillity. It was an environment of concord and harmony with all around. Not only however was this sea peaceful, it was also clear as crystal; ie pure and precious, Job 28:17, clear and shining Revelation 21:11, 22:1. This is 'clear' as we use the word symbolically in English as in 'clear of any impurity' for example. As glass it is quite specifically transparent Revelation 4:6 and 15:2 as being open, authentic, nothing hidden or unknown. It speaks of all these spiritual qualities that alone must typify all those that can stand before the throne, see Revelation

15:2. This also is the Holy Spirit of Christ Himself.

The 'Sea' may also be an allusion to the 'sea' of bronze before the altar in 2 Chronicles chapter 4 verses 1-5.

SECTION 2: PART 4

A Fanfare of Trumpets

Revelation Chapters 8:7 to the end of Chapter 9

The Events on Earth that are Portrayed as God's Warnings to Mankind of Impending Judgement

The sounding of the trumpets is the second great sequence of events to issue from the opening of the scroll, the scroll of authority given to Christ to bring in the Kingdom of God throughout the world. In the last part of this section we considered the scene in Heaven prior to the breaking of the seals, which will be considered in the next section, section 3, of this study; the breaking of the seals exposes the order of things in the world at present that prevent the majesty of God's Kingdom being implemented. This section considers the sounding of the trumpets that follow, which will call mankind's attention to what is happening to the world because of his moral incompetence, together with a call for repentance. With part 5 of this section this forms the backdrop to section 3, where God enlightens mankind as to the moral conditions in which He can reside with mankind and what must be removed before He can preside over a world of peace and justice.

Logically the breaking of the seals has to occur however before the trumpets; it must first be made clear to mankind what prevents the peaceful and ordered rule of Christ coming into effect. It is then that God announces, following the trials of the seals that beset mankind, the moral basis for His kingdom. The trumpets announce the moral setting for all that is to come in removing everything that prevents Christ's reign at the present time, that is the whole immoral political system of all that is contrary to Christ, that rules this world at present; this we consider in part 2 of section 3.

In the trumpets however God would now inform mankind, through this next sequence of events, that not only is He merciful but also that He is Holy and righteous and that judgement will come if man does not relinquish his course of belligerent independence from God. Mankind will finally be shown that this course of action will lead to his ruin; in the Bowls of Wrath that follow after the trumpets, mankind will then receive its last chance to repent before it is finally held accountable for its explicit position of rejection of God's authority over them.

The trumpet call generally is a call to attention for the people, both in ancient and modern cultures; it is notification that someone of significance has something important to call to their notice. Here it is a messenger of God Himself that calls to mankind's attention the significance of the events that are to follow. The trumpet gives intelligence as to the significance of those events. It is necessary first of all to understand the essence of what is being averred in this passage. Each trumpet speaks through a particular aspect of experience; here they represent different aspects of our physical experience of the world and thus speak symbolically of our innate personal experience of what constitutes life itself. Here each innate aspect of life is compromised, life goes on unsatisfying and incomplete; it is this principle that through suffering personal emotional and spiritual distress that God speaks directly to our hearts, to show us our need for His salvation.

To consider these things helps us in two particular ways. First it helps us to understand typically these different aspects of our natural life and how each one can unwittingly taint our relationship with Christ. A direct correlation with us personally is that this helps us to understand more fully the relevance of Christ in each area of life itself. It is a very intimate and insightful analysis and enlightening for all of us.

A poignant feature of five of the trumpets is the limited effect that they have upon the Earth. In each case it is a third of something that is consumed, with the first three it is earthly amenities that are lost, with the fourth and sixth trumpets it is the heavenly bodies and mankind respectively. Now the metaphor of a third here is ostensibly significant and widely inclusive. Three in scripture represents the relationship of the parts of a particular entity to its whole. Frequently in scripture that implies the Godhead, but here that is plainly not relevant. Here the content in each case where it is employed, relates to a certain aspect of life. If then three represents a full complement or set, for a part or a third to be missing or destroyed then the entity is incomplete, lacking that which gives it identity, meaning or certainty. Such is what is being portrayed in each of these scourges that are inflicted on the world. Through these afflictions, in each case, God is saying directly to the heart of all mankind that life lived in a vein of alienation from God has no meaning or security. The warning is not only gracious but clear and unequivocal.

It is important to note that the trumpet sounding does not come from the event, but the other way round, signifying that it is God alone who presides over everything that comes to pass, that His purpose shall be fulfilled at the right time. It is God speaking to our hearts that causes the loss of confidence in life, not the events themselves or some great natural insight into events. The events are a consequence of what God seeks to communicate, albeit we may perceive it the other way round. If 'God's voice' were incidental to events, then the expression would only be a euphemism. It is first that God speaks to us directly, albeit through what He decrees must happen or allows to happen on this world stage.

There is an obvious correlation between each of the seven trumpets and the seven bowls of wrath in chapter 16, except perhaps the first in each case. This is because they are both about the same aspects of life, although the outcomes are different. Appendix 6 to this study gives a comparison between the seven seals, trumpets and bowls of wrath,

The first trumpet sounding brings about a great hailstorm, with blood mingled with it. Bearing in mind that hailstorms are usually localised, this one we might assume covers at least one third of the Earth's surface. The effect is also very unusual with a third of all trees and all grass being burned. Whatever the physical manifestations at the sounding of these trumpets, it is rather evident that these effects at least have significant symbolic meaning, even if they are not in themselves just allegories. Now trees in scripture signify what is salubrious and fruitful in life, that is providing food and sustenance, suggesting that quality of life that provides comfort, fervour and vibrancy. This is what is being compromised; this is what is losing its cogency and worth. In the West today we enjoy a high standard of living, taking this aspect of life for granted, so that we can easily disconnect from its vulnerability to loss or scarcity. We are therefore also challenged here to abandon our reliance on this physical quality of life for our wellbeing, being reminded here that it can so easily desert us. Likewise the grass speaks to us of healthiness and of the flourishing ambience of life, which can also be so quickly confounded by misfortune or ill health for example.

The second aspect of life that is interrupted again is represented typically and will be experienced by each person according to his or her own milieu interieur, that is their own hearts and minds. Here a great mountain is cast into the sea. It is easy to imagine this happening literally; volcanic activity can cause such phenomena, causing landslides, usually resulting in a tsunami with disastrous consequences. Nothing like that is implied here though; rather the result is that part of the sea is turned into blood. A mountain here, as usual in scripture, is an analogy for authority, institution or influence, a particular government or social order. The sea usually in scripture implies a mass of something often the mass of humanity. It intimates the disintegration of social order and identity, perhaps even the annihilation of a nation state. It is easy to understand in today's global economy how such an event would have ramifications throughout the world, warning everyone of the vulnerable nature of human institutions. The effect on society is dramatic, with a deficiency in the quality of communal life and the curtailment of public affairs. Thus God patiently allows mankind to see that the course of this world will only tend towards confusion and chaos. The warning message then of this trumpet is the transient and uncertain quality of human civilization per se and to the ideals to which it aspires. In these days of increasing uncertainty and tension in the world, politically, socially and morally, together with the global issues of pollution, terrorism, overpopulation and their effects it is not difficult to see how all these things can destabilise governments and institutions.

> 'Do not lay up for yourselves treasure on Earth,'
> said our Lord in Matthew 6:19-20,
> 'but lay up for yourselves treasure in Heaven,'

The third facet of life to be affected is, typically at least, the rivers and springs, those facilities of physical wellbeing that are both needful and sensually cheering. It is not necessarily just the tangible objects in this regard that are compromised, but maybe the appreciation alone of anything that supplies our wellbeing that is being harmed. As with all these issues it is something that we all experience to some degree individually at times, through deprivation or illness for example, something that is essential discipline to

God's family in leading us to ever greater dependence and faith in our Lord. It is something however to which one day the whole of the world will have to submit, not just the faithful, and acknowledge the prerogatives of God.

Here we are given a picture of what it is that inflicts this trouble. The event that calls for mankind's attention is a burning star, suggesting an angel, a messenger from God, a physical condition, entity or being that is coming in consuming judgement; albeit limited judgement at this stage, as it is simply a call to mankind to face the facts and their responsibility to the Almighty. The effect on the quality of the experience of life is to make it rancid, bitter, poisonous even, as death figuratively, or literally, ensues. This is reinforced by the name of the star, wormwood, emphasising that its whole character is toxic.

The fourth trumpet and last of what we might call the ecologically-based warnings is for the major heavenly bodies to be inflicted, the things that bring light and meaning to the world and structure to the days and seasons, having lost their completeness. A third is lost, life becomes merely functional and mundane, and the joy and warmth that the sun brings to daily life is degraded. Likewise the moon that rules over the night, that time of obscurity, from which renewal comes with the new day, is also debased. Life becomes confused, meaningless and uncertain.

The fifth trumpet is not only of different character but receives a special warning as to its severity and the anguish that it brings. Here we have depicted in considerable detail a supernatural event that unequivocally implicates what is spiritual and experiential. The picture is graphic, surrealistic to our materialistic notions, and yet if we consider each part of the image in the light of scriptural similes, it becomes clear what is being revealed to us. Again it is a warning as to the real nature of life apart from God and what that will come to. Again it is a call to rational mankind generally to forsake a persistent course of self-destruction. To us it is another call to take stock of the quality of our lives, to ask ourselves if we live for what is temporal or for what is eternal.

Perhaps the first point of interest is the sphere in which these troubles take place. The air here is not the word in the original that is used in scripture for the arena of the birds, more usually rendered as the Heavens, but a word simply meaning the atmosphere. It is the same word as used in Ephesians 2:2, describing the devil as the 'prince of the power of the air' and where those that love the Lord Jesus will meet Him when He returns for them. It can just mean the empty space all around us, but more directly the air that we breathe, both literally and metaphorically, meaning ambience, feel or environment for example.

In a biblical context it often implies more specifically the worldly spiritual environment, the ethos of this world, the whole ambience of this life. There it is a totally hostile environment to the holiness of God, the antithesis of the 'Heavenlies' in Ephesians 1.

The second significant focal point is this aspect of life, which like the other elements of life that are presented here we usually take for granted when all is well. Now however it become polluted by a plague from hell itself, a place of darkness, the antithesis of life: Lamentations 3:6. Clearly it is something that has been sanctioned by the Almighty, as it is an angel that opens the pit to release the plague; it is something that up to this point has been restrained. There is a lot of detail given here as to the nature of this great affliction on mankind, which gives us insight into the modus operandi of the forces of evil. A list will most clearly and succinctly summarise the connotations of this dramatic imagery. Together they speak eloquently of the appalling quality of life-experience that emanate from the sounding of this trumpet.

- Smoke – what is pungent and unpleasant; Proverbs 10:26.

- Locusts – what are destructive, prolific, all pervading, a plague.

- Power of scorpions – inflicting severe pain, to the extent that mankind will want to die, life is so intolerable.

- They harm all but those that have been sealed by God, ie the 144,000 of chapter 7, they are exempt, reinforcing the view that this plague is solely a spiritual affliction

- The shape of horses ready for battle – their attitude is belligerent.

- Crowns like gold – They have a pseudo regal or Divine façade, assuming a false privilege.

- Faces of men – displaying intelligence of purpose.

- Hair of women – A covering of modesty, disguising their real nature and intent; deceiving the unwary.

- Teeth like lions – rampageous and inexorable.

- Breastplates of iron – hardness of heart.
- Wings – Mobility, Jeremiah 48:9.
- The sound of – the menace of horses and chariots going to battle.
- Sting in the tail – the suffering is in the aftermath of the affliction.
- For five months – what is more than sufficient (5), for the full allocated period, suggesting that a specific purpose is required with full implementation.
- The army's king, Abbadon – means destroyer.
- From the bottomless pit – hell, the place of no hope or comfort.

There is a noticeable difference here between this plague and those of the other trumpets. There is not a loss of an essential part of life here but a great suffering as this aspect of life becomes prey to what life apart from God will ultimately lead to. Broad or easy is the road, said our Lord, that leads to destruction, Matthew 7:13. This plague though is not the end; it is a salutary warning of that impending end.

It is significant to note that not only does this infernal horde emanate from the bottomless pit but so does the charismatic leader of chapter 13, the 'Beast'. Here is a distinct irony; those who choose to follow after this charismatic monster because they are seduced by his charm, now suffer the grief inflicted by trouble emanating from the place from which he emanates. Most importantly though to ourselves is to note the consequence of following after the 'Beast', that is anything in this life or ourselves that is contrary to all that Christ can be in us, for us and to us; this is to be conformed to this world: Romans 12:2.

The next of the three particular woes announced by the angel then follows. What is threatened by the sounding of this sixth trumpet is perhaps the most basic aspect of life. This is the arena of our awareness of security and confidence; this is about physical life itself. It means to live in fear not only of our own lives but also of the uncertainty for the future of mankind and the horror that seems about to engulf the world; cp Luke 21:26.

This is an issue that had been in the making for some time; in fact the scripture here alludes to several significant historical backgrounds to this time of retribution. Firstly it was prepared for this specific time, that is the hour and the day, this is the time of Jacob's trouble, the Day of the Lord that had been foretold many times in the Old Testament. It is also described as being determined for a divinely-set length of time to fulfil a definite purpose, that is a month. Lastly it is said to have been prepared for a year, possibly inferring here that it is a dilemma that has been accruing for the whole cycle of time, ever since the time of Christ at least, the time that the scriptures refer to as the 'last times'. Up to this point the four angels have been restrained, but what has happened that they can now be loosed?

The authority comes from the horns of the golden altar, verse 13, the altar that we meet in chapter 8:3 after the breaking of the seventh seal. The altar expresses the principle of sacrifice, the surrender of all that we have and are; the principle of Divine acceptance that defines the only way that we can approach a Righteous and Holy God. It is from this altar that the prayers of the saints were offered up to God in chapter 8.

This is an implicit reference to Exodus 30:1, the altar of incense in the tabernacle. Now the tabernacle and sacrificial law are in themselves symbolic and prophetic, referring in type under the covenant of God with Moses, of the new covenant to come, namely to Christ and His redemptive sacrifice. The golden altar was made of acacia wood, which symbolises humanity, and was overlaid with pure gold, symbolising the divinity of Christ.

The altar then is a picture of Christ as man, though as the embodiment of His Divine nature. It is as man and God that He can act as our great high priest, the intermediary for His saints, those that by their prayers show their worship and dependence on God Himself, that is the incense that is being offered on the altar, the place of sacrifice. It is then the fire of consuming and the incense of worship that is directed at Earth as a testimony against it. This is what calls for the trumpet warning to sound, calls that are preceded by thunder and an earthquake.

It is this context that the trumpet calls, particularly to those that know God's Law, namely Israel and the Latin nations, in warning of the consequence of continuing on a path of alienation from God.

The authority for the warning to be issued to mankind comes from the power invested in the golden altar, symbolically represented by its horns – see Revelation 8:3. If the golden altar then represents Christ in His sacrificial character, then this effect emanates from who He is, not from the delegated authority of the scroll.

Four horns and four angels indicate the universal character of this trauma that is released upon the Earth.

The result is that a third of mankind is killed. Again there is a limited loss of life, a third, albeit this is unprecedented in its magnitude. What could possibly be the reason for this horrific carnage?

We have a clue in verse 20-21 where it says that those that were not killed did not repent of their idolatry, sorcery, murders and adultery. But we might think the action by the Almighty rather arbitrary and vindictive to kill a third of mankind when the link between the cause and effect may not be obvious.

To find an answer to this we must look carefully at the constitution of this remarkably army to see why it perpetrates this massacre.

The first thing to note is the location of these angels that are waiting to be deployed, by the river Euphrates. Probably the most significant feature of the river Euphrates in the scripture is the fact that it defined the northern boundary of the land promised to Abraham and Isaac, Genesis 15:18. Beyond that is where historically Babylon, Assyria and Persia were situated. These are the nations that before Christ, God allowed to chastise His people and bring them back in repentance to Himself. It is then from these Arab nations of the Middle East that the armies are released alerting the apostates of His people, from both Jew and gentile, warning what will be the consequence of their disaffection towards God. It is only those that have the Word of God that are overcome, and should know from the Bible what traditionally such affliction signified in the past.

Next the size of the army; this is translated often as being 200 million, though as the world population when this was written was about 250 million it would have been difficult to conceive at that time that the number was meant to be literal. Today however with the world population at about thirty-five time that number it is not difficult to credit this size of army. The bible however does not furnish us with incidental information; the number is not given just for the sake of curiosity or dramatic effect. The original text says that the army is two times myriads of myriads, signifying something like 'twice innumerable x innumerable' or saying symbolically the 'witness or emphasis of what is overwhelmingly irresistible'.

There is a similar picture in Daniel 7:10 with regard to the number of people that waited on the Ancient of Days. It would perhaps signify two things; firstly as in the example from Daniel, it would indicate the majesty and dominion of the one that they serve or commands their action. Secondly it would indicate the irresistibility of the force in its overwhelming constraint, but not in this case to execute final judgement, rather to give a warning, a warning that cannot be ignored, that this course of disobedience against God will lead to judgement. The probability however that this army is at least connected with the armies of Armageddon, Revelation 16:16 and the armies of chapter 19:19 should not be overlooked. It is probably the same event, just seen from three different contexts or perspectives. Here it is respect of the threat that it poses to the security of life. The second reference is much more sinister in that it portends the end of everything. Finally the context is the end of the age when Christ returns.

Now the breastplates of the horsemen, those that perpetrated this action, the breastplate signifying their motive and intention, is of fiery red, hyacinth blue and sulphur yellow. There is an obvious correlation here with the breath of the horses, showing that the intention of the riders is synonymous with the menace of their charges.

It is the horses then, that which carried the force, which breathed out the fire, smoke and brimstone, which is disseminating their consuming anger and devastation. These horses have the heads of lions indicating their predatory and dominating thought. This is not to say that this is not a physical force, undoubtedly it is, but these terms are evidently used allegorically to describe character and motivation.

Their power is in their mouths, implying that it is the threat that they convey that is effective.

Their power also lies in their tails, that is what ensues from their menace,

The 'snakes with heads' intimates the satanic purpose of the aftermath that they leave behind.

The practical details of how people were killed are not given; it is the spiritual character of the invasion, its Divine purpose and its consequences that the scripture always intends to show us. Cp Isaiah 9:14-16.

The contemporary view of morality is that it is merely one of empathy with those that we live and work with, a simple matter of cooperation that can be reduced to a scientific description of the action of a neurotransmitter in our brains; a definition that sits easily with a random evolutionary concept of mankind. This is a definition that implicitly denies the existence of a higher morality and the God that defines it. God does not reveal Himself to those that repudiate Him, but shows Himself unequivocally to those that will accept Him for who and what He is. Mankind however instinctively seeks a life of self-gratification and mankind's own concept of morality fits easily with that. It is however totally alien to that absolute righteousness that God desires, the standard of righteousness that Christ averred in Matthew 5:21-22 and 27-28 and in Mark 12:30-31; the only standard that can and will deliver real world peace and contentment.

The six trumpets however, with all their allegoric detail, demonstrate that God does warn in mercy that His life is the only viable life, that it is only those that refuse to accept His principles that will be banished from the life of His Kingdom. Those that listen and obey are accepted.

SECTION 2: PART 5

The Majesty of God and His Mission

Revelation Chapter 10

A Deeper Insight Into God's Moral Position; His Directive to Mankind is Asserted

The imagery of chapter 10 of the Revelation is difficult to understand at first until we read it carefully and openmindedly. Firstly we cannot understand any of this Book out of context in which it was written and it also helps to follow the themes that recur repeatedly through the book, themes on which this present study is based. Preceding this chapter, in chapters 8 + 9, the trumpets announced the failure of mankind to manage his own destiny and warned them of the need for God's standards to be adhered to. It tells us of the imminent end of the rule of mankind on Earth and the need for God's moral order to come in as the only hope of mankind for salvation from destruction. The beginning of chapter 11 then emphasizes the witness of the eternal holiness and faithfulness of God, which we will come to in section three of this study, when we consider how God will bring about His purposes for Mankind. Chapter 10 however gives us an important background scene to this that demonstrates the way that He will implement this, firstly by showing how He will display His own might and majesty and then how He will make known His final message to mankind; before time runs out.

We see then some very dramatic imagery when we come to chapter 10, a picture that is very easy to visualise and remember, though we must remember one whose meaning is to be interpreted as a word picture; as a visual image it has little or no meaning. These are spiritual realities that are being spoken about here, written for a heavenly minded and destined people, cp 1 Corinthians 2:16 '...we have the mind of Christ', also Romans 8: 6.

These are abstract ideas, verbal significations that cannot be put adequately into mundane language, so it is portrayed in this beautiful picture-language. We can think about them, discuss the images and make comparison with other scripture, though ultimately it only the Holy Spirit of God that will make them meaningful to us. What we cannot do though is introduce other ideas external to the Bible, philosophical or historical, as this can sidetrack us, distorting the meaning and diverging from what God is saying to us.

The scene of activity here is set in Heaven, though it opens at first with its significance in relation to Earth. With both feet on the sea and land, we see an angel as a representative or messenger of God in His Majesty establishing complete rule on Earth, having all things under His feet. This is pictured so succinctly in the description of his feet as pillars, which describes the strength and permanence of his standing in relation to 'all things that are under his feet'.

The angel has his right foot on the sea and his left on the land. Now as we have seen, the sea in scripture symbolises a mass of something, geographically as here representing the nations surrounding the place of habitation. The sea is a dark restless mass, heaving and battering the land. Just as the sea was not viewed in ancient times as a place of beauty or recreation but as a threat to peace and security, so the nations around were a constant 'thorn in the flesh' to the children of Israel and were used of God on many occasions to punish His people and bring them back to Himself. The land though in the Old Testament often denoted the land of Israel, the area of focus of God's working on Earth; the one particular nation that God favoured for Abraham's sake and from whom would come the Messiah.

The fact that the angel has his foot on the sea signifies that his standing is in complete sovereignty over the restless nations that surround the 'Land'. It is the angel's right foot, the executive foot specifically, which implies that the nations are not just kept under control but also managed or manipulated, so saying that the angel controls the nations to fulfil the purposes of God, particularly in relation to the 'land'. Now his left foot is on the land, still signifying his standing, but in sovereignty over the land as well now, not to control this time so much as in help and support, as the left implies his holding in security and protection. We have a beautiful picture of this idea in the Song of Songs in the relationship that Solomon has with his beloved, chapter 2:6.

His feet are described as pillars of fire, standing for the devoted purpose of the refining of God's chosen people; or in the judgement and annihilation of all that offends God's Holy nature, on 'land' and 'sea'. God's call is ever to repentance and then to blessing, both to the nations and to Israel albeit that His Holy purposes differ for each of them. God is ever gracious and longsuffering, but He will never, He can never, compromise in all that is perfect in personal standard and government.

Who then can this angel possibly be, seeing that he has such great authority and power? If we consider his description, his true identity will soon become quite apparent. His face is described as the sun, which is a very powerful image. The sun is that which gives light and makes it possible to live our daily lives, in fact for all life to exist at all. It is that which gives light, substance and meaning to the entire creation. Spiritually it means perception and understanding of eternal issues, particularly of the scriptures.

We know that angels are messengers, agents of God, in fact 'ministering spirits sent forth to minister to those who will inherit salvation' Hebrews 1:14.

This angel though seems to have almost total responsibility in all that God is accomplishing on Earth, just on his own. If we look at the description however we shall see that really he stands as a representative symbol of God himself rather than only being a representative instrument of God's purposes. He is portrayed as being clothed with a cloud, which is symbolic of the glory and majesty of God, or what conceals that glory and majesty. Next he has a rainbow around his head, which tells us that which surrounds His thoughts in the action that is being realised here. Now the rainbow signifies the promise of God in relation to His covenant with mankind, through Noah, then by extension to the other promises, or covenants that God has made to mankind, namely through Moses and in the New Testament through Christ Himself. God's thoughts and purposes then are inherent in the meaning of this vision, nothing less than the fulfilment of His promises to mankind. The awesome majesty that this angel displays then is a reflection of his mandate rather than any inherent qualities that he possesses in himself.

We have more though. From God's Holiness and general intentions towards mankind, we now move to His specific purpose displayed in this vision. God is ever gracious; it is notable that before the angel is introduced as standing in judgement or refinement over the Earth, the angel is portrayed as holding a little scroll in his hand. The implication is that in the little scroll (not to be confused with the scroll given to the Lamb in chapter 5) is written the words that the angel says as evidence of their Divine authority; that the end is imminent.

The fact that it is in his hand, not specifically either hand, suggest that it is in connection with God's work generally towards mankind; that is here in His mission to mankind of salvation from the destruction that mankind has brought upon himself since the garden of Eden, as we shall see. The scroll, as we saw previously, represents a permanently recorded and established declaration, in this case by God Himself.

The angel cries out as a lion, ie he 'speaks' in witness of the power and authority he possesses, which is then confirmed by the seven thunders, these denote the voice of God testifying of the completion in the matter of what the scroll establishes. Cp Genesis 2:2.

Thunder appears 10 times in the Revelation conveying an impression of the power and awesomeness of God; 1 Samuel 12:17, that we may perceive and appreciate what God requires, and turn to Him – verse 20. It is at this time a command for respect and attention to the message of the seventh trumpet to follow.

The actual penalty for disobedience of God's laws and decrees is not to be revealed until it is time. Therefore John is told not to write what they actually say, suggesting that although the thunders were comprehensible and decided, that part of the mystery of God must remain a mystery until the final time of revelation. Cp.2 Corinthians 12:4, Daniel 8:26, 12:4-9, Mark 13:32. God does not threaten or bully mankind into submission, but graciously warns of danger and patiently pleads.

In His wisdom God does not reveal times and seasons either, for example, while we are still in this temporal scene, that would encourage us to merely see prophecy in terms of times and seasons only. We would then become complacent regarding its significance and what we should be concerned with during our time on Earth. Our time here should be one of watching for the return of Christ and occupying with His work until He does come; which will be at an unexpected time; Matthew 24:44. Our time here should be as it will be for all eternity, spent in faith and dependence on God alone, trusting His omnipotence and wisdom from moment to moment and learning of and from Him. The angel however lifts up his hand in proclamation to Heaven to confirm by the Eternal One, that the time was at hand, God is about to fulfil His promise after one further proclamation. The final proclamation in Heaven of the fact that now Christ was at last to be fully instated as King of Kings.

The angel swears by 'Him who created the Heavens, Earth and sea and all that was in them'. It was the creator of all things, that gave this declaration authority. Not only had He power to create all things, but power to determine the course of history on Earth and to govern how all things should be finally settled.

So after this declaration by the angel has told us no more than what we ought to know regarding when the Lord shall take up His rightful position on Earth, a voice, the same voice that stopped John's impulse to write what was not authorised to be written, cp. 2 Corinthians 12:4, now tells John to take the scroll from the angel's hand and to eat it. This may seem a strange instruction if we fail to remember that these are word pictures here describing important spiritual issues.

The judgements of God are sweet to the taste - Psalm 119:97 - giving us reassurance that God will prevail, but to comprehend their consequence to those that rebuff the message is to fill us with regret or bitterness, with the bitterness that will encompass all that reject God and His message.

John now no longer is just an observer and recorder of what he sees; he is told to take an active part in the heavenly occasion. John like the church to whom he is writing these things will take part in the heavenly process.

John is told to take and eat the scroll, which will be bitter to digest, although it will be sweet at first to his taste. This is an indication that he is to fully assimilate the contents of the scroll and that will qualify him to carry out the task which follows. The content of the scroll then was what the angel had declared in verses 6&7. Now however John, having fully assimilated and digested its message, is to continue with this declaration; he must prophesy, that is publicly expound, before many people, nations, tongues and kings. The nature of this prophecy becomes apparent at the beginning of the next chapter, which is made by way of demonstration, as were often the prophecies of the Old Testament eg the prophecy of Hosea.

Now in chapter 1 John was told to write all these things in a book (The Revelation) and send it to the seven churches. It is clear then that what was revealed to John was primarily for the edification of the churches, which we infer was not just to those particular seven churches mentioned, but also by extension to the whole of the Church throughout the age. John was just the scribe who was to write the message. If that is so then the voice that tells John to take and eat the book, that is to spiritually ingest it, was giving instruction to every true church member, as much today as at the time the Book was written. In this sense we are saying that John represents the Church in this respect.

It is then very significant that the Church has an active role now in the measuring of the temple, although we might say that the context for this is just before the sounding of the last trumpet at the end of this age, which will declare that the mystery of God is now fully revealed, that this present world order is about to be swept away and the kingdoms of this world will be ruled alone by Christ. First though the Church plays an appreciative role in 'ingesting' the scroll and its contents, but also in having done that she now has an active function, that is in measuring the temple, the dwelling place of God amongst man. The significance of this is considered in Section 3.

It now begins to become clear why this chapter appears between the trumpets of chapter 9, where Heaven itself is declaring to mankind its failure to manage the creation as God had given charge to Adam to do, and chapter 11 where John's prophetic demonstration is carried out. This chapter not only signifies a special mission for the church now, but also puts into perspective the tremendous significance that this work has now and in the future, now where God stands in full control of things on the Earth and when Christ returns as King of Kings and Lord of Lords.

How though does the commission given here to John, and by inference to the Church, differ from the commission given to Christ's apostles before His ascension to go into all the world and preach the gospel, again a commission that we infer was implied to the whole Church throughout all the age? This we will consider when we come to consider how God will bring to pass His great purposes for Mankind in Section 3.

SECTION 2: PART 6

The Sinister Beast

Revelation Chapters 13 and 17
Daniel Chapters 2 and 7

The Monster that Gives Us a Picture of the World System, Exposing it as a Dominant, Satanically-Inspired Empire

The vision that John has at this moment is very dramatic, surrealistic we might say today; though of course this is another word image from the point of view of understanding it. Its dramatic sinister image however helps us to remember it easily and remember its evil characteristics that affect us all, not just some people at some future date. Its immediate characteristics however will be referred to in the next piece of this study, now we will correlate what the scriptures say in the Revelation regarding this creature with what we have extensively in the book of Daniel in the Old Testament.

Devout Jews at the time of Daniel must have been most perplexed at the plight of their nation in 600BC. They had God's promise to Abraham to make them a great nation, one in whom all the other nations on the Earth would be blessed. God had miraculously brought them out from the slavery they had suffered in Egypt and brought them through the forty years of wandering in the desert to their own land, a land 'flowing with milk and honey', just as He had promised. Now everything seemed to have gone wrong. Now they were back in captivity in a heathen land. The faithful of God's chosen people must have wondered what was going to happen to them, even perhaps if God had forsaken them.

Such was Daniel. The first chapter of the book of Daniel tells of his devotion to God and his refusal to indulge in the pleasures of this world and to eat with those people that stood in opposition to the God of Israel. He would not defile himself by eating the food of his captors.

It was however because of this fidelity that he was able to testify to Nebuchadnezzar that his God was in command of this world, not only of his people Israel but also of Nebuchadnezzar's empire and those empires that followed after him. It was only Daniel and his colleagues that could understand and interpret the King's dream in chapter 2 because they, and not the heathen wise men, knew of the prophet Isaiah's foretelling of the fall of Babylon to the Medes, see Isaiah chapter 13 etc., and also that in the end times, God would set up His own kingdom that would never be overthrown. It was only such a man of God as Daniel that could explain to the King not only what his dream was but also the interpretation, that his kingdom would fail and that successive kingdoms, progressively inferior in excellence to his own would all fall until eventually God's own rule would prevail.

This though is just the beginning of the book; the themes of these writings is more than just the foretelling of future events, indeed more significantly it is the telling-forth of God's purposes for mankind through the course of the history of this world. However, it is even much more specific than this. It is God's foretelling through the collection of writings of Daniel, how His purposes will be brought to pass in relation to Israel particularly. The identity and constitution of the empires that would be instrumental in determining Israel's future had now been foretold in Nebuchadnezzar's dream. They were described as five aspects of a giant image, head, chest, thighs, legs and feet; one empire in essence, that is in relation to its instrumental function, though diverse in manifestation. It is this particular essence or abstraction that is referred to several times through scripture, each time building on its character, significance and context so that we can progressively come to understand the better what is being portrayed here, and elsewhere, and its significance. In Nebuchadnezzar's image it is the succession and quality of the dominions that are presented, though the account gives particular attention to the nature of the feet of the image, the final phase of secular power, relevant to Israel's sanctification, to have dominion on Earth, prior to the coming of God's Kingdom.

The next vision is in chapter 7. It is Daniel himself who receives a revelation from God about the future of empires, which were to be the predominant political and military powers on Earth. Daniel's vision however is quite different; this was not about a sequence of world empires as was

Nebuchadnezzar's dream, but four kingdoms or states, characterized by four different predatory animals each with particular and unusual features. These were all states that would arise in the future (verse 17) and come from the four winds of Heaven, ie they would be universal, between them covering the whole of the world, and not just part of it as did Babylon and subsequent empires that arose from it. Verse 3 and especially verse 12 imply that not only do they all arise concurrently but also that they will all co-exist together at the end when 'The Son of Man' receives dominion from 'The Ancient of Days' to rule over all these empires, ie the whole world. The first three beasts are all diverse from each other (v.3) though all rapacious, predatory animals. The fourth however is particularly fearsome and which receives special attention and more detail is given of it.

Not only did this mythological type beast have strange physical traits that symbolically could clearly identify it, it also made war and overcame the saints of 'The Most High' (v.21). This made it of specific significance to Daniel and all the faithful, those both of the Jews and of the Church. Thus it was that Daniel wanted to know more about the beast, what the strange features of this animal represented. Again (v.24) it all relates to something that will happen in the last days. The ten horns, he is told, are ten kings, three of which are vanquished by another that shall arise after them. This terrible beast shall devour the whole Earth, which would include the empires of the other rapacious beasts, trampling and breaking them to pieces. Thus it will be the whole world that will suffer at this time, not just God's chosen people. All these beasts represent earthly empires that are associated in some way with God's final purposes for His world of peace and universal righteousness.

In Nebuchadnezzar's dream image it is the feet that are given special mention and detail as this will be the kingdom that will predominate just prior to God setting up His own Kingdom. In this Daniel makes distinct mention of the ten toes in his interpretation to Nebuchadnezzar, though no reference is made to what they represent in chapter 2; in the king's dream it is just the outward features of the kingdom that are mentioned, its spiritual attributes having no significance from a temporal orientation. Here in chapter 7 Daniel is given more detail, here it is its particular constitution that is in view. Now its character is focused upon and its significance to God's people, Israel in particular.

The next time we see the beast in scripture it is revealed in yet another light in Revelation chapter 13. We can tell without doubt that it is the Beast of Daniel seven because not only is the imagery given there carried over, but also it is defined as the final empire on Earth, prior to end of the age and the coming of the Messiah to reign.

Each time this brute appears it emerges in a different way, presenting new features building up a fuller picture of the same creature, but with aspects that give us greater insight into God's purposes for mankind through the state of things on Earth. Here this creature probably represents the whole empire; in other scriptures however sometimes it refers more directly to a single man, the king or dictator of that empire. Either way however it does not change the character of what pertains at the time; the king and the kingdom can be synonymous terms.

The first point of contact, which is common to all of the prophecies, is the ten toes or horns as they are variously described, but in each case they are an oligarchy of ten kings that shall rule the world at the end of the age. They are to hold power under delegation from a sinister figure variously represented, but always as a single power and more specifically an all-powerful and evil autocrat. The particular characteristics, relevant to the context, are presented in each passage to help us understand the significance of this Beast, what it represents and how we should respond.

In Daniel chapter 2 we had the external representation of the beast, the empirical aspect, the environmental figure. We are told that the kingdom will be partly of iron, just as the previous empire of Rome, had been; strong, perhaps ruthless and rigid as well. Probably strong in structure, that is well ordered and with strong government, but also paradoxically that it will be weak. Its weakness is described as being as potter's clay, as soft clay, completely fluid, not having any ability to hold together, least of all to mix or bond with the iron part of its culture. These are the members of that society, 'the sons of men' as they are described. This is the fifth style of empire that is seen in Daniel's image, though some expounders consider it to be just an extension or development of the previous one.

Chapter 7 of Daniel, looks beyond just the social presentation of the beast as an empire, it looks more deeply at its nature; particularly the character of its authority and nature of its government. It appears this time as a fearsome and belligerent beast, distinctly different in dreadfulness and style to its contemporary beasts. It is identified as being centred in one man alone rather than just a kingdom, a cruel potentate who subdues three kingdoms and dominates seven others in his quest for absolute world power. His character is described as anti-God, which speaks out against God and wars with his saints and changes the very basis of society, its laws and times. Persecution of Christians is something that has occurred throughout the time of the Church on Earth, in latter days particularly in communist and Arabian countries, showing that the spirit of antichrist is prevalent in the world even now, as John reminds us in his letters

When this horrendous beast is mentioned again in the scriptures it is nearly seven centuries later when it again appears with new characteristics describing deeper, more spiritual aspects of its character in the book of the Revelation chapter 13. This time we see its real modus operandi, its motivation, even its character and spirit within that drives it on. It is described as a leopard, rapacious and fast in moving to his goals, though moving resolutely as a bear and speaking as a consummate politician, talking 'as a lion' with cool confidence and ruthless persuasion. It blasphemes the 'Most High' Himself, misrepresenting, hating and cursing the name of God and assuming God's position himself towards men, commanding their complete devotion, obeisance and loyalty to him. Jesus Himself refers to this point particularly in Matthew chapter 24:15. He is inspired by Satan himself, obtaining from him the complete power and influence that he has throughout the world, Revelation 13:2.

Finally in Revelation 17 we see this awesome beast for what he actually is; the fullness of being in his historical identity. This is not just a man, albeit the most sinister that ever lived, that has just appeared on Earth at the end of time; this beast represents a continuity of kings or kingdoms that have appeared through time. Now the Beast is described as having seven heads, representing seven kings, each with his own outlook and agenda, but all forming the character of this beast. These kings are also described as being seven hills or mountains, which in scripture can symbolize several different things, depending on the context. As heads they suggest the mind or purposes of the brute, with his declared action and objectives, along with his oligarchy of kings.

Then as 'hills' they perhaps represent powers, authorities, or specifically in respect of Israel under their domination, as adversity. They are seven dominating or persecuting powers that guide Israel's fortunes from the first captivity in Babylon until the coming of their Messiah to reign. Five of these kings, or heads have already fallen, that is passed into history at the time of the prophecy. These in fact can be traced back through the historical books of the Old Testament and prophetically in the book of Daniel particularly, see section 4 part 9. The sixth head was the one that was extant at the time of the prophecy in 90 AD when all Israel, even the Jews as a nation, had been dispersed by the Roman armies among all the nations, as also had been prophesied would happen in Ezekiel chapter 6, verse 8 in particular. This head, or hill, this state of affairs remains to this day, the Roman Empire having long ceased to exist, its function complete. The seventh kingdom then has yet to come in, a fact that could presumably happen at any time since Israel has been restored as a nation for more than half a century. When Israel then does come under domination again, by this evil tyrant this seventh king, whoever he is, will only remain for a 'short space' possibly just while the final conflict, the time of Jacob's trouble, endures or for a period before that as well.

Now the fact that the heads represent kingdoms or periods of repressive rule seems reasonable. However, we are told that the beast himself is 'an eighth' but of, that is belonging to, the seven. This only make sense if we see this as meaning that the 'beast' is a man, a dictator of awesome power representing all the sinister characteristics of the seven consecutive kingdoms or periods of suppression of God's people. Somewhat incongruously the beast is the king and its heads are kingdoms, but this makes perfect sense in its metaphorical meaning.

In Revelation 13:3 we are told that this beast had a mortal wound to one of its 'heads' that was healed; this is reiterated in verse 12 and 14 to emphasize its importance and relevance. What does this mean though, what is its significance to Israel, the church and to us all individually?

To simply surmise is simply to introduce ideas into the interpretation; we have to seek the interpretation from the scriptures themselves if we are to be sure of keeping on safe ground.

- The healing of the mortal wound is something so dramatic as to cause the whole world to be in awe of him, except those whose names are written in the book of life, see chapter 17:8.

- It doesn't say which 'head' was butchered, so it could be anyone of them. It is not until we come to chapter 17 that we are told what the heads represent.

- People are mesmerised by the fact that this creature has been healed of this mortal wound, with such awe that they worship him, verse 12.

- Their wonder extends to them making a representation of the creature, verse 14, one that was able to kill anyone that did not follow after the beast; a sinister killing machine.

- Generally in scripture symbolically a 'head' represents the mind, that is, purpose or attitude. Clearly this head or king was an influential political figure so this head seems to represent a political entity with diverse principles, style or history. It was one of these concepts that was impaired or destroyed but was then revived.

In Genesis 3:15 God speaking to the serpent says, 'He shall bruise your head and you shall bruise His heel'. The reference 'He' refers there to the Messiah, the woman's seed. Now this alludes to Messiah destroying the serpent's power and purpose; the first prophesy in scripture to the Messiah's work of salvation. In Revelation 13 we have a similar idea of curtailed power or influence, though here it is one of seven 'heads' of resolve, which is restored to this charismatic figure. The healing of this wound was therefore something that was very dramatic, high profile and important to us as the fact is reiterated twice in the text. It relates to some great purpose of mind, probably a political ideology for it to have such a magnetic and popular significance to the masses.

Anti-Semitism, the promise of world government, the end of all wars? We can speculate, but that is pointless. All these things have been promised or perpetrated before. The significance for us is that whatever the world promises, however hopeful and exciting, it is barren and will leave us disillusioned, but in the meantime lead us away from a pathway of faith and obedience, seeking after other 'gods'. We are not told what the head or its deadly wound is, as far as we are concerned it could be any archaic beguiling philosophy or purpose that has been 'revived'. Ecclesiastes 1:9 tells us there is nothing new in this life; whatever beguiling attractions are presented as new, the world has seen it all before. It will fail and disappoint as it did before. As the seven heads are also seven kings, that is empires, or more correctly the culture of those empires that were a time of adversity and purification for Israel, then the 'head' that is revived may be a particular time of difficulty in their history that had become quiescent or seemingly ended.

To Israel though the beast will be a cruel, ruthless tyrant that will visit them with all the troubles that they have suffered as a nation up to that time, Daniel 12:1. This will be though their final period of purification by fire that they will suffer, then their Messiah shall come and deliver them, establishing His Kingdom on Earth.

There is however a very important lesson for us all here. We sometimes know this 'fearsome beast' in terms of his spiritual name, that is its character, antichrist, 2 John 7. As a principle this is anyone or anything that is incompatible with Christ. We know Christ if we walk, that is persevere, in love and that means continuously living according to Christ's commandment to love one another, 2 John verse 5.

'Antichrist' however, or rather the spirit of antichrist is effective even now, 1 John 2:18 and 4:3, and is anything that:

- Opposes or is contrary to Christ.

- Induces us to worship, that is admire or follow after, the thinking, interests and values of the world.

- In John's letters, it is anything that denies the deity of Christ, His unique relationship with God His Father or of His manhood as God with us. Implied also in the second letter particularly, is not just what we believe but the effect that it will have on us; compromising the indwelling of His Holy Spirit, anything that discourages us from keeping His commandments, namely that we love one another with the same spirit of love that God has for us in Christ.

The importance then for us is insight as to what the scriptures mean by separation, keeping ourselves unspotted from the world and the insidious forces of antichrist in it that are hostile to Christ. In chapter 17 we are told specifically what those heads represent and what they signify spiritually to us, though there is no mention there of the mortal wound, despite its reiteration in chapter 13. There we saw the heads, not as beguiling sophisticated mind-sets, ostensibly opposing, but effectively acting as agents of our sanctification, bringing about God's purposes in ourselves and in Israel.

In section four of this study, in chapter 17 of the Revelation, this unsavoury creature re-emerges, not now as the background to Israel's sanctification and by extension our own also, but in respect of his character and influence. It is his annihilation that prepares for the coming of Christ.

A table summarising the troubles that Israel has and will suffer under the various periods of oppression and the scriptural references where they are described are summarised in appendix 7. These are also explained in more detail in section four and are typical of the way that the world imposes on us, testing and refining our faith. We are vulnerable when we fall away from that faith and become occupied with sensual and worldly interests; all that this beast stands for.

SECTION 2: PART 7

666

Revelation Chapters 3: 13-14

Further Insight into the Character of this Monster and its Significance to Us All

666. What sinister undertones this number has now, even in our popular culture. But what does it mean? Many different meanings and identities have been attributed to this number, though most of them perhaps have been assumptions to support a personal agenda, or the result of doubtful mystical methods of interpretation. This is not the proper interpretation of the scripture though but adding to it, merely abuse and therefore impiety to say the least. Again, as with every meaning of scripture including symbolic and poetic meanings, the scripture will interpret itself. The passage reminds us that it is only those that have wisdom or spiritual insight who will understand the meaning, so we should approach the interpretation, as with

every quest to understand the scriptures, with deep humility, worship and an attitude of seeking and dependence upon God. It is the Holy Spirit alone who makes known the deepest meaning, truth and most of all the relevance to our hearts and lives because we must appreciate these things personally, spiritually, not just rationalise them, to fully grasp there meaning and significance.

Now the fear, that is a deep reverence, of the Lord is the beginning of wisdom, Psalm 111:10; it is seeing things from His perspective of humility and total honesty that enables us to see the truth. That truth can and will be revealed to us through the study of God's word, if we maintain that attitude of reverence. The first thing that the text here tells us is that the number is the number of the bearer's name. Now this means in scripture that the number here refers particularly to his character and disposition, which we are told more about in the book of Daniel. We also have specific details in chapter 13 of the Revelation, where the profane creature is first introduced in the book.

- He arises from the sea; the sea being literally a dark restless mass, heaving and battering the land. As mentioned, the sea was not viewed in ancient times as a place of beauty or recreation, but as a threat to peace and security. This could then symbolically suggest simply that he will be a gentile, from the heaving hostile masses of the nations. Significantly though, it suggests a ruthless and belligerent origin.

- He has the 'character' of blasphemies on his head; that is in his mind and intentions. Now the OED defines 'blasphemy' as 'profane speaking against God or anything held sacred,; slander, evil speaking, defamation'. In scripture the meaning is broader than that and would include any thought or action that would intend to displace God from His rightful place of respect and glory.

- He is miraculously healed of a fatal wound to one of his heads, symbolically that is to a mind or intention of his that had, in the past, been defeated and maybe eradicated. The fact that we are not told which head suggests that this is not what is significant. What is significant is that the world will see this as a miracle or sensation and cause them to worship or esteem and believe in him. Whatever this deadly wound is, this will no doubt be an identifying feature of the 'beast' when he is manifested.

- He instigates and accepts the worship of everyone in the world that reject God; 2 Thessalonians 2:4.

- He is like a leopard, bear and a lion, that is agile, aggressive, regal and also eloquent, both intimidating and charismatic.

- He has his position and power conferred by the devil himself.

- He desecrates the Temple of God in Jerusalem; Matthew 24, or perhaps the Temple here refers to the spiritual temple, the church or its members. This interpretation would at least have relevance directly to us now.

- He persecutes those that are faithful to God: Daniel 7:25, Revelation 13:7.

To summarise, he will be an arrogant, belligerent, evil, devious, deceiving, impious, blasphemous, heathen, seeking to frustrate and destroy all those and all that is of God and bring all glory and power to himself, epitomising all indeed that is contrary to the character of Christ. Albeit charming and convincing, all those that choose to follow and serve him are likewise imprinted with his 'name' or number, that is his character. This is not to say that this will not literally happen in the future, there is sufficient evidence in scripture to accept that it could, but rather it is to say that it is the spiritual significance that matters as this decides what and why their destiny will be, as warned in chapter 14:9-11, and this is relevant to us all.

The scripture however summarises what his character is, in a way that conveys so much of the significance of that character from God's perspective, in this cryptic phrase, the number of his name. There is only one other instance described in scripture where this number is used and that is in 1 Kings 10:14 and 2 Chronicles 9:13. There though this is in reference to Solomon's income which is expressed in talents of gold, a context opposite in meaning to here. This shows us though that the number itself has no moral implications, just the value or nature of the features that it is applied to.

Six also would seem to have a diverse meaning in scripture, where numbers are often clearly used symbolically, for example most usually in the poetic books of the scripture, such as Job, Psalms, Ecclesiastes, Proverbs but often the prophets also. A typical selection, to get a broad use of meaning of the number 'six', would be for example Exodus 29:9, Job 5:19, Proverbs 6:16 Isaiah 6:2 and Ezekiel 41:1-8. Work or works, achievement or the capacity of man, of other created beings, even of God Himself would seem to be implied in these verses. It does not just refer to man alone for three main reasons.

First that would just be simplistic and would better be expressed in a straightforward manner. It would also just be a coded message and the word of God explains mysteries to mankind, it does not create them. God in His wisdom and His servants that wrote down the scriptures used symbolic meanings to express broad spiritual meanings that are best articulated in that way as they are more easily understood and envisaged in that literary format. Lastly the text here tells us specifically that this number is the number of a man, it relates in particularly to a man; if that was simply the meaning it would be an unnecessary reiteration, a truism. It is not a number meaning man but the attribute of a specific man.

Sixty however refers to the full strength or expression of work. (Typically it would refer to the aggregate of man's efforts, as with man generally this is the age of full maturity, the age of retirement from work; when he became an elder of the people in the culture of that day.) Six hundred however would suggest the full sufficiency of working or striving, for example this was the age of Noah when he entered the ark. God had striven with the evil of man for the full sufficiency of time. Judgement was then destined to fall; the implication of judgement may also be implied then in this passage by association with the day of Noah, cp Luke 17:26.

To show all these three numbers together as the scripture describes them in this context, we see that the number expresses the concept of all that the beast represents:

- It is all that mankind in their natural state can devise or effect,
- It is the full intensity and maturity of man's effort,
- It is also the complete finality of all that could be achieved by man after the flesh.

Thus it is that we then reach the next chapter when immediately the judgement of the beast begins to unfold. It is not until man has reached the consummation of his degradation and enmity with God, will God rightfully bring in justice and judgement. Before we are told the number, the significance of the name, the character of the beast though, we are introduced to the second beast.

Now this second beast seems in many ways as culpable as the first beast, in that he promotes the deception of the nations, to beguile them into delusion and sin. However, he has certain other distinct features that will identify who he is and what other scriptures there are that refer to him. We will first consider all the features described in chapter 13:11-17, 16:14 and 19:20; that are said to be attributes of the second beast.

- He comes up out of the 'Earth', possibly indicating that he will be an Israeli, in contrast to a gentile. The Earth though usually signifies what is human, of secular culture or worldly, see John 3:12; James 3:15 and 2 Corinthians 4:7. This man will not be a cruel dictator albeit a great orator, but he will be well cultured, suave and eloquent, pious even, though worldly-wise.

- He has two horns, that is twin authorities or identities, cp. Daniel 8:20.
- He looks like a lamb.
- He speaks like a dragon.
- He has the same power as the first beast and convinces or forces the populace of the world to worship the first beast.
- He performs miracles or tricks that make fire come down from Heaven, to deceive the people into making an image to the beast.
- He has power to give 'life' to the image so that it speaks and causes the death of anyone that does not revere the first beast.
- He makes all mankind to have the mark, or the name or the number of the name of the first beast in their right hand or forehead, that is, to adopt his character in both achievement and mind.

To summarise the characteristics of the second beast, he is possibly a Jew or Israeli with double potency.

- He counterfeits the lamb, Christ.
- He speaks lies like a dragon, the devil, is a seducer, deceiver and a treacherous intimidator.

Christ refers to the first beast in Matthew chapter 24 as the 'Abomination of desolation', quoting from Daniel 9:27. In the following verses he then speaks of false prophets, particularly in the verse from Mark's gospel, where we are given details of his modus operandi, one way of how he can be identified.

Matthew 7:15 - Christ warns, 'Beware of false prophets who come to you in sheep's clothing' (ie is like a lamb) 'Many false prophets will rise up and deceive many'

Mark 13:22 - 'For false Christs and false prophets will rise and show signs Matthew 24:11 and wonders to deceive, if possible, even the elect.'

The title 'antichrist' is used in scripture to describe anyone that is contrary to the character of Christ or working in direct opposition to Him. The term actually comes from the letters of John, Christ's disciple and apostle. Now clearly these false prophets and false Christs are also 'antichrist' in character. Christ spoke only the truth; He was the truth, these prophets speak lies. They seek to seduce mankind; Christ sought to save mankind from sin and devastation.

- 1 John 2:18, 'Little children, it is the last hour; and as you have heard that the Antichrist is coming, even now many antichrists have come, by which we know that it is the last hour.'

- 1 John 2:22, 'He who denies that Jesus is the Christ? He is antichrist who denies the Father and the Son.'

- 1 John 4:3, 'Every spirit that does not confess that Jesus Christ has come in the flesh is not of God. And this is the spirit of the Antichrist.'

- 2 John 7, 'Many deceivers have gone out into the world who do not confess Jesus Christ as coming in the flesh. This is a deceiver and an antichrist.'

Christ is Prophet Deuteronomy 18:15-19, priest Psalm 110:4 and king 2 Samuel 7:12-13.

Antichrist is identified in John's epistles as an apostate, one who refutes the prophet, priest and kingship of Christ, the divinity of Christ, and one who repudiates also that the Son of God has become a man. He is a false prophet in this respect. In 1 John 2:18 though he is spoken of as a particular individual, the epitome of the spirit of antichrist. He is a false priest in that he prevails on people to worship the first beast, Revelation 13:12, instead of God and is 'antichrist' in this respect.

The first beast though supplants Christ, he is a false Christ, presides over people's lives as a king, directing and making laws. He counterfeits the lamb, he has all the characteristics of the second beast which are the antithesis of Christ; he speaks lies like a dragon, a seducer, deceiver and a treacherous intimidator.

The second beast fulfils the image of antichrist as prophet and priest. The first beast personifies Christ as king and seeks to impersonate God; in this respect this is the ultimate blasphemy and is therefore also 'antichrist'.

These two villains having now been presented and shown for what they are, the narrative now turns towards their final destruction. However, before that is actually announced we have a piece that would appear to be a digression at first. It is though highly significant as we shall see.

Suddenly we have a dramatic contrast, the antithesis of all that the beast stands for. There is not only evil in the world at this time, God has also provided a testimony to Himself that anyone may follow if they will, rather than follow the beast and all he stands for.

Chapter 14 opens with the scene of the true Lamb standing on mount Zion with the 144,000 that have been saved from hurt, during the time these two 'beasts' are operating, by being sealed with their Father's name, see chapter 7:3-4. They sing a new song before the throne, which only they are qualified to sing. Their relationship to their Messiah and their joy is unique. The reason for their fitness for this distinction is then described as their virginity, that is their single-mindedness and moral purity now that they are redeemed.

Note that it is Christ as the Lamb that is presented here, as the one who has redeemed that great company of Israel. They are the first to be redeemed from the utter apostasy and corruption into which the whole world has descended under the dominion of the beast. The company stand on Zion, which figuratively now and one day literally is where Messiah will rule amongst His people on Earth, Psalm 2:6.

Back in chapter 11:3 were the two witnesses, typifying Moses and Elijah, implying that it is the law and the prophets that are a testimony to the world following the warning of the sixth trumpet. Now in chapter 14 it is the peerless life of 'The Lamb' and the virtuous lives and faithfulness of those of Israel that are redeemed as first fruits from the Earth that are a living witness to the coming rule of righteousness.

There is also more than just the testimony of their lives. Thirdly in verse 6 there is the angel, a messenger from God, preaching the everlasting gospel of repentance to every person on the planet. Perhaps this is the good news of salvation from judgement by giving glory to almighty God; a gospel that is preached by the 144,000, or the message being expressed through the witness of their lives. Whatever the physical means, God is still faithfully calling for mankind to repent and be saved, even during this final time of turmoil.

As if that is not sufficient grace from almighty God, there follows the witness of the inevitable and imminent fall of 'Babylon' as a testimony against the evil and degradation that mankind has fallen into, calling again for repentance and salvation from sharing in its destruction and from eternal separation from God. The warning is clear that all those that worship the beast and his image will suffer the agony of eternal separation from God. It is a warning to which we all do well to pay heed that we separate ourselves from anything that 'Babylon' represents.

Finally, after this threefold witness to humanity, the actual judgement day comes into view. No man can say that God did not give clear indication of the state that man had gotten into and his need to turn back to their maker. They cannot say that their stubbornness was not tolerated with exhaustive patience. They cannot say that they did not have repeated opportunity to repent. Now finally after all this, before the judgement actually finally and irrevocably falls for eternity on them, a clear vision, an unmistakable warning of what is about to fall on the world is granted to the whole world, that the end of all things is immediately to hand.

Then comes the end. Here the reference is to the implications of the second coming of Christ in judgement and the events that are a precursor and preparation for that. The angel thrusting in the sickle is a clear picture to all those that reject and militate against God and His anointed; they are cut off without remedy. This is a clear representation of the spiritual situation of those on whom the judgement of God will fall. Later in chapter 16 the same situation is referred to but in a different manner; there we are given the place of the 'harvest' referred to in chapter 14, namely Armageddon. The context in view there though is in respect of the satanic influences that inspire the leaders of the nations to assemble for battle against God's people and His Anointed. Lastly in chapter 19 the context in prospect is the actual, physical second coming of Christ and His final overthrow of all opposition and rejection to God and the eternal torment of the beast and false prophet in their separation from God.

Returning to the implications of chapter 14, the harvest and destruction of all that secedes from almighty God. We are shown at the beginning of chapter 15 the response of those that had also gone through the terrible torment of the years of massive tribulation, but instead of resisting God, revolting against His warnings, they repented and sought His mercy and received salvation. They now stand before the throne as a testimony, as representing their heavenly status. Most prominent is the spiritual significance that is in view here, because we are told of their activity and the subject of their worship. It is the same hymn that the children of Israel sang, when they were delivered from Egypt centuries before. They give glory to God for His mercy, thanks for their deliverance and praise that God has acted in righteous judgement.

Some find the troubles and carnage in the Revelation difficult to reconcile with the concept of a loving God. Here though we have the consummate answer to that dichotomy.

The number of people saved from sin and eternal separation from God is probably far greater than at any time in history. The polarising pressure exerted by the beast towards obvious evil and the opposite witness of the 144,000 sealed of God, causes perhaps the majority of Mankind to turn to goodness. There are only two choices now, no middle ground, receive the mark of the beast and be damned or suffer persecution and martyrdom but receive eternal glory. It is this stark, polarising choice that not only leaves no middle ground but refines and defines the purity of true faith. We now see further the wisdom of God in allowing Antichrist to exist in all his evil manifestation. This is producing what is perfect, uncompromising for His Kingdom, which brings us to the final part of this section.

SECTION 2: PART 8

The Return of the King

Revelation Chapter 19: 11-21

The Arrival of Christ and His Entourage to Establish God's Kingdom on Earth

The unrivalled time of celebration and joy of the heavenly wedding feast cannot take place on Earth in a state of compromise; it cannot exist alongside what is selfish, malevolent or sinful. Just as in our own lives the Kingdom of God, that is the life of Christ, cannot reside within us alongside our instinctive nature and the values of this world, but has to be eradicated; likewise all that is antagonistic in society to the holy and virtuous life of God cannot be accommodated but has to be removed. Thus when the Heavens open to reveal a white horse, the image there is not only one of purity it is also one of militant power that would sweep away all that would stand against it.

He that sat on the horse, directing its vigour is 'Faithful and True', literally steady and sincere; what He is here He has always been, Hebrews 13:8. This is the way He has always been known by His Church through faith; the scene now is being set though to show that this is the way He now is to act overtly throughout the world.

He makes war against all that is evil with the sole purpose of establishing righteousness. This is the Lamb that was alone found worthy to 'open the book', it was He alone that had lived a perfect, spotless life and through death destroyed him that had the power and influence of death. He alone has the character of humility and mercy and also the Divine authority to institute universally the life that is the Kingdom of God.

Next follow the armies of Heaven; those dressed in white linen, that is the saints clothed also in His righteousness, cp verse 8. They are 'clothed in fine linen, white and clean'; they are clothed in excellency and purity of character, cleansed from every impurity, cp Ephesians 5:27. They followed Him on white horses. They act in perfect submission to His command in execution of their delegated role.

Incidentally the word 'righteousness' in verse 8 means a judicial sentence whereas in verse 11 it means 'justice'. Christ therefore is the Lord and Judge; it is His army that implement His will and judgement.

We then get a poignant picture of Him; His eyes were like a flame of fire, cp 1:14 and 2:18 suggesting a piercing insight into our inner most being, cp Hebrews 4:12

On His head were many crowns; that is His Kingship extends to the whole of our lives, not just our outward allegiance and this will apply on a global basis when His Kingdom is no longer a spiritual kingdom only but also a sovereign state.

'He has a name written that is known only to Himself'; it is written, that is it is permanent and apparent, but its quality and meaning is not apparent to anyone but Himself. As Christ Himself said in Matthew 11:27, 'no one knows the Son but the Father'. Christ has many names in scripture, many expressions of what He represents but they all reveal His Father and the way that He reveals His Father. His own personality is never revealed. His saints likewise reveal the righteousness of Christ alone, their particular private being is known only to Christ; see Nahum 1:7 and John 10:14, cp also Revelation 2:17. Thus the Kingdom of God is perfect because only the life of God pervades that happy place, in all and lived by all.

However His name is also called The Word of God. This is His Divine, eternal name; see John 1:1; This is Christ as He represents God to us, in His person, life and work and in everything that the scripture says about Him. It is Christ alone that is the expression of God Himself, it is His life and character that is revealed in substance to and in us through His Spirit. This name though is not written; it is inherent in His being but apparent only to those to whom God discloses Him.

He wears a robe dipped in blood, that is He is dressed in sacrifice, He has assumed that disposition, see Philippians 2:6-8. This signifies His fitness to reign, Philippians 2:9. The Kingdom of God is not established by force or violence but by self-sacrifice and gentleness; there cannot be any opposition or competition that prevail in this life. It is in a similar way that His saints are dressed in white linen, His righteousness, except that is not what we take upon ourselves but what God alone confers, ethically and practically.

Now out of His mouth goes a sharp sword. It is not through violence and belligerence that the kingdom of God is established but by the authority of His word that all that would stand against Him are swept away. Every institution that is contrary to His Will has in fact already disintegrated following the bowls of wrath, mankind must now accept that God's Kingdom is the only viable civilisation that can really deliver what man has always really longed for, perfect peace and contentment, individually and corporately. All the old institutions must be rejected and swept away though and all that will still refuse to accept the new dispensation.

This sharp sword we can compare with the two-edged sword of Hebrews 4:12. There the Word of God is a double-edged sword in that it discriminates between what we are and what motivates us, our actions and self-indulgence, our thoughts and feelings. This is relevant to us now, during our walk here as the Kingdom of God is being implanted in our hearts. This is something which education may help us to do to a certain degree in practice, but not to bring us to a true knowledge of ourselves and establish the Kingdom of God within us. Likewise to establish the Kingdom universally within every creature, the Word of God must lay bare every secret motive.

At this point though in Revelation the sword that goes out of His mouth is just a sharp sword. We have been told at this point that this rider is the Word of God and as such He has that innate authority to declare the person and will of God. His sharp sword though is not one of enlightenment as is the two edged sword, but one of executing the will of God:

- Smiting the nations; that is to inflict on them His word of authority.

- Ruling them with a rod of iron, that is, without compromise.

God is Holy and Christ will do His Father's will alone. We know from our own experience that the Kingdom of God is not established in our hearts without the removal first of anything and everything that stands in opposition to it. That is why the two-edged sword is first necessary to separate that which is corrupt from that which is our innocent being. Then must come judgement on what is sinful so that what is good can then be grafted in untainted. This is the winepress of Almighty God. God is above all righteous and must establish this principle universally; that which we learn from experience individually now, must be set up on a worldwide basis if the Kingdom of God is to be established globally. The winepress then will not just be a spiritual metaphor as to us now, albeit a profound one, but will then be a physical metaphor also.

Then to leave us in no doubt who this person is once His credentials and authority have been established we are told, 'On His robe and thigh', that is in His appointed role and personal strength, He is 'King of Kings and Lord of Lords'.

The scripture refers to what we are by nature as 'the flesh', what we are physically. Flesh implies all that is foreign to God's nature. It is in this way that God is Holy, that is, entirely separate. The 'flesh' nature must not only be displaced but ultimately also consumed. Likewise when Christ establishes His Kingdom on Earth all that is of the 'flesh' will be removed at His coming. The birds, that is here scavengers, vultures, are a symbol in scripture of those natural agents that consume what is bad, compare Genesis

40:17 -19. These are to consume all that has opposed the reign of Christ, whatever their status in life may have been. Ironically these birds are called to 'the great supper of the Lord Almighty'. It is ironic because 'supper' is the same word used for the marriage supper; one was a promotion of love and rejoicing, this one though one of annihilation of all that is hateful and detrimental. Ultimately God is righteous; all that is unrighteous, all that stands against Him must be removed and consumed. This must be true in our hearts individually, the Holy Spirit convicting us first of sin that brings us to repentance, but then builds and confirms in us the righteousness that is alone of God, cp John 16:8. The Holy Spirit though also convinces us of judgement; if we judge ourselves we will not be judged. If we do not judge ourselves then what remains unjudged will be consumed. For those that have never acknowledged the Lordship of Christ in the day that He comes physically to reign on Earth, they will be totally consumed, there will be nothing to salvage.

God is yet again revealed in mercy in the next image, in the context of the Lord's coming to establish His rule of absolute righteousness throughout all the Earth. Here is an angel standing in the sun, a Divine messenger sent to show those armies that would presume to stand against that Divine rule, the macabre consequences of their folly. He stands in the sun, a place of prominence and enlightenment and calls to the scavenger birds, those creatures that will completely devour that which is dead. The message here though is spiritual as well as factual; they are called to the great supper of God Almighty. God will only accommodate what is pure and upright, any self-interest is foreign to His

Nature, all which is of the flesh, whether physically or spiritually cannot inherit the Kingdom of God. In this life we are subject to troubles for that very purpose, to 'put to death' what is natural in us, that the glory of Christ may be revealed in us, Romans 8:35-36. This will apply universally in that future dominion.

We are then told what it is that these voracious birds were to remove, 'that you may eat the flesh of kings and the flesh of captains', that is they consume all earthly authority; then they are to devour 'the flesh of mighty men, the flesh of horses and of those who sit on them'; they devour all earthly might and all that is natural of this world. Lastly to consume the rest of the army, 'free and slave, both small and great', anything that still remains in defiance of Christ after all the explanations and warnings that have been given.

Typically that is what these birds, these purifying agents that purge what is odious, do in our lives for us individually. These 'birds' will be different for each one of us; illness, poverty, misfortune for example, all these things can work towards our salvation if we humbly allow the Lord to work His grace in us. 'And all the birds were filled with their flesh,' that is the work is satisfied, complete, no putrefying remnant of the old order will remain.

This is what prevails as a matter of principle; this is a fundamental spiritual necessity. This exposition though does not preclude a simple physical fulfilment of this terrible scene; rather it shows why it must happen.

Divine judgement though is executed on the beast and false prophet first, then comes the killing of the satanic inspired army, the mighty and also the insignificant, all those that have stubbornly refused to repent through the time of trouble but have remained belligerent. God is longsuffering and merciful but justice must eventually prevail. It is the influences of evil that have deceived the world that are first removed, the agents of Satan that are banished forever from God's world, though they remain forever as evidence of God's absolute righteousness and witness to His mercy.

> 'And I saw the beast, the kings of the Earth, and their armies,
>
> gathered together to make war against Him who sat on the horse
>
> and against His army'.

That is all who, despite God's mercy and patience, still stand in defiance of all that is pure and good.

> 'Then the beast was captured, and with him the false prophet
>
> who worked signs in his presence,
>
> by which he deceived those who received the mark of the beast
>
> and those who worshipped his image'.

The complete removal of everything that stands contrary to, and at present prevents, the Kingdom of God being established.

'These two were cast alive into the lake of fire burning with brimstone'. They are removed but not annihilated, judged and separated forever. They and their judgement must for ever remain a witness, to eternally vindicate and emphasise the holiness of God.

'And the rest were killed with the sword, which proceeded from the mouth of Him who sat on the horse.' That is the sword of His mouth. Even here it is His word that slays, the emphasis is on the effect of who He is, not on His action. That is ever the Divine way, what is spiritual is what is of consequence, what is outward is merely transient.

SECTION THREE

The Spectacular Realisation of God's Purposes as the Old Order is Removed

PREFACE TO SECTION THREE

God Explains How a New Kingdom Where Only Love and Righteousness Reside Will Be Implemented, but in His Mercy Warns That All That Would Be Contrary to That Must Be Removed First

In this third section of this study we will consider how God will bring in His universal Kingdom as revealed in Matthew's gospel chapters 24:15-51 and in The Revelation, chapters 6, 11, 15-16 and 20. Section one considered what were God's objectives for this world and mankind; section two sets the stage for those intentions to be realised. This section explains the manner in which His purposes are realised, through the five episodes or themes that each section follows.

Each of the five parts of this section follow the themes of what those purposes are, firstly in Matthew's Gospel and then from four more angles in the Revelation. As mentioned in the introduction, they follow the spiritual themes or perspectives in sequence, temporal, heavenly, moral, judicial and the Divine objective.

In Matthew Gospel chapter 24, Jesus answers His disciples' question as to how this present age will end. Jesus had explained in chapter 21-23 of Matthew's Gospel what God's intentions were for mankind and this was not going to happen initially through Israel as they had expected but that Israel was to be set aside temporarily while God brought His plans into fruition. Part one of section two then looked at what life for His disciples would be like while these plans were developed directly within their hearts. Now from verse 15 of chapter 24 though Jesus then returns for a while to Israel and how they will be affected by the time of great trouble on Earth just before He returns to them as their king.

In part two of this section, the breaking of the seals in Revelation 6 are considered as they explain in detail the reason for the present state of the Earth and what it is about mankind and his natural life and culture that prevents the Kingdom of God from being realised globally now. It is the breaking of the seals that highlight each of those things and sets in motion the next stage to the bringing in of the Kingdom. The manifestation of what prevents the Kingdom of God being realised results in a great multitude being saved as we consider in the next section.

In part three of sections one and two we considered the moral aspect of God's working with mankind, how it is the sacrifice of Christ that is the moral basis for the bringing in of the Kingdom. It is His Spirit of perfect sinlessness, absolute humility and sacrifice that alone can be the foundation for that Kingdom. It was also necessary that that Spirit should indwell, without compromise, the hearts of all His subjects. It was therefore in answer to the heart-felt longings and prayers of His saints that the Kingdom of Heaven would come in. This could only happen though for those that listened to the angel's message that the end was near, for those that repented and in turning to God to seek His mercy would ensure their part in the Kingdom.

In part three of this section though the temple in Heaven is measured, signifying the basis and conditions on which God can live with and in mankind, showing us intimately and spiritually the character of that relationship and that model must also pertain to mankind as a whole. The action here is the actual measuring of the temple, that is the actual personal evaluation and appreciation of it, what we, and all that would live in God's Kingdom, must do to accommodate to it.

The next aspect of the process of the bringing in of the Kingdom is for all that is contrary to God's will and Holiness to be judged and destroyed. The practical, spiritual and moral proceedings have been presented; now it is the practical removal of evil that we are presented with. All that is contrary to God's nature must now be completely removed so that His Kingdom of absolute righteousness can alone hold sway. Now in chapters 15-16 it is the bowls of the wrath of Almighty God that are poured out on Earth. If we just consider chapter 16 though out of context with chapter 15 we get a distorted view of what is going on. Chapter 16 is the effect that the pouring out of the bowls has, on their own they would seem to be just arbitrary and vindictive.

Chapter 15 opens with the angels with their bowls of wrath, but they are seen in context of all those people that had gained victory over this world's system, worshipping and praising the God of their salvation. We then get another glimpse of the temple, that spiritual symbol that shows how it is that God dwells with us individually and corporately. It is from this that the angels emerge to pour out their bowls; the picture here then is a contrast of how God in His love and mercy will dwell with mankind, but also that necessarily implies that anything that rejects the 'temple' order must be condemned and suffer the natural consequence of that rejection. This is particularly dramatically displayed in the destruction of the city Babylon, that domestic and commercial world entity. Again, the two systems cannot coexist to even the slightest degree.

Chapter 19 begins with the scene of the heavenly wedding feast as representing God's plan of love and happiness for mankind, which then continues into the coming of Christ as King as being the stage on which this would be put into practice. This is what we considered in the first two sections.

The way that this will be done though is the subject of the last study in this section. This will be effected over the thousand-year reign of Christ; 'for He must reign until He has put all enemies under His feet,' 1 Corinthians 15:25. That will begin though with the first resurrection when all those that had been faithful to God's word and to Christ will rise again and reign with Him on Earth. After this unprecedented millennium of peace and relative harmony though a final rebellion ensues, followed by the final judgement of all of mankind throughout history. This is then the prelude to the final stage of God's realisation of His scheme of salvation for all creation in Revelation chapter 20, which is considered in section four of this study.

SECTION 3: PART 1

The End of an Era

Matthew 24: 15-51: The Olivet Discourse

There Shall Be a Time of Great Trouble Such as Was not From the Beginning of the World

Matthew chapter 24 has been a source of much difficulty for some due to its compound structure, but also because they have been discouraged from giving it the attention it deserves due to the obsession of some of searching through the scripture for end of the world scenarios. Certainly chapter 24 is different from much of the rest of this Gospel in that it deals more with the facts of things as they will occur, rather than just the principles and issues of the Kingdom of God with which most of the Gospel is concerned. There is however a very significant message implicated in this prophecy and reasons for Christ to say what He did.

Verses 1-14 of this chapter were covered in part 2 of this work; Jesus telling His disciples what the character of this present age would be and that it would feature the preaching of the gospel of the Kingdom right up until the end came. At the end of verse 14 it then says, 'and then will the end come.'

We can tell from verses 9 and 14 that this time up to the end time would be relevant to the church age particularly. But does this mean that the beginning of the 'The End' is preceded or even initiated by the end of the church era as some believe, that the church will no longer feature in God's purposes on Earth and have been taken from the Earth? This proposal is put forward in a postscript in the epilogue for consideration at the end of this study, but would be a deviation to include it here.

Clearly from verse 15 down to verse 35 then concerns another group. Verses 15, 16 and 20 state clearly that what Christ says here is what concerns Israel. In v15 it is the Jewish temple that is being sacrileged, in v16 the instruction to flee is addressed to those in Judea, in v20 He says to pray that your flight will not be on the Sabbath day, a matter of concern to Israel only. The events foretold though will involve the whole world v30.

Verses 36 down to the end are addressed primarily to His servants, v45, which describes the relationship that members of Christ's church in particular as having with their Lord and Master in the New Testament. So what was Jesus telling His disciples here? Was He just simply answering their questions to satisfy a somewhat facile curiosity on the subject or was He telling them something that was rather more multifaceted? What conclusions can we draw from this passage and the rest of scripture, without making presuppositions?

All through this section and the rest of this chapter however, Christ addresses His disciples, verse 33 for instance, 'so you also, when you see all these things...' and in verses 15, 20, 23 and 26. If it is His followers alone He is identifying in these verses then plainly the whole of the chapter involves them directly as well. If however Christ was using the word 'you' generically as we do in English to refer to anyone to whom it is relevant then it may not necessarily include His followers. This interpretation would be reinforced by the fact that in the original the personal pronoun is used in verse 44 when He was calling specifically for His disciples to 'Be ready', but it is not used elsewhere.

Servants and friends

Clearly verse 15 is the sign that the 'End had come', to quote the previous verse and so we can deduce that what Christ was telling His disciples was that in respect to 'The Day of the Lord' and His coming again in particular, the Old Testament scriptures would be fulfilled; with several references to them in His answer here. Now the disciples were of course Jews as well, but why is this reported in the scriptures if its only relevance was their own interest in what would happen to their people, the Jews, at the end of the age? The answer may lie in part at least in considering the nature of the disciple's relationship with Jesus. In John 15:15 Christ, when talking about the nature of that relationship, had said:

> 'No longer do I call you servants,
> for a servant, does not know what his master is doing;
> but I have called you friends.'

Christ was telling the disciples of God's purposes for all mankind and how everyone will be affected by the traumatic events that will transpire, not just them personally.

In John 14:22 Judas – not Iscariot – asks Jesus how He will manifest Himself unto them, the disciples and by extension all that should believe on Him through their word, John 17:20, that is the whole church since Pentecost, and yet not reveal Himself to the rest of the world. Jesus answers Judas to say that it will be through the Holy Spirit that He and His Father would be made manifest to us, John 14:26. This first occurred of course at Pentecost and has been the experience of believers through the centuries since; it still is the experience of all that truly trust and acknowledge Christ as Lord and Saviour.

Christ however will be manifest to the entire world eventually. Matthew chapter 24 gives us a detailed answer to the disciples' question following Jesus' account of the destruction of the Temple. The questions, v3, go further than what Jesus had said up to that point, to ask about the end of the world, thinking probably that this was directly associated with what He had been saying:

- When shall these things be? ie the destruction of the Temple
- What shall be the sign of Your coming?
- And of the end of the age?

His disciples had linked all these things together, perhaps expecting an early fulfilment, as they showed that they still thought this right up to the point of Jesus' ascension, Acts 1:6-7. Jesus therefore starts by saying; let's get all these things in perspective, yes all these issues are related but not in the way that you might think. He starts His reply with a preamble down to verse 14 to explain that as far as they were concerned the final fulfilment of His prophecy would not be until this present time, described in verses 4-14 of chapter 24, the age that St. Luke describes as the 'Time of the Gentiles', is complete.

A trouble shared

Now Matthew doesn't report what Christ said directly in relation to the disciple's first question, 'when is the temple going to be destroyed?' We know that He did address that point directly as it is reported in Luke 21:20-24. He mentions in Luke's account the trauma that will befall the city and that it will be overrun by the gentiles until 'the time of the gentiles is fulfilled', ie this present time when anyone of any race can come into the blessings that God has made available in Christ. The sacking of the city was fulfilled in AD70 when the Romans laid waste the city of Jerusalem and the temple and killed many of the city's inhabitants. History records that those that had believed in Jesus' prophecy and heeded His advice to flee the city when they saw it surrounded by armies were saved from the massacre at that time.

Matthew though does not report this part of Jesus' discourse to the disciples but refers to a second part of the prophecy when the temple will be profaned as prophesied by Daniel. This time though it will also be followed by a time of strife and turmoil with the same advice as before to flee the city, but this time the conflict will be the worst there has ever been in history and will be followed shortly afterwards by the second coming of Christ to rescue His people. The two incidents, in Matthew and Luke, are linked thematically with some similar characteristics but separated by nearly two millennia at least.

When however the time of the end does come, when this time of turmoil starts, you will know says Christ because Daniel's prophecy will then start to be fulfilled. Up to this time everything will continue as He had explained in verses 4-14 with the gospel being preached during this time of confusion and conflict as it has continued up to the present time. Then will Daniel's prophecy - Daniel 9:27 - herald the end of the present age; the age that is the 'Time of the Gentiles' as Luke mentions in his report, the time when the gentiles are coming into God's blessing. The apostle Paul also refers to it in another context, Romans 11:25. This time, from verse 15, however regarding Daniel's prophecy will affect Israel primarily as this is the beginning of the 'Day of The Lord', as mentioned by several of the Old Testament prophets in calling for Israel's repentance. That is why these verses 15 – 35 are addressed to Israel. Our Lord was talking to the disciples, but this was to answer their questions, the answer though was to cover a lot more than what was to involve them personally, it was to explain the events that God had fore-ordained to fulfil His purposes on Earth.

All this would have been of interest to the disciples, but what of the rest of the church, all the gentiles, non-Israeli, that have been added to the body of believers since then? Why should they have any interest in what happens ultimately to Israel? The answer partly, as we considered, is that God wishes to make known His plans for all mankind to His servants, but we can also see it from another angle. In his letter to the Romans, at the beginning of chapter 11, Paul asserts that God has not discarded His people Israel but rather that they are temporarily set aside so that the gentiles can come into blessing, v25. This point there, however, is made to remind the Christians at Rome that what God did for Israel in cutting them 'off from the vine' because of unbelief, He was well able to do for those who had reneged on their profession of faith in Christ. The significance here however is that both Israel and the Church (which some today see as a continuum rather than separate identities) are both of the same root whether naturally or by being grafted in. God will though fulfil His promise to Abraham and in the Prophets, that Israel will come into blessing and will be the centre of world administration during the reign of the Messiah on Earth, Zechariah 9:9-10.

Times of Confusion and Testing

It is apparent that the Temple must be standing at the time of verse 15, for the 'Abomination' to be standing in the Holy Place, that is the Holy of Holies, something that will scandalise every devout Jew when fulfilled literally. Paul also refers to this incident in 2 Thessalonians 2:4 when he is explaining to the Thessalonian Christians that the Day of the Lord could not have happened at that time, as they had been erroneously told, because this particular event had not yet occurred. A feature of this time will be false-christs and false prophets as Christ spoke of earlier in verses 5 and 11, however in verse 24 they are spoken of in a detached, impersonal manner, whereas He was addressing His disciples directly in the earlier verses, telling them of their personal involvement. This is to be a time of suffering unparalleled in human history, such that if God did not intervene and stop the carnage, all of humanity could be eradicated. Such a scenario is conceivable today, given a modern nuclear exchange.

The scriptures though in the Old and New Testaments foretell that it will the Messiah Himself coming to set up God's kingdom on Earth that will be Israel's salvation, a time when many nations will be poised together to annihilate them, eg Zechariah 14:1-9. Both this present time as well as the time of great trouble talked about in this chapter are particular times of testing for everyone on the Earth, not least for Christ's own personal followers, a time to prove really where their loyalties lie.

His coming will be very open and dramatic. Immediately prior to Christ's coming though, just following the great time of trouble, there are several very dramatic cosmic phenomena that occur, such as the sun being darkened and stars falling from Heaven before He comes, verse 29. The coming of Christ Himself will be even more dramatic, as the lightning shines right across the sky; His coming will have the same impact. Everyone in the world, every tribe, will see Him and recognise Him. Then also will come the re-gathering of Israel to the land of Israel, not just the Jews, the tribe of Judah, but all the lost tribes of Israel as well. All this Christ tells us will happen within a generation from the beginning of the time of trouble. Then there follows the selection process for every inhabitant on Earth at the time, in Matthew 25, if they will be accepted or rejected as citizens of God's Kingdom.

Christ emphasises that His coming will be when we don't expect it, when life in the world will be carrying on as normal, in His words, 'As it was in the days of Noah,' verse 37, the world was carrying on its normal business, oblivious to God and His warnings through Noah. People will be out at work, in the field or grinding corn to use the illustrations of the economy in Christ's time. Some will be allowed to stay in the Kingdom, others taken away out of it, as the flood eliminated the dissolute in the time of Noah. Then His faithful servants will be rewarded with responsibility within His Kingdom. Those that fail to continue faithfully to the end though will have proved that their faith was not real and will be rejected.

Different Aspects of the Advent

There is however what appears to be a subtle but profound contradiction on the face of it within this chapter. Christ has said unequivocally in this chapter that no one knows 'the day nor the hour', the era or the specific time, we might say, when the end will come. In respect of His coming, that is in the context of His coming to hold His servants to account, He is even more explicit: 'at a time that you think not' reiterated three times, vv 42, 44 and 50; Many have tried to predict Christ's coming or the end of the world; they have had a following publicity for a while but are left with egg on their faces when their prediction passes without incident. My words shall never pass away Christ says, so it is the height of presumption and impiety to contradict Him and to presume to know when He is coming.

However He says Himself that from the beginning of the troubles to the gathering together of His elect will be within a lifetime in which time His coming will be realized. Also in Daniel chapter 9 we can infer that Christ's coming as King will be within a few years of the event that Christ refers to here, the desecration of the temple by 'the prince who is to come', as He is referred to there. We can understand that we might have no idea when this 'prince' might be revealed in the Temple, but once that has occurred, then His second coming in Glory to Israel as King is imminent. It doesn't accord at all with 'at a time that you think not'. This phrase though is conspicuously more adamant than 'no one knowing the day nor the hour' saying quite categorically speculation will be misleading. If when at some time in the future the first event of verse 15 occurs, how then can both statements then be true, His coming to be within a few years and that we cannot then have any idea when it might be?

In verse 36 Christ is speaking about His coming in glory, when everyone will see Him, v30. Then before He says that no one knows when that will be, He tells the little parable of the fig tree to clarify the fact that He is talking about a sequence of happenings that will all occur immediately after each other, the desecration of the Temple, the time of tribulation, the omens in the sky and then His return.

In verses 42, 44 and 50 however, He is talking about the consequence of His coming on His servants, those He has left to take responsibility for The Kingdom while He is away, something that Christ said is within us, not external yet, a place intrinsically personal that we all have to serve

Him. Here He makes no reference to anything but His coming as Lord to examine those that are particularly answerable to Him, His servants. Here He says:

> 'Watch therefore (give strict attention, be
> cautious and active)
> for you do not know in what kind of day
> (whether a near or remote one) your Lord is coming'
> v42 Amplified Bible.

This is reinforced three more times in vv44 and 50. We can have no idea when that time will be. If we think we do, we will be wrong.

The point of Christ saying this is then made apparent. He gives a promise to those that are genuine and faithful to Him, a promise of promotion! To those however who are unfaithful and duplicitous, they are disgraced and 'sacked'. If we could be sure of a few years' notice of His arrival, that would give us ample time to get ready for His arrival. The picture here though is that of the master walking through the door unannounced and finding His servants either on the job or slacking. The scripture seems explicit.

Maybe His coming to hold His servants to account will be at a different time to His coming to reign on Earth. There is a strong precedent for this to happen; many Old Testament scriptures talk about the coming of the Messiah but don't mention that the fulfilment of the prophecy will be over two different occasions, His first and second comings. This is graphically illustrated in Isaiah 61 verses 1 and 2. This was the passage that Christ Himself read in the synagogue at the beginning of His ministry, Luke 4:18,

'The Spirit of the Lord is upon me because He has anointed me… to proclaim the acceptable year of the Lord'. He then sat down and said, 'today this scripture is fulfilled in your hearing', having left out the second part of the last sentence, 'and the day of vengeance of our God'. This was because this very last part He had not come to fulfil at that time. This is yet to be.

To speculate when the time will be that He will come to call His servants to account is simply to add to the scriptures what they don't reveal. The reason why it is not revealed is explicit, it is to prove our loyalty. To speculate and create scenarios that seem to fit what the scriptures foretell simply mars and confuses our faith and faithfulness and distracts from our real purpose, the Kingdom of God being formed within us now; that is what should receive our full and undivided attention continually.

The Kingdom Within

So to summarise, Christ starts addressing His disciples with warnings and encouragements addressed to them. He then tells them about what will befall Israel, largely reiterating the prophets, before returning to addressing them directly again with warnings and encouragements, in verse 42, regarding His return to His servants personally as their Lord. Nothing is said here that this might imply that it will be the same or a different event to His coming to Israel as their King and deliverer from their enemies.

The question of His coming is referred to many times in the New Testament in many different contexts in respect to our lives and faith at this time; it is also cited in respect to

His coming as King over all the Earth. Clearly the message is here that we should be concerned with the work of God's kingdom now, something that is within us now, Luke 17:21, so that is where the work should begin.

'The Kingdom of God is... righteousness and peace and joy in the Holy Spirit', Romans 14:17; this is what the Kingdom of God is and therefore what concerns us as His servants. This is the business of the King whom we serve and therefore the business we are concerned with.

'Work out your own salvation with fear and trembling, for it is God who works in you both to will and to do for His good pleasure' Paul writes in Philippians 2:12-13. Let God do His work within you, he is saying, through His Holy Spirit, but also let us seek to let these qualities govern our minds and lives.

The coming of the Lord then informs that work, putting it into perspective to keep us on our toes, as it were. The prophecies are not just given to us to satisfy our curiosity about the future, but rather to preside over the whole course of our salvation. Our lives are a pathway of faith, trusting and relying on God in every detail. Explicitly, that is why we do not have an exact temporal account of Christ's coming, we should not be absorbed by the event but by the substance and its implications to us. To be absorbed with a partisan interpretation of scripture or to be engrossed in a temporal view of the scriptures is simply a distraction from how God would have us be engaged. It also tends to breed complacency. If we have a 'time line' all worked out, or a very liberal re-interpretation that nullifies what Christ was saying we can miss the true import of the discourse. If we have everything settled in our mind what will happen even relatively we can easily disconnect from what the address is really teaching us to focus on.

SECTION 3: PART 2

Where Are We All Going?

Revelation Chapter 6

The Evident Features of This World that Indicate its Failure

The scroll, as we saw in chapter 5, was the written authority of God conferred on the 'Lamb as it had been Slain': He alone has defeated the power of sin by living a perfect life on Earth, while His death has made it possible for anyone to live in the same perfect obedience to God. Hence now, 'all authority in Heaven and on Earth is given to Him' as He Himself foretold as recorded in Matthew 28:18. This perfect obedience to God is the modus operandi, the protocol by which the coming Kingdom of God on Earth will function. The scroll however is sealed with seven seals, concealing its contents and preventing it becoming operational. Then just as Christ was the only one in Heaven and Earth who was worthy to open the scroll, so only He is worthy to break the seven seals so that the scroll can be opened and the power that is deferred on Christ can be revealed to all in Heaven and on Earth.

It is evident that the seals represent something that prevents Christ exercising that authority until they are broken. Each of the seven seals tell us of the morally decadent position of mankind that must be made fully apparent to and accepted by mankind if they are to be reconciled to God, this is the 'breaking' of those seals, when those things are revealed. This does in fact proves very effective as we see in the next section of this study.

It is one of the living creatures which invite John to 'come and see' in a voice that spoke as with Divine power, represented by thunder, what it is that must be made apparent to mankind. It is the breaking of those seals that bring something to pass, so that the scroll may be opened; the first of three sequences of events where God patiently seeks to lead mankind to turn from there natural inclination towards self and self-seeking and to seek after Him. It is God in His mercy who will not bring judgement on mankind until:

- First, the seals make apparent to mankind what their fault is.

- Secondly in chapters 8-9 following the opening of the 7th seal the trumpets have given sufficient warning to mankind of the consequences of continuing in their present course unchecked. This precedes the measuring of the temple, which declares to mankind the moral imperative that will be the basis of a totally true and just world.

- And lastly not until the pouring out of the bowls of anger to make known the judgement and condemnation of God, declaring to mankind his last opportunity to repent. It is though that same judgement that must precede the time when 'The kingdoms of this world have become the kingdoms of our Lord and of His Christ', Revelation 11:15.

Most of the book of Revelation cannot be seen to happen consecutively in time as it is about eternal issues, moral and judicial mostly. However, those scenes in this book that relate to God's dealing directly with mankind on Earth, such as the seals, trumpets and bowls of wrath, probably do happen successively as mankind are temporal creatures. There is then a partly temporal basis for this book though for the most part it is a sequence of overlapping themes.

It is God who is so rich in mercy that He will not:

- Inflict His final judgement on Mankind until they are fully aware of their shortcomings before Him.
- Until they are then forewarned of the consequences, as we are told in chapters 8 and 9, and
- Finally, after experiencing the effects of their waywardness
- They are given every opportunity to repent.

The seals expose to us individually and collectively what must be condemned so that Christ can be revealed in all His glory as the only one that can rule in equity, and so fulfil all the purposes of God in antithesis to all that has gone before. If we do not then condemn sin in ourselves when it becomes apparent to us, then God will warn us of the consequences, in ways that will disrupt our lives and cause us discomfort, as in the sounding of the trumpets that we considered in section 2. If then we still persist in defiance of God's warnings, then His anger will be made manifest through severe personal dilemma. It is in this form that God shows His mercy and patience with everyone in calling to turn to Him and His integrity. This is an eternally abiding principle throughout all time and personally throughout our lives as we are schooled in the only principles on which the Kingdom of God functions.

The seals give us, and ultimately all mankind, insight into the nature of our moral distance from God, and God's mercy in then allowing a full disclosure of the consequences of what this course inevitably leads to. Jesus will not take full authority until judgement on mankind has been executed, and judgement will not be executed until the full course and consequences of his path of alienation from God has been fully demonstrated. Indeed Jesus cannot exercise His right to reign until all has been fulfilled, if God is to act wholly according to His nature of absolute righteousness and mercy. This is what the seals here represent and it is the opening of them that demonstrates to mankind the full dreadfulness and immorality from God's perspective of what his intent and direction is leading to. It is a conspicuous account of what by nature resides in the heart of each one of us, separating us from the Holiness of God and an active and intimate knowledge of Him in every part of our lives. It is a picture of everything that we must judge in our own hearts, if we are not to be judged (1 Corinthians 11:31). Hence the seals do not just represent an 'End of the World' scenario, but rather something that is relevant to the world as it is now, as it always has been and will continue to be. It is a challenge to all of us to condemn in ourselves the very nature that Christ died to deliver us from. It is only then that we can live His life in the power of His Spirit by which He then rules our lives, as He will rule throughout the world at His coming.

The breaking of the first four seals reveal four dramatic images of horses, cp Zechariah chapter 6 verses 1-8. The most striking aspect of these images is their colour. Now their appearance is the way that they represent themselves and superficially the colours seem to represent the dilemmas that they create. The drama here though is not superficial, as in the rest of scripture the images here reveal what is laying beneath the surface. The meaning here will be spiritual; namely the colours signify something of their character, their inner energy, what motivates and inspires them to produce the respective effects.

A horse then is the first thing that is seen as the first seal is broken, the first of four. Four is symbolic of what is universal. It is a horse that carries the first four characteristics of mankind that are to be exposed. Each one is introduced by one of the living creatures, suggesting perhaps that it is the whole of the living creation on Earth that call attention to man's depravity and failure, though compare this idea with chapter 4, section 2 part2 of this study where they also appear to represent an attribute of the Throne of the Almighty. Now any image used symbolically in scripture represents a certain characteristic or spiritual quality that some thing or person would epitomize, and scripture itself will usually demonstrate the meaning there or in other places where that word or image is used.

A horse is no exception, with God Himself speaking to Job in Job 39:19-25, showing the dynamic that resides potentially in the hearts of us all. Strength is the obvious physical quality that he possesses, and the emotional and spiritual qualities that emanate therefrom: assertiveness, fearlessness, pride, aggression and a cavalier attitude are perhaps some that we can glean from this passage. Also that which instils confidence in Psalm 33:17 and that which is at man's disposal or inclination in James 3:3.

The first horse then was a white horse, the colour signifying a qualifying feature of those dynamic features of a horse. Now white in scripture is often taken to simply indicate moral purity, though in this case this interpretation would scarcely be pertinent. White in scripture, as well in our own language, would indicate something more characteristic, a distinct and spiritual property, with the context giving the best application. Unadulterated, unqualified, absolute, complete, unmodified would be more accurate or from the active perspective as we have here, single-minded, totally self-absorbed. Later in the chapter we have the same word used again symbolically in respect of raiment. Here it is expressly a picture of moral purity, but there it is a quality of the raiment that is given to us, not something we inherently possess. There we are dressed in a quality of life that is not natural to us but conferred upon us. There it is pure in that it represents an unadulterated and unqualified character that we are dressed in.

The rider then who represents the central thought in verse 2 is characterised by these qualities. He carries a bow, which indicates as we are told, his propensity to conquer, seeking pre-eminence for himself. There is no indication that this rider is a specific person, but rather in the context of the scroll it seals it is typical of a spiritual characteristic endemic in the world as a whole, a characteristic of each and every one of us. It is man's grasping and exploitive nature, seeking to take precedence over others in status and self-determination to the exclusion of God and others; self-assertiveness, necessary in all creatures for self-preservation in this natural life but something that leads to deficiency for others.

In addition to this he is also given a crown, indicating not only a predisposition but also the ability to dominate and rule the world, in a social context and over the physical world. This power we may suppose was granted by God Himself in the garden of Eden, see Genesis 1:28, though first given to mankind for him to care for and govern his environment, not to exploit and abuse it. It is this, man's self-absorbed and empirical nature, his grasping and dominating predisposition, that is the first seal that prevents the scroll being opened so that Christ can reign supreme. This must be broken, and it is Christ alone who is qualified to do this. Note that it is in Heaven, the sphere of Divine authority and rule, that the seal is broken. On Earth it is what lies in the heart of man that still continues in being fully realised at this present time.

The next horse though does not represent the 'pure' self-determination and assertiveness of man in his natural state, but is red or fiery in his outlook. As in our language, fiery in scripture in relation to man indicates passion or belligerence according as the context suggests. Here man's proud and forceful disposition is fuelled by belligerence, aggressiveness and violence. Here his self-seeking is cruel and inconsiderate of the consequences on others. This is not just a predisposition either, something that is potentially resident in the heart of all, it is also given to him to take peace from the Earth.

The great sword that is given to him indicates the nature and extent of the aggression. Here again we can suppose that this status is God-given. With this also man has responsibility for his own action; God in His mercy will allow man to follow the devices of his own heart until it is shown what the fullness of his actions leads to. The seal will then be broken; war, cruelty and hatred will then be fully realised to be inexcusable. We may think that this propensity of man has been well demonstrated through the centuries and millennia, but man has not yet shown fully what he is capable of and the dire consequences that his actions will lead to. We are used to the media often presenting an optimistic outlook towards the future, despite the obvious common perils that loom on the horizon, such as global warming, increase in terrorism and moral decline in societies. In modern society of course these are all issues that the world is waking up to now, though mankind seems powerless to adequately deal with these matters. God however has a wholly different perspective, as we can see here and later on in this book.

The third seal, like the second and fourth seal, is in a sense sequential to the first, in that war, famine and indeed death all follow directly from man's self-centred nature. They are not the same thing though; they are treated and indeed judged separately. They all individually present an obstruction to the scroll being opened.

The third horse then is black. Now black in scripture can mean slightly different things depending on the context; threatening or angry, 1 Kings 18:45; fearsome or awe-inspiring, Hebrews 12:18; incomprehensible or bitter, Job 3:5; harsh or hostile, Job 6:16. All or any of these traits could be implied with respect to this horse, a heart that resides at the deepest level with all creatures, including ourselves. Black can also signify what is putrefied, scorched, degraded or inferior and so can represent a quality or value that arises from a cold-hearted disposition.

The consequence of this is quite clear from the imagery, the scales signify the shortages and inflated prices that result from famine. Moral and spiritual dearth leads to deprivation of the weak and vulnerable. Physically this no doubt will be a feature of the world until the end of this age, as it has been in the past, perhaps more so as we continue towards the end. This in itself though is not what prevents the scroll from being opened; it is what is in the heart of man that leads to such conditions. Driven on by the assertiveness of the 'horse', it is the selfishness and ambition of mankind that leads to the dearth of society and the essential resources that exist for the good of everyone. It is this that is described here as blackness, primarily the corruption that is in the heart of mankind, something that has yet to be fully developed before its cause and effect are unequivocal and ripe for full condemnation. It is the essential necessities of life though that are rationed as the cryptic line suggests, 'And do not harm the oil and the wine', suggesting that luxury commodities are still freely available for those that can afford them.

The breaking of the fourth seal would seem to contain a slight paradigm shift at first in what is exposed, but if we consider it carefully we shall see that it is similar in character to the other seals that we have considered. The NKJV describes the horse as pale, with a specific reference here to its rider as being Death. The paleness of the horse however is not just a dramatic word picture of death; the horse is what is driven by death but also disseminates death. The literal meaning of pale here is pale green in the original.

The visual image of pale would imply here then what is ashen, deathly pallor or anaemic. As a metaphor though, it is here something that is ridden by or driven by death rather than representing death itself, 'pale' would indicate for example; fear - Jeremiah 30:6, humiliation - Isaiah 29:22, vulnerability, weakness and timidity, cp Psalm 31:17.

It is difficult perhaps to think of weakness or fear as a dynamic spirit as is single-mindedness or aggression, but when we think that what we are talking about is the natural spirit that drives all creatures, it is not difficult. The principle of 'fight or flight' is a modern idiom, though it is perfectly appropriate here. It can produce a very powerful emotion to save ourselves and our possessions from any situation that we see as being harmful. As a passive mindset of alienation it is just as significant. As a spiritual metaphor this is what death is, lack of life, existence without incentive. From a biblical point of view this means life apart from God, not being motivated by His spirit or being separated from a communion with Him. His Spirit though is probably not being implied here directly, more our vulnerability to such discouragement when life is daunting. Commensurate with this is a sense of inadequacy, heartlessness and unfeeling for others. Ultimately it is death, spiritual and physical, and the fear of death that emanate from these things.

Many will think that this portrait of humanity is pessimistic, puritanical and distorted. We can all be kind and compassionate as well, and for the most part we are. This is true, but God does not look on the outward appearance but on the heart. It is our most inward nature He sees and what 'fruit' that produces. Everyone that loves is born of God and knows God, 1 John 4:7. That love though is a totally self-sacrificing, an unconditional love for anyone and comes from God alone by faith and with faith. The underlying natural love that we all have for others is always variable and uncertain and will not stand up to every demand made on it. Some there are who are motivated by an unqualified love from God; they are the salt of the Earth that Christ speaks of in Matthew 5:13. Such as have that Spirit also have those other characteristics; joy, peace, patience, gentleness etc., Galatians 5:22. None of us are yet perfect though, until His Spirit fills us completely and exclusively we shall all continue to fail on occasions. It is those failings though that gives away to us where our need is, if we are humble enough to admit it.

To return to our text though, just as sinister as death riding the horse of moral-weakness is what is added, Hades follows close behind. Physical death is the end, physically, but Hades claims the departing spirit until the day of Judgement; Hades not having so much a physical location perhaps as being an inert spiritual state.

The fifth seal does not present so much a characteristic of man however as a moral position; it is the call for justice for those that have been killed for the word of God and the testimony they held and therefore the call to mankind to recognised this. This however raises the question of how this prevents the reign of Christ being fully realised. The existence of the martyrs themselves though implies the very disposition that precipitated their killing, it is a rejection of God, His word and all that testifies to Him. All that would reject God and His Christ must be exposed before Christ can reign as king throughout the whole Earth. This does expose a further spiritual feature endemic in man, that is what is of human nature, that is what the flesh is, at enmity with God Romans 8:7. The redeemed of God still have that old nature warring against the life of God within them, as Paul points out in Romans 7:23, which needs to be identified and progressively removed by the Holy Spirit. The answer the martyrs receive however is for them to be identified themselves as righteous, the putting on of the white robes, to be clothed in what is unequivocally pure, the righteousness of the saints Revelation. 19:8. The testimony of God must be complete though before God will finally 'read the charges' to the defendants. Again He stays His hand in mercy until all is revealed, when the number of their fellow servants and brethren, who would be killed as they were, was completed, verse 11.

Penultimately then, before the final warnings of God are declared by the angels, we have the sixth seal broken by the 'Lamb'. Here we have reiterated what Christ Himself spoke of in Matthew 24, as we considered in the previous piece quoting from the Old Testament prophet Joel 2:10 + 31,

3:15, namely the colossal disruption of personal and social activity. Now however it is seen not in the context of various aspects of the Day of the Lord as in Joel and Matthew, but now in its fulfilment and the impact that it will actually have; the phenomena that will occur on the Earth before Christ come in glory to reign. The imagery here suggesting a breakdown in social order and that the world becomes a confused and threatening place. Again on the face of it we are presented with an image of Divine action against man and of man's terror at these events. This though again begs the question of why a righteous God would do such a thing. It is not implied that it is in judgement or some form of retribution, however, so what could it be? Quite apart from the fact that all these things are the inevitable effect of mankind's self-seeking, it tells us at the end of this chapter why God allows these catastrophic events to continue. All men from kings to slaves call on the mountains and rocks to fall on them and hide them from the face of Him that sits on the Throne and from the wrath of the Lamb. Mankind is finally forced to face up to the realisation that the world is imminently facing catastrophic disruption and disintegration, and that God in His Holiness must be acknowledged, but mankind's reaction is to refuse to recognize Him and to vainly desire to be shielded from Him, even at the expense of their own hurt or sacrifice. Matthew 24:21 + 29 tells us that the tribulation with all its woes is now just past and the coming of the Lord is imminent.

Mountains in scripture often represent powers and governments, the rocks places of firmness and security, so the text could be seen to be symbolic in this sense or literal, perhaps both. It can easily be conceived that all these things that are promised to come upon the Earth will in fact literally occur, though if this is all it is telling us then all the passage can be is merely a harbinger of doom. God however is a righteous God, loving and merciful to those that fear Him, not a vindictive being at all. The message of this image is spiritual as is the rest of scripture. God is a Spirit and wishes to make known His will and nature. The full meaning of this text lies in its relationship to the rest of scripture and in particular other places referred to where these events are foretold. In the character of apocalyptic literature the imagery is symbolic, not just metaphoric of some other event that we may imagine, but clearly defined moral and spiritual values and realities.

So what are these convulsions that are described in verses 12-14 signifying, that should cause all of society or societies to recoil with such dread? What is it that is happening that informs them that the one whose existence they have denied or refused to accept is about to finally come and execute judgement?

First of all there is a great earthquake, the first of several in this book. It means much the same in both Old and New Testament, and indeed our own language, a shaking or trembling. It has more significance in scripture however as signifying more than just a frightening physical event that we would assume. To the ancient people in Isaiah 29:6 it was seen as a punishment from God. Here though the earthquake seems to represent a shaking of all that is secure and established in daily life, the foundations of the Earth or fundamentals of life itself. We can deduce this from what follows; the sun is darkened, understanding, insight and comfort curtailed.

All the heavenly bodies represent the influences that govern our lives and so give meaning and purpose. So the moon signifies what is enduring, Psalm 72:5, that which rules the night, bringing brightness and reassurance at the time when life is dark and fearful. Here though the moon is turned to blood, indicating that that quality of life is ended, it now threatens death and has become repulsive and sinister. Likewise the stars, the lesser influences and lights in our life, fall from the Heavens, and their place of rule and control over the world crumbles and disintegrates.

It is not surprising then that next sequel is for the sky to depart, 'rolled up'. The sky here is the Heavens, that is where government on Earth derives from, cp Acts 7:49. Law and order now collapses, complete anarchy now holds sway; the mountains, that is authorities, are moved out of their place, as are the islands, those individual communities with their particular cultures and identities within which we all live. We have a vivid picture of the complete collapse of all that makes for life and contentment as we know it.

It is the weak that are mostly affected by the first horse, as they are the ones that are manipulated by the domineering of the stronger. It is those that are politically insecure that suffer from war and it is the poor that suffer from a state of famine and shortages. It is the vulnerable particularly that are affected by man's heartlessness and exploitation of his environment and the virtuous that suffer for their devotion to God. When we come to the sixth seal though, it is the whole of society that are affected; the complete breakdown of all they lived for. This is the end. This is what no man can face when he is faced with the inevitable result of his rejection of God and His principles.

There is nowhere left to go, he must face facts, he must face Him that sits on the Throne either as Saviour, if he will accept Him on His terms, or as censor and judge.

SECTION 3: PART 3

The Irresistible Presence

Revelation Chapter 11: 1-14

God Will Make the Entire World Aware of the Need for His Values to Be Established on Earth

The book of the Revelation is filled with strange images and expressions, and chapter 11 is particularly mysterious. Sometimes, taken literally, the language would be nonsense, yet it is clear that what is being said is both serious and profound. As with this entire book the terminology is mostly symbolic and conveying spiritual truth, as God Himself is a Spirit, what is spiritual is therefore of primary significance. This is the Word of God and therefore every word is true and relevant. This is something ultimately that we can only prove for ourselves, individually by experience, but we must always appreciate the literary style the text is written in. The language is often allegorical and is typical of apocalyptic literature of the time.

Verse 14 describes these affairs as the second woe, that which is causing great sorrow or distress throughout all mankind. In other words, the happenings themselves represent, or at least have, spiritual consequences, so it is not surprising also that the images used are themselves spiritual analogies.

The first word image that we are presented with here is threefold: the Temple, its altar and its worshippers. John is given a reed, an implement representing a standard, with which he is told to get up and measure these three things. This we may infer means that he is being charged with taking note of and evaluating the importance of these three things, to become cognisant with their significance and implications. Now the temple in the Old Testament was where God lived among and met with His people; see 1 Kings 8:13.

In the New Testament the temple of God has a much fuller and intimate meaning. Here the Temple of the Old Testament takes on a typical meaning in respect of individual believers that are indwelt by the Spirit of Christ. All the symbolism that is detailed in respect of the tabernacle, which was the forerunner to the temple before Israel came into their own homeland, typifies the way in which we can know and experience God personally, in the deepest spiritual sense. See 2 Corinthians 6:16.

Here in the Revelation it is the Temple as a witness to mankind as a whole that is in view and so it could be represented either by the actual building itself or the evidence of the indwelling of God in the lives of people, depending on the circumstances.

The intimate presence of God was in the Holiest place

of all where the Ark of the Covenant was, behind the veil. This though is not mentioned here as in verse 19 of this chapter, so the holiness and law of God is not what is significant here; rather it just speaks of God's presence among man. The altar though is mentioned, the place of sacrifice, atonement and offering to God, the recognition that we cannot meet with Him except in the appropriate manner. It is on God's terms of acceptance alone, complete surrender and personal sacrifice and not according to our own ideas and wishes that we can appreciate His presence and being. However it is not only the principles of encountering God that are being brought into focus in this text, but it also gives respect to those that profess to know and worship God and the quality of their devotion and understanding of who they worship. It also directs us personally to understand how we should worship, Hebrews 13:13-15, what true worship is, John 4:23, and what empty worship is, Matthew 15:8-9.

There is a parallel passage to Revelation 11 in Ezekiel chapters 40 to 47 where Ezekiel is told to consider very carefully the measuring of the temple. There, in very great symbolic detail, is indicated the way that God is made known to us, how we can understand Him, commune with Him and Worship Him.

Significantly though, John is told to leave out evaluating the outer court of the temple. In Herod's temple at the time of Christ this outer court, but no further, was as far as the gentiles could come. Gentiles were not allowed to enter the temple itself as that would pollute it, see Acts 21:28-29.

However it would seem unlikely that it is Herod's temple that is being referred to here, as there is no mention in scripture of this temple other than its existence in the gospels at the time of Christ and its prospect of destruction. There is also the fact that Herod's temple had been laid in ruins for the past two decades when this prophecy was written.

Ezekiel chapters 40–47 accord much more with the vision here, as the Ezekiel temple was also a very detailed vision where Ezekiel is also told to measure it with a reed. This temple is unlikely to be a physical prescription for a future temple because of its dimensions and should be understood in the first place at least as a spiritual allegory, describing exactly the terms and conditions by which God will dwell with mankind in His Kingdom. Now the outer court of this temple was where the ordinary people came to. The inner court was for the priesthood only, where they would perform the rituals of sacrifice and worship. To come out of the inner court to the outer court they had to remove their ceremonial robes.

The emphasis then in chapter 11 seems to be simply that what is in mind here is the function of the inner court, the testimony of what it represents. The presence of God Himself in the Holiest of all, the ark of the covenant and specifically the presence of the people in the outer court are not relevant to the point that is being made.

The image of the temple then represents here:

The testimony of God's presence in the lives of the people of God and the testimony of their worship.

The sacrifice that they both celebrate as the way of salvation and that they practically demonstrate in their own lives.

This is the context that is being focused upon and the

substance of the message of the two witnesses, which we meet in the second part of this scene.

There is however a specific reason given for the outer court to be left out of the reckoning; to be trodden underfoot, that is, despised and ignored by non-believers, for a definite period. Had God been accepted by mankind they would be included in the benefits that the temple provided, but as it is spurned, it then becomes a testimony against them. In Luke 21 it is Jerusalem that is trampled underfoot until the time of the gentiles' ascendancy is completed. Here it is only the outer court of the temple that is in view and for considerably less time than the 'time of the gentiles'. In Luke 21 it is the administration of Judea that is set aside, here it is the blessing of the gentiles, both though for a specified period.

It has often been remarked that the 42 months that the outer court is trodden under foot is the same period as the 1260 days in verse three and also the time, times and half a time, the three and a half years of chapter 12:14. This begs the question why it is described in these different ways. Again the answer lies in the symbolic application of the words themselves, or else the different expressions are hollow.

Verse three refers specifically to the time of the prophetic witness; verse two though refers to the time that the gentiles are disqualified from blessing because of their disrespect of the Holy City. This is a time of universal rejection for the entire world, to all that snub God's majesty. This is emphasised by the statement that it is to be left out, literally thrust or cast out of benefit. It is a matter of Divine ordinance no less. This emphasises that we cannot come into

God's blessing or indeed have any understanding or knowledge at all of Him if we rebuff Him and anything that witnesses to Him.

Where the word 'a month' is used in scripture it is where emphasis is made on what is being advocated during that time. A month then calls attention to the purpose of the time and is a period of responsibility for those implicated, cp 1 Kings 4:7

A 'day' however just refers to a specific occurrence or era. Emphasis here is in respect of the events that are occurring at that time. In the context here it is the witness that is being effected by these two individuals. Emphasis then is on the significance of what is achieved.

It is then against the backdrop of the measuring of the temple that we are introduced to the two witnesses. No indication is given as to who these individuals might be or even if they represent a group or class of people. The point is that the scripture here does not focus on their identity but on their character, purpose and testimony, so that is what is significant. The miracles that they perform here are an obvious allusion to Exodus 7 et seq. and are typical of what Moses performed in Egypt when He led the children of Israel out from the slavery that they had endured in Egypt. It was the indication to Pharaoh that he was defying the God of Heaven. Likewise Elijah caused the rains to fail during the days of Ahab, 1 Kings 17:1, this was because of Ahab's evil ways, see the last five verses of chapter 16 of that book. God continues to speak in the way that He has always done to show man the error of his ways and to persuade him to turn from his propensity to evil and to honour Himself. Again we have to look deeper than just the physical signs that are portrayed if we will understand the significance of the deeds that are made to happen. Now fire in the scriptures speaks of Divine purging, in judgement or purification, so what proceeds from their mouths, their witness, is more than just censure but renders their adversaries completely susceptible, they cannot escape the challenge that the witnesses present, cp Jeremiah 23:29.

Now the period of their proclamation is 1260 days, the same period that is in the next chapter, cp Revelation. 12:6. There it is in respect of the period that the woman spends in the desert, protected from the dragon and where her sustenance is provided. There seems no obvious similarity between the two scenarios though, if we would understand what the significance of the number is. However, if we consider the full context of these scenes we can see the metaphoric meanings quite clearly.

The first reference to the 1260 days is what relates to the gentiles. A period of call to repentance to those who spurn God, to those that live outside of God's government and independently of Him. What is in view here is a specific period of universal witness against this natural mindset and conduct that characterises all human and animal life, as we considered in the previous chapter of this study, this is the context here in chapter 11.

The next reference then to the 1260 days is to 'the woman' who clearly represents Israel as the 'mother' of the Messiah, see section 1 part 4. Both these groups, the witnesses and Israel, are those that have been chosen by God for a specific purpose, verse 3 of this chapter and see Deuteronomy 14:2. These are people that are called to live by faith, Galatians 3:7. These are those that live day-to-day in dependence on and obedience to God. This period of protection and supply is for them one of complete Divine government, whether they are living in the realisation of and cooperation with that or not. Cp Romans 8:28.

That is why, no doubt, that man would harm these witnesses, to neutralise the prophets and bring an end to their own discomfiture and embarrassment. Why though is their message not recorded here? It does not even say that they preached a message, only that fire issue from their mouths to prevent their enemies harming the witness that God maintains, we do not know for sure that they are two individuals, they are described as two witnesses. Now the 'two' in scripture is symbolic of emphasis or guarantee, cp Matthew 18:16.

A witness is someone or something that gives evidence or verification, by their testimony or by virtue of their existence. What is it then that they are validating but the context in which they are placed in the scripture here? It is the Temple, its altar and the worshippers as above, bringing to light their significance and testimony. Who or what the witnesses are is not relevant, that is why we are not told. It is the fact that God will not judge man on what he is not culpable of or has not been convicted of and given opportunity to turn from in penitence. Cp Luke 12:47.

God will leave adequate testimony to Himself and on what basis we can know Him; on how we must revere Him alone and bow to His supremacy. We are in fact told of the way that these witnesses demonstrated their message, they were clothed in sackcloth, displaying the call to repentance. They are also described as 'the two olive trees and candlesticks' in position before the God of the Earth. Now the olive tree is the source of the oil that gives the light in the lamps or candles. As witnesses then they are not only shining as lights to the world, displaying His message vis à vis the temple etc, but also they are the source of the oil, oil that is burned to give the light, and informing the understanding, cp Psalm 119:105 and 2 Peter 1:19. Maybe it is because in this way their witness is twofold that they are described as two witnesses.

We can compare this also to what Christ said about anyone that followed Him that is living according to His principles and Spirit: 'You are the light of the world' Matthew 5:14. The world sees and takes note to what we are in this world.

Their testimony seems quite innocuous, even passive and yet it is not they that speak but God who speaks through them. God is ever patient and merciful, yet He is ever faithful also and will not let His message be nullified or ignored. Hence the fire from their mouths, a symbol of consuming judgement, prevents their witness from being stifled, cp Rev. 19:13-15.

God's testimony of righteousness must be maintained and has been maintained through the ages. Christ Himself exemplified this on Earth, He suffered endless rejection and abuse of Himself and never protested, yet He continually spoke out against sin and against hypocrisy in particular, cp Matthew 5:14.

We are also told of the signs that they perform, to demonstrate to those that are treading underfoot those blessings that God extends to all that will accept Him, the consequence of their despising the witnesses and all they stand for.

Rain is a blessing sent from God. Either physically as evidence of the Goodness of God to everyone, or as a source of growth and sustenance, gladness and pleasure itself, those spiritual states of mind that give such benefits to us, so to prevent the rain from falling is to curb the enjoyment of life itself. Cp Matthew 5:45, Acts 14:17. and Ezekiel 34:26

The image of water however represents something different from the rain; rain makes the world around us, or metaphorically our hearts within, to flourish. Water though is that which we drink to give us life and comfort, Psalm 107:35. All the sources of drinking water in Egypt were turned to blood (signifying death) in Exodus chapter 7 so that Pharaoh would acknowledge that he was dependant on God for his very life. The rivers in Egypt stank, the scriptures tell us, and the life in it died.

The life we are told is in the blood. Cp Gen. 9:4. Lev 17:11 Gen. 4:10 Rev. 18:24

Shed blood not only exhibits death but also in itself is loathsome. The act of drinking it to sustain life for the Egyptians in ancient Egypt would have become repulsive. This is the same picture here in Revelation 11, that life itself and the refreshment of maintaining life becomes fraught with revulsion and death. To deny God is to refuse the source of real life, to live to one's own satisfaction is to bring about disillusion and death. To be faced with the reality of the situation, which is what the witnesses here facilitate, brings us to face responsibility for our own destiny.

The third sign that the witnesses are empowered to carry out is to bring plagues upon the masses that spurn the Temple, those that despise the presence of God in their midst. Again it is in Egypt that we see plagues permeating the dwelling, the home environment, of those that sought to oppose God and show contempt for Him; typically this is the mind-set that we naturally reside in when we are in detachment from Him. This affects not life itself or the source of life as above, but the conduct of activity in whatever situation we are in. The very course of life as well is now frustrated and made wretched. Cp Gen. 12:17 and Ex. 7-12

Generally most people know how the vicissitudes of life can yield such agonies. How much the more when through them God brings individuals face to face with the reality of God and their responsibility to Him through accepting the privation of their situation. To be faced with the reality of the situation brings us to face responsibility for our destiny.

The witnesses though are not invincible; it is God's message that will of certainty be manifest and ultimately all will have to confront it. At the end of the 1260 days, their final witness is their martyrdom by the beast that ascends out of the place of demons, cp Luke 8:31. – 'He makes war and kills them,' cp Psalm 140:2 and Psalm 2:2

Chapter 13 of Revelation denotes the character of this beast, which we met in section 2, as being altogether evil, altogether opposed to everything that is good and of God. He is sanctioned to kill the witnesses and to leave their bodies on display. The significance of this is partly in the length of time that they stay in the street, which is the place of the ordinary course of life in the 'city', the three and a half days that we will come to, and partly in the fact that they continue to be a witness even when in apparent demise and defeat. Cp Dan. 7.

There are then further details that are added to this

account, which make us realise that even this is not all that is pertinent here. The Street they lie in is described as four different places. Clearly we need to dig a little deeper to see what is being typically presented. The scriptures themselves define their symbolic meanings; it just takes diligence to study other references to these places to see what they represent. Now Babylon is described as 'that great city' eleven times in this book of the Revelation, a place that represents commerce, the kingdoms of this world and the materialistic and idolatrous religious aspirations and tendencies of us all. The origins of Babylon are recorded in the first book of the bible, where man sought independence from God and tried to insulate himself from the future possibility of another catastrophe like the flood that God had inflicted on mankind in judgement.

This city, representing the attitude of all in our distance from God, is also pictured in other ways, each highlighting a way in which we are naturally alienated from Him.

It is also described as Sodom. Now Sodom is also featured in the book of Genesis as being a place of sin and immorality, so much so that God rained fire upon it; as we have seen in this passage a sign of God's purifying Judgement. Cp Jude 7 and Isaiah. 13:19

Next it is described as Egypt, which is portrayed in the scripture as a place of pleasure, opulence and a place to find physical sustenance and satisfaction. It represents a position of disharmony and independence from God; a place also of bondage, a place where we are prevented from appreciating God in worship and thankfulness, Cp Acts 7:34. It also portrays us as strangers there, Acts13:17, a place of distracting pleasures and riches, Heb. 11:26, and the place where we find natural or worldly resources, Is. 30:2 and 31:1.

Lastly it is described as the place where our Lord was crucified. Again this is speaking metaphorically. Where our Lord was crucified was where He was hated, rejected, mocked and spat upon. Such also is the environment that we live in today. Religion maybe is respected on the whole, but Christ in all His grace and majesty is only accepted by those that honour Him and all that witnesses to Him; cp John 19:6 and15, Acts 4:10 and 5:30, 1 Cor2:8.

All four of these positions represent a facet of what the New Testament calls the 'world' as regards to its character. In many places we are encouraged, not to be conformed to this world, to be separate from the world, to come out from it, that is to have no association with or contamination from it, cp Rev.18:4. The 'city' described here exemplifies well the traits that we should seek to be liberated from, if we would sincerely seek to communicate with God in full fellowship. Not to be isolated from the world but to be kept from that which is evil and its influence upon us; cp John 17:15.

The testimony of the two witnesses is for a preset time only: 'My Spirit will not always strive with man'; the number of days is specified, whether this is exact or typical makes no difference, though numbers in scripture do have a symbolic significance, as long as we look to see what the scripture implies elsewhere rather than making assumptions or just using our imagination. After their days are finished they are killed by the beast that comes from the place of demons, this character that we meet in chapters 13 and 17 of the Revelation.

Our text then tells us that every kind of community will

see their dead bodies and gloat over their demise. Again we are told the specific period, which must be either incidental or meaningful. Cp Rev.12:14, Luke 4:25.

Now a half in scripture in itself implies no more than just a division of something into two parts, its context conveying the specific matter that is being referred to, here a half of 'seven' as we shall see. Here it would suggest that they lie dead for three and a half days and then after that they are raised to life and ascend into Heaven.

Earlier, in chapter 11:3, the two witnesses carried out their prophecy for 1260 days, which is the period described in the next chapter, verses 6 and 14, as a time, times and half a time, 3½ years (refer back to section one, part four for more details). This is that three-and-a-half-year time of trouble that will end this present age before Christ comes again physically to reign on Earth. It seems striking then to find that number 3½ again in respect of these same individuals in verses 9+11, albeit as days. What then is the relevance of this number?

The 3½ years refer to the time of desolation of Israel, half the period of their great apostasy (see epilogue 2 for an explanation). It is a time of great distress and disillusion when they are betrayed; when as the prophet Isaiah foretold in chapter 28:17-18:

> 'The hail will sweep away the refuge of lies,
> and the waters will overflow the hiding place.
> Your covenant with death will be annulled,
> and your agreement with Sheol will not stand;
> when the overflowing scourge passes through,
> then you will be trampled down by it.'

In a similar way those that were troubled by the witnesses put their trust in the fact that they had disposed of them, only to be disillusioned when they come to life again. Their resurgence is now the testimony of God that their prophecy cannot be dismissed. It is a message to us all; 'If God is for us, who can be against us?' Romans 8:31. Likewise we cannot escape His reprimand if we put our trust in our own efforts or the institutions of this life for our security and wellbeing. Only trusting in Him can we find real peace and rest.

Evidently for three and a half days their presence is then a testimony in itself to the hatred of the people of the city and their refusal to accept them. During this specific time they become the testimony to God's overt endorsement of all that they had demonstrated. It is a time of trial, first to demonstrate how man is in his attitude to the things of God, then for God to demonstrate His authenticity and vindication, by a Divine acceptance and endorsement of their testimony to Him by their being taken up into Heaven. This is the second half of this issue, the coming to life again of the two witnesses and their going up into Heaven. After the declaration and then the authentication there then follows judgement. First an earthquake, the shaking up all that is familiar and secure in one's natural life.

- The result is that one tenth of the city fell. A tenth in the Old Testament was the amount paid to a priest or a ruler in honour or obligation and particularly under the Mosaic Law was the amount to be paid to God.

- Again seven personifies Divine standard of consummation or completeness, when 7000 were slain.

- A thousand is emblematic of or representing all or everyone in a group, which here is all the residents of the great city. The result then confirms God's purpose will be completely effective in what transpires through the witness, men give glory to God, recognising His absolute authority; challenging their refusal to honour Him.

SECTION 3: PART 4

Broken Promises

Revelation Chapter 11: 1-14

Trusting in Any Promise or Institution in This Life Will End in Disillusion and Betrayal

This period of 42 months that we considered in part 3 has a very significant consequence; not only because of its symbolic meaning but because it also relates to a particularly significant and sinister time to come, the consummation of this age. It relates to the sinister prophecy of Isaiah 28:14 –15 that foretold of a national and total apostasy:

'Therefore hear the word of the Lord, you scornful men,
who rule this people who are in Jerusalem,
because you have said, 'We have made a covenant with death,
and with Sheol we are in agreement.

> When the overflowing scourge passes through,
> it will not come to us,
> for we have made lies our refuge,
> and under falsehood we have hidden ourselves.'

This prophecy was made about 40 years before the northern tribes of Israel were taken into captivity in about 760 BC. After another 150 years the southern tribes, the Jews, had also been taken into captivity, though it had been foretold by the prophet Jeremiah, chapters 25:11 and 29:10, that it would only be for a period of 70 years. Later, Daniel the prophet understood that this period was coming to an end and so he prayed earnestly to God to know what was going to happen to his people after that. In chapter 9 of this prophecy it is revealed to him the next phase of Israel's history, the times through which Daniel's people, the Jews, would pass to bring in the Kingdom of their Messiah. In verse 27 this outstanding covenant referred to above in Isaiah 28 is put into its context as being at the end of this next phase, a much longer period of time that was allocated to his people to make complete their suitability for God's Kingdom on Earth.

Earlier in Daniel 7:25 there is a period of time cited as the time, times and half a time of the exploits of the ruthless king that will be destroyed at the end, just before the kingdom is given to the saints of the most high. 'Time' here is literally an appointed time, a period which is defined more clearly in chapter 9 where this period, just before the Kingdom of the Most High comes in, is referred to again, this time in the context of the process of salvation of God's people.

In verse 27 of Daniel 9 it is in the middle of the final period of 'seven' that this period becomes a time of blasphemy, persecution of the saints and the changing of the structures of society. This is literally at the half of the 'seven,' numerically three and a half but spoken here as the dividing of a period of completeness, seven, into two. The first half was a period of security and reassurance, implying that it is a period of complacency, the first half of the 'covenant with death'. The second half is the one that is focused on though as being one of a great holocaust, the second part of the prophecy from Isaiah 28, referred to above. This period is spoken of again in Daniel 12:1+7 where it is referred to in respect of the unprecedented time that shall bring about the final and complete salvation of God's people.

The time, times and half a time, that is 3½ times, arises first in Daniel chapter 7:25 in the context of the persecution of God's people. Chapter 9:27 of that book then explains that this period in fact will be the dividing in half of a specifically-appointed-period of 'seven.' This will be the last 'seven' of the whole appointed time of Daniel's prophecy which was 70 'sevens', that is sabbatical years (see epilogue 2 for a fuller explanation) making 490 years that spanned its implementation. However, all but the last of these 70 x 'sevens' were consecutive and were fulfilled when Messiah was 'cut off,' that is rejected and crucified in approximately AD 33; Daniel chapter 9, verse 26. This last 'seven' then is in respect of this broken covenant in verse 27, which we mentioned in section 1/4 on chapter 12 of the Revelation, and is yet to happen.

This then implies that the significance of the 3½ is that it is the dividing of a 'seven' that is a sabbatical seven-year period. Now seven in scripture is commonly used symbolically in respect of what is complete, finalised or perfected. The Sabbath rest then, which was a prominent part of the Mosaic Law, was commemorative of the time that God rested after His creation. This then shows that this Divinely-appointed period of completeness connotes perfect peace, security and rest; cp Hebrews chapter 3 and 4. Here the 'seven' is a period of expected peace and security but it is based on a lie, dependant merely on what mankind has fallaciously promised to deliver. The breaking then of such a period here implies the breaking of peace and security. As the apostasy of this covenant is radical the effect of its failure is also sweeping, leading to the greatest time of conflict this world has ever seen, see Matthew 24:21. 3½ then, in these contexts at least, denotes dissimulation and disillusion, leading to distress and insecurity.

In Revelation, the other great apocalyptic book of the scriptures, we come to this period of time, times and a half time again in chapter 12:14 where the period is mentioned in respect of the period in which God's people will be protected from the massive onslaught that is projected against them, emphasising again that this is that particular appointed time of their deliverance from this great persecution. In chapter 13:7 there is a further mention of this persecution of the saints, though the period is not mentioned there as it is just in the context of recounting who will be the persecutor.

However in chapter 11 of the Revelation this period of three and a half times appears again but in two different contexts and is described differently. The first is the period that the outer court of the temple is left out of the reckoning; see section 3/3. In verse two it is described as being 42 months; it is not here though regarding just an appointed time for some great purpose as above but rather an allocated-period-of-purpose, as a month in scripture implies. Emphasis being on what the period is for, here its mission or duty, presented here as one of universal witness. In the next verse though it is 1260 days, which is the period of prophecy calling for repentance. A 'day' however suggests a specific occasion with regards to its effect, much as we can use the word metaphorically in English; thus making clear the concurrence with this appointed time of time, times and a half but calling attention to the event rather than its purpose. The symbolism of the number 1260 here perhaps signifies the full extent of effort, presentation and sufficiency. (Cp appendix 4)

Also there are poignantly another three and a half periods in this chapter, in verses 9 and 11. This is in respect of the period that the two witnesses are allowed to remain dead in the street of the city. This is a time of great rejoicing by those that suffered under their witness, though the same thought is conveyed as with the three and a half times. It is the disappointment and frustration that come from the failure and futility of trusting our natural inclinations to bring peace and rest. The witnesses are raised to life, their testimony cannot be killed off by repression and murder; they are given heavenly status, effecting judgement on those that refused to submit to their prophecy.

It is apparent from all this then that the scriptures are conveying a particular message:

- That what is particularly important is not dates and measures of time but their significance to people and their life experiences and to the various plans and purposes of God in their various spiritual contexts. It is clear that all these things relate to a specific period of history though and it is much of what the Book of the Revelation is about.

- The symbolic use of words adds meaning to the word images that are presented in scripture, but they do not add facts or ideas to the basic text but add colour and spiritual understanding to their significance. Even with that qualification the actual figurative meaning is always consistent with scripture generally and not a matter for speculation.

- The main lesson here is that to trust any promise or institutions in this life will end in disillusion and betrayal. Only God can deliver complete security, satisfaction and rest, can and will, but only according to His ways and principles. To trust in man is apostasy, a scenario that will be played out at the end of this age on a dramatic scale, culminating in unprecedented chaos and conflict on a global scale.

- Finally, that God is faithful. Following the passage from Isaiah 28 at the beginning of this piece, in verses 16 –18 of that chapter God promises to rescue His people from the dilemma that they have descended into if they believe, but that His purposes will be established either way:

> 'Therefore thus says the Lord God:
> 'Behold, I lay in Zion a stone for a foundation,
> a tried stone, a precious cornerstone, a sure foundation;
> whoever believes will not act hastily. (ie panic)
> Also I will make justice the measuring line,
> and righteousness the plummet;
> the hail will sweep away the refuge of lies,
> and the waters will overflow the hiding place.
> Your covenant with death will be annulled,
> and your agreement with Sheol will not stand;
> when the overflowing scourge passes through,
> then you will be trampled down by it.'

Whoever believes then, trusting in their God and acting in obedience to Him, even after all their apostasy and unfaithfulness to their God, God will deliver and re-establish them and bring in peace and security for them. Only destruction, disillusion and judgement though will be the outcome for those that will not accept God's provision of a sure foundation to govern their lives.

This chapter is rather dense and difficult to follow, but seeks to summarize those important spiritual issues outlined in previous chapters. They are details that give deeper insight and understanding of the scripture.

The Four Horsemen, Ottheinrich Bibel

The Sealing of the 144,000, Ottheinrich Bibel

The Seventh Seal, Ottheinrich Bibel

The Temple and the Prophets, Ottheinrich Bibel

The Triumph of the Lamb, Ottheinrich Bibel

The Whore of Babylon, Ottheinrich Bibel

Vision of Heaven II, Ottheinrich Bibel

Vision of Heaven, Ottheinrich Bibel

SECTION 3: PART 5

Mankind's Last Chance

Revelation Chapters 15-16

The Condemnation of God on All That Is in Opposition to Him Is Made Apparent Before It Is Removed in Judgement

Chapter 15 opens with an ominous portrayal of God's wrath, a dramatic picture that we are rather inclined to shrink from. We think of God as omnipotent, all-knowing and loving, not vindictive as we might be inclined to consider from this first verse of chapter 15. If we look at the wording carefully however, we can see that there is much more here than we might at first assume. The original word here translated as 'wrath' does not just mean fury but rather the indignation and opposition of God; a God who is, above all His other attributes, a just and holy God. To continue on a course that is in opposition to God and His life of peace and goodness will inevitably be at variance with His holy outlook. God is the only true God, the creator and upholder of all things; it is only His way that can sustain all things, any other way or the slightest compromise must lead to demise or destruction.

God then is merciful to expose mankind's shortcomings and give him opportunity to amend. A life that is lived outside the bounds of God's principles will inevitably turn foul and end in destruction and death. God has made it plain for all to see what prevents His rule of peace on Earth at this present time in the seven seals. He has warned mankind of the consequences of his current course in the sounding of the seven trumpets and now He will demonstrate to all the consequence and futility of that life of antagonistic obduracy towards God. It is mankind's last opportunity to turn from his self-centredness and self-destructiveness and find favour and deliverance with the Almighty.

The breaking of the seals meant that mankind gained insight into his own erroneous outlook. The trumpets conveyed their message through the loss of amenity of life on Earth. The bowls of wrath though are described as plagues, meaning stripes or wounds, implying censure inflicted or sanctioned directly by God Himself. It is then in mankind's deepest interests to turn from his path of self-destruction, he cannot claim ignorance any longer as all these troubles are the consequence of his path of independence from God. It is his last chance to accept that his natural self-absorbed lifestyle must finally end in despair; the quality of life turns fetid and disintegrates. This is the last chance to repent before judgement, before all that this world stands for and all the challenges to God's rule of righteousness are swept away in the coming of Christ to rule the nations; when: -

> Out of His mouth goes a sharp sword,
> that with it He should strike the nations.
> And He Himself will rule them with a rod of iron.
> He Himself treads the winepress of the fierceness and wrath of Almighty God.'
> Revelation 19:15

What then are these plagues that are portrayed here that will have such a dramatic effect on the quality of life for everyone? To understand what they are fully we have to consider these 'Bowls of Wrath' in their context to get a grasp of what is happening morally, that is from a heavenly perspective; the place from which they are poured.

The context of these plagues, that is these indications of God's complaint at the quality of the lives led by mankind, is the scene in which they are immediately placed. It is those people that had gained victory over the beast of chapter 13, those that had triumphed in a time of 'great tribulation' as our Lord describes it, that stand, that is are established in a state of purification, depicted as a sea of glass. In chapter 4 it was just a continuous expanse of crystal, that is pure and untainted, here it is mingled with fire, indicating what had created that purity, the sanctifying effect of the troubles they had suffered through tribulation.

The fact that many had repented and gained victory over the perpetrator of the trouble is itself a vindication of

God's patience, righteousness and might, in saving those that are penitent. They are in full appreciation of God's righteousness, His Holiness and worthiness is to be feared and worshipped by all, because His condemnation of all that is contrary to Him has been made evident. We can compare these individuals with the innumerable crowd in chapter 7:9 that came out of the great tribulation, verse 14, these are they that have obtained salvation through the wisdom, honour and might of God as they acknowledge what God has done for them. They have 'washed their robes and made them white', through the troubles of the 'tribulation' they have turned from personal sin to serve the living God.

The difference there is that they are not in the same depth of appreciation of God's righteousness as those that have obtained victory over the fully matured evil of the 'man of sin'. Those that are before the throne on the sea of glass though have a more profound appreciation of the character of the Almighty and so can worship Him more fully. Cp chapters 7:vv10, 14-17 and 15:vv3-4.

Now the scriptures here give us a detailed account of what it is that they gained victory over, described in verse 2 as various aspects of the despot that holds the whole world mesmerized and in idolization of himself.

First of all, it is the beast himself that they gain victory over, the satanically-appointed dictator that rules over all mankind, cp chapter 13:7. It is all that he represents politically and morally in his sway over the minds and aspirations of mankind. They are over-comers of all that he stands for, ironically, in that it was he that made war with the saints and overcame them; yet they are the final victors because they refuse to bow to the world and remain faithful to God and to the Lamb. It is a spiritual victory that they gain; compare the differences and similarities in chapters 2 and 3 of Revelation of the rewards promised to the overcomers; also:

> 'He who overcomes shall inherit all things,
> and I will be his God and he shall be My son,'
> Revelation 21:7.
>
> 'And they overcame him by the blood of the Lamb
> and by the word of their testimony,
> and they did not love their lives to the death.'
> Revelation 12:11

- Next they resist the image that is set up to remove all that reject or resist this evil ruler. There is no middle road, they cannot abstain and avoid trouble; all those that will not actually revere him will be eradicated. They resist then not only the tyrant himself but also the pressure put on them to conform from that icon which promotes him.

- Their rejection of the world and all it stands for though goes still further. They refuse to accept his mark, something that superficially would suggest identification or association with him, but at a deeper level it would mean to deny any contamination with his character or spirit. As always God looks upon the heart, it is not what is superficial but what is spiritual that is of significance to Him.

- Fourthly they have refused to take the number of his name, 666. As we considered when looking at chapter 13, this number represents his value or special significance. It is the number of a man; the number six signifies work or what is brought into being, for example as when God created the world in six days. Here it is expressly applied to man or a man, however it is this attribute of all that mankind has achieved and can achieve in his distance from God that is in focus, all that is destined for judgement. All this is now epitomised in one man and all that follow him. The fact that this number is also multiplied by ten and by one hundred denotes totality and full representation respectively. These individuals on the sea of purity have victory over all that characterises this man, the epitome of aggression, pride, idolatry and deception; all that militates against the holiness of God.

To contrast this, in chapter 13:17 we have another attribute that is associated with the beast and those he deceives, and that is his name itself, that is his identity, his innermost self, his ego. Now a name as we have seen earlier is all that a person is in character and essence; in relation to man, all that is in all of us naturally and potentially. It is this aspect of all that is contrary and antagonistic to Christ which resides in all of us by default. It is this nature that the scriptures refer to as the 'flesh', that is our innate, self-orientated nature. It is this nature that we see in full flower and development in this evil character.

If however this disposition in ourselves is systematically put to death through the influence of the Holy Spirit within us, then we gain victory over this nature as we find examples detailed in the second and third chapters of the Revelation, 'to him that overcomes'. It is through the ordinary difficulties and trials of life that we are brought face to face with our failure, weakness and shortcomings in respect to God's absolute standard of holiness and righteousness, through the Holy Spirit's enlightenment of scripture and the work of the Holy Spirit within us directly. It is He that changes us into the image of Christ. Such is the subject of much of Paul's writings in the New Testament, the process of which is called sanctification. Holiness is an attribute the Church is called to, the putting away of sin on a day-to-day basis.

It is not said though to be a feature in this group in chapter 15 that they had victory over his name. They resisted him and all that he stood for, but the actual name (his nature) of the beast is not mentioned in connection with them. It may seem pedantic to make these distinctions between his name, mark and number, but as the scripture clearly delineates them we do well to try and understand the distinctions and significance between them. The sin of every generation has been put away by Christ; salvation is only possible for all or any generation and age through faith in God and His Christ. To replace our sinful nature in this life with the glorious nature of Christ however is only possible through the indwelling of Christ's Holy Spirit. This is a lifelong process, having deep and immediate consequences, something that has eternal importance but not something that is spoken of in scripture in respect of everyone that will inherit the Kingdom of God. This process is very profound, very secret and fundamental in the lives of all those that belong to Christ in this age and will have eternal and very profound implications in God's final purpose for mankind. God however has a different purpose for us all, individually and apparently collectively in this life and in the ages to come. This we will see dramatically exemplified at the final chapters of this study.

This is to digress however from the function of this particular group of the saved in chapter 15, which is articulated in verses three and four. Their purpose is just to appreciate and joyfully proclaim God's wonder, righteousness and awesomeness, to sing of His holiness, omnipotence and manifested justice. They do not however have the appreciation of or witness to Christ's glory, honour and power in all creation that the elders do in chapter 4; their function is different. This is not to say that there will be different group identities in the Kingdom of God and the life hereafter as far as we know, rather that we will all be individually qualified for those different roles according to how Christ has been manifest in us at this time.

In chapter 15 it is in the context of the great company before the throne that another image is also brought again to our attention; it is the Tabernacle of the testimony, the representation of the Covenant of God with mankind. The law of God here also will be emphasised now to all mankind, through the seven plagues.

The focus on the tabernacle here is not as in chapter 11:1; there is no altar or worshippers here but the ark of testimony, which is central. Now the Ark of the Covenant represented primarily God's covenant and provision for Israel from the time of Moses. Here it is exhibited to all mankind, thus it lays bare the effect of breaking the Law of God on all followers of the beast and what life becomes as a result. This covenant does however have the complementary meaning:

> 'To love the Lord your God, to walk in His ways,
> and to keep His commandments, His statutes, and His judgments,
> that you may live and multiply; and the Lord your God will bless you;'
> Deuteronomy 30:16.

More than that however, the Ark of the Covenant is in itself symbolic, giving us a picture of another covenant:

> 'For this is the covenant that I will make with the house of Israel after those days,
> says the Lord; I will put my laws into their mind, and write them on their hearts;
> and I will be their God, and they shall be My people.'
> Hebrews 8:10

It presents in great detail how the law of God, symbolised by the ark, can be written into our hearts through the work and character of Christ Himself. The practical nature of this salvation is exemplified by those that are featured here as having obtained victory over the beast, indicating the exceptional relationship between the crowd of the sea of glass and the Ark of the Covenant.

It is from here that the seven angels we saw in verse 1 emerge to pour out the plagues upon the Earth. They are dressed in pure linen, which signifies that it is the pure righteousness of God that characterises their actions. The gold belt around their chest signifies that it is Divine motivation that occasions their actions; there is no malice here. Cp Revelation 1:13.

The next thing to note is that the bowls are given to them not by God Himself but by one of the four creatures. This is another detail that is very significant, but one we could easily miss. In chapter 4 of this Revelation we saw that the living creatures are that which testifies to the authority, strength, wisdom and grace of the Throne that they encompass and that the function of their wings was the providing of a covering or protection. The text doesn't say which creature it was that gave the angels the bowls of wrath, so we conclude that he is representative of all of them. What is relevant is that it was not a unilateral action by God for some inscrutable reason, but rather by that which openly testifies in creation to God's wisdom and justice. It is these attributes of God, wisdom and justice, rather than His mind or judgement, that require these terrifying actions.

It is a voice from the temple however that authorises the administration of these plagues. It is the holiness and justice of God and the way that He dwells amongst mankind that the temple stands witness to and thus it is those attributes that sanction these actions. The commissioning of the judgements alone then results in the temple being filled with smoke, something that continues until the outpouring is complete. Now smoke is the evidence of the unapproachable holiness and glory of God in the context of the temple:

> 'And the posts of the door were shaken by the voice of Him who cried out,
>
> and the house was filled with smoke,' Isaiah 6:4,

Or the evidence of its consuming power -
'As smoke is driven away, so drive them away:
as wax melts before the fire,
so let the wicked perish at the presence of God,'
Psalm 68:2,
'For my days are consumed like smoke,
and my bones are burned like a hearth,' Psalm 102:3.

As a result the Temple, the place of meeting of man with God, cannot be entered into by any man until the wrath of God is revealed against the beast and all those that follow after him. God is unapproachable in this role, we can only approach Him in the context of His love and grace, never in His position as judge.

The quality of life turns bitter and loses purpose

We now come to the plagues themselves, to discover their implications and deeper and intimate meaning. As throughout this book, it is how God Himself is being revealed to and acknowledged by the entire world, through the opening of the scroll by Jesus Christ. It is how His holy character and His glory must be made fully make known to all Mankind before His Kingdom can be put into practice. Everyone then must recognize Him or be eternally excluded from His presence.

Each one of these plagues encompasses a different aspect of what life itself epitomises. The first plague that is 'poured out' on all of rebellious mankind is a painful sore, all those that have the character of antichrist and all those that follow after him. This is life at its most obvious; the simple physical experience of life becomes painful and repugnant, the very tangible quality of life is abhorrent during this time of horror and tribulation that has come upon the Earth. This is a time when loyalties are clearly exposed; there are those that seek prestige and fulfilment through coercion and immorality and those that seek to do only what is right in the sight of God. The former way of life ends in pain and distress, 'the painful sores'.

The other way may elicit persecution and testing but leads to the gates of Heaven itself.

The second plague that is poured out is upon the sea. Now as we have seen, the sea in scripture symbolises a mass or expanse of something, much as it can in English, the context indicating to what this refers to. Here we have a picture similar to the second trumpet, which could be significant. In chapter 8:8 the sea refers to the multitude of human life and the general affairs of mutual daily living, community life in other words, the collective and interactive course of national daily life. In chapter 8 a third of the creatures and ship were destroyed, a representative part of this quality of life is lost; see section 2/3. It is not only part of the 'sea' though that now succumbs, following the second trumpet, but rather also the whole of life becomes completely congealed and dead. Community life has ceased altogether; such is the catastrophic effect of this global war. Life in a practical, active social sense expires, all who follow the beast are now isolated and alone, emotionally, psychologically and spiritually.

The third plague is much closer to home however, much more intimate, affecting not just communal life but one's individual experience of life. Water is life sustaining for every creature. It is also our source of refreshment; for the springs and rivers to yield revulsion and death, implies that personal existence becomes meaningless and nauseating. Here then it is emotional life that ceases to have any value. The scripture does not say if these later plagues involve all human life or just of those that live according to the course of this world, those that worship the beast etc., but the implication of scripture, 1 John 2:17 for example, is that it is all life that is in alienation from God will fail and end in death. Those that are living for God will find all their contentment in Him, the spring of living water.

To this account of the third plague we have an addendum, a proclamation attributing this result to the judgement of God, that He has caused or allowed this outcome. There is a distinct irony here, that as they have murdered those that lived virtuously then in consequence they must now swallow the effect of their malevolence; having shed the blood of the saints and prophets they are given blood to drink. Such is the Divine principle: -

'I will make justice the measuring line, and righteousness to the plummet:

the hail will sweep away the refuge of lies,

and the waters will overflow the hiding place,'
Isaiah 28:17.

and

'Do not be deceived; God is not mocked:

for whatever a man sows, that he will also reap.

> For he who sows to his flesh will of the flesh
> reap corruption;
>
> but he who sows to the Spirit will of the Spirit
> reap everlasting life.'
>
> Galatians 6:7-8

With the fourth plague this chapter continues to explore analytically the different facets of what makes up the experience and meaning of life and the effect that God's censure has upon it. This time it is the 'icing in the cake' of living as it were that is affected. It is what those that enjoy a more prosperous life style regard as 'life', our day-to-day enjoyment and appeal of living. Now though the source of that quality of life, the sun, is turned from a life-giving resource and a supply of warmth and happiness to something that burns and consumes. Again there is an irony here; that which advances life is turned into something that blights it. Today, with the problem of global warming and loss of the ozone layer, we can easily imagine this effect literally, though what is presented here has ramifications for the whole province of one's experience of living. But what is the response of mankind but that which is usual; they blame and curse God for their discomfort, refusing to accept any culpability for themselves or to honour God as God and the true source of pleasure to those that seek Him.

The fifth plague, like the first, is directed solely at those that stand in direct opposition to God; it is directed on the throne, that is the reign, of the beast, the whole realm that spurns the authority of the rightful sovereign. It is the whole integrity and ideology of the government that is thrown into confusion; there is complete darkness throughout the whole realm where evil reigns. This is the intellectual life of all that form part of that dominion, of all that conform to that regime. Anarchy now reigns.

Life now is meaningless; full only of blackness, despair and agony of soul. They gnaw their tongues in pain; continued existence gives no moral insight or understanding, it offers no meaning or reason to live for. Once again man's response is to blame God for his troubles, as if God was responsible for his wellbeing rather than they being responsible to Him for their conduct and accountability. They blasphemed God for their pain and sores, which they had effectively brought upon themselves.

The penultimate affliction to strike brings further erosion in the essence of life.

Now it is the failure of the security of life and the confidence and peace that give life any direction and confidence. All that mankind toils for each day, the drive to create, to establish a foundation and refuge for himself, is under threat. Everything that one lives for in this life and our drive to succeed that is so crucial is at risk.

The river Euphrates forms the northern boundary of Israel as defined by God to Abraham, Genesis 15:18. This border is with Assyria, with Babylon built on the river. This has historical significance in the captivity that Israel suffered at the hands of the Syrians. It also has symbolic significance in all that Babylon represents in the scriptures, particularly in the final judgement of it, which features so much in the Revelation.

In chapter 9:13 it was the sixth trumpet that called for the angels to release the massive army from the river

Euphrates; the army that was to inflict such widespread death and destruction. Here it is the warning that God is giving of the impending disaster that is about to engulf the world, the final conflict that will be the end of this age; one that would emanate from this river, this barrier that separated Israel, the Land of God's promise, and Babylon as symbolic of the kingdoms of this world. Morally it is figurative of the barrier that has existed between good and evil since the beginning.

Now though the barrier that provided security for Israel is removed. Even morality itself loses any meaning; there is no distinction in life between what is pleasant or vile any more, good or bad. More than that the nations of the Earth are incited and deluded by signs from the spirits of demons that emanate from the mouths of the satanic trio, the dragon, the beast and the false prophet.

- They are spirits because they have evil intentions.
- They come from their mouths, implying that evil intentions are articulated.
- They are like frogs. The image given here is of the way that they permeate through the Earth, as did the frogs in the plague of Egypt penetrating even the most personal areas of life, destroying the Egyptian's composure and way of life:

> 'He sent swarms of flies among them,
> which devoured them; and frogs,
> which destroyed them,' Psalm 78:45

We are told in chapter 13:5 that the beast was given a

mouth speaking great things and blasphemies; here with his allies he incites all the world to collaborate in battle against God and His people, to bring them to the valley of Armageddon, a large plain west of the Jordan river. What a presumption! But this mindset emanates from the three forces of evil that rule the world, typically now in that it is prevalent in the spirit of antichrist, cp 1 John 2:18.

The whole world is now united in one objective, to finally remove all influence of God and His people Israel from the Earth; such is the hatred that is inflamed throughout the world.

The last bowl finally brings about the destruction of the one remaining aspect of life on Earth, social life. Here finally the whole world order, commercial, political and religious, all that Babylon stands for, standing in united hatred and opposition to God, is finally brought down completely. This is the dissolution of all the secular social structures that we take for granted in the conduct of everyday life. The angel pours the bowl into air, suggesting that the primary targets of God's wrath are the principalities and powers that prevail in this world; all that holds sway over every aspect of civilised and secular life, Cp Ephesians 2:2. As with all these disasters, it is not necessarily the outward physical or material entity only that is destroyed, but the primary focus is on the experience, the spiritual appreciation and character of that particular quality of life.

A loud voice calls from the temple, 'It is done!' At last, all that stands in opposition to the rule of Heaven is removed; now the temple itself stands witness that in righteousness God's own administration can now be established on Earth; the old order has been completely removed.

The effects of the last plague however are many:

- The first outcome from the meting-out of this bowl of God's wrath is noises, that is sounds, or voices as the original word is translated most frequently, suggesting that there is a particular message, presentiment or ambience being articulated, for example:

> 'Like the noise of many waters,
> like the voice of the Almighty,
> a tumult like the noise of an army.'
> Ezekiel 1:24, also see 3:13 and 10:5.

- There were thunderings, indicating the voice of God to mankind in scripture

> 'Hear attentively the thunder of His voice
> and the rumbling that comes from His mouth ...
> He thunders with His majestic voice,'
> Job 37:2+4.

- Lightning indicates the arrows of God, fired in resistance to all that this worlds order stands for.

> 'He sent out arrows and scattered them;
> lightning bolts, and He vanquished them.'
> 2 Samuel 22:15.

- Next there is a massive earthquake, greater than anything previously in human history. This is the most significant and radical disruption of the earthly order since Adam. This would indicate a great shake-up of the daily order of life, a total transformation in every institution on the planet, the Kingdom of God now reigns supreme over all the Earth, bringing every other realm into subjection.

- The great city Babylon is divided into three. Three in scripture implies a fully-integrated set, for example the Godhead. For the city to be divided into, literally 'to become' three, would imply that the earthquake entirely disrupted the integrity of the worldly civilisation. It is now defunct.

- 'And the cities of the nations fell' - that is the places of habitation, the social affiliation of all secular civilizations. No longer are there different alienated national identities; in future all national identities and states will be united in their recognition of the sovereignty of the one true God.

- Great Babylon is kept in mind to feel the anger of God, which is all that it has represented for many millennia; although it has been something that God has tolerated out of patience and mercy to mankind, despite its abhorrence to Him.

- 'Every island fled away' - every isolated and independent faction or society has been brought down to their lowest common denominator. Every mind-set that divides and segregates communities has been broken up.

- 'And the mountains were not found' - all authority, influence, arrogance and places of false worship have been swept away completely; there will be just one authority now throughout the Earth, God's Holy Mount Zion, Jerusalem.

- But first God's Divine judgement against mankind in their waywardness from Him must be seen and recognized; there is a great hail (a Divine instrument of destruction).

'The weight of a talent' is about 30 kg, the heaviest measure of weight in biblical times. Some of mankind has held out to very last, after every aspect of life has been exposed, censured and judged, yet still mankind stands in animosity and defiance to God. They do not repent and accept God's mercy but simply blaspheme God for the great plague. Human nature is incorrigible.

We passed briefly over verse 15 of this chapter. There is a parenthesis after the 6th plague with a message direct to the seven churches in Asia Minor to whom the Revelation was written. It is a message that is very important to everyone that knows and loves Christ and is looking for His return. The context in which it is given here couldn't be more dramatic and yet significant.

'Behold I am coming as a thief. Blessed is he who watches, and keeps his garments, lest he walk naked and they see his shame'

The 'Revelation' has one main theme, the revelation of Jesus Christ, though an essential prerequisite for this to happen is that all that is of antichrist, all that at present exists that is against or stands in place of Christ, must be openly judged and removed first. This is true of us individually and spiritually, as it will be generally and globally. Christ will be revealed in the future in all His glory to and throughout the entire world, but not yet. God is at present revealing his Kingdom within us individually, day by day, but this also includes revealing to us the principles that must one day apply throughout the world and how this will be universal.

This begs the question though how the breakdown of life in all these aspects globally reveals the nature of Christ in us, in place of our innate instinctive 'fallen' nature. The answer is that it doesn't, directly. The breakdown of spontaneous life through the loss of amenity in any way, temporal or personal, teaches us that life is finite and subject to corruption and eventual death. We can cling to that in a forlorn hope that all will work out for the best in the end, or we can renounce it in despair, or we can turn from it and embrace the risen life of Christ, which He freely offers. The prerequisite to receive that risen life though is always to renounce both this world, 'Babylon' in the imagery of this book, and also what we are in ourselves by nature. The emancipation from our self-centredness and the giving to us of the life of Christ that then follows however is the work of God alone. Anything that we might try to do for ourselves to emulate this is doomed to failure and disappointment.

This 'new life' of Christ however is something that must emanate spontaneously from within us, deep within our being. This then becomes evident in the quality of our demeanour and disposition, the lives we lead; this is the testimony of salvation, this is being in Christ, this is the believer being a witness to the existence of Christ for all the world to see: cp Acts 1:8. This then in verse 15 is the 'garment' that we are exhorted to keep, showing us that is something we can lose if we neglect it. This 'garment' does not refer to salvation as in the wedding garment in Matthew 22:11, but to this new life in Christ. To lose that means to become preoccupied with this natural life and neglect the new. Hence all this detail as to the different aspects of life experience implicated in the bowls of wrath is directly relevant to ourselves and to our relationship with Christ now, practically, morally and spiritually. It is a help both as a reminder that this is how everything will end and as an encouragement to continue in a path of faith.

In chapter 17 we meet one of the angels of the bowls of wrath again, first in showing us the judgement and destruction of Babylon as an adulterous and constitutional entity, standing in opposition to God and His purposes on Earth. Next in chapter 19 again it is this angel that reveals to us the bride of Christ in all her glory. In the next section of this study we will look at the significance of that.

SECTION 3: PART 6

The Die is Cast

Revelation Chapter 20

Only Those that Have Deferred to God's Principles Can Have any Place in His Kingdom

As we have already seen in this book John is not just a detached observer, reporting for curiosity's sake what will some day transpire. In 'seeing' he is becoming fully acquainted with what is being revealed with all its implications, something that was only partially disclosed before in scripture but now here something that affects us all directly and intimately. What is not always so obvious is how these things concern us directly and why we should understand their significance. As always in scripture we cannot just use our imaginations to interpret the details or assume a standpoint to construe all its meaning, but should rather read it in the context of other scripture to understand all its ramifications. The more we read and compare, the deeper will be our understanding. We can then know what the will of God is for us personally and how that can be effected in us and for us.

In the New Testament Christ Himself, in the first three Gospels, expresses the subject of His reign upon Earth. In Matthew chapter 25 for example, He tells three different parables to illustrate the character of the Kingdom of God on Earth and the qualities that will be required in those that are citizens therein. The next section of this study examines these qualities in detail. Here we will just be concerned with how this compares with Revelation 20 and what light it may shed on our understanding of that chapter.

In 1 Corinthians 15 the details of the nature of the resurrection of those that belong to Christ is explained in the context of how this will happen. Verses 23-24 of that chapter also show us that the resurrection will precede the time of Christ's coming and the Divine purpose for His coming, that is, when He will then rule on Earth until everyone and everything is in subjection to the will of God. After this only can the new Heaven and Earth be established, where only righteousness can exist.

Revelation chapter 20 then also reveals details about the setting up of Christ's kingdom. Here the detail is not about the resurrection itself but the qualifications of those that are resurrected to live and co-reign with Him for the whole of the time of His reign. There is no conflict between these three different accounts; the first in the Gospels tells us of the spiritual attribute of those that will be a part of that realm. The second, in 1 Corinthians 15, reveals that those that will be brought back to life will be those that are chosen and loved by God. Lastly in Revelation 20 those that are spoken of as being co-regents with Him are those that have suffered and died for His sake and have rejected all that constitutes this world's temporal ideals, that is, all that is contrary to the will of God and the person of Christ.

At this present time it is a principle of the Kingdom of God that those that know and love Christ will suffer for Him. They will reject and suffer all that does not glorify Him in this world, that is all that is of antichrist, described here as the Beast, which we can remind ourselves is an implied reference to the attributes of the great and terrible beast as outlined in Daniel chapter 7. It is this theme that only through such suffering and rejection can the Kingdom of God be cultivated, a theme that appears in different contexts throughout the New Testament. Christ's Sermon on the Mount is perhaps one of the most detailed accounts of this. When Christ returns this present time of suffering will be complete and in coming back to Earth, as He promised, He will establish the principles of that kingdom universally.

For Christ to reign supreme though, all that stands against Him must be removed first. Nothing physical or spiritual that is contrary to Christ can be allowed to remain. Babylon, that which represents the religious and material culture of the nations, has gone completely by this chapter. However the evil influence and disposition of Satan must also be excluded. If this were not so then the perfection of Christ reign, illustrated throughout the bible, would not be possible. Christ must reign until He has put down all rule and authority. Christ reigns now, in the lives of those that are His, but then it will be in the context of the continuous absence of everything that is contrary to Christ and His kingdom, everything that would displace Him as Lord. That rule is not yet universal and cannot be until all that is adverse to Him is removed.

Hence the first mission of God to be established is the eradication of evil from the Earth. Satan's power had been limited to Earth in chapter 12. Now Satan is incarcerated for the duration of the reign of Christ, for as long as it takes for Christ to achieve His remit contained in the scroll of authority given to Him in chapter 5. This is said to be a thousand years. To debate whether this time is literal or just typical is futile and just causes us to miss the significance of the administration. A thousand years certainly has symbolic meaning but that does not mean that it will not be a literal period as well; we will return to this point later.

It is an angel from Heaven that implements this state of affairs. It is not popular to think these days of immaterial entities such as angels and devils that exert influence on us for good or evil, but that is just to ignore or reject the significance of what is spiritual and therefore what is of God. If we believe that the world has no inherent purpose but that everything happens arbitrarily, then evil is just incidental to life. If however the cosmos and all that is in it does have a consummate created purpose, then it is difficult to account for evil unless it is an active force that is tolerated at present as part of that created purpose. Cp though Romans 8:20.

Satan then is that active force for evil, evil that is not passive or just relative but is fundamental, determinate and manipulative, the antithesis of goodness, which likewise is a moral absolute not just a relative quality, as our postmodern culture advocates. It characterizes intentions (what is intellectual), and effect (what is creative).

That function of evil though will end when it has fulfilled its time. An angel is simply an agent or messenger of God, here with a key and chain, symbolising that Satan is to be contained completely in the abyss. The literal meaning is that he is completely restrained in a very deep place. He is far removed out of the way, unable to exert any influence in Heaven or on Earth. No longer is he able to deceive or corrupt mankind for the duration of Christ's rule on Earth. To debate whether this pit has a physical or abstract location can be just to miss the spiritual significance of the concept. The world is now to be a completely different place where only righteousness reigns; so how then will the new administration be instituted?

'I saw thrones', John records in verse 4; the first thing that is seen is the primacy of authority. This administration will not be a democracy, as we are inclined to believe is the fairest form of government. Christ will have absolute authority and discretion; He will rule the nations with a rod of iron, Psalm 2:9 tells us, that is without compromise, but in absolute righteousness, mercy and integrity; no dissent will be possible. The will of man will no longer find expression in the affairs of state or social intercourse. This will be the state of world peace that mankind generally has always craved but never been able to deliver; it is the Divine order that now predominates. A democracy is always a compromise at best, and perhaps when mankind runs his own affairs a compromise is the best that we can attain to. Christ however will reign in absolute righteousness, unequivocally and without compromise, as He reigns in the hearts of His people to the extent that we are committed to

Him now. When evil is removed however, peace can hold sway completely and universally.

John then saw those that sat upon the thrones, to whom judgement was given. The thing that is now brought into consideration is that this authority is delegated. These thrones are in respect of Christ's Kingdom upon Earth and so represent a different character from those thrones in chapter 4. Here these vice-royals have responsibility on Earth; we might consider them as Christ's senate, each having a particular place within the administration. We are then told who they are; 'then I saw the souls of those who had been beheaded for':

- Their witness to Jesus, for living lives that were a demonstration of Christ Himself.

- The word of God, that is they had lost their lives for being faithful to the word of God.

'Beheaded' could mean literally killed or that their lives were given up for the sake of Christ or both. There is an obvious correspondence with the souls under the altar in chapter 6:9.

That faithfulness essentially meant also that they refused to worship the beast, typically anything that is contrary to what Christ is in this world, or to worship his image, that is to give place to anything that even resembled him. Their dissension is uncompromising, untainted by any attribute in thought or in practice, in that they did not receive the mark in their forehead or hand. When we consider the spiritual implication of the picture presented in the scripture we realise what a challenge it is to ourselves, something that we can never achieve by ourselves, that it can only be the exclusive work of God alone, to 'make us walk in the paths of righteousness for His name's sake.' What is written in the scripture here may just be in respect of an exclusive group from a particular era, but its spiritual significance is relevant to every believer of every age.

Verse 6 tells us specifically what their role is in this administration: 'they shall be priests of God and of Christ,' they are those that speak and appear on behalf of God and of Christ towards the rest of mankind. From being the outcasts of this present world system they are now promoted to a ruling elite, acting in the prerogative of God alone. This contrasts with the 24 elders in chapters 4 and 5 where their priesthood was in relation to God only. This does not mean necessarily that they are a discrete identity or entity in time but those that possess those spiritual qualities enumerated.

They lived and reigned for a thousand years. The thousand years is reiterated six times in this chapter, so we can glean from that that it is significant. Now a thousand in scripture denotes the full extent or magnitude of an entity, here being years, that is phases or ages. What is expressed therefore symbolically is that the period of this millennium will be complete in itself to attain to its Divine purpose, as mentioned earlier.

All this though requires in the first place a supernatural God, a God that is simply above all that is natural. To deny such a being relieves us from any sense of responsibility that is implicated, but it also excludes from us any knowledge of Him that we could experience through loyalty to Him.

Blessed, contented, set apart is he, God's people are every one of those that are resurrected. Death in scripture can imply several different concepts, depending on the context. The second death referred to in this chapter is spoken of in connection with those that have been resurrected, and so this term suggests a comparison with the first death, their physical demise. The second death is mentioned a couple of other times in the Revelation, in chapter 2:11 and in verse 14 of this chapter where it defines it as the lake of fire. Note that this is the second death, not a particular aspect of it or a situation somewhere, literally or mythologically. It is describing the suffering of eternal separation from God; it is the agony of existence without living; this is the second death, the Lake of Fire. It is a state of existence, not just a place. Those that know Christ however will forever enjoy intimate association with Him and cannot be separated from Him, Romans 8:38-39. They will have, not a natural life as now, that could only ever be temporary; they will know only that Divine life which they first began to appreciate when they accepted it as a gift through faith.

The purposes of God in salvation are revealed here in two ways. Firstly the purpose of and the necessity for the millennium become apparent as has already been alluded to. Secondly it becomes apparent why God ordained that we should be saved from sin, in the environmental context of a sinful and evil world. It is said of the early patriarchs that they looked for a city whose constructor and public benefactor was God, Hebrews 11:10. They looked for a world where only righteousness reigns, this is the New Heaven and Earth that are revealed later in chapter 21. That new order of affairs though could not be achieved until all that was in antithesis to it was checked. This can only happen though when the reign of Christ on Earth has completed its purpose.

Now God is in Himself Love; it is a fundamental characteristic of His Divine nature. It is love that is intrinsically based in and emanates from His absolute goodness. This in turn may be defined as unqualified moral rectitude, one aspect of His complete nature of righteousness, which in turn defines His Holy Status. Thus this is the complete integrity of God; it cannot function apart from these principles and cannot relate to any other, except in judgement. It is only mankind that can be capricious and deceitful.

Therefore that new order could only be according to the nature of God Himself, a nature that is not only righteous but also loving, pure and unqualified selfless love. Now to love essentially implies independence of will in all parties, or it is not love in any degree. This in turn implies the possibility of rebellion, which is what sin is, and this is what inevitably transpired after mankind was made in the image of God; that is as having His nature, having moral sensibilities so that he could know and love God. So God must first put away all rebellion and corruption to make this new order of things feasible.

In this present age He is redeeming back from a state of rebellion all those who will be resident in that eternal state. The prerequisite though is for every candidate to reject ego and self-will and be filled with the Spirit of Christ instead. This is what God is achieving through this age in transforming individuals who lay down their own wills and way of life to adopt the life of Christ alone. It is then in this way that they are essentially qualified to be part of the administration of Christ's reign, bringing about the state of affairs where Christ has introduced a world where all rule in independence from God has been eradicated. Then will God alone be supreme throughout all perpetuity.

And so comes the age that mankind has dreamed about since civilisation began; an age of peace and contentment will at last come to pass. Not by any thought or design of mankind but only by the work of God Himself, after many eons of time through the salvation of a people that first had to be allowed to go their own way before renouncing that futility and assuming the endowment of the mantle of Christ. However, when that age has achieved its purpose, after the allotted period of that preparation, time now really will come to an end. Time is essentially about change. When all is perfect, time will become obsolete. However, first one further matter has yet to be completed, that of justice.

The Final Reckoning

For all the players on the great stage of history, that is all mankind, the die is now cast. The vision here is one of a great white throne, white representing purity and candour. Heaven and Earth as we know it are now gone, all the great principles and laws that govern our world including that very sphere itself are now no longer of any significance, there is no place left for them. This is the greatest social leveller of all time, everyone, great and small, standing equal before the throne.

The redeemed will live with God eternally; those however that consistently refused to accept the reality of God and therefore their responsibility to Him, those that persisted in excluding God, His values and His people from their reckoning cannot now be reformed. The age of grace when the offer of salvation was extant is now past. Time is no more; the door of opportunity is now closed. All must be judged according to 'what is written' about them. The criterion is simple; all that have been accorded life, all those that have lived according to His life and principles, that is all those recorded in the Lamb's Book of Life remain. All those that that are strangers to God and His principles have no part in an afterlife. They are judged according to their attitudes and activities in the natural life.

This brings us to the other moral dilemma; why a righteous, all-knowing and loving God could allow anyone who has sentient existence to ultimately be barred from the life that God alone gives. It is easier to accept that only those who love God can receive His life, than it is to accept that anyone who has existed at all should continue to exist in a state of hopelessness forever. From a moral perspective it is simple. We cannot make a choice if we do not exist in the first place. If we make an independent choice it could go either way, the choice to love and accept God must be independent or it cannot be really mutual; it would not then be real love. It is not then a rational choice that can be made out of self-interest but rather one of affection, based on our disposition. If we choose self, then we are on our own. If we elect for God's summons and renounce self-interest, then He will reveal Himself to us and progressively in us. We cannot accept and love God out of self-interest, to secure a better future for ourselves; that would be an inherent contradiction and so patently false. Faith must come before experience in this matter, not the other way around as in life generally for the most part. Moral responsibility then is an essential constituent of any positive relationship, particularly so in a Divine relationship where that love has to be unconditional.

There is however one more principle that is dealt with here before that final and irrevocable polarisation of destinies takes place. Satan is released on Earth for one last brief moment, the purpose, to prove that mankind is ever susceptible to evil, even after 1000 years of virtuosity and peace. God never judges anyone unless His principles of justice are apparent. The weakness and vulnerability of natural flesh will always ultimately fail as it did in the Garden of Eden, and so can never find a place in a perfect world. As scripture says, flesh and blood cannot inherit the Kingdom of God.

As above, God has allowed evil to exist so that His grace can be shown to those that trust Him and to prove what is absolutely genuine. It is also only through an environment of evil and confusion that man can truly choose the good and be made perfect and faithful to God alone. After that is fulfilled, to then disregard that evil which had to exist to accomplish that perfect state would be gross injustice. Verses 7-10 of this chapter by their direct reference to the greater detail of the whole of chapter 38 of Ezekiel illustrate this perfectly. Verse 16 of that chapter explains that judgement must fall on Gog and Magog because of their belligerence against His defenceless people. Thus is God shown to be Holy and just in His actions in defending those that trust in Him, but meting out destruction on the belligerent and treacherous. This is the principle that pervades the final judgement. Those that have rejected God and His people are themselves rejected, those that persecuted His people are themselves afflicted; see also Matthew 25.

PS: Gog was simply the king of Magog in ancient times; Magog is mentioned in Genesis chapter 10 as the grandson of Noah; the tribe that descended from him are thought to have occupied the northern regions of what is now Russia, what would have been recognised as the farthest reaches of the world at that time. The north in scripture in relation to Israel usually signifies the direction from which invasion for the Divine purpose of discipline and correction emanated, which would further illustrate the point made in the previous paragraph.

SECTION FOUR

**The Earth Shall be Filled with the Glory of the Lord:
The Kingdom of God on Earth**

PREFACE TO SECTION FOUR

―――∞―――

What God Achieves Through the Troubles of This World: the Fulfilment of His Plans in Salvation

In this fourth section of this study we will consider what God's Kingdom on Earth will be like and what His eternal purposes for mankind are, as revealed in Matthew's gospel chapter 25 and in The Revelation chapters 7, 11, 17-18 and 21-22.

Each of the five parts of this section follow the themes of what those purposes are, firstly in Matthews Gospel and then from four more angles in the Revelation. As mentioned in the introduction, they follow the spiritual themes or perspectives in sequence, temporal, heavenly, moral, judicial and the Divine objective.

In Matthew chapter 24 we were given a picture of how the world would be from the time of Christ until the present day and then during the time of unprecedented trouble that will engulf the world at the end of this age, just before Christ returns in glory. This forms the background and then the process by which God is implementing and will continue to implement His objectives for the Kingdom of God on Earth. In section 4 part 1, chapter 25 of Matthew, now arrives at that position where Jesus outlines the outward aspects of that Kingdom, who will be accepted into it and the basic spiritual qualifications for acceptance and positions of privilege within it. Jesus tells three parables to illustrate the fundamental aspects of the kingdom and the basic principle on which it will be set up and function.

Having clearly established in Matthew 25 that the Kingdom of God on Earth will be a physical establishment with total and worldwide rule, Revelation chapter 7 is also about how the Kingdom of God will be but from a heavenly, that is spiritual, perspective. This is not about the basic outward features of the Kingdom but about the character and lives of those that live and function within that Kingdom. It focuses on those of Israel that have been protected by God during the time of troubles for special service and those that have been saved out of the troubles to enter the Kingdom. This scene then is analysed in detail to see what it is telling us about the character that those from Israel possess and how these characteristics are pertinent also to all those of the present time that love and serve God. From the simple symbolic language of the meaning of the names of the tribes of Israel and from other detail is revealed not only the spiritual characteristics of its citizens but also the spiritual benefits that will be experienced in that Kingdom; Part 2-5 of this section.

The character of those that inhabit the Kingdom has now been revealed, and the benefits that will be found there, through all the adversity that the redeemed have had to suffer. This though now presents a moral issue; what will happen to those that are incorrigibly perverse in refusing to relinquish their antagonism and to acknowledge the claims of God. In the first part of chapter 11 the prerequisite to God residing with mankind had been made clear to all the Earth and the need for repentance, the turning from sin and self-serving. The scene from verse 15 though is the sounding of the seventh and final trumpet to tell the world that all the kingdoms of the world are now under the dominion of God's own King; there is only condemnation and banishment left for those that destroy the planet. The trumpet also announces that the law of God is now established on Earth as the basis of God dwelling among mankind. This causes great rejoicing and worship amongst the 24 elders on their thrones

All those that are unfit to live in this Kingdom of righteousness, by virtue of their pernicious stubbornness, have been given their last chance to yield. However there is a further matter to be dealt with before all the new institutions and administration can be set up for this new world order, where only absolute peace, honesty and holiness hold sway. The old institutions have to be removed, three in particular. There are the great idolatrous practices of the world, atheism, materialism and all false religion for example which are represented by the great harlot of chapter 17, together with the evil political and commercial systems of the world which are characterised as the Beast and Babylon respectively in chapter 17. These are destroyed completely, by infighting, earthquake and collapse of the whole world monetary system. Again there is rejoicing in Heaven that the peace and joy of Heaven can now replace the injustice and distress that was endemic in the old order of things.

Peace and justice now reigns throughout the world; Christ, that is the Lord's anointed, is now King. He has now reigned for a thousand years, quelling any remnant of dissention from His rule, then that was followed by the final assize when everyone that has ever lived was judged. Even death is now abolished forever, 1 Corinthians 15:24-26. This of course is what occurs in chapter 20. God's eternal state of perfect peace will now exist for eternity; it will never come to an end. The world as we know it will have ended its turbulent history with the reign of peace being actively and uncompromisingly maintained. Even that episode is now complete; all sin, that is dissension from God's perfection, is now gone forever. All sorrow and obscurity are therefore things of the past; even death has ceased. Now there is a new Heaven and Earth where only righteousness dwells. No one rules this enlightened state to impose order because only the life of God Himself pervades everything and everyone; no dissention exists. These last two chapters in the Bible now give us much detail as to how this new cosmos functions and how its structure and institutions are ordered. This is the place that Abraham that great patriarch of faith was looking forward to; Hebrews 11:10: 'The city which has foundations, whose builder and maker is God'.

SECTION 4: PART 1

Parables of the Kingdom

Matthew Chapter 25: The Olivet Discourse.

The Earth Shall Be Full of the Knowledge of the Lord as the Waters Cover the Sea

Now at last we are to find out what this long-promised Kingdom of God will embody. In chapter 25 of Matthew's Gospel, Jesus is explicitly telling us what the Kingdom of Heaven will be like, that is what features will characterise it. In chapter 22 He has explained who it will be that enter the kingdom; it will not be those that assumed that they would qualify on the strength of their own virtue but the humble and despised that come in faith. Chapter 24 tells of how all that is in the world at present will end in confusion and finally be removed. We now come to what will replace all this, something that is certain, confident and altogether beautiful.

Now in chapter 25, Christ tells us not who will enter the Kingdom but on what grounds individuals will be eligible. Each of these parables tells us different requirements that must be fulfilled for entry into that realm and the basis on which the whole will function. It becomes apparent therefore that this present time for us is a period of preparation and proving for that coming time when the Kingdom is established.

In 2 Thessalonians 1:10 Paul explains the purpose of Christ's coming, how Christ will come to be glorified in His saints. The glory of Christ alone will be what fills that realm, but it will be displayed not in the trappings of power, grandiose buildings and public adulation as in this age, but His glory will be replicated in the character of the lives of His subjects in that kingdom. Each one will, by their particular personal relationship to Christ, partake of and reflect His Glory.

As usual, Christ teaches us what these spiritual qualities are and how they will function through the means of analogy, that is, in parables. In the first parable the advent of the Kingdom is likened to the drama of a procession to a marriage celebration. His coming with His bride, He says, will not be just be to impose His authority, but also to celebrate His marriage. This will be the beginning of an intimate relationship with all mankind; this will be the new administration, His life, His Glory permeating throughout the world through the lives of His faithful servants. This marriage relationship itself is not pertinent, however, to this chapter. This chapter is not about identifying different parties either, that is, those who are selected to go into the kingdom, but only the grounds on which anyone is acceptable. It is these principles that are being presented, not specific individuals or groups.

The scene then in this touching and rather beautiful drama is a typical Jewish wedding party of a bridegroom coming with his espoused wife and an entourage of friends of both the bridegroom and his bride, to be met by the bridesmaids who will lighten their path to the celebration. The bridegroom has just been to the house of the bride to bring her to the house of his father. The focus here, however, is just on the bridesmaids, particularly on their function, their qualification and their readiness to act. It is easiest for us to think of the ten virgins here as representing the Church of Christ, though that is not to say that it does not apply to other groups that are spoken about in scripture that will inherit the Kingdom of God. To reiterate, it is a principle that is being presented here, a principle that applies to all that would be acceptable in that heavenly society.

The bridesmaids represent in the parable all those expecting the Messiah and to then accompany Him to the celebrations, that is the advent of His reign on Earth. They give dignity and pageantry to the event, making public the status of the bridegroom and the importance and wonder of the occasion.

There is however a sudden crisis. The bridesmaids have become indolent in their duty and in the privilege of their calling and have forgotten their purpose. They have fallen asleep and their lamps have gone or are going out.

The significance of this parable centres on the fact that five of the bridesmaids had oil for their lamps, but five did not. Not only that, but this was of vital importance as the foresight of taking oil for their lamps was an essential qualification for their acceptance into taking part in the procession and in the celebrations. Typically of course in the application of the parable it is even more onerous, in that it illustrates the central and essential basis of acceptance into the Kingdom of God, having sufficient oil. What then could this oil represent in this parable, and what is the meaning of taking oil in a vessel? Oil in scripture, that is oil that is obtained from crushing olives, is used in the application or anointing for many purposes, healing, soothing, softening and symbolically as a sign of the conferring of authority or some other benefit on individuals, ceremonies or objects. It was used for instance in the tabernacle in the Old Testament ceremonies, namely in cereal offerings figuratively signifying that it was an essential part of God's salvation for mankind.

In Genesis chapter 28:18 we are given a clear understanding of the figurative meaning of oil in Jacob's use of it. Jacob had just had a dream where God had appeared to Jacob and repeated to him the promise that He had made to his grandfather Abraham. When Jacob woke up he took the stone that he had used as a pillow and poured oil on it, calling it 'Bethel', meaning the house or household of God. The oil signified there then was the spiritual presence of God Himself, the place where He dwells with mankind as in a family. It is a picture that appears consistently many times throughout the Old and New Testament, often implying the grace, beauty or might of God that may reside with and, in respect of individuals, within mankind. It is such a widely-used analogy that any spiritually-minded person would have understood to some degree what Christ was saying when He first spoke the parable.

Here, however, it is used as a fuel for the lamps, as indeed it was in temple worship and in everyday life. The picture is simple though profound; those that had oil with them were in personal possession of the Spirit of God Himself; they were pervaded by His grace and dignity. Thus it is that which is hidden that distinguishes between what is acceptable and what is not. Outwardly they all appeared qualified for their role. All had lamps that at one point were lit, so at that time all would have appeared to be the same. Now the light that is produced when the oil is burned is another picture that we are presented with in this parable. The meaning of this Christ clearly gave earlier in His ministry.

'You are the light of the world... let your light so shine before men, that they may see your good works and glorify your Father in Heaven', our Lord says in Matthew 5:14+16. The witness of our lives in Matthew 5 , however, is in respect of this present era, something that in this parable had fallen into decline while they were waiting for the bridegroom to come. The warning of our Lord at the end of this parable, however, shows that it is important to maintain continuity of testimony until the coming of the Lord, both corporately and individually. The following two parables will illustrate the reason why this is important.

The lamps then represent the witness of all those that own the name of Christ, though it is the grace of Christ that is manifest in us for others to see, this is the oil that is burned in the lamp. In Acts 1:8 our Lord says that you will be witnesses, literally martyrs; you will be a living evidence of me, not just having a profession of faith. A profession is something rather different and is displayed by all the 10 virgins. All had their lamps burning at first while they were waiting. An outward profession of faith, however, is not in itself enough to qualify as a herald of our Lord's return.

The warning here is sinister: all 10 had been chosen to meet and publicize the expected Messiah and all had lost their sense of mission, none are watchful though all are aroused by His coming.

The message here is plain; the waiting naturally tends us towards becoming detached from our purpose. If we are watching for the 'bridegroom', if we are longing for Him to come, then this informs all our actions and interests in the meantime. If we lose that single-mindedness then we become engaged in our own pursuits and our true purpose is neglected, that is we fall asleep. If this happens it could signify one of two things. Either our relationship with Him is faint and vulnerable to becoming superseded by other interests or pressures, or that our affirmation of faith was merely an outward display that did not emanate from the heart.

All had oil at one time, but the test of time shows that it is only those that were ready with a supply of oil who could perform their intended purpose. Those that just 'burned' with enthusiasm for an ideal had no supply of oil; they had oil in their lamps but none in their 'vessels', their hearts; their true motivation lay in their own will, not the Holy Spirit of God. Only those that were genuine, that is that had a supply of oil with them, a depiction of their true affections and purpose, proved to be ready when the moment of truth arrived. The pretenders were now motivated to remedy their remission but now it is too late, their motive now is not pure, it is self-interest that now inspires them, not true devotion.

The five wise virgins are not penalised for their frailty, though our Lord emphasises that vigilance is important. He summarises the significance of the parable right at the end by saying, 'Watch therefore, for you know neither the day nor the hour in which the Son of Man is coming', and immediately continues to explain why.

It is not what we believe or profess that is suitable but that our 'vessel', our hearts, are filled with oil, that is the grace of God Himself, which we can see and know in Christ Himself. Galatians 5:22 gives us a beautiful description of the Spirit that is progressively manifested in us when we are living humbly in Him and He in us. 'You are the light of the world', Christ had said in Matthew chapter 5... 'That men may see your good works and glorify your father in Heaven'.

It is those characteristics described by Paul above as the fruit of the Spirit that are evidenced in our conduct, it is this fruit that is our 'works', as the scripture sometimes describes them, not just the outward actions that can be from any motive.

So it is those described as wise that took oil with them, not just in their lamps; the lamp is that which is visible to others and provides overt testimony, but that which represents having the truth of the testimony is what is in their hearts. It is a grace that is real and profound, one that is essentially from the heart, not one that is fabricated and just affected for ulterior motives. Hence when they needed a true testimony at the coming of the bridegroom they had the genuine faculty to provide the light that would be alone acceptable, the Spirit of Christ Himself.

However when the bridegroom came they were actually asleep; their lamps had gone out. They had oil but no testimony at that time; they were in a state of inertia, their lives were not characterised by the Spirit of Christ until they awoke. The lack of testimony , however, up to the coming of their Lord does not preclude them from going into the celebration.

The qualification for that is not what they profess but that they were in a state of preparation, having the grace of God ready in their hearts. The indication here is of great reassurance; our acceptance does not depend on our own consistency to be accepted into the Kingdom but what God has done for us and in us and through us.

We are saved by grace alone, though that salvation will be evidenced in our disposition and conduct if it is genuine, but not if it is just faked or imagined. This we can only know by being honest with ourselves; again Galatians 5:22 tells us what will be apparent, within and to ourselves and to others.

The foolish however did not have that essential character that fitted them for their role. They did not have the grace, the Spirit of Christ, in their hearts, that is in their real being. They had been called to be bridesmaids but they had never been prepared for the responsibility they were called for. They acted only out of natural motives, but the message here is that we are unable of ourselves to be what we need to be or correctly do what we need to do without the grace that is altogether beyond our own nature. 'Without Me you can do nothing', Christ said in John 15:5. The foolish had appointment and the equipment but lacked the true facility.

They did obtain, but too late; the market indicates morally a position of entreaty, humility and prayer. If grace is to be obtained it takes time and moral exercise. Without His Spirit, when He comes He will not own us.

Their request for a gift of oil from those suitably furnished is refused. It is personal quality that is being spoken of, not an idea or entity. Grace of the heart is not assignable; it has to be obtained by each of us through a state of contrition and supplication. This is only efficacious during this present time of waiting, a time of faith and opportunity; a time when the wise virgins had been to 'the market' to obtain the oil in penitence and faith.

When faith becomes obsolete, the grace that is only acquired through faith cannot then be imparted; when that which we expected transpires, opportunity also ceases. Motive is now one of self-pity, not true affection. 'Many are called but few are chosen,' Matthew 22:14.

It is very important to note, however, that the witness here is that shown at the coming of the king, and continuing into the administration of His Kingdom. The witness at this present time, while the bridesmaids waited, is deficient but they are not criticised for that. It is after the bridegroom comes that their witness is their raison d'être. This is their function in the new administration of the Kingdom of Heaven on Earth, something for which they will ever need that oil.

Christ's final exhortation, however, may seem surprising at first after the message that the parable has brought home so clearly. The foolish bridesmaids are rejected as being counterfeit: 'Watch therefore,' He says. If we are watching, we will be conscious of our relationship with Him and longing to see Him. If we remain alert to the Lord's coming yet do not know Him in truth, then will we be filled with fear or apprehension. We will know then that we need to 'go to the market and buy oil'. If we sleep, that is if we become preoccupied with natural things, then we will become anaesthetized to our spiritual state, whether we are genuine or impostor.

It is not just to make sure , however, that we are eligible for God's Kingdom, but also to be clear in our minds that our salvation is genuine, that we should stay awake, being ready and anticipating our Lord's return at any time. This parable shows us that what we just display of ourselves makes no difference as to our being chosen or not to play a part in Christ's kingdom. It is only by having His Spirit in our hearts can we enter the Kingdom and that is granted by God alone to all who will accept Him in complete humility. However the role that we play in that Kingdom will depend on what our lives have been characterised by in this life, that is if we have also lived according to His Spirit or not. This is explained in the next parable, which describes another aspect of this great event, the coming of our Lord, and needs to be read in conjunction with the first parable to get the full picture of what Christ is saying. In this next parable He tells them another reason why they must be vigilant.

Responsibilities and Loyalties

In the parable of the bridesmaids, the relationship that they had with the bridegroom was one of friendship. They were doing it out of a mark of respect for the fact that they had been asked to perform that honour, because they had been chosen for the privilege, but also out of personal regard and admiration for the bridegroom and such an auspicious event. In the second parable the relationship spoken of is primarily one of servant and master. The attitude that each servant had towards his master is of central importance, but this is not known until it is tested, that is it is not until after the master has gone away does their true regard for their master become apparent. The image shifts here from the waiting for the bridegroom to the waiting for our master's return.

In this parable it is not what we have that is important, that which qualifies us for the kingdom, that which we obtain in the market place, an appropriate spiritual disposition; rather here it is what is given to us by our Lord after we become His servants, after we have properly entered into that Divine relationship. The central theme of this parable is the testing of the servants' fidelity by the master's departure, to prove where their loyalties lay. In the previous parable the theme was proving who was properly qualified for their commission. The servant relationship that we have with Christ, however, is as important as the other aspects and qualities of our relationship spoken of in the scriptures, such as friends of Christ, as brothers and corporately as His bride. As servants, however, this denotes particular responsibilities as well as privileges. In Luke chapter 19 we have a very similar parable to this one, told shortly before this one. The theme is rather different however, as we shall see later.

In this parable here in Matthew the implication is quite clear that the duty of each servant is to work with and develop their master's interests. Each one is given a talent, that is a weight, a balance, a fixed measure of his possessions, a resource for the servant to develop. The point of the parable is to illustrate the fact that Christ gave something to His servants before He left them, something that He continues to do to all those that become His servants. We sometimes speak of natural abilities and skills as 'talents', though what is meant here is rather different in substance and quality.

What Christ preached about and demonstrated through His miracles while on Earth was the nature and substance of the Kingdom of Heaven, which He spoke of then as having arrived. He is the King of that Kingdom which He now shares with His servants, that is, He imparts the treasures of Heaven; spiritual riches such as are alluded to in Christ's sermon on the mount in Matthew chapter 5, and spoken of in various ways in the rest of scripture.

If then we receive a measure of that kingdom, we are, as Paul says in Romans 8:17, 'Joint heirs with Christ.' As also James asks the rhetorical question in chapter 2:5; 'Has God not chosen the poor of this world to be rich in faith and heirs of the Kingdom which He promised to those who love Him?'

Each of us is given a measure of the master's wealth, that is His life in us; that is the substance of the Kingdom of Heaven; 'The Kingdom of Heaven that is within you', Luke 17:21. This corresponds to the oil of the previous parable. It doesn't come in a word, that is in speech, or as a matter of reason, but in power, cp 1 Corinthians 4:20.

'The Kingdom... is righteousness and peace and joy,' Romans 14:17, these are the true treasures of Heaven. It is, however, Christ Himself that mediates that truth, peace and comfort through the presence of the Holy Spirit.

To each of us is given a measure of the master's wealth, a variable quantity according only to the master's discretion it would seem, if we apply this parable as a tangible commodity. Christ, however, is speaking of spiritual issues as He does in all His parables, He is talking here of a 'measure' of His Spirit, the number of talents given, however, relates directly to boundaries of our own being and not to any limited portion of His gift. Each one given a gift according to their measure of faith, cp Romans 12:6

Now five in scripture signifies complete sufficiency of provision, for example David's five stones that he chose to fight Goliath or the five loaves with which Christ fed the 5000. It represents what is complete for every aspect of our personal being, that which is intrinsic. The first servant in this parable shows his master a 100% return on his investment. This is where the life of Christ is fully reproduced in ourselves, if we are completely faithful to our master alone until He returns for us all.

This is the 'measure of the stature of the fullness of Christ' as Paul describes in Ephesians. 4:13.

The second servant, however, received two talents. This does not mean that he only received 40% of what the other servant received. Two in scripture signifies witness or emphasis, that is, testimony of the outward evidence of a life of righteousness, peace and joy; that which is extrinsic rather than what is intrinsic. Again the return is 100%, indicating that the two different amounts given are thematically linked, in spiritual terms they cannot exist independently.

There was however another servant representing a third position. The first two servants showed confidence in and loyalty to their master; they knew and understood him to be entirely faithful and trustworthy. They understood that their master was giving them the opportunity to prove their devotion to him and to exercise their gifted abilities for his benefit.

Those that had the five and two talents traded with their endowment were involved in active promotion of growth of spiritual treasures. It is their faithfulness and conscientiousness that is rewarded, whatever the magnitude of that which was given initially. The reward is by grace alone, not on that which was achieved.

The third servant however shows a spirit of fear, doubt and unbelief, which from our personal perspective can co-exist with a spirit of commitment and affection. We can be ambivalent, not totally committed even in our love for our Lord. It is a spirit of resentment and cynicism that can be a response in every one of us on receiving the gift. What is important is that it is recognised. Ephesians chapter 6 details 'the whole armour of God' whereby we are able to resist the attacks of doubt, sin and sloth, the wiles of Satan; it is through victory in these very things that our faith is fortified and deepened. This servant however despises the gift, 'buries it', ignores it, regarding it as useless. To him it is just one talent that is given, one signifying identity, that which just relates to himself. He displays a negative, self-centred response to being given the gift. He shows no respect for the gift or to him that had given it. His understanding of his master is distorted, bigoted and false. He is resentful and cynical, lacking in faith and truth and so the truth lay buried. It is this that informs his actions and thus determines his fate.

The lazy servant is not condemned for not actively trading with his gift, but he is condemned for not respecting his responsibility and at least passively allowing its effect to prosper by giving it to the bankers, that is giving it credit to 'bring forth fruit', represented in the parable as interest on the money. In the first parable it is not having the oil that is the selected party's failure. In the second it is despising the resource and suppressing it that is his downfall, not allowing it to flourish.

In Luke 19 there is a similar parable that Jesus told of a nobleman that left his servants to go and receive a kingdom for himself. There are similarities to the parable in Matthew 25 but also some profound differences. In Luke the gift is not a quantity, a certain weight but a value, a quality, a sum of money. Typically the gift is the same as in Matthew, which is eternal life in Christ through the Holy Spirit. In Luke, however, it is not faithfulness as an absolute that is in view but the dutifulness or industry of each servant. It is not concerned with the totality of the resource given to each servant but rather the return that each obtains. Here it is an equal amount that is given to each servant, that is, its objective value. Subjectively, however, its value differs to each servant. To the first its value is overwhelming, the significance of ten being that which is comprehensive in effect and typically referring to what bears fruit in every aspect of our lives.

In Matthew the reward is the same for every faithful servant, it is a place in the joy of the kingdom. In Luke it is responsibility towards the master that is rewarded, a reward commensurate with the degree of dutifulness, diligence, tenacity and industry that is demonstrated during the master's absence. In Matthew it is the servant that didn't apply the gift but suppressed it that is excluded; in Luke the responsibility was just hidden, kept safe but not used. Typically in both cases the gift was rejected; it never bore fruit in a changed life and so the consequence is the same, they are branded as hypocrites; they appeared to be respectable 'Christians' to others but had no true affiliation with their master and Lord. In each parable, however, it was the talents and the sum of money that were recognised as having made the increase, not the servants. Any spiritual harvest in our lives is always the work of God, anything that comes from our own doing is of no consequence. Philippians 2:12-13 tells us however how we are involved in this in practice:

'Work out your own salvation with fear and trembling; for it is God who works in you, both to will and to do for His good pleasure.'

There is also in this chapter another parable that Christ tells us that describes who will inherit the Kingdom of Heaven on Earth. The first parable was about those that are chosen to give testimony to the coming king, secondly it is his servant that is in focus; not that these are separate identities necessarily but different qualities of being. The last parable here is also about the spiritual qualities that are needful in those that accede to the kingdom. Here, however, no formal relationship is implied between these individuals and Christ. Strictly speaking this story is not altogether a parable but a simple analogous account of how all individuals will either be chosen to enter into the kingdom or be rejected.

It would have been a common sight in Israel at the time that this story was told to see shepherds separating the sheep and the goats into separate folds at the end of the day. This then is used as an analogy to describe the way that everyone alive at the coming of 'The Son of Man' as king will be divided into one class or into another. The message is very direct and straightforward. Christ replied on one occasion when someone spoke to Him about His natural human family, 'Whoever does the will of My Father in Heaven is My brother and sister and mother,' Matthew 12:50. Those that do the will of the Father have a familial relationship with Christ; they are those that know and love Christ personally and they are a living testimony to that. Without the life of Christ it is impossible to please God, it is only His life that gives testimony to Christ. These then are the brethren of Christ spoken of here, those that demonstrate the character of Christ in their actions and disposition. These are those particularly that are despised and scorned by the majority, those that generally people do not identify with. In the parable those classified as sheep are those that show a familial attitude to those having the character of Christ, those that show an affinity for them by demonstrating compassion on them when they are in any sort of trouble. Typically sheep are those that follow the shepherd and recognise and trust his voice. This is what is being implied here; they follow Christ in disposition and action and therefore are acceptable in the Kingdom.

The kindness given, however, is to 'the least of these My brethren,' Matthew 25:40, not just those that we personally identify with: our 'friends' or those we have any natural connection with. It is a matter of the heart, of character and of disposition and motive. To love and accept my brethren, specifically those that I identify with and who identify with me, is to love and accept me, the king is saying. Those then that display the character of the Kingdom are therefore citizens of it.

The essential nature, that of showing compassion and relieving suffering, is to display that self-sacrificial love, to be motivated alone by it, that is the oil that animates the Kingdom of God. This oil is the life of Christ and that is the common theme of all three of these parables,

Those likened to goats however are of a different disposition. They do not recognise the shepherd or his voice but simply follow their own inclinations. They herd together with their own kind for security, for their own protection, but goats do not follow the shepherd, they must be herded.

They would not have any pity for those whom they regarded as divergent from themselves, albeit that they were suffering in some way. These are those that identify only with their own kind, and lack true faith and compassion, the true oil of the life of Christ; those characteristics that are foreign to our own nature and so cannot be manifest in those that have not the spirit of Christ. They may act with kindness to others in trouble out of other motives, civilised behaviour or what they would be expected to do, but true selfless compassion informing our action comes from the heart, not a sense of obligation. Everyone that loves is born of God and Knows God, 1 John 4:7, whatever their outward character, creed or denomination.

SECTION 4: PART 2

The Kingdom of God Within Us

Revelation Chapter 7
Establishing the Kingdom

In Matthew 25 Christ revealed to His disciples and thence to ourselves what is of fitness to God, that is on what grounds anyone will be acceptable for the Kingdom and what that involves; essentially, the process of the proving and instilling that necessary character within us and in everyone who will inherit the Kingdom of God.

In Revelation 7 the perspective is different. Here we are shown what is fitting from a Divine perspective, here it is the revelation of God's action in salvation, the mind and manner of God's working, seeking always to secure mankind's thankfulness, love and worship, rather than imposing judgement. Here the intricacies of salvation are revealed, how the receiving of the Holy Spirit, as a central element of salvation, works in us to create that work of grace that is essential to salvation. In this passage it is revealed in practical terms how God will save a great multitude through the sealing of His servants. Underlying this, however, a deeper truth is revealed, the significance of the 12 tribes enumerated here, helping us to understand in a nutshell the grounds and principles of our salvation; what it is that we are saved from and the benefits that we receive in their place.

The chapter starts, however, with the words 'after these things', that is, the outcome of the 6 seals, the actions that must work to the demonstration of Christ's authority and the revelation of the need for that authority. We recall that the breaking of the first six seals relates to this present age, as the effects of opening the seals would seem as being typical of every age, the last two millennia in particular.

Before the breaking of the seventh seal, however, which we consider in part 7 of this section, there is an interlude explaining what is to transpire during the breaking of this last seal. This will be the end of this present age, being a period of calm followed by an unprecedented time of chaos.

The four corners of the Earth in v1 is a figure of that which encompasses the whole Earth. The four angels are the Divine agents appointed to hold back the breaking up of the natural order of the world so that the new order can be introduced. The winds of change, the forces of destruction, are held in abeyance until God's final and dramatic act in salvation, which is described in chapter 7, is completed. The Earth, sea and trees here could mean symbolically the natural order of life, the mass of humanity that is, and the functional vitality of life overall, all that which will suffer as the trumpets are sounded at the breaking of the seventh seal.

It is then that the angel with the seal of the living God from the east, that is from the direction of the rising sun (which gives us light and understanding), explains what is about to happen, how God will use His chosen people on Earth, His servants, to effect His purpose. They are sealed on their foreheads. Whether this is a physical mark or just a symbolic expression does not matter; it is the significance, the meaning of this mark, that is important to consider. The word 'sealed' is used a lot in the Revelation and means preserved, confirmed, closed or finalised; as it is the seal of God here it is therefore irrevocable. They are sealed; their status and position cannot fail, so it is completely secure. It is all five angels that carry this out, meaning that they are also charged with protecting them from the effects of the judgements that they will later administer, Revelation 9:4; cp Ezekiel 9:4-6. However, as the mark is on the foreheads it could also imply that they are endowed with constancy of mind, faith or testimony; that they are being marked out as distinct in character, as a witness during the chaos that is about to encroach upon the Earth, cp Revelation 14:1.

The total number is given as being 144,000, that is, 12,000 from each of the 12 tribes to whom the promise of Abraham was delivered. Now 12 symbolizes the Divine administration amongst mankind; twelve thousand would suggest that administrative function in the whole compass of God's government on Earth, details of which are reflected in the meaning of the names of the tribes which we will consider here and in the next few parts of this section.

Twelve for example is the number that features in the heavenly city New Jerusalem at the end of the Revelation. 1000 however represents the whole of a group or class, for example, 'the cattle on a thousand hills' in Psalm 50:10. Here perhaps what is being suggested is that this is the full extent of God's work and testimony in mankind. The promise to Abraham was that through him, that is through his progeny, would all the nations of the Earth be blest. The book of Hebrews points out that this was fulfilled through Christ alone, as the one that procured salvation for all. This is consistently born out through the prophecies of Isaiah, for example, that the blessing of the nations would be through Christ, also many other Old and New Testament texts do the same.

What then are the tribes of Israel doing here as a prelude to the salvation of a multitude of all the nations? They are primarily of course as God's servants representing and advancing that salvation, but there is also a deeper significance in that the names of the tribes allude to the plan of salvation itself.

Further down and in the next two piece of this section an outline of the meaning of all the names of the twelve tribes is given, together with the rudimentary significance of those meanings from a spiritual perspective. The order that they are given here is not the same as their birth order, nor indeed does the list here coincide with the tribes as listed in the Old Testament. The reason for that is simply that the birth order is not relevant here, though their name meanings here are in respect to their service in salvation, the bringing of salvation to countless numbers throughout the world. Chapter 7 then is broadly a succinct summary not only of all that God gives in salvation to mankind, but also the way that it is accomplished and demonstrated through the testimony of His servants. This chapter then is not just an account of what will happen as a result of this time of trouble, described here as the great tribulation, but also the full character of the spiritual harvest that God will effect through it and as a principle in the way that God acts in Salvation throughout time. This is of course relevant to us.

The polarising effect of these troubles will be that everyone will have to show allegiance, either to the evil beast and to receive his mark, or reject the beast and choose what is right and to honour God. The whole world will be in awe of the beast (see chapter 17:8) except those that are written in the book of life; they will suffer great persecution and martyrdom. This choice will transcend all religious and social differences; there will be no middle ground either.

This group of 144,000 are referred to again at the start of chapter 14. Here further information is given regarding them in the context of their association with Christ, specifically in His position of authority in the Kingdom; that is standing on Mount Zion. Here they are said to be those redeemed from the Earth, the first from among mankind. These are virgins in the spiritual sense in that their dedication to the lamb is absolute, undefiled by any other matter. They are true Israelites indeed, like Nathaniel, in whom was no deceit, John 1:47. Do these servants then represent the church, as some have supposed? To ask the question misses the point; scriptural symbolism and allegories always represents some spiritual truth; they are not enigmatic riddles that require a good imagination to decipher. They are simple, plain truths that are expressed consistently in analogical form. Often the meaning is explained, as Christ did for His disciples when He told Parables. In other places where the image describes a particular thing, albeit an abstract entity, like the great prostitute in chapter 17, the text then tells us simply what is being portrayed; the metaphor used there for example simply describes the immoral character of the world system.

Here, however, it is Israelites that are spoken of, we must not assume that they enigmatically represent some other group without clear indication or sound authority; this is the word of God. Paul, however, does explain in Romans chapter 9 that the true spiritual seed of Abraham are those that are faithful, like those virgins in verse 4 of Revelation chapter 14. It is their qualities that are an example to us and that is what is important to us, as being essential features of all God's servants, of every age or era, of all those who would follow the Lamb wherever He goes, without equivocation.

Now the scene of the 144,000 and the next scene of the great multitude of those saved during the time of great trouble are interposed between the breaking of the 6th and 7th seals. What then is the significance of this and what is the relationship between the two groups?

- Implicitly the 144,000 were sealed to shield them from the harm that is to come upon all upon the Earth. It is during this time that the 'great multitude from every nation' is saved.

- Both groups have a special relationship with the Lamb.

- Those from the twelve tribes are inherently pure, the multitude however are made pure.

- The servants, verse 3, impart God's plan of salvation,

representing the blessings that God promised Abraham that his progeny would bring to all the nations. The great multitude is the recipient of that blessing.

- In this case their setting together is not coincidental; clearly both scenes are set from a heavenly, that is spiritual, perspective and signify what God is doing practically through all the trauma that is being acted out on Earth. This chapter describes what the revelation of Jesus Christ will achieve spiritually, that is in the hearts and souls of individuals. The details of the distress that occurs in previous and subsequent chapters is the account of how it will be achieved. Chapter 7 then gives us the Divine rationale for or benefit from all that chaos.

This then is the fulfilment of God's promise to Abraham, but adding detail and perspective to that original promise as described in Genesis 12:3. This blessing was of course procured and sealed by Christ alone, as Paul points out in Galatians 3:16, but here the servants of God are the living testimony to what that blessing extends to.

Salvation is bestowed to people from every nation, tribe, people and language, that is, it includes every ethnic and cultural group. They are all clothed with white robes signifying that they are unadulterated by any pollution; that is anything that is tainted by sin or the natural mind. It is a universal feature of salvation that we can only stand before God having been 'dressed' in the Divine life of Christ. The graphic scene here then gives us a picture of the effects of salvation. If the servants of God, the twelve tribes, testify to what God confers in salvation from a spiritual dimension, here we see what is achieved from a practical standpoint.

There are, however, other ways that these two groups of people are similar. First we note that the response of the multitude, the basis of their relationship with God, is one of praise, that is, gratitude and worship. They exclaim with a loud voice, that is, presenting a powerful witness that salvation is to the honour of God and the Lamb alone; 'salvation to our God who sits on the throne,' that it is He that has effected it in justice and in power and that secondly salvation is attributed to the Lamb who Himself performed the work. Praise is a universal feature of all the redeemed, that their hearts are filled with love and praise to the one that loved them enough to make possible a way for them to come into such a relationship. This blessing is a particular feature of the servants of God as we come to consider the tribe of Reuben.

Then we see what are the rewards of salvation. He who sits on the throne dwells among them; it is a place of privilege and acceptance for them. The suffering that they have endured during the time of the great rebellion is now contrasted with a place where only peace can exist. There is no suffering or sorrow either, God will 'wipe away all tears'; their faithfulness in tribulation is rewarded. Persecuted no more, the Lamb will shepherd them, leading them to fountains of living water, that is in a state of continuous satisfaction, cp John 4:14. This also is a feature of the servants of God, the tribe of Manasseh for example represents that blessing of release from all the bondage and affliction that is past.

The manner of salvation is the same in every age from a basic position, although the outward religious form may differ. They stand before the throne, that is in absolute righteousness; salvation is the complete removal of all stain of sin, their robes are washed in the blood of the lamb. This is a profound description of a spiritual process; we are 'accepted in the beloved' as the name Simeon conveys. Not only is the death of Christ the only way God could effect salvation for us, but we note that we also must involve ourselves in the process; they 'washed their robes and made them white' indicating an active cooperation in their own salvation, cp Philippians. 2:12-13.

They also have a purpose in salvation, to exalt and honour their God, signalled by the palm branches in their hands, actively and publicly attributing prosperity, strength and eminence to the God of their salvation. This is their special relationship with Him. For this reason then they are qualified to 'stand before the throne of God and serve Him day and night in the temple'. This is their role, to serve God in the sphere of His dwelling among mankind. Levi presents that blessing of being at one with the Lord as Leah felt she would be with her husband. Here it is the great multitude that knows that special relationship in their priestly role, typified in the sons of Levi in the Old Testament.

Next there is another character that appears on the scene, one of the elders that first appeared in chapter 4. His role is to enlighten us as to how this group came into salvation, one that himself had been redeemed at another time, see chapter 5:9, but one that had completed the course and now understood the principles of God's ways. He displays the spiritual maturity to have understanding of the physical process of salvation. God made the way possible but the way of salvation is one of difficulty as was Pilgrim's journey in John Bunyan's 'Pilgrim's Progress'. 'These are they that have come out of the great tribulation'. It is through many tribulations we enter the kingdom of God, Acts 14:22. Naphtali presented the same picture from a slightly different perspective in the earlier verses of chapter 7; the name means 'wrestling.'

We then come to another group that joins the elders and the four living creatures in full appreciation of the unique power and majesty of God. The angels, the ministering spirits of God that fulfil His will through Heaven and Earth. Angels, elders and the four creatures can all appreciate the blessing that the multitude has received. 'Amen! Blessing and glory and wisdom, thanksgiving and honour and power and might be to our God forever and ever', the angels say, showing their response to and insight into salvation and the glory and nature of God. Their appreciation is fuller and more extensive than that of the multitude.

It becomes apparent then that not only are there several different group identities in this chapter, but they all have distinct characters and purposes within the Kingdom, in salvation and in the unveiling of the King. It is to become sidetracked, however, if we just consider their identities from a human perspective and miss what the scriptures are telling us. It is the spiritual quality of these individuals that is significant in understanding what is the mind of God for His creation. Salvation is sufficient for all mankind, though not all will appreciate what it is and profit from it. Those that do may differ in the extent to which they enter into the glories of the King Himself; these are spiritual blessings that we can only become acquainted with in Christ. 'Blessed be the God and Father of our Lord Jesus Christ,' though, 'who has blessed us with every spiritual blessing in the Heavenly places in Christ,' Ephesians 1:3.

SECTION 4: PART 3

The Heavenly Life Within Us

Revelation Chapter 7 vv 4-8
Establishing the Kingdom

The Old Testament is full of stories, images and rituals that illustrate how God works according to spiritual principles in creation and in particular with mankind. In Hebrews chapter 8 verses 4 - 5 for example there is an explanation how that the old covenant that God made with Israel was the archetype of the covenant that God would bring in through Christ.

'There are priests who offer the gifts according to the Law,
Who serve the copy and shadow of the heavenly things'

As Moses was Divinely instructed when he was about to make the tabernacle.
For He said, 'see that you make all things
According to the pattern shown to you on the mountain.'
The tabernacle and all the ceremonial law in the Old

Covenant then were a visual pattern of the New Covenant, that is Testament, where God would 'write His Law upon the hearts' of believers. This new covenant then was of a spiritual character so that mankind could keep His Law instinctively, something that under the Old Covenant mankind had not been capable of doing to the standard that was necessary. This takes us back to the parables of Matthew 25 again, which symbolically signified that it is only through the indwelling of the Holy Spirit that we can please God, for it is the presence of the Holy Spirit that writes God's Laws on our hearts, giving us the power and predisposition to keep them; as Paul says in Galatians 5:16, 'Walk in the Spirit and you shall not fulfil the lust of the flesh'.

Likewise we find that the account in the Old Testament of the trials of Israel from their time in Egypt until their coming into the Promised Land is a detailed analogy of the experiences of the Christian life. The time of Israel in Egypt is symbolic of our living in the world, as a holy chosen people living in slavery to a worldly system. The Passover in Egypt was the time when, through the sacrifice of a lamb, each family of the children of Israel was delivered from slavery in Egypt. They then wandered in the wilderness, where they received the Law of God, both their civil law and the religious law as referred to above.

Likewise in the New Testament Christ is sacrificed for us to deliver us from the corruption of the world and the sin that is inherent in us. In 1 Corinthians 5:7 Paul uses this analogy, speaking about Christ our Passover being sacrificed for us as a direct parallel. In that particular verse it is in the specific context as regards to our practical dissociation with anything or anyone that continues to live in a sinful way.

Symbolically the picture is of the believers coming out from Egypt; the children of Israel are lead out through the Red Sea into the wilderness, which is referred to by Paul in 1 Corinthians 10:2 as a figure of the Christian discipline of the conquering of our sinful nature in baptism. The symbolism then extends to our wandering through the wilderness of this life, no longer at home here, but at the same time assimilating God's Divine nature as the Holy Spirit 'Writes the Law of God in our hearts'. The antitype was when Israel wandered in the dessert where they were given the law of God, externally on tablets of stone.

The tabernacle which was 'a sanctuary that I may dwell among them', as it is portrayed in Exodus 25:8, the Ark of the Covenant particularly in which the Law resided, represents Christ, the only one that ever fulfilled the Law of God completely. In the crossing of the Jordan, which represents death, the waters are held back by the 'Ark of the Covenant', signifying that death can no longer have power over us; that is now we can be free spiritually from the power of sin, both morally now and eventually, when we die physically as resurrection will follow at the coming of our Lord. The 'Ark of the Covenant' represents the Law that now indwells our hearts as Christ indwells us.

The book of Joshua in the Old Testament tells us of the battles that Israel endured to conquer their Promised Land, that they fought in faith, Heb. 11:30, trusting in God and giving us an archetype of the spiritual battles we face to enter into and possess that heavenly land, even that heavenly inheritance that we can know in Christ. It is an outline of this heavenly inheritance that we are given in Ephesians chapter 1, which chapter we will compare with our text in Revelation 7.

We now come back to those verses in Revelation 7 and to what is represented here, in verses 4 to 8. It is in the servants of God here that signify the names of the twelve tribes of Israel to whom the Promised Land was divided among. We started this piece in Hebrews with the Old Covenant being a shadow of the New; we now come to another aspect of that shadow, a picture of God's detailed plan of salvation for mankind, the substance indeed of that New Covenant.

The story begins with Abraham's grandson, Jacob, or Israel as he was later called, and his marriage to Laban's two daughters, Leah and Rachel, together with their respective handmaidens, that is their personal servants, also given to them by Laban. The names of the twelve tribes of Israel get their names from the twelve sons of Jacob, that were then born to him from his wives and their maids.

Christ said to His disciples in John 15, 'I am the vine, you are the branches. He who abides in Me, and I in him, bears much fruit.' This is an antitype of the picture of the marriage relationship, in the scripture as a whole, but in particular here of Jacob, his wives and the children born to him.

The sexual relationship in particular, being the most intimate and devoted part of marriage, the becoming 'of one flesh', is when we are united in a common bond and attitude to each other. This is an illustration or a type of the profound relationship that we can know with Christ. The 'children', that is spiritual qualities then that are 'born' of that relationship are the fruit or qualities that come from our bond with Christ through the indwelling of the Holy Spirit in our hearts and lives.

'Rachel and Leah, the Two that Built the House of Israel'

Ruth 4:11

Jacob's two wives are typical of the church as a whole, though more immediately as regards to believers individually and two aspects of our personality, so we can see immediately how significant their story could potentially be to us. A modern concept of marriage is that of two partners of equal standing, the scriptural concept though is one in line with the culture of that day, that the wife lived to serve the interests of her husband alone, which is how our attitude to Christ will be if it is truly healthy. Now Leah was the first wife that Jacob married; you will remember the story in Genesis 29, how he intended to marry her sister Rachel. Leah, her name meaning 'weary', is typical of our innate human consciousness, our mind, emotions and bodies, weak and susceptible, (all that we are humanly speaking, that is apart that is from our innate sinful nature, the nature that the scripture refers to as 'the flesh', the nature we are by default).

Rachel on the other hand, her name meaning 'a lamb', represents that spirit within us which is born of God as having His nature, a Divine essence, that which is beloved of Christ as Rachel was of Jacob. This is that being, or spirit, which is born of God by His Spirit, it isn't that Holy Spirit in Himself but that which is part of us, created in us by God and that can relate directly to the Spirit of God, as Adam did in the garden of Eden before his disobedience. The handmaidens then given to Jacob's wives are also part of our beings that serve both our innate sensibilities (Leah) and also the newborn spirit (Rachel) within us.

There is also another beautiful picture in the scripture of the marriage relationship, found in the Song of Songs, the title of it suggesting that it is the most profound and joyful natural experience we can know. There is much detail in that poem that accords with that deep, yet all-embracing relationship that both we can have in Christ and that He has in us, one that grows in beauty and completeness as we progress in the spiritual life in Christ.

The twelve sons that are then born to the wives, just as they go on to form the character of Israel as a nation, so it is in our relationship with Christ, in its close intimacy of being both 'in Him' and 'He in us.' The names given to the twelve sons that are born to Jacob characterise all the blessings that God would bestow on us in Christ. These are those spiritual blessings that are outlined in the first chapter of Paul's letter to the Ephesians and then developed in the letter's later chapters. These blessings then are also suggested in the meaning of the regions of the Promised Land as they take their names from the sons of Israel.

The two wives of Jacob, together with their maids, then represent different aspects of our being in our union with

Christ. Christ said, 'Come to me all you who labour and are heavy laden and I will give you rest,' Matthew 11:28. It is only when we are weary of ourselves that we can come to Christ and make Him our refuge, in our appreciation of Him with us. Jacob worked seven years to win and marry Leah. Leah then denotes our conscious being, our souls, minds and emotions. Her maid servant Zilpah's name means 'myrrh dripping,' signifying the 'spice' or pleasure that permeates our souls and give life value for us. By the Holy Spirit that pleasure is so much purer, fuller and more abiding than the pleasures of this life. It is our awareness that we have an inheritance from God, His glory in us, and this will fill us with praise. This is our reward for first trusting in Him. In this way we serve God in true praise and worship.

Jacob then worked another seven years before he could marry Rachel. The name Rachel means 'a lamb', a meek and unassuming disposition, that same disposition which enables us to possess the Kingdom of God. It is then the Spirit of Christ Himself in us that causes us to have 'sons' that is to gain those qualities that make us beneficial to Him and His Kingdom. Rachel's maid Bilhah then serves that disposition; her name means 'tender,' signifying our submission and susceptibility to His will, leading to the knowledge that our desire to be complete in Christ is fulfilled.

A table showing the figurative meaning of the wives of Jacob, and their personal servants; all figurative of our make-up and the meaning of their sons' names born to them.

Bride and maid	What this represents about us	The Aspect of our personalities that give Birth in our Relationship with Christ	Meaning of the Sons' name born to them
Leah	Our Human Consciousness, Our Souls,	Meaning - **Weary**; weak and vulnerable, with a constant desire to be loved as Rachel was; it represents our innate being, our normal thoughts and feelings; our consciousness of our relationship with Christ	• Praise • Behold a Son • Hearing • Joined
Zilpah Leah's maid	The pleasure and joy that gives life value	Meaning - **Myrrh Dripping**, (cp S.S. 5:13) used for perfume, preservation and pleasure – symbolising the Divine pleasures that can be manifest in human awareness – first manifest in Christ and given to us by His Spirit.	• Fortune • Happy • Reward • Dwelling
Rachel	Our New Being, Born of water and the word	Meaning - **A lamb**; meek and trusting in nature. As Rachel, it has a constant desire to be fruitful and represents our new life, 'the Lamb' bearing 'increaser' (Joseph) and true 'spiritual sonship' (Benjamin); epitomizing our Divine function.	• Increaser • Son of my Sorrow/ Son of my Right Hand
Bilhah Rachel's Maid	That new spirit born within us	Meaning – **Tender**; our susceptibility to spiritual transformation through grace,	• Wrestling • Justice

Throughout the scriptures specific significance is attached to the meanings of names. The multitude of names given to Christ throughout the scriptures for example, describing His Divine and human character, bear this out. Many place names in the Old Testament indicate the special significance or character of that place. Here it is no different and the names of the tribes all indicate the significance and character of the Promised Land, both historically from the point of view of Israel, but more especially here where the promised land is a metaphor for the heavenly state that we can experience in Christ. It is typically the character of and experience of God's detailed plan of salvation for mankind in every generation.

Now the tribes as listed in verses 5-8 of Revelation 7 are as follows in the order they are given there, with their meaning and why those names were given as recorded for us in Genesis chapters 29 and 30; this would have been about B.C. 1752. The names of the tribes are all mentioned individually in Revelation 7 and so they are each ostensibly significant, so let's look first at the meanings of the names of the sons of Jacob and why they were given. You will note that their birth order is quite different, but that is not relevant in the context here. It is the order of the meaning of their names as given that is significant.

Tribe	Son of Jacob	Name Meaning	Significance of name
Judah	4th, by Leah	Praise	Leah's last son: 'Now I will praise the Lord'
Reuben	1st, by Leah	Behold a Son	'The Lord has surely looked on my affliction, now therefore will my husband love me'
Gad	7th, by Zilpah	The seer, lot, fortune	Because she said, 'A troop comes'
Asher	8th, by Zilpah	Happy	'I am happy for the daughters will call me blessed'
Naphtali	6th, by Bilhah	Wrestling	'I have wrestled with my sister and indeed I have prevailed'
Manasseh	Eldest of son of Joseph	Causing forgetfulness	'For God has made me forget all my toil and all my father's house' Genesis. 41:51
Simeon	2nd by Leah	Hearing	'The Lord hath heard that I am unloved'
Levi	3rd, by Leah	Joined	'My husband will become attached to me', because I have born him three sons'
Issachar	9th, by Zilpah	Reward	'God has given me my wages'
Zebulun	10th, by Zilpah	Dwelling	'Now my husband will dwell with me'
Joseph	11th by Rachel	Increaser	'God has taken away my reproach'
Benjamin	12th by Rachel	Son of my right hand	His mother died in childbirth naming him Ben-oni 'Son of my sorrow'

Now the list of names that we are given here does not coincide entirely with the tribal areas of the land as defined in the book of Joshua either; there is an important reason for this. The Promised Land was a physical inheritance, given to the children of Israel alone. The whole land was ruled by the Law as given to Moses, both the civil law and the religious law. Now the religious law was a detailed instruction regarding the atonement for sin and was in itself a picture of how salvation would be effected by Christ at His first coming for all mankind of every age.

The Promised Land was given to the families that descended from Israel's sons, each being allocated a particular region, though each region is also a picture of the various parts of the spiritual inheritance that is given to all those that are in Christ, those that have received His life through His Holy Spirit. There is however an essential difference. The old promise, that covenant made with Moses, was governed by the Law. The new Covenant or promise that is fulfilled in Christ is administered by grace alone. It is now the Life of Christ in us that fulfils God's Law in us; it is the only thing of significance. The life that we lived to our own ideals and ourselves is gradually replaced as we grow more in Him and He in us. This is our being joined to Christ, enjoying His life as joint heirs of Christ, becoming His brethren and therefore sons of God. Now 'sonship' in scripture is very specific in its character and inherent in the culture of that time. Typically in the New Testament it is a relationship with God that we all share, both male and female for in Christ there is no difference. It is not right therefore to talk of us as sons and daughters of God because that would imply that women have an inferior status in Christ as daughters did in the culture of that time. It is a case where political correctness trips itself up.

The list here in Revelation 7 is telling us, not about the physical land of Israel, but the connotation of the tribal names themselves and the principles of the inheritance that anyone may inherit in Christ, that is a spiritual inheritance; each name signifying an aspect of that life of Divine character. There is a direct parallel in the New Testament in the first chapter of the book of the Ephesians, where Paul outlines the elements of this spiritual inheritance. That chapter is really the counterpoint of what we have in summary in the Revelation. Ephesians however presents what God gives us in Christ; it defines those treasures only found in Him and so they are presented just from a Divine perspective. The position we have in Revelation is presented from our own perspective, the actual experience of that spiritual inheritance that we have in Christ, what that Divine life means to us experientially. A point for point comparison is therefore helpful which we now come to in the next piece of this study.

Jacob's fifth son Dan in Genesis 30:6 appears to have been replaced by Manasseh in the List in Revelation. In the second half of the book of Joshua the land of Canaan is divided among the twelve tribes, though there the tribe of Levi does not inherit an area of land but inherits the priesthood and tithes from the rest of Israel. That leaves eleven tribal areas. The tribe of Joseph, however, receives two areas, assigned to his two sons Manasseh and Ephraim, so making twelve areas in all. The land assigned to Dan, however, was never conquered from the Philistines, which has spiritual significance for us see part 4d. This is why in Revelation 7 Dan and Ephraim do not appear, though Joseph and Levi do.

SECTION 4: PART 4

'Christ in Us, the Hope of Glory,' Colossians 1:27

Revelation Chapter 7: 4-8
And Ephesians Chapter 1: 3-10

Establishing the Kingdom

This study is about the meanings of the names of the tribes that we met in the previous piece and how that summarises our deepest spiritual union with God as our Father. These 12 tribes seem to classify into three groups of four each. As mentioned in more detail in part 3 of this section, the meaning of the tribal names summarise these blessings from our own perspective. The description of those blessings in Ephesian's chapter 1 are the counterpart from a Divine perspective.

The first tribe mentioned here is Judah, meaning praise. Our first encounter then with the heavenly realm will be for us to be filled with appreciation of God, to be filled with awe and praise at who God is and what He has done for us. It is praise alone that lifts us into that heavenly realm through God's Holy Spirit filling our hearts and consciousness with an outpouring of admiration and honour. When we come to Ephesians 1:6 however, we then see that it was in fact God Himself that first selected us for that purpose, to be 'to the praise of the Glory of His grace'. The joy that it gives to be filled with a heart overflowing in love and worship then is God given by His graciousness and a heart of thankfulness and humility that the God and sustainer of all things should favour us so.

The next tribe in Revelation 7 is Reuben, named so because he was the expression of Leah's delight at having given birth to a son and how she saw that as bringing the fullness of relationship with her husband that she longed for. Our encounter with the heavenly realm is to be preoccupied with the understanding of our privileged position that we enjoy as the adopted sons of God and the unhindered access that we can realize in coming into and enjoying the glory of His presence. From a Divine perspective however, the parallel in Ephesians is in chapter 1 verse five, explaining that in fact that it was God's choice to 'predestine us to adoption as sons by Jesus Christ to Himself'. Again we realise the reality of our standing in Christ. Maybe it is some time before we appreciate the significance of the fact that it was not anything that we did but that it was God alone that first selected us and that is the only reason we can know that wonderful assurance and confidence in our standing and realise that our security doesn't depend upon ourselves. This is why we can know Him as and call Him 'Father', because He begot us; a spiritual new birth; John 3:3.

Thirdly then we begin to grasp the substance of the life in Christ, how it is that we are changed to be like God Himself in nature as true sons and know the wealth of that relationship as a result. Leah's appreciation in type was 'behold a troop comes', this being her seventh son, albeit by her maid; as she could foresee a material blessing that would result from the birth of her son Gad, calling her son 'fortune'. In Ephesians it is the realisation that we were 'chosen in Him before the foundation of the world to be holy and without blame before Him in love'. It is our growing experience to have God's own nature, holy and righteous and loving, and the unrivalled rapport that it brings with God Himself, to know from experience the 'fortune' of the richness of quality of that life, being 'holy and without blame before Him in love'

Jacob's next son in this passage is Asher, that is, 'happy', denoting Leah's response to the birth of another son. In Ephesians one it is in verse three that Paul exults, 'Blessed be the God and Father of our Lord Jesus Christ who has blessed us with every spiritual blessing in the heavenly places in Christ.' This blessing is simply that radiant emotion, that 'joy unspeakable and full of glory'. It is a state of complete contentment with all that God gives us in Christ, such that nothing else even compares with it. That, however, comes directly from God Himself blessing us, which is why it transcends anything that transpires from self-fulfilment or satisfaction from the advantages of this life.

Now although all this is undoubtedly true, it is not true to say that life in Christ now is one of unmitigated bliss. That state will one day be ongoing when we meet Christ face to face, but it is not something that we attain to instantly, it is something we come into progressively. In the biblical type, we do not just walk into the Promised Land and life after that is perfect; 'possession of the land' is an on-going course. The land first has to be conquered which is the image that we are presented with in the next four tribal names of the Land.

In the first four areas of the spiritual kingdom we had a summary of all that we can obtain in Christ through the grace and favour of God alone. You will note that the order in Ephesians is in reverse to the order in Revelation in respect of these 'tribes', that is because our understanding progresses into appreciation of the depths of what God has already planned and provided.

The next four regions of the heavenly land that we discover is not what we receive by grace alone as an absolutely free gift, but the actual experiences that we are actively engaged in as we appropriate those gifts and the depth of meaning that they then give to us. This involves our daily walk with Christ, seeking ever to 'walk worthy of the calling with which you were called;' Ephesians 4:1.

Verse seven of Ephesians one says, 'In Him we have redemption, through His blood'. This is the work that Christ did for us once at Calvary; this is God acting on our behalf. Redemption literally means God 'buying us back' from the life that was alienated from Him into companionship with Himself. From our perspective, however, it is something that we actively participate in, it is not just part of a belief system or something that we only give mental assent to. Nor is it just a single act of faith; it may commence that way from the viewpoint of our experience but it is an ongoing process throughout life, through faith, as each of us is changed into the image of Christ. Faith then is substantiated or corrected by experience. This is how we mature spiritually in faith and understanding.

Naphtali is the first tribe that we have in this next group in Revelation seven; his name means wrestling, as Rachel, his adopting mother, said: 'I have wrestled with my sister (that is Leah) and have prevailed.' This is what redemption means for us in practice in our daily lives. Paul tells us to 'work out our own salvation with fear and trembling, for it is God who works in you both to will and to do for His good pleasure', Philippians 2:13. We have to 'work out' what God works in, in practice through the trials of life and also through study and meditation of the scriptures. Wrestling is a very poignant picture of both aspects of that process. Our Lord said 'strait', that is restrained, 'is the gate that leads to eternal life'; it is not easy but always a struggle. Paul said, 'I discipline my body and bring it into subjection', in 1 Corinthians 9:27; and again in Ephesians 6:12 that we wrestle not against flesh and blood but against principalities and powers etc. We are always in conflict with all these, the course of this world, with our natures and with the spiritual powers that impinge upon us, but in all these things 'we are more than conquerors through Him who loved us', Romans 8:37. The redemption then that we have in Christ through His blood, Ephesians 1:7 is a life of wrestling but also a life of victory as we can only prevail as we prove the power of God in our lives. 'His blood' then has a double meaning; firstly it is through His death that we have His life and secondly the wrestling is also the putting to death of our innate nature, the flesh, so that Christ can be formed in us, that is our innate conscious being that Rachel's sister Leah typified. This is stepping out on the path of faith, as Pilgrim did in Pilgrim's Progress.

Verse seven then goes on to say, 'the forgiveness of sins, according to the riches of His grace'. This is not the same thing as redemption; though it is essentially dependent on and subsequent to it of course. Sins here are all our acts, thoughts and feelings that are contrary to the mind and character of God, every imagination that is motivated from our own self-will, self-promotion and self-interest; everything that separates us from an intimate relationship with God. 'Sins' are all those things that result from our innate sinful nature. Now God is able and willing to forgive us all those transgressions, past, present and future, but as in the other provinces of our life in Christ, there is always our own response to that.

This correlates with the next region of the Promised Land we come to, Manasseh, who was Joseph's second son. His name means 'causing forgetfulness', because as Joseph, elevated to a position of power and dignity, realised that his life of slavery and imprisonment in Egypt, such as was the whole nation of Israel to suffer after Joseph's death, was now for Joseph past with no more influence on him. Slavery and imprisonment in Egypt is a type in scripture of our enslavement to sin, the guilt, regret, doubt, shame and bitterness etc. of which we can be freed from in Christ; as Paul says regarding his own background, 'forgetting those things which are behind and reaching forward to those things which are ahead', Philippians 3:13. Forgetfulness then is a synonym in this context for the complete freedom from the oppression that sin has on our minds, freedom from that moral imperative. Thus in a practical way we are both redeemed spiritually from and freed practically from the tyranny of sin.

We then come to Simeon, that is hearing, as his mother said, 'the Lord has heard that I am unloved, He has therefore given me this son also'. Now Leah's complaint was that she felt unloved by her husband, just as the nation of Israel felt forgotten by God during their years of exile or occupation; as we can feel ourselves at times when passing through difficult times, times of discouragement, despair and suffering, for example, and always, if our life of faith is healthy, in longing for a fuller and closer relationship with our Lord. To Leah her joy was the fulfilment of an emotional need, the hope that her husband would now love her because of what she had done for him, given him another heir. From our own deeply personal experience in knowing Christ the longing that our hearts have for a deeper and fuller union with Christ also 'bears fruit' as we know that we are in tune with Him and that He hears us. Thus, like Leah who continued to produce children, we also grow in our resemblance to our Lord as we grow in grace and in the knowledge of our Lord and Saviour Jesus Christ. With God however, our whole state has already been fully implemented, in verse 6 of Ephesians 1, 'by which He made us accepted in the beloved'. It was God who put that desire to know Him in our hearts and then waits patiently as we learn to fully enter in to that relationship that God has planned for us.

Finally in this group we come to Levi, the tribe that was given the priesthood instead of a region of land as their inheritance in the land promised by God to Abraham. Now

Levi means 'joined' as Leah said, 'now this time my husband will become attached to me, because I have borne him three sons'. At every stage of our progress to 'inhabit the heavenly land' we are inclined to think that we have arrived and that in future our lives will be in tune with our calling, not realising how much further we still have to go. This life is ever growing more into a greater apprehension of and closer attachment, a joining to our Lord. In verses 8-10 of Ephesians 1 we realise this from a Divine viewpoint in 'making known the mystery of his will... that He might gather together in one all things in Christ'. This then goes way beyond our own narrow horizon of just our relationship with Christ, but it extends through Him to our relationship with each other and indeed all (things) in Heaven and on Earth. 'All things' in verse 10 is the same meaning as in verses 11 and 22, suggesting that this includes not only each other but also the whole of creation.

There remain then four more tribes that outline the blessings that we obtain only in Christ, which we come to now in the next part.

SECTION 4: PART 5

If Anyone is in Christ He is a New Creation, 2 Corinthians 5:17

Revelation Chapter 7: 5-8
And Ephesians Chapter 1: 11-22

Establishing the Kingdom

We turn now to the four remaining tribes that outline the blessings we obtain only when we are in Christ and through Him alone. The first of these tribes mentioned in Revelation 7 is Issachar, the first of this final group of four that refer not primarily to our special privilege that we can enjoy in Christ or to the course of our union with Him but now to a complementary view, our appreciation of the riches that Christ has in us, something which the scripture tells us we can be fully cognisant of. It remains for us to prove it empirically in our own hearts, awesome as the idea is. As Christ is established in us, so it is that His inheritance, which is part of His Kingdom, is formed within us. This is how it works.

In verse 11-13a of Ephesians 1 the next blessing we receive from God is an inheritance, namely that we should have our existence for a special purpose, our inheritance is that of being to the praise of His glory. This means that not only do we exist as evidence of His grace to us, but that we ourselves should also both appreciate and express His glory. To do that we have to be filled with that glory ourselves, that is, to share in Christ's own glory. This can only be a supernatural gift, inherently spiritual and overwhelmingly wonderful. In this remarkable way our inheritance is what Christ first received, then we can experience that in our own Divinely-appointed role as 'being to the praise of His glory'. In no way can we even imagine this state of being, let alone synthesise it in our hearts; it is the gift of God alone that comes with all these other blessings as the risen life of Christ is brought to us by His Holy Spirit.

In Revelation 7, however, the corresponding tribe is Issachar, which means 'reward', as Leah said: 'God has given me my wages'. On the face of it there seems a paradox between the two ideas, a reward and a heritage. This is especially so seeing Leah perceived her gift as remuneration for something that she had done whereas the Divine antitype is clearly a pre-ordained innovation of God Himself. How can we reconcile these things if we are to adhere to the parallel interpretation of these two passages? With Leah it was an aspiration, not the fulfilment; this was yet to come. The answer is that this is a matter of perspective, something that is given by God purely as an act of graciousness on His part. It requires, however, a reciprocal response on our part for us to be able to appropriate it, albeit that this response is inspired of God Himself, see Philippians 2:13. This 'reward', however, as perceived on our part by some action or response, is in practice an inheritance something we receive ex gratia, 'that we should be to the praise of His Glory'. This then is the inheritance that we can appreciate, the fact that we exist, by the pre-ordination of God, to be both evidence of the Glory of Christ and to live a life that is to His praise, in thankfulness and heartfelt worship.

After Issachar, Leah has another son by Jacob, his tenth son Zebulun, meaning 'dwelling', because Leah hoped that her husband would now live with her because of all the sons she had borne him. She longed for the contentment and reassurance that this would bring her. Although this would suggest initially that our motive is seeking God's approval and acceptance by our own endeavours, we get a clearer understanding when we realise how it comes from God alone working in us.

In verse 13 of the comparable passage in Ephesians we get another perspective on this need that we all have. 'You were sealed by the Holy Spirit of promise who is the guarantee of our inheritance', that is giving us the security for the promise that He would stay with us until we live with Him altogether. At this present time, however, He lives within, which we know from experience and in confidence when His Spirit directs us. This consciousness of His indwelling then is another spiritual endowment, as is the inheritance itself. It is something that lies above just any thought or feeling; it is that intimate experience, a knowledge deep within our hearts that God has already provided what we were seeking. It is something that gives us complete assurance, when the Holy Spirit provides this guarantee.

Now the last two of Jacobs's sons were his favourites, the sons of his beloved wife Rachel. We must not impose on this idea any modern sanction of the correct way to treat our children, as a spiritual allegory it is perfectly correct, as was the original situation no doubt in that culture.

The first of Rachel's son's was Joseph, meaning 'increaser' because as she said, 'God has taken away my reproach' and 'The Lord shall add to me another son'. Her life was now fulfilled and looking forward to being even greater service to her husband. As the bride of Christ we all have the counterpart in our relationship with Him: 'The spirit of wisdom and revelation in the knowledge of Him,' Ephesians 1:17. This is a blessing, not something mediated to us as are our inheritance and position of dwelling with Christ, but it is something that is infused directly in us and which becomes part of us, that part of us which was initially born of God alone, cp John 3:3. This is knowledge in the scriptural sense as being a full appropriation, extending, increasing the experience of His Spirit within us as in Ephesians chapter 4:13:

> 'Till we all come to… the knowledge of the Son
> of God, to a perfect man,
> to the measure of the stature of the fullness of Christ'.

It is a matter of us becoming the same standard and character as Him. This is the testimony of much of the New Testament. It is not just what we believe, it's the becoming like our Lord, as the analogy our Lord Himself used, that we should bear fruit. This knowledge becomes a feature of our innate characters; for example as Paul says also in

Galatians, 5:22 + 23, listing nine characteristics that that knowledge constitutes. Like Joseph, who sustained God's chosen family as well as much of the known world at the time, we bring increase in blessing to ourselves, to others, particularly those of the same spiritual 'family', but above all to our Lord.

And so we come to Jacob's youngest son, Benjamin. This was also Rachel's last child as she died in giving birth to him, naming him Ben-oni, 'Son of my sorrow'. Jacob's name for him, Benjamin, however means 'son of my right hand', which was not to despise the name that his wife gave him, but to indicate that for him to be born who he was, she had given her everything. For Jacob he meant so much more to him because his beloved Rachel had given her all to provide him with another son. This made Benjamin much more precious to him, so now he would confer on him complete trust and authority to act on his behalf, one who would be entrusted with all he had, as the expression 'son of my right hand' would indicate. This is an amazing parallel with the next part of Ephesians 1, in verses 18-20, where Paul prays for the Christians at Ephesus, 'that you may know what is the hope of His calling, what are the riches of His glory of His inheritance in the saints; and what is the exceeding greatness of His power towards us who believe.'

Here we are transported to a different realm, this is not just that understanding of the inheritance that we have in Christ, wonderful as that is, but rather the complement to that, what Christ has in us is altogether far more glorious and yet it is possible for us to not only comprehend it but also to enter into the reality of it, because it means that we are no longer living for ourselves but that Christ is living in us, full time, to achieve the purposes of God alone. Christ's inheritance of course is the Kingdom of Heaven, which is what He has in us now. Just as Christ did only the will of His Father, so we attain to that standing, this is the Kingdom of Heaven in us, being the 'Son of His right hand.' We not only have the spirit and ethos of God's Kingdom within us but we are also the administrators, executors of that Kingdom, bringing about its principles in our everyday lives and in our interaction with others.

Ephesians 1:18-20

'That you may know what is the hope of His calling.'	To grasp what is the prospect and confidence of our vocation. To realise just what it is that we are appointed to do, cp v12, and 1 Peter 2:9
'What are the riches of the glory'	His majesty and supremacy invested in His 'bride'. This is the power of His Kingdom that is in us who believe, though which one day will be in every creature: Philippians 2:9-11
'Of His inheritance in the saints'	'For so an entrance will be supplied to you abundantly into the everlasting kingdom of our Lord and Saviour Jesus Christ,' 2 Peter 1:11. 'The Kingdom of God is within you', Luke 17:21. 'It is your Father's good pleasure to give you the Kingdom,' Luke 12:32
'And what is the exceeding greatness of His power towards us who believe.'	His power invested in us to administer it as well, potentially until we fully appropriate His Kingdom, His inheritance in us.
'Which He worked in Christ when He raised Him from the dead.'	Essentially a resurrection power, the life of Christ is the Kingdom and the power given to Him vv21-22

Rachel died giving birth to Benjamin, the ultimate service she could give to her husband and that is the stark reality for us, that is if we are to become fully equipped to achieve what God would do in us and through us; that is to show out the richness of Christ's glory, that glory that is evidenced in the inheritance that Christ received and which resides in His Church, v22. The life that we receive from God when we first submit to Him is not what dies. That is the life that Adam lost when he disobeyed God in the Garden of Eden and is then reinstated in Christ when we first become acquainted with Him, by faith. 'Dying' here is the action afterwards when we relinquish our own self-existence and interest so that Christ may be fully realised in us and expressed through us. This is a most profound and usually painful or traumatic process as all sense of personal importance, self-righteousness, dignity, identity, self-will and earthly loyalties are 'put to death', to use Paul's term, through the Holy Spirit, so that the life of Christ can be refreshed within us until it possesses every part of our being.

We are then His body; His will and dynamic then replaces our own. The death of Rachel then represents the fullness of what is also portrayed in the rite of baptism, it is the ending of what we are so that the risen life of Christ can be realised within us in all its power as 'expressed through Benjamin'.

Whenever we come to the end of ourselves, realise and accept that we cannot fulfil the standard that God requires of us, we can come to Him in failure and submission, waiting upon Him for salvation from our insufficiency, then will we be delivered from the bondage to our desires and our efforts to keep His Laws and ways. His grace then is experienced in victory, this is the spirit of wisdom and revelation in the knowledge of Him, wisdom to guide and understand, a personal revelation to realize and engage that knowledge.

To serve Christ unequivocally, however, requires something more. It requires the complete end to not only sin and our sinful human nature and the 'putting on' the nature of Christ but it requires the end of all self-interest and personality. As Rachel died giving birth to Ben-oni, the son of her sorrow, who was then renamed Benjamin, 'Son of my right hand', so we also as we perish as a self-being become a servant of the highest calibre, to serve Christ absolutely. Then we will do perfectly the work of God. John 6:29 tells us what that is, 'this is the work of God that you believe in Him whom He sent', that is believe, trust and depend on Him entirely in everything that we do, think or say. Then do we truly know His mind in us, not our own interests, opinions and outlook, but a humble lowly and contrite heart. Then do we truly live in Him and He in us.

To be a 'son of Christ's right hand' then is the end result of our sanctification. Christ fully formed in us is the Kingdom of God within us. This is the inheritance that Christ has in us, thus we exist only for the purpose of displaying the praise of His glory.

For the most part this chapter has been a very brief outline of all the treasures that we have in Heaven. It has been little more than just joining up the dots as it were between the different scriptures to give us a basic picture. Little detail or shading or colour has been applied to fill this out, to do so could have created another book in itself, it is such a vast subject; it is no less than the purposes of God for mankind as revealed in His word. This may all seem rather overwhelming, unreal even or incomprehensible at first, but in terms of the Old Testament antitype, 'entering the promised land', this is something we grasp more completely as we grow in grace and understanding of the scriptures. Next though, to know the reality of it all, to fully take possession of it there are many spiritual battles to be fought and won; this is being an overcomer as we have examples in chapters 2,3 and 12:11 of this Book.

> Eye has not seen, nor ear heard
> Nor have entered into the heart of man
> The things that God has prepared for those that love Him
> But God has revealed them to us through His Spirit
> 1 Corinthians 2:9

Addendum

Jacob in fact had another son who received an inheritance of land in Canaan, his fifth, Dan, by Bilhah, Rachel's maid; this meaning 'Justice or discernment'. He was named by Rachel as she said 'God hath heard my case, that is He has vindicated me'. However, in the list in Revelation 7 his name has been replaced by Levi. Now Levi received no land in Canaan as his tribe's inheritance was the priesthood in the tabernacle and later the temple.

Dan signifies giving birth to righteousness by doing what is right and fair, that is the fulfilment of the Law of God, which was the case under the Mosaic covenant, 'If you will do these things then shall you live.' This is vindication by our own effort. This, however, patently failed; what we are by nature can never achieve, that which we also know from experience, just as the tribal area of Dan in Canaan was never conquered. The spontaneous righteousness of Priesthood, however, comes by grace alone, through the mediation of Christ as our Great High Priest. This was prophesied by Jeremiah, in chapter 31 verse 33:

'But this is the covenant that I will make with the house of Israel after those days, says the Lord: I will put My law in their minds, and write it on their hearts;
And I will be their God, and they shall be My people.'

This is accomplished through the work of Christ. Thus the change from God's Old Covenant to the implementing of the New entailed the setting aside of Dan as a region of the Promised Land, to the installation of Levi in the new, in the spiritual antitype.

SECTION 4: PART 6

Spiritual Maturity

Genesis Chapters 29: 16-30 and 30: 14-24

The Story of Leah and Rachel: Establishing the Kingdom

There are two aspects to any relationship from the point of view of our own spiritual experience: how we connect to the other and how we are affected by their rapport with us. This is particularly true with a fully-committed marriage relationship for example, though in our relationship with Christ this bipolar relationship is even deeper. Here these two aspects can in fact conflict, as in any relationship, depending on our perceptions, expectations and level of commitment. Our relationship with Christ is of course different from the physical, emotional and spiritual interaction that we have with other people; with Christ it is entirely spiritual, through faith and learning from our experience of how God cares and communicates with us. Our feelings for Christ can be both possessive and adoring; our perceptions and expectations of Him, however, can be misguided. Christ's standing towards us however is always that of master and always entirely consistent, something of which we are ever coming to a better understanding.

These two positions are what we have in our relationship to Christ. Christ Himself described them as being 'we in Him' and 'He in us', John 15:4. These two positions can be fully integrated, merely complementary, or they can be dissociated.

First Christ in us brings the whole of Heaven to our inner experience, to our conscious and emotional awareness. This is 'Christ in you, the hope of glory,' Colossians 1:27. When He abides in us, His quality of life is instilled in us, transporting us to the 'father's house' where He dwells. This is 'all the spiritual blessings in the heavenlies in Christ Jesus' that we had earlier in this section. The 'sons' born of this fellowship that we can know through 'Christ in us' are those very intimate and personal blessings that we experience and are the manifestation of that state. Christ in us is His glorious life of worship and unity, it is the life we are conscious of that streams from within us.

Christ in us is not somehow Christ controlling us from the outside as the depiction might be construed, with us just acting as automatons, but what we experience of Him from the source of our being. It is Christ rooted and grounded within us and as part of us, not just His life being acted out within us. He is the 'ground of our being' is the term Bishop John Robinson used to describe it.

To be in Christ, however, is the counterpart; it is actively living according to His character and principles, according to God's own life of holiness, righteousness and peace; it has moral dimension rather than just acquaintance.

To be in Christ is not somehow us appropriating His quality life for ourselves according to certain ideals as we might think, but rather our whole life-force being the same spirit and character of Christ, informing every part of our being. It is we being rooted in Christ, not just assuming His quality of life. This is His Spirit within us, not we trying to emulate His nature.

'Therefore, if anyone is in Christ, he is a new creation; old things have passed away; behold, all things have become new,' 2 Corinthians 5:17.

This is the way of the cross, abiding in Christ, the path of sanctification as we are changed into His image and character. In Galatians 2:20 Paul describes it this way: 'I have been crucified with Christ; it is no longer I who live, but Christ lives in me.'

In John 15:5 Christ said, 'He who abides in Me, and I in him, bears much fruit.' With our hearts residing in Him we are ordered by His principle of holiness, righteousness and submission. As Galatians 2:20 continues, 'and the life which I now live in the flesh I live by faith in the Son of God, who loved me and gave Himself for me...'

J.B. Stoney describes it this way:

'There are two ways in which Christ occupies the heart, one in reference to what He is to me, the other in which I live to Him. The first is necessarily the greatest, because it is infinite. The more I am occupied with Him as He is to me, the more I am entranced with the boundlessness of His grace and goodness and wisdom. His love passes knowledge, and I am filled with all the fullness of God. I am surcharged with the vastness of what He is to the saints and in which I share. The practical effect of this occupation is to so engross me with Him that I lose sight of myself. Self is distanced and I seek to apprehend my portion whereof I am apprehended by Jesus Christ.'

The story of Jacob and his two wives, together with their maidservants, is an intimate analogy of that relationship that we have with Christ, including the difficulties we often have in integrating our perceptions and feelings, our hopes and aspirations. The relationship between Jacob and his two wives also typifies more generally and collectively the relationship between Christ and His Church. Particularly, however, it is the relationship that Christ has individually with each one of us and we with Him, as described in John chapter 15.

Jacob had to work for seven years for Laban in lieu of a dowry before he could marry Rachel with whom he had fallen in love. He had first to marry her sister Leah, however, and then work another seven years for Rachel. What does this then tell us about how we come into the blessing of knowing Christ?

First it tells us that it is something that is initiated by Christ alone and that we are 'married' to Him before we are drawn into a relationship to Him. Secondly that it is Christ who works for us to bring us into that relationship, not something we do ourselves. We then respond to that love and devotion of our Lord and so experience His grace and grow in faith ourselves. If we neglect that love and occupy ourselves with our own interests, we don't grow in grace and understanding.

Next it tells us that the relationship is entered into in two ways and these are not simultaneously experienced. At first Christ is made known to us, our relationship with Him and as sons of God is established. It is only then that our personal devotion to Christ is espoused and later begins to bear fruit, that is generates spiritual characteristics that are beloved of God.

Leah represents that side of the relationship where we are dwelling in Christ, with all that the Spirit of Christ is working in us, our faith in and desire for Him and those blessings conveyed to us so intimately and confidentially by His Holy Spirit.

The name 'Leah' means weary, that is, exhausted by toil, yielding to discouragement or lassitude from disappointment. This is our mundane human existence, our bodies as described in scripture, our physical and emotional constitution. Leah was sensitive and retiring and represents our contrite compliance to Christ, longing for His love but often not finding it as a sustaining and fulfilling joy in our hearts, as was the Shulamite in her early love for Solomon in the Song of Songs, see Canticles 3: 1-3. It typifies our human longing to please Christ and our efforts to do so to be accepted, efforts that initially leaves us with doubts and disappointments.

'If anyone is in Christ then, they are a new creation; old things have passed away; behold, all things have become new.' 2 Corinthians 5: 17. This is growing in grace and in the knowledge of our Lord Jesus Christ.

The 'sons' that are then born of this relationship indicate, by the meaning of those names, the specific blessings that come from that relationship of being in

Christ. When we are amenable to Christ, looking to Him in dependence and faith, then we receive spiritual blessings from our communion with Him.

This is the true spiritual life of being 'raised up together, and made to sit together in the heavenly places in Christ Jesus,' Ephesians 2: 6. They often at first, however, seem to be just promises that are received rather than immediate, appreciable and fulfilling blessings.

Rachel however represents the other side of that relationship; there it is the Spirit of Christ abiding in us. All that we may know of Him intellectually, emotionally and spiritually, all that we know of Christ both in us and for us. Christ abided in His Father, but particularly here His Father in Him, doing His Father's will alone, representing Him to the degree that He could say, 'he that has seen me has seen the Father,' and then laying down His life in complete obedience to Him, as in type Rachel also did. Likewise with ourselves, Christ abiding in us means to 'let this mind be in you as was also in Christ Jesus' etc., Philippians 2: 5-8.

Rachel represents the character of spirit of the divine grace and beauty of Christ that is imparted to us by the Holy Spirit. This is the spirit that Christ loves, the character of the 'lamb', meek, gentle, obedient and self-sacrificial. This new disposition that is born within us however is also the work of God alone, we cannot produce it ourselves because then it does not come from the heart and soul but at best is only an amelioration of our natural behaviour or thinking.

This analogy in itself does not however refer directly to the removal of our old nature and the spiritual warfare that follows, although this is implicated in practice, but it is just about our new nature, which is brought to life through Christ living in us and we in Him. When Christ is living in us, we are sensitive and receptive to Him. When we abide in Christ then His nature is formed within us and our personalities reflect the nature of God Himself in Christ.

The blessings that come from our appreciation of Christ's love for us – Rachel - then is of a different type than from our love for Christ - Leah.

From a knowledge of Christ's love for us comes an appreciation of all the blessings that come from Christ being in us.

From our love for Christ comes increase in the grace and beauty of Christ and His Spirit within us, within ourselves, as we become more like Him and more devoted to Him, and that is then imparted to others through our witness and testimony.

These two aspects of our being are different and tend to coexist independently and complementarily but not necessarily reciprocally at first.

The Mandrakes

As we experience the joys and splendour that we find from 'Christ in us' and also as we grow in grace and in the knowledge of Him from 'being in Him' there comes a time in our experience when these separate positions become blended together.

The blessings of Christ that we know in our souls then informs our whole being and service, our new nature and function; what we are for Christ. Then what we do in love and service for Christ comes from what He is in us and not from what we do spontaneously. This is a subtle transformation but a very profound one, one that is illustrated for us in a picture that we are presented with in a story in Genesis 30 of Rachel and the mandrakes.

The story is that Reuben, Leah's first son, was in the field at harvest time and picked some fruit, or possibly they were flowers, and brought them to his mother. Now these mandrakes, as they are called, are described in the New Bible Dictionary as 'love apples, a stemless perennial of the nightshade family having emetic, purgative and narcotic properties. Aphrodisiac properties were also ascribed to it at an early period'. Rachel saw Reuben and asked Leah for some of these 'love apples'; perhaps believing that would help her conceive. Leah, however, resents Rachel wanting to share the blessings of her family.

Reuben represents to Rachel the joy of motherhood, of bearing fruit to her husband as Leah had done. The mandrakes or love apples that he brings to his mother is that filial love and joy that comes from that relationship of sonship. Rachel wanted to share in Leah's fertility; being jealous of it, her intentions and desires are apparent even if her understanding was somewhat superstitious.

It is Leah's nature, however, that makes her fertile and fruitful. Leah, however, wanted to know the experience of her Husband's affection and was jealous of Rachel who enjoyed that happy and harmonious relationship. It is Rachel's nature that makes her beautiful as a spiritual analogy. In the story in Genesis the two wives make a reciprocal agreement, a mutual arrangement that gives transitory satisfaction to both parties. The story on the surface, however, seems simply a trade-off between two rival wives, each wanting what the other had got.

As a spiritual analogy, it can show us the way for our personal being and our spiritual lives in Christ to become fully integrated, a position that can become much fuller and more significant than the antitype in Genesis: Leah agreeing with Rachel to share her realization of sonship, Rachel conceding to Leah to share her position of favour.

For us to know from a practical experience both the security and assurance of being 'in Christ' and to know the joy and fellowship of Him dwelling in us, we need to know from experience Rachel's position of favour, just as Leah needed to. This is something we already know by faith, something that is a moral position that we can appreciate in our hearts, but not necessarily something that we are living in the full practical outworking of in everyday life. This is a life where we are living day by day in the will of God, living practically the life of Christ from the heart and not just from conviction. This is being 'guided by His eye', so that we 'see' by His Spirit of love and truth what course we take through life, being guided by His wisdom and understanding. This is what Paul meant in Philippians 2:12-13:

> 'Work out your salvation with fear and trembling
> for it is God who works in you both to will and to do of His good pleasure.'

What God has worked in us as Christ lives within us, we let Him work out practically in our lives. Just as in the antitype, however, there is a reciprocal relationship, something that at first may seem to be an unrelated matter, but one that essentially must happen at the same time for Philippians 2 to become meaningful. With Rachel her standing is rather different. She does not wish to adopt her sister's position as Leah had done; that would be to degrade what is Divine to what is human. Reuben in the story is what is born of Leah the relation of sonship that we have with God. It is the harvest of what that brings that Rachel shares in. Now sonship in scripture implies an attitude of compliance to the Father, of living to serve Him and promote His interests. This is the nature of Leah, this is the fruitfulness or fragrance that the mandrakes represent; true sonship now informing our service for Christ.

Paul explains this how this works in practice in Romans 12:1:

'I beseech (come alongside) you therefore, brethren, by the mercies of God,

that you present your bodies a living sacrifice,

holy, acceptable to God, which is your reasonable service.'

This is where it starts then in practice, through the Holy Spirit, resigning our own wills and desires more fully and completely to those of our heavenly Father, then His will becomes our will and we live to serve God alone; altogether a new creation. Then just as both sisters, by assuming each other's disposition became united in outlook, had further blessing, or sons, as a result. We also, by reaching a fuller commitment to our Lord and Saviour, can realize further blessings in a deeper relationship with Him and to the glory of His holy name.

The significance of the sons respective to their 'mothers'

There tends to be then this disconnect between our everyday mundane life and religious and spiritual life, which causes tension within our lives; between our ideals and ordinary experience and outlook, between conscience and freedom of spirit. We have a desire for full assurance and enjoyment of what we believe in and also for our righteousness and service to come spontaneously from the heart and not just carried out from conviction or self-interest.

Before this matter is resolved, however, our spiritual life in communion with the Father will bear fruit when we seek His approval and blessing in that realm. As with Rachel, who had children attributed to her by her maid, likewise the Holy Spirit will work within us to vindicate and fulfil that desire to be fruitful in our spiritual lives; the Holy Spirit doing a work for us, strictly speaking, not here changing our hearts in conformity to Christ. The first son that Rachel is credited with through her maid is Dan, meaning justice, as she said 'I have been judged and the Lord has heard my case.' She felt confident that her prayers had been heard and accepted, that she was vindicated and declared right and rewarded with the productiveness that she sought. Likewise with ourselves our confidence and propriety before God will be assured, our expectation and prayer for our love and devotion to 'bear fruit', that is to produce the peaceable fruits of righteousness in our hearts, will be answered, spontaneously living according to the laws and principles of God, albeit imperfectly at times.

Her second son she named Naphtali as she said, 'I have wrestled with my sister and have prevailed'; as Paul said, 'I discipline my body and bring it into subjection,' 1 Corinthians 9:27, describing the ongoing conflict that exists within ourselves between our own hearts' desires and our new nature, between our ordinary lives and our religious ideals. This is a sequel to 'Dan' as above, though is also the activity of the Holy Spirit within our lives, the benefits of which we are the recipients. Our spiritual life, with its expression through our religious convictions, takes precedence over our natural emotions and desires, bringing it into subjection.

Both these sons then were not born to Rachel herself; to us these illustrate the services of the Spirit within us, they are not changes of our whole being and relationship with Christ as are the sons born to Rachel herself.

Next in the story of Jacob's family comes the incident of Reuben's mandrakes when the two sisters are reconciled. Subsequent to this both women have further children. Leah first bears Issachar, meaning reward, the reward she got for sharing the blessings of her family with her sister. When our mundane life becomes fully consecrated to God, as in Roman's 12:1-2, then our ordinary experience bears spiritual fruit through the Holy Spirit of God. The reward of His glory in our hearts and lives brings such a deep satisfaction and fulfilment that nothing in this world even comes close to. Her next and last son by her maid was Zebulun, meaning dwelling. This is what Leah longed for more than anything, that her husband would live with her as her companion and beloved. As our hearts and souls are committed more fully to Christ, as our own desires, interests and ideals are displaced, then we know the joy of His indwelling companionship, a fellowship that is more profound and satisfying than any human relationship, however good.

Last of all however, Rachel had two sons of her own. When our religion and spiritual being becomes active in our everyday lives, then the life that is hid with Christ in God bears fruit in our common experience and course of our life.

Our whole being becomes progressively sanctified for the Lord's service; 'a vessel for honour, sanctified and useful for the Master, prepared for every good work,' 2 Timothy 2:21. With Rachel her first child of her own was Joseph, meaning 'increase'. Rachel's expectation in naming him was that she would have more children, though Joseph would fulfil the meaning of his name in other ways through many trials and troubles, ever maintaining his candour and faithfulness. He rose in prestige to feed and serve many nations including his own family and save them from starvation. Likewise when we are suitably qualified by the supremacy of the Holy Spirit in our hearts, living holy, righteous and sober lives, we are then vessels fit for the master's use, to serve Him as He would choose.

Rachel's second and last son and also Jacob's last was Benjamin, meaning 'son of my right hand.' If Joseph had learned complete submission and dependence upon God to serve the world and his family, 'Benjamin' would indicate from the meaning of his name an even greater position of conformity to God's purposes for us. As 'son of my right hand' Benjamin would be entrusted to be his father's chief executive, acting not only as living exclusively for his father's interests, furthering his affairs and ends, but also conforming entirely to his father's will. Such is that biblical cultural concept of sonship; as Christ said in John 6:38, 'For I have come down from Heaven, not to do My own will, but the will of Him who sent Me.'

This He did absolutely, without demur or compromise. This then when fully realised is the final objective of our sanctification, the total demise of our own personality and will so that the Spirit of Christ is completely sovereign.

The biblical story	The significance to the analogy	The antitype – our relationship with Christ
Laban	Father of Leah and Rachel and uncle of Jacob.	Leah and Rachel were of the same family of faith, that is great-grandchildren of Abraham. Similarly we are also of the same family of faith, cp. Galatians 3:7
Leah, the older; retiring disposition	Our mundane physical and emotional lives on Earth, with our human hopes and aspirations, which Christ will indwell and transform	The quality of the life of Christ we appreciate; The blessings that we receive from God as we acknowledge Him and seek to please Him. Having a constant desire of assurance and security in knowing the love of Christ that comes only from 'being in Him.'
Rachel, Leah's younger sister, ie having the same father; gentle and beautiful.	Our religious and spiritual lives in fellowship with Christ and our occupation with Him	The way of the Cross, the Divine character of life that is instilled in us, as all that stands contrary to it is displaced. Having a constant desire to bear real fruit to Christ, which we cannot do until it comes from 'Christ being in us'
Rivalry between them	'The flesh lusts against the spirit and the spirit against the flesh' Galatians 5:17	Our spiritual lives develop ideologically at variance with our everyday lives. The full reconciliation of these two spiritual positions is a feature of Christian maturity
The Maids that serve their mistresses	The manifestations of faith 1. 1. Zilpah meaning - myrrh dripping, 2. Bilhah meaning - tender;	Faith... is the gift of God; Ephesians 3: The peace and joy that comes with a daily life of communion and occupation with Christ. The privileged standing of being in Christ, doing His will in serving Him

Mandrakes –	Love apples bought by Rueben from the harvest	The ability to bear fruit in our life in Christ comes from our level of commitment and sacrifice to Him
Leah wins a share of Rachel's privileged position	Leah gains the intimate position that Rachel has already with Jacob	When our mundane lives become sensitive to Christ, His Spirit directs us fully in our ordinary lives as well as our religious; then we experience a deeper and more satisfying relationship with Him
Sharing the harvest between the wives	The blessing of knowing God as his obedient children, doing His will and sharing that rapport from which true service emanates	Our ordinary lives become a daily sacrifice to God, thus knowing that He dwells with us. Our religious life of service and devotion becomes based on that true relationship of sonship, stimulated by our Father's will alone.
Sons born to Jacob	Six sons born to Leah, two to Rachel and two each to their two maids	It is Christ in us that yields fruit, what is born of Christ from fellowship with Him. Rachel had no children of her own until after she had learned Leah's position of being fully yielded to her husband and lord.
Joseph	Jacob's favourite because he was born of Rachel, as having her nature	The first son born of 'full maturity', one that lived a life of complete obedience to God, service and benefit to mankind; true Christ inspired service.
Jacob leaves Laban	Jacob separates his herds and family from Laban's residence and influence	Christ calls us to separation from all things of this life, not only from the world but all family ties, natural and spiritual, everything that distracts from unqualified devotion to Him.

SECTION 4: PART 7

The Kingdom of our Lord

Revelation Chapters 11: 15-19

'The Kingdom of This World is Become the Kingdom of Our Lord'

The Elders Give Testimony to How the Moral Position on Earth is Now Prepared for the Reign of Christ

We have now come to the third stage of God's full implementation of His purposes in creation, something that has been an ongoing process since the beginning of time. Christ at His first coming revealed how this would be a universe that harmonised with God's own being, a nature of mutual self-giving love and absolute righteousness. He enlarged on what prophets in the past had already told of the coming Kingdom, something still hidden and developing in the hearts of individuals now but soon to become evident throughout the world.

The first stage of this physical and external revelation was foretold by Christ Himself, as reported in Matthew chapter 25 in particular. This explained what the essential resource was for everyone that can be a citizen of the Kingdom of Heaven, that we should be motivated by His spirit of self-giving love and absolute righteousness alone. This is the nature of salvation; we are saved from our intuitive human propensity of self-determination to live instead only according to His Spirit.

In Revelation 7, parts 2-6 of this section, we realised the particular spiritual blessings of the Kingdom from the point of view of our own experience and compared this with Ephesians chapter 1, the Divine perspective. This is the substance of the 'Kingdom Within' that Christ referred to in Luke 17:21. This is living the life of Christ; it is the essentially spiritual constitution of the whole of the Kingdom of God.

The first few parts of this section then are concerned with the founding of God's Kingdom, something that God is bringing to pass secretly in the hearts of individuals even now. The third part that we come to now, however, sees the Kingdom coming to pass from a global perspective and could not be known until, in the language of the 'Revelation', the scroll is fully opened and its contents declared. This aspect of the Kingdom is nothing short of a new Divine world order, a complete and perfect theocracy, in its truest sense. It describes the universal effects and implications of the coming of the Kingdom. Now that the scroll is fully open in this scene, the effects of man's rebellion against God is completely exposed. God in His faithfulness will not condemn man for what has not been made patent and given him the opportunity to repent.

Thus in the previous chapter of the Revelation, chapter 10:7, it was announced that at the sounding of the 7th trumpet the mystery of God would be finished, the mystery that is disclosed by His servants but understood only by those that fear God. It is a mystery to all others at this present time because the natural mind cannot appreciate the essence of a spiritual kingdom; it can make no sense of it. At the sounding of the 7th trumpet, however, its imminence at least is understood by all.

This is the final prophecy, making known the primacy of the Almighty – see Chapter 10:7; the angel standing on the sea and the land – making known to the whole Earth that which has been a mystery up to that time to mankind generally, that now the days of mankind's autonomy are at an end. This is a mystery that has been understood by those that have known and trusted God. They have known what was to come, that this present age is a time of testing, responsibility and transformation. If we had not known that, then the message of the time of reckoning would also be ignored or disdained and so it would have remained a mystery.

For this reason the immediate effects are seen in Heaven, the spiritual realm, and appreciated by the spiritually mature, the elders. This is not the full implementation of the Kingdom, palpably on Earth as yet, there are further issues still to be resolved before the tangible kingdom is realised, namely the elimination of the old world order with all its secular values and practice, referred to as 'Babylon' in the Revelation and other prophetic and apocalyptic scripture. What we see here is that morally everything is established. The mystery that God revealed to His servants the prophets, that is that the

Kingdom of God, the secret of Christ in us as it is spoken of in several places in the New Testament particularly, is now fully realized. So the course of secular history is now complete; all that God had planned to fulfil in salvation through this time of testing and proving is finished.

This is what those ancient ones with wisdom and understanding and with full maturity of life in the Kingdom, the twenty-four elders, now celebrate. At last has come the time for the restitution of all things. This now begins with the removal of all that stands in the way of universal peace and righteousness being introduced. This is the beginning of a sequence of epic events that reaches its final conclusion in chapter 22 of the Revelation.

The primary effect of the 7th trumpet sounding is in Heaven, loud voices making an announcement, that is giving clear, forceful and eloquent revelation; 'The kingdoms of this world have become the kingdoms of our Lord and His Christ and He shall reign forever and ever'. This then speaks not just of Christ's coming but the 'Day of the Lord' as a whole; the outlook is looking forward from the end of this present era on to the final consummation:

- The demise of the kingdoms of this world, those empires that function through self-interest and self-promotion must be eradicated.

- Then the Kingdom of our Lord, a realm that seeks to exalt God alone as the only one that can bring universal peace and respect, can be brought in. A realm that will be governed by the principles first made known by Christ Himself in Matthew chapters 5-7, for example.

- Christ will then reign supreme as the unassailable monarch until He has put down all authority that would stand against the Almighty, see 1 Corinthians 15:25.
- Then He, that is God alone, shall reign for ever and ever.

It is the twenty-four elders that are in the full appreciation of all that is being proclaimed, they as elders are the aged ones, wise ones, rulers; they understand and have been waiting for this greatest ever transformation of history. They sit before God on their thrones, denoting their position in acknowledgement as to where their authority devolves from. Indicated here as well is their qualification to take such a position of authority, which comes from the spiritual maturity implied by their title of 'elders'. They are those that have gone in and conquered the 'Promised Land,' they are the overcomers of chapters 2 and 3 of the Revelation, they are the ones who understand the purposes of God, who long for them to be fulfilled, who are fully schooled in the ethics of the Kingdom such that they are now co-rulers in God's Kingdom. They are as Joseph, living the life of Christ to the benefit of all, and Benjamin, true 'sons of God's right hand'.

Their actions and prayers here indicate their suitability. These are people that understand the purposes of God and that He will implement them. Like Jeremiah and Ezekiel of old, however, they have entered into the experiences themselves, the joy of knowing what blessing God will bestow on those that love and obey Him, but they have also identified with the pain and anguish that will befall those that deny and reject Him. Their immediate response to the announcement is for them to fall on their faces and worship God in self-effacing adoration; their perfect loyalty to God comes from their being of one mind with Him, their judgements and intent are born of the Spirit of God alone. Therefore their hearts are filled with thankfulness that at last the answer to their prayerful longing, 'Thy Kingdom come, Thy will be done', is being established. Their understanding of the ramifications of the imminent kingdom is complete, signified by their sevenfold response in worship.

The Sevenfold Response:

- They proclaim God's existence beyond time, 'The One who is and who was and who is to come'. They appreciate the magnitude and splendour of His being: the eternal one, the one who connects to and gives purpose to time.

- 'Because You have taken Your great power and reigned;' they recognize that the time of allowing sin and nature to run their course is now over. As 2 Peter 3:9 says, 'The Lord is not slack concerning His promise, as some count slackness, but is long suffering towards us, not willing that any should perish but that all should come to repentance'. Christ's coming is delayed until all His children have come into the Kingdom.

- What man is fully capable of when unrestrained has also been revealed. It is now for the day for God's Kingdom to be revealed and His King to be installed.

Psalm 2 asks the question, 'Why do the nations rage?' speaking prophetically about the coming Kingdom of God that David anticipated in 1000BC. He pointed out the futility of such an attitude, to rage against God when He is omnipotent and intends to bring about His Kingdom of universal and eternal brotherhood and peace. 'The nations were angry' v18 because their autonomy and self-interest has been reined in, the time for giving account is come. As executives in God's Kingdom, those that have been redeemed from that corrupt life and are morally members of God's kingdom, enter into David's disappointment at the belligerent rejection of God's government by mankind, but are filled with praise to God to see David's prophecy fulfilled after more than three millennia.

- There is, however, an irony here. The nations are angry because of the frustration of their own ends, but that very attitude has precipitated the anger of an omnipotent God. 'And Your wrath has come' they announce, not the resentment of the nations but the vehemence and intensity of almighty God. Only those that have known God personally, that is to know God in accepting for oneself His uncompromising integrity and principles, can vindicate the necessity for His complete removal of all that would stand against Him.

- Those that have known God's forgiveness and reconciliation also know that God demands justice. If anyone will not be reconciled to Him, despite the fact that the way is open, they must be separated from

Him when time and the opportunity for reconciliation is over. The die is now cast; 'the time of the dead that they should be judged' has now come, the elders say. This now looks beyond the time of Christ's reign on Earth to the judgement of all those that have ever lived; cp chapter 20:12. It is after this that God alone shall reign supreme forever and ever. This looks on to chapter 22 of Revelation; see 1 Corinthians 15:25 as referred to above.

- Those that know God, that know His absolute righteousness, also know from experience that He is absolutely faithful and will bestow blessings and recompense for faithfulness to Him. 'And that You should reward Your servants the prophets and saints and those who fear Your name, small and great'. Three classes of favoured ones are mentioned according to the faithfulness to their calling.

  - First there are the prophets, those that publicly declare God's truth, in true testimony, that is, in word and in action. These are the servants of God that we met in Matthew chapter 25.

  - Next there are the saints, those that are separate, holy, set apart. It is not the outward manifestations of conduct and purity of life that is highlighted here but the inward soul, the affections and attitudes that are recognised by God and acknowledged accordingly.

  - Finally there are those that acknowledge Him in fear. Those that honour His unqualified right to their loyalty and respect Him thus. All these, however, are not mutually exclusive groups but all qualities of those that truly know and believe in God, though we may all differ in the extent of our faith. This is not just outward or private religion and belief, but it is what true religion derives or emanates from, see James chapter 1.

- The final insight of the elders into the significance of the change in the world order is that God 'should destroy those who destroy the Earth'. It was Adam's commission, his created purpose, to have dominion, that is to control and rule, over the creation. He was created in the image of God for that purpose, see Genesis chapter 1:28, to look after and care for it. This of course man has failed dismally to do, rather in the past two centuries particularly he has exploited it for his own glory. He therefore finally loses his responsibility and is destroyed; destroyed here means marred or corrupted thoroughly, not just to be annihilated.

The sounding of the seventh trumpet, however, also has another consequence. It is the third great woe that is to fall on the Earth, v 14, so the implications are dire for the whole world and we must realise the import of verse 19. The third woe follows immediately the episode of the two witnesses, which was the second great woe that is to befall the world, the testimony that censured their impiety and antagonism to God's messengers and blighted their consciences. In this third woe the temple of God is opened in Heaven. Before it was the measuring of the temple, its evaluation in respect of mankind's behaviour, which was focused upon. This time it is the presence of the temple that is pressed before mankind's awareness; not only the temple, which speaks of the presence of God with mankind, but also particularly on this occasion the Ark of the Covenant is seen in His temple. Now this is the only reference to the Ark of the Covenant in the New Testament, though there are 15 other references to the temple in the Revelation alone. It is the Ark of the Covenant that presses home the inescapability of the law of God. The calling to account is imminent and so those that have not escaped condemnation through faith must now be censured by God's impeccable standards. The witness of the Ark is accompanied by dramatic natural events, lightning, thunder, earthquake and hail; these phenomena traditionally symbolise the voice and judgement of God and the social dislocation that that brings, with all the fear and insecurity that engenders in the human heart; cp Revelation 4:5, 8:5 and 16:18.

This now then is finally the full revelation of the mystery of the Kingdom; it is a mystery no longer. What prevails at this present time is what Christ said to His disciples: 'It has been given to you to know the mysteries of the Kingdom of Heaven, but to them it has not been given,' Matthew. 13:11. This will then become history and the whole world will know the ethics and standards of the Kingdom. There now just then needs to be the removal of all of the old regime that stands in contradiction to all that is of God and His Kingdom. God is not arbitrary but patient, ever pleading within mankind to give up their pernicious and self-destructive ways and embrace His way of peace and righteousness.

SECTION 4: PART 8

Spiritual Adultery

Revelation Chapter 18

The Insidiousness of the World and How it Refines Or Impairs Our Faith

'Adultery': the very word inspires a medley of emotional responses from most of us, of anger, disgust, embarrassment or even personal hurt, for example. Chambers' dictionary defines adulteration as the 'making impure by the addition of something else' and in this sense it is not emotionally loaded. The normal meaning of adultery though is being unfaithful to one's marriage partner and both of these definitions, being intrinsically related in meaning, are relevant in the same way in one's relationship with Christ as Saviour and Lord. Adultery is an analogy used of Israel's behaviour frequently in the Old Testament when they wandered from following the God of Israel, their forefather, and to worshipping and praying to the gods of the nations around them. To fulfil their own lusts and inclinations, they turned to gods and idols of their own choosing, breaking the first commandment of their Mosaic covenant with their God. Adultery with regards to one's relationship with God is specifically defined in the scriptures as idolatry. For example:

> 'So it came to pass, through her casual harlotry,
> that she defiled the land and committed adultery with stones and trees.'
> Jeremiah 3:9

> 'You erected your shrine at the head of every road,
> and built your high place in every street.
> Yet you were not like a harlot, because you scorned payment.
> You are an adulterous wife, who takes strangers instead of her husband.'
> - Ezekiel 16:31-32.

The New Testament takes the meaning even wider by defining the love of money as idolatry and therefore by extension from this is 'adultery' for the true disciple as it is the mixing or addition of the love of this world with a profession of love for God:

'No covetous man, who is an idolater, has any inheritance in the kingdom of Christ and of God.' - Ephesians 5:5

'Covetousness, which is idolatry.' – Colossians 3:5.

It is popular in our culture to worship possessions or people, either out of love, greed or admiration. This is simply idolatry, so the worship of anything other than the true God is idolatry and for those that have been redeemed by Christ it is therefore adultery. Covetousness is contrary to the last commandment of the old covenant, see Exodus 20:17. Christ Himself showed us that this meant the love of our own possessions as well as the desire for those of other people:

> 'And He said to them, 'Take heed and beware of covetousness,
>
> for one's life does not consist in the abundance of the things he possesses.'
>
> Luke 12:15

And also in the Old Testament:

> 'For the wicked boasts of his heart's desire;
> he blesses the greedy and renounces the Lord,' Psalm 10:3.

It is the love of possessions that is the popular meaning of 'materialism' in its mundane sense in our society. It is what our Lord was warning us against when He said, 'Do not lay up for yourselves treasures on Earth... but lay up for yourselves treasures in Heaven,' Matthew 6:19-20. The Book of the Revelation puts the message very graphically. Babylon represents the empirical and political aspiration of man, as explained in Daniel 2, but also in Revelation chapter 18 it is Babylon's material and commercial endeavours that are regarded as significant in its destruction. In Daniel 2, Babylon is described as the Head of a series of world empires that would culminate in the 'Most High' setting up His kingdom. In Revelation, as in numerous passages in the Old Testament, the message is very clear, Babylon in both respects is reserved for judgement and complete destruction, see Jeremiah 51. Both aspects of course are directly related, secularly and spiritually. It is the antithesis of all that is of God; it is the persecutor of His saints and a place that Christ warns His saints now to come out of:

> 'And I heard another voice from Heaven saying,
> 'Come out of her, my people, lest you share in her sins,
> and lest you receive of her plagues." Revelation 18:4.

This by way of introduction to Babylon, we now turn to its significance, at the same time returning to our main theme. Adultery, or fornication to the unbelieving, is the worship and emotional attachment to this world. This is 'Babylon' or secularism as in 1 John 2:15:

> 'Do not love the world or the things in the world.
>
> If anyone loves the world, the love of the Father is not in him.'

The world has a seducing power that insidiously draws mankind into its clutches. None of us are exempt, though for some perhaps it seems more insidious than for others. This is why 'Babylon' is also personified in Revelation chapter 17 so eloquently as a prostitute. As a prostitute she is introduced at first in a way that denotes her true character and qualities, but then as the Book progresses we are told specifically in chapter 17:18; emphasising also the vast extent of her influence:

> 'And the woman whom you saw is that great city
> Which reigns over the kings of the Earth.'

Babylon's particular qualities display its character of a prostitute, implying the analogy of sexual allure and selfish indulgence to portray the powerful effect that all aspects of the material world can have on us. This concept is then again affirmed in the next three verses of the next chapter. These verses liken Babylon to a prostitute – that which seduces the kings of the Earth to commit fornication. As a harlot it corrupts men from fidelity to their true spouse. As a whore it seduces men into an adulterous relationship, fulfilling a transient desire in a brief period of excitement, whatever the consequences.

Certainly this is a picture of materialism in the West today, though historically also it was in Babylon that actual pagan worship of idols prevailed, and the Chaldean Mystery Religion first originated, ideas that were continued in many ancient cults and religions in antiquity. Even in the West today there is a revived interest in pagan religion. This is of course still as much idolatry as materialism. Passages such as Jeremiah 51 make it clear that it is judged for its idolatry, as was Egypt and Samaria for example (Isaiah 10:10-11 and 19:1-2). The apostle Paul was anxious about the tendency for this to happen in the early days of the church when he expressed a concern for the Corinthian Christians that they should be chaste and free from the corruption of false doctrine in 2 Corinthians 11:2:

> 'For I am jealous for you with godly jealousy; for I have betrothed you to one husband, that I may present you as a chaste virgin to Christ.'

The worship of idols, however, in any form is adultery – for the true disciple, as it was for Israel in the Old Testament – or fornication for those not 'married' to Christ, that is non-believers. Anything that takes the place of God is an idol; anything that takes the place of true devotion to Christ in a person's own spirit is idolatry. Any image of Christ is an idol if that is what is worshipped rather than it being to us just an artistic representation of whom it is speaking. It is a matter of individual status and responsibility and is the same for every denomination that professes Christ, ie it is not a physical but a spiritual matter.

Religious ritual, religious art, religious iconography and majestic church architecture can all speak to us of God and His truth and encourage us to worship Him. It is probably true to say that some find such expressions helpful, even vital, to worship; others do not. It is a matter of individual association. The enticement, however, at a natural level of ritual and ceremony, the allure of religious sentiment and the comfort that it brings is mystical seduction if it just gives us emotional satisfaction rather than promoting true worship. This is as much seduction as the attraction of the material things of the world, if it is to become engaged in for its own sake, that is for our own comfort, admiration and interest rather than the worship and comfort of Christ alone. It is then adulteration of the absolute lordship of Christ, the adulteration of the pure life of Christ in us by our own natural life and desires; the flesh.

To regard these prophecies in the Bible referring specifically to a particular religious organisation or practice as being the great prostitute, as has been suggested by some, is a most deceptive and dangerous interpretation for the true believer and does not hold up to careful analysis. It is deceptive because, although this could be partially true as explained above, it limits its relevance to something apart from ourselves. It is dangerous then because it not only alienates us from other true believers, it tends to cause us to be judgemental and complacent in that it refers only to someone else. Quite to the contrary, it is possibly the most widespread and emasculating influence within the churches today. Perhaps the most profound warning for the true Church today is 'Come out of her, my people,' Revelation 18:4. Not out of any particular church or other organisation but out of that spiritual entity that the notion 'Babylon' embodies.

Modern 'historicist' understanding has said that the prostitute is an apostate system, though why a system is not apparent from the text; it is to introduce an idea that is a mechanical interpretation of the symbolism here. A corporate identity is not necessarily implied. Also suggested has been that she has an 'ecclesiastical' identity, which is again an assumption that the symbolism here is to be taken as being a physical or corporeal representation rather than a spiritual one. The discernment of scripture, however, is to be spiritual:1 Corinthians 2:14.

> 'But the natural man does not receive the things of the
> Spirit of God,
> for they are foolishness to him; nor can he know them,
> because they are spiritually discerned.'

The scripture itself defines very specifically the way that we should read it. Paul when writing to Timothy says in 2 Timothy 2:15, encouraging him in 'Rightly dividing the word of truth', Dividing, that is literally meaning correctly separating out, that is from its context, and then applying it in its true meaning. Again in 2 Timothy 3:16-17:

> 'All Scripture is given by inspiration of God, and is
> profitable for doctrine,
> for reproof, for correction, for instruction in righteousness,
> that the man of God may be complete,
> thoroughly equipped for every good work.'

Its purpose then on us directly is to sanctify, not make us judgemental! This is not to 'spiritualise' the meaning of the scriptures either, in the sense that is as the OED defines: 'To expound or understand in a spiritual sense, to explain away in this manner', or in a more popular sense to vaguely generalise, abstract or obscure. Spiritual in our usage here is not meant to be the popular meaning of supernatural, esoteric, emotional, or concerned vaguely with feeling. It is quite specifically that which is concerned with personal truth and integrity generally, rather than just certain facts about us. It is concerned with our spiritual growth rather than just imparting information. Spiritual here means the inner self, that which moulds our character and attitudes and directs our thoughts and feelings. In the scriptures it most often refers to what is of God and the grace that He imparts to our spirit. It does also refer sometimes to unsanctified influences, what is of Satan, the world or what is natural, human or otherwise, the context defining the moral calibre and substance of that reference.

None of us are totally immune from these influences and love of the world and worldly practice may adulterate the churches or some of its members but this is nothing new. Self-indulgence and seduction of disciples is something that has always been prevalent from the early church in every age to some degree. In the Old Testament from the time of the golden calf in the desert until the northern tribes were taken into captivity in about 720 BC, and later in Judah, Israel consistently turned to false gods in superstition and self-indulgence. Witness also in several of the letters to the seven churches in Revelation chapters two and three; Christ though there did not just cut Himself off from those that were not living perfect lives, rather He came to them, first commending them on what they did have that was good, then He pointed out what was wrong and called for them to repent. Remember the words of our Lord in Luke 6:41-42:

"And why do you look at the speck in your brother's eye, but do not perceive the plank in your own eye?
Or how can you say to your brother,
'Brother, let me remove the speck that is in your eye,' when you yourself do not see the plank that is in your own eye?

Hypocrite! First remove the plank from your own eye,

and then you will see clearly to remove the speck that is in your brother's eye."

In chapter 16:19, and about a dozen times in chapter 18, Babylon is referred to as 'she' or 'her'. In verse 7 Babylon 'sits as a queen and no widow'; verse 16 describes the city in exactly the same language as the prostitute in 17:4. The reason that the city is also described as a prostitute is in respect of the relationship that the kings of the Earth have with 'her'; so money, the world and politics replace God in their affections, hence the idea of 'fornication'. Her seduction is the allure of the world. 'Adultery and fornication' are love of the world, assimilating its material values and being preoccupied with its goods.

The 'Revelation' is about Christ and His glorious putting down of all that is in opposition to Himself, in the process of His complete revelation to the world.

Chapter 17 of the Revelation opens with the matter in view as being the judgement of the great prostitute. It is not expressed as the judgement of Babylon, though that is what receives judgement in chapter 18. Then in chapter 19 it is the prostitute that is celebrated as being judged for corrupting the whole Earth. The first name on the forehead of the prostitute is 'Mystery' (ie what is known only to the initiated and usually is used in the New Testament to that which is known only to those that belong to Christ), Revelation 17:5+7. This is explained by the angel; namely, the woman is 'That great city' – ie Babylon. It is a mystery because it is a spiritual concept; it will only be appreciated by those with heavenly sensibilities. That it refers to the mystery religions associated with it, that is, those practising secret rites, may be implied as mentioned above, though the only other scripture where 'mystery' is used in respect to what is corrupt is 2 Thessalonians 2:7. In western culture it is capitalism, that which might be described as the militant arm of materialism, which 'rides on the back of' the Beast, driving and controlling it. It is what embodies domination, conquering and empiricism, ie abstract concepts, spiritually significant features. These are characteristic of all societies to some extent.

Materialism, and even its offspring capitalism, however 'reigns' over most if not every kingdom on Earth, even in Islamic countries that ideologically abhor it. Likewise it is quickly adopted by primitive societies when exposed to western culture. 'Reigns', v.18, is in the present tense, so it would have been as relevant to Christians contemporary with John as it is today. This is emphasised by the fact that the rest of the explanation given here by the angel, in respect of the 'Beast', is either in the past tense or future. It is a dominion that will be hated by 'The Beast', the antichrist that will rule the world in abject evil for a short while with his oligarchy of ten 'kings'. It will be something that will 'ride the beast', control the direction it goes and yet is dependent on the Beast for its 'status quo', its 'modus operandi'. It will be hated by the (ten horns of the) Beast perhaps because it will threaten his absolute control,

'These will make her desolate and naked,

eat her flesh and burn her with fire,' Revelation 17:16.

On two occasions Jesus indicted the Pharisees particularly for religiosity and hypocrisy, for just an outward form of religion, and then went on to say:

> 'That on you may come all the righteous blood shed on the Earth,
>
> from the blood of righteous Abel to the blood of Zechariah.'
>
> Matthew 23:35, see also Luke 11:51

In verse six of Revelation 17 however it is the prostitute that is drunk on the blood of the saints and martyrs of Jesus. How can we reconcile these three passages and the foregoing analysis of spiritual adultery? Is the prostitute just the whole of apostate religion after all? I think we need to dig a little deeper.

Hebrews 11:4 tells us that it was by Abel's faith that he was accepted by God and it was the witness of the fact that he was accepted that Cain killed him (Genesis 4:5-8). Likewise it was the witness of the life and message of the prophets, calling for repentance and faith in God, to turn from their false gods and evil way of life that resulted in their martyrdom. The Jews of Jesus' day were again rejecting the message of the Kingdom of God and instead just following their self-made, self-fulfilling religion. Knowing that He would be executed by them for His witness, Christ therefore says that they were of the same spirit as Cain and those that executed the prophets for the witness of their faith and so they were just as guilty as their predecessors. Now there have been many more martyred saints since Jesus first came to Earth, notably first by the Jews, then by the Roman armies during the early days of the Church. Subsequent to that we have had the inquisitions of the Middle Ages, ostensibly by the Church itself. Since then there have been many missionaries killed for their faith and devotion to their Lord, of all denominations. Although since the Enlightenment there has been outward tolerance of all Christians and other faiths in the West, even today there are many who are killed in different parts of the world because they stay faithful to Christ.

What then is common to all those that have been tortured and slain for their loyalty to Christ from Abel to the present day, and what is the common motivation for these martyrdoms? It is of course contained in the meaning of the word 'martyr', which means simply 'witness'. Witness for their faith by word and example against the evil, indulgence and idolatry of the world and those that are of the world. Again we see the prostitute as Babylon in its disposition of seducing men away from God to lives of self-fulfilment and self-indulgence, hence the image of a prostitute as one who induces infidelity in her clients. We may still be tempted, however, to take a personified interpretation of the Prostitute inasmuch as she is 'drunk with the blood of the saints and martyrs'. Usually one thinks only of a person being drunk, though not of the analogy being applied to inanimate entities. However, Deuteronomy 32:42 uses the analogy in an abstract context:

> 'I will make my arrows drunk with blood, while my sword devours flesh;
>
> the blood of the slain and the captives, the heads of the enemy leaders.' NIV

Being drunk here does not imply inebriation or elation, ie human emotions, but as with the prostitute being disinhibited, fully gorged with revenge. There are several other details within the text here which, taken in the context of the scripture as a whole, give us further confirmation on this particular subject. A cup in particular refers to one's deep individual experience or participation in something pleasant or evil:

'You anoint my head with oil; my cup runs over,' Psalm 23:5
'If it is possible, let this cup pass from Me;' Matthew 26:39

The golden cup of the prostitute, verse four, in this case full of abominations and filthiness (idolatry and lewdness), signifies the amusement, the personal occupation and indulgence of kings and suggests that this is what she is providing. This particular reference has resonance with Jeremiah 51:7 as the imagery is the same, though it is Babylon that is specifically in view here.

> 'Babylon was a golden cup in the Lord's hand,
> that made all the Earth drunk;
> the nations drank her wine,
> therefore the nations are deranged'

Again in verse two it is the prostitute that has made 'the inhabitants of the Earth 'drunk with the wine of her fornication'. In Jeremiah it is Babylon that is held responsible.

It is the prostitute that is spoken of in verse 1 as sitting on many waters, though it is Babylon that is spoken of in the Old Testament as the one who sits on many waters:

> '...Babylon. O you who dwell by many waters,
> abundant in treasures, your end has come,

the measure of your covetousness.' Jeremiah 51:13

The 'great prostitute' can be compared with another idolatrous city in Assyria in ancient times, Nineveh - see Nahum 3:4-7.

It is then the 'World,' as a degenerate system, that is such a great immoral influence on the whole of mankind being described variously as Babylon, Nineveh or a harlot or prostitute depending on the particular characteristic that is being emphasised. It is the whole atmosphere mankind breathes, the environment he lives in. An influence that holds all in its control and affections – that is all except those who have given their lives entirely to Christ. It is something that claims to give self-fulfilment and happiness, though something that flouts God's claim to obedience. Something that is insidious but compulsive to 'man after the flesh'. Something that we are warned to guard against, again and again in scripture: The World: the materialistic world of capitalism and the love of money. The 'World' that offers entertainment, sensual and sexual pleasures. The philosophy of evolutionary and other scientific theories that exclude God, for example atheism and enlightened thinking that sanction men to reject God totally from their lives.

'For all that is in the world, the lust of the flesh,
the lust of the eyes,
and the pride of life, is not of the Father but is of the world.' 1 John 2:16.

This is simply saying that our relationship with, our outlook and our response to the world, our desires, self-esteem, that is our natural life, are all part of this world.

We cannot fully know the difference until we know the truth (1 John 2:21) and so by abiding in Christ (v.24) we become estranged from the world (1 John 2:3:1). It is only by so remaining, trusting, resting in Christ Himself that we lose the hold that the world has over us. From Matthew chapter 5 the New Testament is so full of the theme of personal holiness and separation from the world. Paul returns to the theme many times in his epistles and we find it through the letters of James, Peter and John into chapters 2 and 3 of the Revelation. We can see then how fundamental and important it is and absolutely central to the Christian life. It is an essential part of:

> 'Pure and undefiled religion before God and the Father is this:
>
> to visit orphans and widows in their trouble,
>
> and to keep oneself unspotted from the world.' James 1:27.

It is the whole of this very world system, Babylon, that is to be removed before Christ sets up His kingdom, firstly from the lives of His saints and then universally with all its trappings and representations. It is though primarily now a matter of individual concern first to withdraw from it, that the life of Christ would purge us from the very evil that would prevent the full revelation of the Lord Himself to us and in us.

SECTION 4: PART 9

Seven Hills and Seven Kingdoms

Revelation Chapter 17: 8-12

The Oppressions and Difficulties of This Life that Refine God's People Israel

In Daniel chapter 2, Nebuchadnezzar was foretold the secular world empires that were to follow his up to the end of this age, though not every kingdom throughout all this time. God's word does not just predict the future but explains to man what His plans are for all mankind and what man's responsibility is then towards Him. Nebuchadnezzar's dream image in Daniel 2 delineated those kingdoms that would fulfil His purposes, specifically in regard to Israel, because it was already prophesied that through Israel would all the other nations of the Earth be blessed. When the Roman armies destroyed Jerusalem and dispersed Israel from the land in AD 70, God's working with them ceased, but only temporarily. In his letter to the Romans chapter 11, verse 25 particularly, Paul prophesied in AD 56, 14 years before the desolation of Jerusalem, that God would take up working with Israel again in the future, just as it had been prophesied in the Old Testament, Amos 9:11.

To Daniel however was given more detail than in Nebuchadnezzar's revelation. To him was foretold not just of the earthly kingdoms that were to rule the Earth but details as to the periods of adversity that his people were to suffer until the end of the age and the specific administrations that would preside over those periods. All these revelations to the king and Daniel were to take place over about sixty years from about 600BC. Some of these prophesied periods that later occurred we can trace through the later books of the Old Testament, Ezra and Nehemiah for example, and are confirmed by general history and in the writings of the history of the children of Israel, for example, in some of the books of the Old Testament apocrypha.

In God's covenant to Israel in Deuteronomy 28:15-68, verses 36 and 63 particularly, God had warned of the consequences of failing to keep His covenant with them.

In 721 BC the ten northern tribes of Israel were taken into captivity because they had failed to live by God's Covenant. Now even Judah eventually failed to stay faithful and had also gone into captivity in 606 BC. God though had a special purpose for Judah because it was through this tribe that Messiah was to come. Throughout their captivity for seventy years in Babylon from circa 606 BC and then again as a nation in their own land until 70 AD, they were to be dominated by foreign powers, though not all these periods would be consecutive. All this, however, had been foretold through Daniel. Not only the fact of their future occupation after their return from Babylon but also what would happen to them, how they would suffer and why this was brought upon them. Returning to Nebuchadnezzar's dream, there were to be five diverse secular governments that would dominate Israel through this period up until the kingdom of the Messiah; one of these secular administrations however was to have two distinct phases in respect of God's planned dealings with His people. There was also another period of suffering for Israel that would transpire, though details were not revealed to Daniel. Ezekiel prophesied this further period, however, reiterating the fact six times in His prophecy, for example Ezekiel 12:15 circa 595 BC, making the completion of God's plan for Israel accomplished through seven periods of oppression.

The first kingdom and period of oppression was Babylon; their captivity of Israel with the impact of that on them in alienating them from their promised land. The people had 'taken God for granted' that He would protect them from their enemies and now they were slaves again in a foreign country. What had changed, from their perspective, to being in Egypt? Why had they, as a nation, gone through all the trauma of crossing the Red Sea and spent forty years in the desert to end up in the same condition? Had God failed in His promise to Abraham? They must have been confused, angry and cynical, but then as we all do in times of extreme crisis, they would have prayed to God to deliver them from their predicament.

Isaiah and Jeremiah had recently prophesied to the nation to exhort them to return to their God, to prevent just this catastrophe, but now it had happened. Then during the reign of Nebuchadnezzar's grandson, Belshazzar, the Medes and Persians took the kingdom. The story of the writing on the wall in Daniel chapter 3 is familiar to us from Sunday school.

The second kingdom then arose after 70 years, as prophesied by Jeremiah, Jeremiah 25:11, see also Daniel 9:2. The Persian Cyrus 1st had issued a decree to repatriate the Jews back to their homeland and not only that but also for them to be allowed to rebuild the temple. Now the temple for the Jews was the place that God would meet with His people, so God had brought back His people, not only to seek after Himself, but also to be able to meet and commune with Him. The facility, however, brought further difficulties; there were those enemies of Judah that sought to sabotage the work. At first they presented themselves as co-worshippers of the God of Judah with offers of help. The work, however, was holy and the people commissioned to do the work were holy, cp Ezra 9:2. Compromise and collaboration would contaminate the holiness of the temple. Frustrated themselves, the saboteurs sought to frustrate and discourage the work, and to stop it altogether. Details of the antagonism are given in Ezra 4:4 and Nehemiah 4:8.

A hundred years were then to pass, with the Jews establishing themselves again in the land, before the third empire that was to dictate their destiny emerged. Now Daniel had a dream many years before of the goat that would destroy the ram, and that had been shown to him as the Greeks that would put down the Persians. In the dream the goat had a single large horn, the horn symbolising in scripture a political power or ruler. It was not the initial attack, however, of the single great horn, Alexander the

Great as it transpired, that is significant he is passed over in scripture in just one verse. It was not he who changed things as far as Israel was concerned, it was when that great horn was 'broken off' in the language of the vision, rather it was the four smaller horns that came up in its place that took Daniel's attention. These four horns it transpired were four generals that ruled the Greek empire after Alexander the Great's death.

It was then just two of those smaller horns that are focused on, the 'king of the north' and the 'king of the south'. This occurred two and a half centuries after Daniel's vision, though in Daniel chapter 11 a detailed account of the campaigns and intrigue that were to ensue between the two show that for Israel, which was poised between the two, it was a time of considerable insecurity. However for a hundred years they were occupied by the southern king, Ptolemy, as history has shown, with tolerance and little interference. Such a state, however, was a constant threat to their peace of mind and anxiety as to their future. Although the politics would not directly affect them, it was significant to them psychologically and spiritually, hence it was prophesied in Daniel's vision. Either the Jews would become unhappy, bitter and disillusioned again with their plight in their promised land, or they would have turned to their God in dependence on Him, and trusted Him to carry them through their never ending insecurity.

Matters, however, were not to get better. The fourth period of occupation was about to break upon them, though technically still part of the Greek empire. This time a truly vicious king was to impose his rule, one whom Daniel had learned quite a lot about from his visions, and one that presented to be a crucial turning point in Israel's history. This was the little horn of the goat that 'waxed exceedingly great towards the south and towards the east and towards the pleasant land,' in chapter 8. In chapter 11:21 he is described as:

> 'A vile person...he shall come in peaceably
> and seize the kingdom by intrigue.'

History has shown this to be the evil monster Antiochus IV, Epiphanies, who persecuted the Jews, trying to stamp out their identity and culture and murdering anyone that resisted him. Only the faithful to their God would stand up and resist him. Only those that knew their God could and would not deny Him. The easier option was to concede and keep one's head below the parapet, to renounce their God and discard His word and worship. Those that studied the scriptures at that time maybe would think from Daniel's prophecies, 7:22+26, 8:25, 11:36-45, that the kingdom of the Messiah was imminent and would have yearned and prayed for that, though chapter 9 would show that another two hundred years were to elapse till the coming of the Messiah. History has shown us that it was the Maccabean uprising against Antiochus Epiphanies that delivered the Jews from perhaps complete annihilation, and offered the Jews a hundred years of independence and recuperation. Then looming on the horizon was another power, an occupying force strong and ruthless.

This was to be the fourth empire, the fifth period of trauma in God's dealings with Israel. This was the 'iron legs of Nebuchadnezzar's image', the fourth empire, that is the legs of the whole sequence of empires, the commercial and political dominions that were to control Israel's destiny and shape them to the quality of relationship with God that He wanted for them. This indeed proved to be the moulding power that was to influence Judah's character for nearly a hundred years, the Roman army. Government was mediated through the ruthless Herod, the Roman procurator under Caesar Augustus at the time of Christ's birth. Order was maintained directly by the Roman army.

Many in Judah were looking for their Messiah to come and deliver them from the Roman yoke at the time of Christ, but when He came they did not recognize Him because they were looking for someone who would exercise military might in defeating their enemy. Also the sect of the Pharisees, which had started as a movement two hundred years before to maintain the purity of the Jewish faith from heresy and compromise, like the rest of their religion, their devotion to God had become stifled in a formalism that focused on mere observance of the details of the law and not on the spirit of it. The Jewish people therefore were caught between the iron rule of their invaders on the one hand and the stifling dogmas of their religion on the other. A faith of love, forgiveness and repentance that Christ offered them was the opposite of what they were looking for and so they rejected it. God, however, had still many years to persevere with Israel before He could fulfil His will in them and for them.

It was therefore less than forty years after the Jews as a nation had rejected God's offer of salvation because it did not fit with their aspirations and beliefs that the next phase of God's working with His chosen people was to be brought into being, the sixth phase. This was the phase that was not foreseen by Daniel, though it is prophesied in Ezekiel as referred above to bring them to recognise their true God. In AD 70, Jerusalem was razed to the ground. The temple was burned down and levelled, just as Christ prophesied would happen in Matthew 24. The Jews, like the rest of Israel were now to be scattered among all the nations of the world, as a nation they would cease to exist. By all outward signs, the Romans had now achieved what others had tried but failed to accomplish, the annihilation of the Israeli nation. It must have seemed to the early Christians that perhaps God had entirely rejected the Jews and had chosen them instead. The apostle Paul, however, affirmed that this was impossible, that God could never go back on His promises. The apostle John however in the Book of the Revelation brings to us the full picture of what God is achieving in Israel and indeed in the Church and the relationship between them both in God's eternal councils. This we come to in the last part of this section.

The Seven Heads, ie Seven-Mindedness

Now scriptural prophecy is not just given to satisfy our curiosity of what will transpire in the future. The prophecies of Daniel were given to Him specifically to tell his people what would befall them in the latter days. God was concerned for them to know what His plan was in them and for them, for them to have faith in Him and to understand His purposes for them when these things came about. By extension it is also both of interest to ourselves in understanding the eternal purposes of God, and the means by which God attains them, and also typically these accounts are significant as well for ourselves in and through our pathway here.

These prophetic words of God in Revelation, however, are given to the Church and are primarily of profound spiritual enlightenment and encouragement to our faith. We see typically for ourselves, in a practical way through God's dealings with Israel, the principles that God employs in bringing His chosen people from their natural state of rebellion into one of complete dependence upon Him through their various periods of defeat and adversity. In Revelation the spiritual implications of these periods of adversity are detailed.

In chapter 13 of the Revelation we saw Daniel's beast emerge from the sea, giving us a character sketch of him. Now the sea is a dark restless mass, heaving and battering the land. As mentioned the sea was not viewed in ancient times as a place of beauty or recreation, but as a threat to peace and security. Sometimes in scripture the sea then portrays symbolically the nations that surround and impinge on the pleasant land of Israel; typically for us the threats and difficulties that we face in life and faith.

In chapter 17 the beast comes into focus yet again, but this time to explain God's purposes in such a beast, what it is that God has been bringing about in and for His chosen people. The first surprise, in chapter 13, was that it was the Devil himself that gave the beast all its strength and reason for being. In the seventeenth chapter, however, its full character is exposed. Its seven heads, that is, its minds, its purposes, its way of working, are described as also being seven hills. Now these hills are symbolic, word symbols, just as the seven heads are symbolic to describe the mind or purposes of the brute.

The seven heads of the 'beast' then are also described as seven hills; it is to describe a different aspect or characteristic of this beast. To interpret 'the seven hills' as referring to a place or other entity as has been done, however, is treating the scripture as a riddle. The scripture here specifically calls for wisdom, though of course so does the interpretation of all scripture, but here it is especially called for; now 'The fear (reverence) of the Lord is the beginning of wisdom;' Psalm 111:10. Spiritual, eternal principles are at issue, not single isolated physical associations however significant they are. This would be just the natural mind at work.

The hill or mountain here refers to a universal authority or power, or by association the oppression, obstacle or adversity caused by them, ie a spiritual concept not a physical one. The 'seven' is the number of completeness. The interpretation then would simply be absolute or complete power or authority. There is a physical interpretation here though as well, but that is given by the angel: 'The seven heads are seven mountains and they are seven kings', or kingdoms. That the Beast has a correlation with Nebuchadnezzar's dream-image and empires, that is the empires that have had significant influential in Israel's history as foretold in Daniel chapter 3, is of little doubt, as we consider in the next piece of this study. That there is implied a religious dimension in this beast's make-up, however, is not apparent. We have to go to the 2nd beast for that, which will arise out of the land. That, however, is another issue that was explained in section 2.

A hill or mountain in scripture simply means an exalted position, though always with certain significant connotations, what particularly being implied by the context. It may mean prominence, for example, Matthew 5:14; or supremacy, Psalm 2:6 and Daniel 2:35 or a position of security or strength. In John 4:20 it is the social religious structure that is referred to, thus it can indicate government or other social structures, these all are descriptive in some way of what derives from some power or entity. However it can have other implications or allusions, such as being a negative force or consequence, for instance in Psalm 76:4 it is an aggressor, implying a threat; in Luke 3:5 and 1 Corinthians 13:2 it can mean any personal obstacle or difficulty, which is the way we sometimes use the word 'mountain' metaphorically in English. In Revelation 17 it refers specifically to social influences; here it is specifically in connection with seven consecutive kings or kingdoms. The social power referred to then is something that supports a corrupt world ideology that is opposed to the Lamb and His saints; this refers to the great harlot, this was explained in the last piece in this section. These hills then embody the antagonism and adversity imposed on God's people through seven phases of history.

This beast, we know from Daniel 2, represents the sequence of empires that will oppress God's people to the end of time, though also in another respect in Revelation 17 it is a picture epitomising the final ruler himself, embodying all the vile characteristics of the seven kings, hence the 'beast' can represent either the king or dictator, or the kingdom depending on the context. The seven hills are shown to be the place where the great harlot sits and would symbolize the adversarial influences that Israel suffers under the dominions and oppressive forces with which we all have to triumph over in this life typically, for us being the worldly influences and difficulties of life. Specifically here it is the rule or structure of life under this great political entity which is motivated by Satan himself. They are also defined specifically as seven kings or kingdoms that relate to the times of oppression on the Jews. Just to make absolutely sure to what they refer the scripture explains that five kings are fallen ie passed into history. We have just seen outlined in the scriptures the five kings or kingdoms that have had specific influence on the fate of God's chosen people These are the Kings that must be referred to here; Nebuchadnezzar, Cyrus/Artaxerxes, Ptolemy/Seluceus, Antiochus Epiphanies and lastly Julius Caesar to Tiberius, or rather the administrations they represent.

'The sixth Kings now is' - that is when the prophecy was made some twenty years after the fall of Jerusalem and has been until within the past seventy years, during which time Israel had ceased to exist. This is the 'hill', ie disruption, which Ezekiel had prophesied when the whole nation would be dispersed throughout the world. However, one king is yet to come. Now since 1947 the Jewish state has been recreated and the Jews are back in their own land, free and independent, albeit without their temple. How long it will be before they are once again under the dominion of the Babylonian image, that is the feet of Nebuchadnezzar's statue, the seventh king of the Beast of Revelation. ie repressed under the sovereignty once again of a pagan state, remains yet to be seen. Indeed what is it that God would achieve in this final phase before the 'abomination of desolation,' the full personification of Daniel's fearsome beast, ascends from the bottomless pit to play out the last few years of secular world history? These will be the years yet to be before Messiah Himself comes to set up His kingdom, just as God has promised to His chosen people many times through His prophets.

All this may seem rather academic and of no immediate significance to ourselves and perhaps even just incidental to the fortunes of Israel. This part of this study has been to explain the historical and symbolic meaning of these visions; the next piece in this section explains then their deeper spiritual significance, particularly now to the Church, but also to Israel and to all those that are called into God's Kingdom.

Appendix 7 is a summary of the periods of oppression referred to here that are relevant through Israel's history of sanctification, both to Israel and ourselves.

SECTION 4: PART 10

Seven Hills: A Spiritual Allegory

Revelation Chapter 17: 8-12

It is Through the Oppressions and Difficulties of This Life That We Are Refined into the People that God Wants Us to Be

What then can we learn from the foregoing piece? What relevance has all this to the Church of Christ? Why indeed was the final mystery of Israel's history made known to the church through John and not to God's prophet Daniel? The answer to both questions comes from understanding the spiritual significance of the whole succession of adverse circumstances that Israel have been through since their becoming a great nation in the land of Egypt. God had made it plain to Israel what His intentions were for them through His prophet Hosea in chapter 14:5-6:

'I will be like the dew to Israel: he shall grow like the lily,

and lengthen his roots like Lebanon.

His branches shall spread; his beauty shall be like an olive tree,

and his fragrance like Lebanon.'

This piece then looks at the successive periods of adversity, outlined in the previous piece, which Israel suffers, past, present and future to bring them into the blessings that God wants for them, then for us to learn how this also works typically for us and all of God's people.

In their time in Babylon they were physically held captive; Babylon, as representing all the world religiously, materially and philosophically. The children of God today as members of the church are also physically in the world, with its outlook and values, though now Christ is risen He has overcome the world, John 16:33, and has sent His Spirit that we might no longer live under the dominion of this world system but live a life of separation to God. This world, however, is still a strong influence on us, testing and strengthening our faith in the same way that God brought Israel through the times in captivity and occupation that He might make His people qualified for His eternal purpose for them, Daniel 12:10. If we through sin or unbelief are separated from fellowship with God we then lose that power to live for God alone and are at the mercy of our circumstances again. We become occupied with the same concerns that all those around us are occupied with, our own wellbeing, making money and the things that money can buy, with gaining prestige and power, and with the entertainments that the world has to offer. Christ becomes no more than someone we give decorous acknowledgement to, typified in the church at Laodicea in Revelation 3. As captive to this present evil world we no longer enjoy our heavenly citizenship, Philippians 3:19-21.

It is not until we again acknowledge our error and ask Christ to forgive and deliver us that He can bring us back again in power and fellowship with Himself; that is He brings us again into the promised land metaphorically speaking. It is there that He can keep us, rebuilding the temple that had fallen down, the temple symbolizing God's dwelling with man. Each day as we persevere with Him in His life, our souls and bodies become His dwelling place with us and in testimony to the world around; just as those faithful Jews that were delivered from Babylon started work on the rebuilding of the Temple. They had those that knew not Israel's God, who for their own motives, possibly mischievous, sought to be involved with the work of rebuilding the temple. So we find that many false prophets and teachers would arise to lead us astray from the pure truth of Christ. If we do not remain totally true to Christ and the truth of the scriptures, the work becomes marred with work that is done from worldly or fleshly motives and unfit for the master's use. That work of 'building the temple' is the work of God in us with which we are intimately involved, Philippians 2:12-13; it is a private, spiritual, Divine work, not one of a certain method or procedure.

After the temple is rebuilt, that is God dwelling with us again by His Spirit and we with Him, He would then test what is of Himself in our lives to refine the gold and burn off the dross. As Nehemiah mourned the fact that the City of Jerusalem still lay in ruins, likewise we yearn to become like Christ, to have Him build His perfect life in us, building us up together in Him, Ephesians 2:22. In Daniel 9 it was the decree to rebuild the city of Jerusalem though that was to be the start of the seventy weeks, that is 70 x 7 years, that were determined, that is assigned, to the people of God before Messiah would set up His Kingdom. Further details are in epilogue 2. The city of Jerusalem is the place where the king reigned, typically for us where Christ is totally sovereign. The first seven weeks or 49 years the city would be in building would be times of difficulty and trouble, Daniel 9:25. The building of what is good and holy in our lives will meet with great obstacle and difficulty, but only that which is the work of the Holy Spirit in our lives is pure and holy. Only that which is of God is suitable for God. Only that will sustain.

However, what Satan cannot obstruct by stealth or deceit he will try and prevent directly. The world will not tolerate the work of God any more than it tolerated Christ Himself, John 15:18-19. Even after the worst fires of persecution and rejection we are not free of Satan's devices to separate us from the God who is ever seeking to draw us closer to Himself. The world will not applaud our faithfulness to Christ; the world will not love us because Christ shines from our everyday living. The world will be harsh and unforgiving, it may applaud good works that are seen as a sign of civilized appearances, but that can catch us off guard and tempt us to merely cultivate such qualities in our own strength and that is of no eternal value, that is merely 'wood, hay and straw,' that is deeds that are done from human motives. These will be burned up, 1

Corinthians 3:11-17. That is the very hollow religion in the Pharisees that Christ expresses woe or sorrow for.

What God has built however, of gold and silver and precious stones, will be tested, tried by fire to refine it further and make its character more pure and beautiful; that or to expose what is false and remove it, ie all that has been put in place by our own effort. When difficulty, when uncertainty predominate our lives, then will the work of God alone shine forth in its purity. Life rarely passes long without some period of trouble and adversity. Grief or temptation, unemployment or loss may be our lot, anything that makes us take our eyes off Christ and look at the heaving waters beneath our feet, but what God has wrought in our lives is equal to anything and we will be more than conquerors through Him who loved us Romans 8:35-39.

Even then there may be worse to come, as it was for the Jews under Antiochus Epiphanies. God may yet test our faith and His work of grace within us even more. Persecution, direct open or even covert hostility will cast us into the furnace of reproach or rejection by our fellow men. Our God, however, can keep us through the worst and He will not let us be tested beyond our strength 1 Corinthians 10:13. Christ Himself told us not to be fearful if we are persecuted, rejected and abused, see Luke 21:12-18. He will be with us in the hottest fire (cp Daniel 3) and not one hair of our heads will be singed, and the smell of the fire will not be upon us. Only what is of man, of our own effort, a show of what we naturally conceive to be morally good, that is wood, hay and straw, will perish.

There is yet though something else, some other circumstance that we can find ourselves in this world that will test our love of Christ; for anyone that has come through the most severe fires of persecution; anyone that has come through the rigors of the uncertainties of life; anyone that has left behind the riches of this world for the unsearchable riches of Christ.

History records what a cruel army the Romans were, though it is only what the scriptures say that is significant to us spiritually. Daniel 2:40 tells us, prophetically in 600BC, speaking of the legs of Nebuchadnezzar's dream-image:

> 'The fourth kingdom shall be as strong as iron:
> inasmuch as iron breaks in pieces
> and shatters everything;
> and like iron that crushes,
> that kingdom will break in pieces and crush all the others'.

Its ruthless destructive character can be seen in the New Testament Gospels and in the 'Acts of the Apostles', for example the way the soldiers treated Jesus once He had been condemned to be crucified and from what was implied when Jesus answered the soldiers' question on how they should behave, in Luke 3:14. The Jews probably hated the way that they were treated, resented the occupation of their country by such a brutal aggressor, and would have despised the fact they were gentiles. The fact that they were ruled by Herod, an Edominite procurator, a descendant of Esau, would have been a continual offence to them also. He also was a very cruel man, as the execution of John the Baptist and his slaughter of the innocents bear witness.

We could easily identify at a natural level with such feelings towards the oppressors, though Jesus Himself taught us how we need to respond to such provocation, Luke 6:29. It is not something we can do, however, from the heart in our own strength; to respond on a natural plane and just try and repress our real feelings is simply to sin and cut us off from fellowship with our Lord. Our religion becomes hollow; an outward structure of formalism or simply keeping laws and rules; something that we defend the more fanatically, the greater the pressure is on us. It is easy to censure the Pharisees for their fanaticism and hypocrisy and yet the act of doing so can make us of the same caste as them.

'Whoever compels you to go one mile, go with him two,'

'Love your enemies, bless those who curse you, do good to those who hate you,

and pray for those who spitefully use you and persecute you.'

Christ taught in St Matthew 5:41 and 44, indicating implicitly perhaps how the Jews felt about the Romans.

However that emotion is not explicitly attributed to the Jews in the scripture, so we cannot assume that this was God's primary purpose in allowing them to be tested by the cruelty of the Romans, as prophesied in Daniel chapter 9, witness verse 26. The culmination of this period of suffering for the Jews would be the coming of their Messiah. Yet He would not come in triumph at that time, rather He would be 'cut off', v.26, from them and not to receive His kingdom at that time.

This was in part the purpose of God in bringing in this occupation, that Messiah should fulfil His work of redemption. John's gospel, chapter 11, shows us that it was anxiety and fear of the Romans that caused the Pharisees to plan Messiah's death. It was Caiaphas the high priest who in suggesting it as a solution to the chief priest's and Pharisees' dilemma, prophesied that Christ would die for His people. Indeed the Jews on two occasions had postured to stone Christ to death, but each time that was because they believed that He 'being a man had made Himself to be God'. It was, however, against this situation of the Jews' fear of the Romans and no doubt Daniel's prophesy as to when their Messiah would come, that led so many to accept Him as Messiah, as we see from the 'very great multitude' that welcomed Him into Jerusalem that first Palm Sunday in fulfilment of Zechariah prophecy (9:9). It had been the great number of Jews that believed in Jesus following His raising of Lazarus that had precipitated the priest's decision to kill Jesus. Again as in other occupations of Israel, this oppression by the Romans had polarized the Jewish nation into either rejecting God's ordained plan or being sanctified the more to His calling.

Daniel 9:26, however, says more. 'Messiah will be cut off', but then the people of the prince that shall come shall destroy the city and the sanctuary and continue until all the destruction that had been determined was complete. This indeed was the position in relation to Israel at the time the Revelation was written. It was still Rome that was in power at that time, but the 'hill' of crisis, the catastrophe that prevailed over Judah was now one of complete desolation of their country and scattering of the people among the nations. The secular power of Greece represented two different periods of repression and phases of His working with His people in blessing through that repression; this was presided over by two different gentile kings. Likewise now Rome had first presided over the repression of fear that had lead the Jews to crucify their Messiah and so bring salvation to the world. Now they had also presided over the dissolution of the nation and their land laid waste.

Now this different direction of and attitude to the Jews was leading them to many centuries of harassment and a longing to return to Jerusalem. This is specified as the sixth king that 'now is', in Revelation 17. Jesus had predicted the desolation at the end of Matthew, chapter 23:38, after having pronounced such sorrow at the hollow religion of the Scribes and Pharisees. In the next chapter He then continues to reveal to His disciples how the temple would be completely destroyed but that the gospel of the kingdom must then be preached throughout the world before the end finally comes. This is how God's purposes are still being fulfilled. The gospel is still being preached in this era of grace, but Israel still remains oblivious to God's purposes for them until the time that Matthew 23:39 is finally fulfilled. This of course had already happened in Matthew 21:9 in one sense, but the context of the prophesy in chapter 23 is after the desolation of the temple; in the context of chapter 24:30.

What are God's purposes for Israel though now, is it possible that He has finally rejected them? The verse from Matthew 23 just quoted belies that. Romans 11:11 answers the question in a nutshell:

> 'Have they stumbled that they should fall?
> Certainly not! But through their fall, to provoke them to jealousy,
> salvation has come to the Gentiles.'

And then from verse 25:

> '…Blindness in part has happened to Israel
> until the fullness of the Gentiles has come in.
> And so all Israel will be saved.'

These verses, profound as they are, are incidental in this respect to what Paul was teaching in chapters ten and eleven of his letter to the Romans. The whole letter to the Romans was mainly to emphasize to them that salvation comes by the grace of God alone, through faith. It was because of unbelief that Israel was 'broken off the olive tree', therefore we need to be vigilant that we remain faithful as we are not in any way inherently superior to Israel and the same principle could apply to us; it is only by faith that we remain grafted into the root. It is only living in Him that we are anything; only by remaining in the vine (to move to the metaphor of John 15) can we bear the fruit of patience, gentleness and goodness. At the best naturally we can merely but control our feelings and make an outward show of goodness.

We may also ask what God is achieving through Israel, and Judah in particular during their time of being 'cut off from the olive tree'; in Amos 9:8-9:

> 'Yet I will not utterly destroy the house of Jacob,'
> says the Lord.
> 'For surely I will command,
> and will sift the house of Israel among all nations,
> as grain is sifted in a sieve;
> yet not the smallest grain shall fall to the ground.'

God is ever seeking to purify His chosen people Israel, as He is also for ourselves and His Church. In chapters 7 and 14 of the book of the Revelation we find 144,000 faithful receiving special protection during that time of tribulation, twelve thousand from each tribe of Israel. Later they are then with the Lamb on Mount Zion, Mount Zion, the place where Messiah will come back to Earth as ruler and King. It is though as a leader of gentleness and meekness, we see Him here, in the character of the Lamb and they follow in His footsteps. No more do they wander from their God, no more do they follow the gods of self-achievement, satisfaction and pleasure; no more are they motivated by natural passions and desires, of status and repute.

To return to Revelation 17, we know that there will yet be a seventh king or kingdom, reign or epoch of the Beast that 'when he comes, he must continue a short time'; the scripture doesn't give us details of the character or corollary of this king. This will perhaps be before the full personification of the beast appears as one man, the man that the Lord will slay with the sword of His mouth, the one that in verse eleven of Revelation 17 is:

> 'The beast that was, and is not, is himself
> also the eighth,
> and is of the seven and is going to perdition.'

This beast personifies all the evil that is inherent in mankind; the anti-Christ, all that is opposite to and in opposition to Christ.

Whether verse 11 means he is literally a reincarnation of one of the seven previous kings, or the epitome 'of them' (all) in character, or both is perhaps not important.

Verse 12 tells us at that time that an oligarchy or confederation of ten kingdoms will constitute the empire at that time. This aligns with the ten toes of the feet of the image of Daniel 2. Daniel 7:24 gives further details in the context of Daniel's vision. This would suggest that this empire might be a 'united states' of Europe just for example or another group of nations, or confederation, such as a 'united states' of Arab nations. That might help to be able to picture it, but it is foolish to speculate as to its actual embodiment, that will be apparent at the time. These kings or kingdoms take their character and instructions from this ruler that epitomises all that is evil in this world. Perhaps the 'hour' that they co-reign with the beast is the hour referred to as the hour of wrath in Revelation chapter 14:7 and chapter 18.

This will be him that fulfils the picture of the terrible beast of Daniel chapter 7:7 and the desolator of the last verse of chapter 9 of Daniel:

'Then he shall confirm a covenant with many for one week;
but in the middle of the week
he shall bring an end to sacrifice and offering.
And on the wing of abominations shall be one who makes desolate,
even until the consummation, which is determined,
is poured out on the desolate.'

That the covenant is something made between the Jews and the 'desolator' of the second part of the verse is implicit, though what that covenant is we can deduce no more than from what is said. Some say that this covenant refers to the Messiah, although the second part of verse 26 would belie that. Isaiah 28:15+18 is probably what is being referred to; here we have it in its spiritual context:

> 'Because you have said, 'We have made a covenant with death,
> and with Sheol we are in agreement.
> When the overflowing scourge passes through,
> it will not come to us,
> for we have made lies our refuge,
> and under falsehood we have hidden ourselves.'...'
> 'Your covenant with death will be annulled,
> and your agreement with Sheol will not stand;
> when the overflowing scourge passes through,
> then you will be trampled down by it.'

The warning is sinister; if we trust in the promises of security in this world, whether they are political or materialistic, we will suffer for it, the overflowing scourge will pass through our lives and trample us down. If we live by the Spirit of Truth then we will be sustained. Thus we can learn from the history of Israel, that we trace through the Old Testament scriptures, a profound analogy of the type of difficulties and trials that we pass through and how that moulds us to become the person that God has planned for us to be, in the image of Christ. It is a very enlightening, reassuring, encouraging and comforting picture.

SECTION 4: PART 11

The New Heavens and Earth

Revelation Chapters 21-22
'Behold I Make All Things New'

From the beginning of Creation, throughout the whole of time up until this point in scripture, God has been showing mankind the way of Salvation and waiting until all His purposes for mankind have been fulfilled. That time has now come at this point in the prophecy, and now He reveals what His consummate plan for creation is, all that has been in the making since the beginning of creation, all that God been effecting throughout the whole of time.

We cannot perhaps fathom the wisdom of God, why in the first place He should create a universe that could be vulnerable to malfunction, but Romans 8:20 tells us that 'the whole creation was made subject to futility', that is without any purpose in and for itself, only what God intended ultimately to achieve through it. It is this final outcome that we are now introduced to, what God had planned in and for creation in the end. God planned also that mankind should have a role in this ultimate paradise, but that to qualify for that role mankind should have to 'through much tribulation enter the Kingdom'

Chapter 21 shows us what those qualities are that He planned to create in us through the difficulty and adversity that, although much of it is common to all mankind, we pass through to reach that final perfect and eternal state.

For this to finally transpire, however, first had to come the removal of all that could oppose it, to establish a state where only God Himself and His Life and Will could prevail.

John now sees a 'new Heaven and a new Earth for the first Heaven and the first Earth had passed away'. The old order of continual change, of birth and then death has now been replaced by a new order of continuity, of universal peace and unity. Christ has put down all opposition to the universal rule of God, the judgement day is past and all that is contrary to the absolute reign of God Himself has been banished. Now is revealed the mystery of how this new order of things will be maintained, the administration that has been prepared to oversee God's mighty creation and maintain its perfect integrity.

> 'Then I John saw the Holy City New Jerusalem
> coming down out of Heaven from God
> prepared as a bride adorned for her husband'

This beautiful simile describes for us so succinctly what it is that God had planned to bring about through the course of the history of time. He then goes on describe all the beauty and glory of its function.

> 'Behold the tabernacle of God is with men',
> a loud voice proclaims from Heaven;
> 'He will dwell with them and they shall be His people.
> God Himself will be with them and be their God.
> God shall wipe away every tear from their eyes,
> there shall be no more death, nor sorrow, nor crying
> and there shall be no more pain
> for the former things are passed away.'

The essence of this city is not in bricks and mortar as the old material Jerusalem, or according the secular politics of its earthly government, but rather its essence and function are primarily spiritual in that it provides for the complete contentment of all mankind, indeed for all creation.

Then He who sat upon the throne said 'Behold I make all things new'. He alone has the authority and wisdom to plan and execute such a thing. It is difficult to conceive a world that is free from sin, death and disappointment, but God asserts that these sayings are true and faithful. It is something that we can only begin to appreciate through faith, a faith that comes from knowing Him whom we believe in.

We are told, however, four things about this new world that help us to grasp its substance; first that it is done, it is now complete in itself, there are no more transitions to a better state, that which is perfect is now come. Next God tells us that it is His intrinsic being that guarantees it. Not only has He been in control from the very beginning to the end of time but also He is in Himself the Beginning and the End of all that He has established. It is His life that is the only vitality in all things, His character of selfless love that embodies everyone; His eternal being that upholds everything.

Next we are told how this new milieu will function: 'I will give of the fountain of the water of life freely to him who thirsts', verse 6. Jesus also said in John 4:14: 'The water that I shall give… will become a fountain of water springing up into eternal life'. 'Water' is used here in the same way, as a metaphor for the quality of heavenly life. Quite the opposite in character to our present natural life of anxiety, self-promotion and competitiveness, this will be of a different order completely, a life that does not emanate solely from within ourselves but from the heart of God alone springing up within us, a life of love, joy and peace; a life that we can begin to experience now in Christ, but then we can know it in its fullness without any hindrance as now, it will be the only life that we can know, the old order is gone completely with the old world.

Thirdly we are told of the benefits that it will provide and to whom they will be given; namely to those that have prevailed in this temporal life, 'He who overcomes shall inherit all things'. Revelation 12:11 tells us of those that overcame the power of Satan by the power of the Lamb's sacrifice for them and in living in them. In chapters 2 and 3 also of this book, seven times Christ promises to those that overcome, that is rising victorious over their present time of trial, will He give some particular reward for their faithfulness. In Chapter 7 of the Revelation we considered all the benefits and rewards that are to be found in Christ. Now in this chapter all these things can be realised in full by those that have devoted their all to Christ, those that have overcome the world, the influence of Satan and indeed their own animal nature of self-interest, can now inherit the fullness of what they had only known in part before.

Finally above all is that intimate personal relationship that mankind will know with God and the perfect contentment that that will realise: 'I will be his God and he shall be my son'. At this present time we have the witness within ourselves that we have that life of God, 1 John 5:10; now we learn obedience day by day to conform to that life that God seeks to realise in us, that obedience that is implicit in the role of Divine sonship. Even Christ we are told, 'though He was a Son, yet He learned obedience by things which He suffered.' When this learning process is over, when that eternal day finally dawns, however, that relationship of complete love and security will be fully grasped and cannot change. The suffering of this present time will no longer be needed, but what it effected will remain.

It is a picture of what Heaven really holds for those that know and love God, an ideal and a fantasy even to some, except for those that truly know the Benefactor. To them it becomes a brighter reality throughout life as we make progress in those heavenly virtues that bring us ever nearer that heavenly city, like Christian in Pilgrim's Progress.

It will only be a true paradise, however, because that previous world of adversity, that testing environment that we now occupy, of all that stands in opposition to the perfect peace and holiness of God, will no longer find any place there; it will have fulfilled its purpose of sanctification and have been eradicated. Those that have not overcome, however, that ever only lived according to the dictates of this natural world and life, can know nothing of the blessings of the life that is found in God alone. Timidity, disobedience, offensiveness, hatred, immorality, drug-taking, consumerism, dissimulation, to paraphrase the list in verse 8, all those characteristics that feature a Godless life cannot be allowed to find any expression; they must depart.

Naturally we do not feel comfortable with the idea that a loving God could create anything or anybody that would ultimately be destined for destruction and suffering. From a superficial human perspective it would seem a contradiction that suggests inconsistencies in the character of God. The Bible, however, is quite explicit that those that persist in unbelief, those that refuse to deny their natural inclinations and accept God's gift of deliverance from that way of life, will find no place in a sphere of holiness, righteousness and Divine love. They will be shut out into eternal blackness, loneliness and regret. Natural self-interest can never have any place in that heavenly sphere, everything there has to be perfect, of God alone, or that place would not be perfect.

It is, however, because God is a God of love, true love that is, not just a sentimental disposition, that God created a creature that was free to make moral choices. If love was programmed into that creature so that it could not do otherwise than love, then it would not be love in reality. Love in its fullness is absolute faith in its object of love. Love in its fullness is total denial of self for the good of another. Love in its fullness is the living for that other alone. Such is the nature of God towards His creatures and it is only that love of God born and sustained within us that can have any understanding or appreciation of Him. If then we are to have the choice to love God, then implicitly we must have the ability and opportunity also to refuse, hence were we created as beings that could choose between obedience towards God, through trusting His goodness alone, or we could choose to be independent and thus essentially and totally be alienated from Him. By default as it were, we have a life that is programmed towards self-preservation and fulfilment; we have to choose between that life, with its failure and disappointments, and the life that God would give to those that sincerely seek it. There is no middle ground or give and take. God is a God of love, but He is also perfect in virtue and holiness and so compromise is impossible.

Thus the cowardly, unbelieving, abominable, murders, sexually immoral, sorcerers (enchanters with drugs), idolaters and all liars shall have their part in the lake of fire, which burns with fire and brimstone; that is eternally consumed. This is the second death. All that is contrary to what is good and glorious is banished, completely and permanently from God's creation, to be consumed eternally in the Lake of Fire. All that is contrary to the perfect character of God must be forever abolished and remain so, so that which is perfect can remain untainted. It must forever remain in distinction and separation from that which is good. That which is perfect can only be so in contrast to all that is impure and unsustainable, so the lake of fire also serves an eternal purpose. All and everything that is unholy is forever consumed and so this then serves permanently to accentuate the glory of the Holy City.

We next come to the picture that begins to explain the mystery of why God created a world that would fall into defection. It is through the difficulties of this present time, this sphere of adversity and antipathy, that the qualities necessary for the government of that idyllic new world are forged and proved, for it is the dispensing of those heavenly features, through His creatures, that constitute this new world. For these qualities to be implanted within us so that we acted automatically would mean they would be performed out of necessity and not by choice. This would be contrary to the life of God within, and we would not then be children of God, having His character and knowing that special loving relationship, but simply servants only as the angels in Heaven. This question is also answered from a Divine perspective in 2 Corinthians 4:7 when speaking about the Light of the Gospel: 'We have this treasure in earthen vessels (ie our weak human bodies) that the excellence of the power may be of God and not of ourselves'.

This new spiritually-constituted government is proclaimed to us now, but then more than now it will be wholly imparted through us. It will not just be partially formed within us as now but then be fully developed and functional.

The description that is now presented is spectacular. The description, however, is not in simple prose; it is in poetic language par excellence. The picture presented gives an aesthetic account of that heavenly organization, emphasising its superlative beauty and worth. It is also an account that is almost totally symbolic in its narrative, so that we need to study and contemplate the vision carefully.

Having done so we realise that what is being described here is more wonderful than we could have imagined and that its ramifications touch upon all of God's purposes for His creation.

> 'Then one of the angels who had the seven bowls filled with the seven last plagues came to me and talked with me saying,
>
> 'Come I will show you the bride, the Lamb's wife'.
>
> And he carried me away in the Spirit to a great and high mountain
>
> and showed me the great city, the Holy Jerusalem,
>
> descending out of Heaven from God.'

Significantly it was an angel that had been involved in the demonstration of God's judgement that also reveals the blessing that God has for those that defer to Him. Blessing can only follow judgement personally and corporately, blessing for both mankind and indeed all creation ultimately.

This great phenomenon that is about to be unveiled, this wonder that transpires to transcend all in this new Heaven and Earth, is presented as the 'Lamb's wife'. It was the Lamb to whom had been given the scroll with the mandate to bring in God's Kingdom on Earth. In this new scene another figure is introduced, one that has a special, intimate relationship with the Lamb, one that is totally likeminded as He in His intent to maintain His Father's will in this new realm. The concept of God's people being like a bride of God is of course one that is found in the Old Testament. In the

New Testament the comparison disappears and our relationship with Christ is spoken of as being one of marriage, eg 2 Corinthians 11:2 and in the Parables of Jesus in Matthew 22 and 25. Here it is Christ that is spoken of as having the 'Bride'; the union is now complete. It is something however that is just spiritually apprehended at this present time, whatever physical or other substance this new world may have. It is its spiritual character and substance that is presented here.

It is something also that is seen from a great and a high mountain. Here a mountain would be a metaphor for a moral position or authority, in the same way as Zion is God's Holy Mountain. This 'mountain' is described as large and elevated, suggesting the grandeur and privilege of the vista, something that we cannot begin to appreciate or understand except 'In the Spirit'; cp. 1 Corinthians 2:14. This detail is not just added for dramatic effect either, this great spectacle is coming directly from Heaven, from God Himself; it is all His plan and creation. It has to be as it radiates His glory alone, that glory that has been revealed to us in Jesus Christ, to apprehend and to reflect on if we live in Him.

The description goes on, however, to give us a portrayal that is rather more independent of just personal experience; 'Her light was like a most precious stone'; her light, this Holy Metropolis, is its most immediate feature, that of giving light, that is perception and discernment as to her real character; 'like a jasper stone, clear as crystal'. This is probably what we would call a diamond today, suggesting moral clarity and purity, like Him who sat on the throne in chapter 4, in all His lucidity and Holiness. Hence also its great and high wall suggests its moral significance and elevation.

There then follows a more detailed account of that city, this bride of the Lamb, which describes its purpose and function. First there are gates, not to keep anyone out because verse 25 tells us that the gates shall never be shut; the gates are there for all the nations to enter into the blessings that this Holy institution confers unhindered. It was to Abraham that God promised that in him should all the nations of the Earth be blessed and here we have an account of how that will be ultimately fulfilled permanently and continuously. It is the Israelites that are the gates to this heavenly economy; they are the people that bring the nations into that heavenly city, with all the blessings for them that place embodies. This is more than just a general pronouncement regarding their corporate role, however; each gate has the name, that is, the characteristic of one of the twelve tribes of Israel.

In parts 2-6 of this section we considered the meanings of each of those names in respect of the blessings that we can receive now in Christ. In that heavenly realm it will be Israel that possesses those blessings; more than that, it will be those blessings that will be the means by which they will be the channels through which all the nations will receive those blessings as well. How profound and far reaching will God's promise to Abraham then be fulfilled,

In this scene it is Israel's heavenly function that will be relevant, that is priestly in bringing others into the blessing of the Holy City. In chapter 7 the names were a picture of the heavenly blessings that those that are born of Christ can now experience. The meaning of the names, though given to the sons by their mothers, for the most part were fortuitous from the point of view of their Divine or spiritual significance, yet they show the very attributes and attitudes that introduce us to the blessings that are to be found now in the heavenly realm, in Christ. In that future eternal day, however, this will be the norm for all of mankind; all will come into blessing, as all will come into the Holy City that they might know and dwell with God Himself.

Here, however, their names do not so much represent a personal access into such blessing, as in Ephesians chapter 1, but rather an active introduction for others into the pleasures of that dominion. It is the possession, however, of these spiritual blessings that enable us to bring others into that same state. Here is repeated what those blessings are that we can know now; then we will know them fully and unhindered.

Name meaning	The Spiritual Blessing
Praise	The joy that it gives to be filled with a heart overflowing in love and worship then is God given, by His graciousness.
Behold a Son	Our privileged position that we enjoy as the adopted sons of God and the unhindered access that we can realize in coming into and enjoying the glory of His presence.
The seer, lot, fortune	For us it is to have God's own nature, holy, righteous and loving and the unrivalled rapport that it brings with God Himself, to know from experience the richness of quality of that life

Happy	This blessing is simply that radiant emotion, that 'joy unspeakable and full of glory'. It is state of complete contentment with all that God gives us in Christ, such that nothing else even compares with it.
Wrestling	A life of victory, as we can only prevail as we prove the power of God in our lives.
Causing forgetfulness	The eradication of all that is past with the complete freedom from the oppression that sin had on our minds, freedom from that moral imperative to be what we were in our natural being.
Hearing	The fulfilment of that yearning to know and live in the glory of knowing our acceptance by God in Christ
Joined	The apprehension of and closer attachment to and joining to our Lord and through Him to each other and all creation
Reward	The beauty and fragrance of a fully integrated spiritual being in God as His sons and the beauty and fragrance that gives to our hearts when we live in the light of that life.
Dwelling	The security of the promise that God will stay with us forever. The knowing from experience the confidence of His Spirit directing us. This consciousness of His indwelling.

Increaser	The Spirit of wisdom and revelation in being like Christ and the spiritual blessings that they create for all.
Son of my right hand	To enter into the reality of what it means to be in Christ, no longer living for ourselves but that Christ is living in us, full time, to achieve the purposes of God alone.

Does this mean therefore that, as some conceive, Israel, the Church and the Nations will all have separate identities and functions in the heavenly state as they do now in time? The answer comes in 1 John 3:2: 'It has not yet been revealed what we shall be, but we know that when He is revealed, we shall be like Him'. We can indeed comprehend that future state as it will be in its spiritual constitution, but we can have no knowledge of any formal structures. When we realise this, many of the differences in doctrine and understanding between different believers disappear.

'Now the walls of the City had twelve foundations on them were the names of the twelve apostles'. The walls are the parameters that enclose that city, the place where God dwells with His people. This concept is also referred to in Ephesians 2:19-20, where Paul writes to the Gentile Ephesians to explain that they have been included in the company of saints, being built on the foundation of the apostles and prophets into a holy temple. The analogy is clear; that the apostles are those that were first chosen by Christ, those that were taught by Him and sent to continue His work on Earth. Being at first grounded in Him, having

His life and Spirit, all those that then receive the Spirit of Christ are built up with them and all the saints to form this great administration of blessing, the Holy City. Built up individually as each of us are transformed into the image of Christ and also built up collectively as being built together as one body, Christ Himself being the head; cp Ephesians 4:13-16.

We next come to the dimensions of that Holy City, dimensions that are given as physical measurements, but as we shall see these are metaphors for its Divine parameters. First they are measured with a gold reed. Now a reed was a standard measuring device of the time, but made of gold it suggests that what is being assessed is the qualities of that city, its eternal character; its incorruptibility. The city, its gates and its walls are all gauged according to the instrument used. To take these measurements as being physical dimensions would claim that the city is a cube about 1,200 miles wide, deep and high, which has no meaning at all. As before, if we consider that these numbers refer figuratively to function or character, twelve thousand would suggest the administrative function as well as the whole compass of God's government; cp 12000 of every tribe Revelation 7. The fact that it is spoken of in furlongs, a measurement of distance, rather than cubits, cubits being a measurement of size, perhaps also goes to suggest that the whole City is not an object but an expanse or area of influence.

If then the city's dimensions inform its style and character of function, next we are told of the extent of its influence. It is laid out as a square; its length is as great as its breadth, in fact its length, breadth, and height are equal.

This tells of the universality of its control, being four-square, literally four-cornered.

Its height however is that heavenly spiritual dimension of exaltation, here what is of God Himself in righteousness, holiness and purity, cp Psalm 102:19 and Ephesians 3:18. This is fully represented in this domain, a province that is the administration of His saints.

Then he measured its wall: one hundred and forty-four cubits to the measure of a man. The walls, the boundaries, are measured in cubits, telling its size so this will relate something of its inherent objective value, 100, 40 and 4, this signifying it being fully comprehensive (40) and universal (4) and having full sufficiency (100) to meet every issue relating to all mankind. It is the Divine perfection of Christ mediated through His people for the purpose of the regulation of all heavenly rule and blessing.

If the size of its walls then shows their innate significance, then the construction of its walls tell of their purpose and integrity The walls are jasper, as was He that sat on the throne in chapter 4:3, telling us that they are of the same character as He, that is being full of light, that is in biblical language, as radiating truth and goodwill. The city, in total, being pure gold says that will never fade, tire or pass; it is like clear glass, ie completely transparent, pure, holy; no dissimulation or eccentricity, having no shade of anything that is not of God Himself.

Now the foundations of this future state of absolute harmony are adorned, that is had the lustre of precious stones. This is so significant to us with regards to our present place in time and also with regards that future state that this aspect of the heavenly Jerusalem is pictured separately in detail in the next piece. Here we will see rather what are the main features of this heavenly realm, why and how this Holy City can exist and that it is not just some capricious fancy.

In verse twelve each gate was focused on as having a specific identity and function. Now in verse 21 we are told of the essence and magnificence of each gate. 'The twelve gates were twelve pearls: each individual gate was of one pearl'. Each one is a complete pearl in itself, having its own importance, a treasure, a cherished object each radiating its individual splendour. The meaning of each name of the twelve tribes of Israel was explored in part two of this study. Each of these spiritual states give us, now and to all mankind in that day, access to this heavenly capital.

'And the street of the city was pure gold, like transparent glass.' Now the street is where the associations and activity of the city take place, the concourse of daily life; here everything is sincere, imperishable and untainted by any impurity.

'But I saw no temple in it, for the Lord God Almighty and the Lamb are its temple.
The city had no need of the sun or of the moon to shine in it, for the glory of God illuminated it; it is the Lamb, however, radiates that light'. It is that Divine spiritual light that only those that are Christ's can know now, but then all shall know that light and live entirely by it; that light that gives complete appreciation and satisfaction and life, cp John 8:12. This is a spiritual realm, which is why a physical source of light to sustain life is not needed.

'The kings of the Earth bring their glory and honour into it'. In this age of darkness and separation from God, anything that is of our human nature can only corrupt and threaten what is pure and holy. The nations now, however, walk in the light of the heavenly city so that their way of life is also pure and holy, now that sin cannot enter that scene. Thus they shine also with that glory and honour, enhancing the city itself. In verse 24 at first it is just the local rulers of the new Earth that are focused on, emphasising that the light of that heavenly regime devolves first to those who preside over the nations. The glory and honour is then seen in all people in verse 26.

The glory and honour throughout this book have been attributed to God and the Lamb. Now the life of God, His glory and honour fills all in that heavenly sphere and they radiate it throughout that setting.

'But there shall by no means enter it anything that defiles, or causes an abomination or a lie, but only those who are written in the Lamb's Book of Life.' This country is pure and holy and can never now be corrupted. Likewise everything that is otherwise is eternally excluded. No one and nothing can ever now change that perfect status quo.

SECTION 4: PART 12

The Foundations of the Holy City

Revelation Chapter 21: 19-20

**The Whole Basis, Character and Purpose of
This Spiritual Metropolis; All Those Qualities That
are Found Inherently in God Alone But Are
Mediated by His Church**

One very important point with regard to chapters 21 and 22 is that there is no mention of Christ as King. In this new Heaven and Earth God is all in all, Christ is referred to as the Lamb and as such He does not rule that realm with a rod of iron, as He will on Earth. He is here the temple and the light of the Holy City, that majestic centre which will serve and lead all of God's creation. The scene here focuses not on the functioning of that place but on the whole basis on which it is founded. Any regime in this world is based on the concept of delegated or assumed authority, which governs its dominion by consensus or force. Not so in that world, the basis of this state will be spiritual, it will be the life of God Himself that will fill all, be in all and will be administered by this city, a city whose fundamental constitution and structure will be based on the quality of that Divine life. Picturesquely these characteristics of that fundamental constitution, the foundations as they are portrayed, are described in verses 19 and 20 of chapter 21; this will be the quality of life, the complete inner character that is the whole basis and structure on which this place functions and the qualities that exist for the benefit of all that enter that city. All the citizens of that place will be all the nations that have been redeemed by the blood of the Lamb. This 'City', New Jerusalem, is spoken of in terms of its dispensation, that is its administration.

The general description of these fundamental characteristics of that city is as 'foundations', emphasising the security and stability that they give to that place, and, being as they come down from God alone, that security and stability is absolute. Scripture refers to foundations in many places, sometimes referring to physical foundations, though usually this will have a spiritual analogy. Often the word is used metaphorically, as Jesus did in His parables to refer specifically to the basis of an individual's character or security for example. Here the foundations are the underlying basis on which the Holy City stands, ie the fundamental principles by which it functions. They are the essence from which the resources of that place are imparted. They are those Divine features that are being formed in the hearts of believers at this present time in the totally alien and adversarial environment of this life, a work which will continue until that work of the Holy Spirit is complete: - Ephesians 5:27. The expression 'foundations' generally in scripture have qualitative or spiritual implications such as stability, 'The righteous have an everlasting foundation' – Proverbs 10:25, or authority, 'His foundation is in the Holy Mountains' – Psalm 87:1. The scripture also refers to Christ as a personal foundation for our being, such as 'I lay in Zion a stone for a foundation' – Isaiah 28:16 and 'For no other foundation can anyone lay than that which is laid, which is Christ Jesus' – 1 Corinthians 3:11.

Now in this City these foundation stones are adorned with precious stones. They are adorned, that is set in order, beautified; in other words, they are endowed with a suitable character. These precious stones are also said to be themselves the foundations of that city per se, which sounds at first contradictory.

On each foundation were the names of the twelve apostles, that is those sent forth to represent the person of Christ, to be His ambassadors, to live His life, letting that light to so shine before mankind that they see our quality of life and glorify God. It does not say which names were associated with which stones, so the implication is that the qualities here spoken of are relevant to all. These attributes are personified in all those that do form this establishment, typified here as the apostles representing the whole of Christ's bride, that is the Church which is built on these foundations. These traits therefore both adorn the saints and also become their innate character; their life is the life of Christ. These are the fundamental attributes that form the basis of that Holy City and must emerge in every saint, those attributes that express the glory and personality of

God Himself as they are found in the person of Jesus Christ. As Ephesians 2:20 says,

> 'Having been built on the foundation of the apostles and prophets,
> Jesus Christ Himself being the chief corner stone.'

The analogy in Ephesians means the foundation of our faith rather than the corporate identity of the foundations of the Holy City, though really the ideas are related. Now these attributes that are being developed in us are summarised in 1 Corinthians 1:30; we are:

> 'Of Him you are in Jesus Christ, who became for us, wisdom from God
> and righteousness and sanctification and redemption.'

It is from these primary elements that the fullness of the Divine nature flows. This is what forms the basis of and also sustains the City, which in turn sustains the whole of His creation, as we shall see. It is in this way that God's perfect life and nature both fill and nourish everything. This was God's eternal purpose and way of providing for a creation in which He could live with His people.

Now 'the foundations of the wall of the city were adorned with all kinds of precious stones.' Some of these stones are only mentioned very occasionally in scripture and some of the names of them have changed since ancient times, so we have to be careful in correctly interpreting what the scripture is telling us. The main features of precious and semi-precious stones are their permanence and security, see Matthew 16:18, and their rarity and hence value, see Matthew. 13:46, but particularly their innate elegance and glory. It is also the aesthetic beauty of the precious stones that is significant and illustrates the testimony that the Holy City radiates, witnessing to the perfection and glory of God's attributes that are displayed, as we shall see specifically with each stone.

Colour particularly gives much of the meaning to each of these stones. The New Bible Dictionary has a useful explanation of what colour meant to those in the first century AD: 'Each colour gained its significance by association with a natural object of that colour, relating also its inherent characteristics by analogy eg yellow implies rarity and perpetuity as that is the colour of gold; blue implies what is Heavenly and scarlet and purple what is noble or kingly'.

These two verses, 19 and 20, contain a wealth of information; they encapsulate all the ultimate purpose of God for His people in this age, to show not just that individuals form the foundation of that dispensation but what is more relevant, what they are in all their sublime character.

Now the wall of the city had twelve foundations, foundations that are laid by God Himself, a city prepared for the family of faith; see Hebrews chapter 11. These are qualities that are being laid down now in the lives and hearts of those that belong to Christ, something that will continue until that work is complete and Christ returns to take His Church to be with Himself. This outcome will be the culmination of all that God has been achieving in creation and for mankind since the beginning of time, the whole focal point of all that He has planned for a sphere where time will be no more. The first point that is being made regarding these foundations is that on them is written the names of the apostles; they have that relevance and function. These are the 'ones sent forth of the Lamb', that is having His character and purpose. This is not a passive or static role that the foundations have, rather they still have a messenger role to fulfil; expressing, presenting, and manifesting the life of Christ in manner, conduct, attitude and word. They manifest the character of the Lamb Himself, the totally and eternally self-sacrificial Lamb; the perfect servant doing only His Father's will. This is what increasingly characterises us now as we ever grow in grace and the 'putting on' of our Lord Jesus Christ. In that Heavenly environment the old order will be gone completely, and this new order that is now in the making will be all that remains, but it will be fully developed and open to see.

It is apparent in many places, in the New Testament particularly, what God has planned with regards to those in Christ. It is to be filled with the fullness of Christ and the foundations of this Holy milieu in all its glory transpires to be His ultimate purpose.

> 'We are called according to His own purpose and grace', 2 Timothy 1:9
>
> To be made 'partakers of the heavenly calling', Hebrews 3:1
>
> 'And predestined as sons', Ephesians 1:5 and Romans 8:29.

These are just examples generally of the fact that what we will be is something foreordained by God Himself. More than that, the specific attributes that do and will characterise that heavenly life in every one of us is also described in the scriptures, and specific reference made as to the fact that that is what we are called, chosen or predestined to be. Each foundational trait is built upon the previous one, or to put it another way, each feature is dependent on another; together they create the picture of Divine perfection found only in Christ and all those in whom He dwells. The only life that will exist in that future heavenly realm is the life of God Himself, imparted to all through Christ.

'Jesus Christ is... made unto us... sanctification,' 1 Corinthians 1:30.

1. Jasper – Holiness

The first foundational quality is the most fundamental and principal foundation of our relationship with God and of our function within His eternal purposes for us. This quality is typified as jasper, a quality that characterises the majesty of Him on the throne in chapter 4:4. Seemingly jasper would be what we might conceive as diamond or crystal, as it tells us that the glory and light city itself was 'jasper stone, clear as crystal', chapter 21:11.

The picture given in the scripture here is a brilliant, clear stone with a shining lustre, its beauty inherent in its radiance. The sense that is being conveyed is one of clarity, purity and radiance, like Him on the heavenly throne, pure, radiant and morally transparent; entirely separate from anything that is of this world order. This is a succinct description of the Holiness of Almighty God Himself.

It is this very characteristic that we are called to, Romans 1:7 and 1 Corinthians 1:2: we are 'called to be saints', meaning sanctified or holy ones. It is this basic intrinsic quality that we are called to advance in day by day until we come into the 'measure of the stature of the fullness of Christ'. Then are we fully equipped to serve our Lord and His interests in true sonship in this world and the next. It is something that naturally lies completely beyond our comprehension, let alone our ability to achieve. It requires a completely radical change to our nature, something that God alone can instil in us, as the scripture says, 'Be Holy for I am Holy' 1 Peter 1:16.

Holiness is a characteristic that defines what we are, or rather will be fully one day.

2. Sapphire – Spirituality

To be holy then means to be separate from, to be entirely other in our interests, behaviour and being. From this emerges the sort of persons we will be in judgement, sentiment, outlook and manner. Philippians 2:5 calls us to be likeminded as Christ in all humility and self-effacement and Romans 8:5-6 calls us to have our minds set on the spiritual, that is to be heavenly minded. This is not something that we adopt or possibly can adopt but rather it is the mind of Christ that is given to those that live in dependency of faith on Him; 1 Corinthians 2:16.

This is beautifully pictured in this precious stone that

is featured in the second foundation, sapphire, an iridescent blue stone, what we would call today lapis lazuli, a dark blue stone with mineral flecks in it that makes it appear like the night sky.

Unlike the shining lustre of the sapphire of today, lapis lazuli has a more sombre, meditative appearance suggesting depth and thoughtfulness. Ezekiel. 1:26 and 10:1 convey a similar image of a heavenly sapphire throne; other more general references to sapphire in the Old Testament imply what is beautiful, precious and highly valued. What is heavenly (that is spiritual; of the sphere where God dwells) suggests what is infinite and timeless, here in the context of the ground of Divine administration that is the rule of righteousness as we see in Exodus. 24:10.

'To be spiritually minded is life and peace,' Romans 8:6.

3. Chalcedony - Priesthood

If then we are called by God to be holy in being and from this heavenly minded in our outlook and affections, then also will our calling have a Divine purpose. 1 Peter 2:9 says that we are:

'a chosen generation, a royal priesthood a holy nation.
His own special people, that you may proclaim the praises of Him
who called you out of darkness into His marvellous light'.

The colour that signified priesthood, that special calling to serve God in the Temple worship in the Old Testament, was blue, see Numbers chapter 4. This then is the colour of the third stone that adorns the foundations, chalcedony, a stone with a blue waxy lustre. Again this does not suggest brilliance but rather a sober and conscientious outlook in a calling of such privilege and responsibility. This is the third foundational character that is based on holiness and heavenly mindedness; first our appreciation and veneration of Him that created, redeemed and chose us for His service and then our inspired response of praise, worship and thanksgiving. In the New Testament we find several references to all God's people being referred to as priests, teaching us that we can come directly and privately into the presence of God in love, worship and thanksgiving, without having to approach through the services of another human being. That of course is the experience of all believers; priests within the established church that lead public worship are a different matter; in this verse it is not a role within the earthly church administration that is referred to, but is speaking of our personal relationship with and service to God Himself.

4. Emerald - Graciousness

Holiness also has another manifestation, not only in what we are in spirit, in our awareness and affections and heavenly experience, but it will also define our whole outward being in our demeanour to the world we live in and those we interrelate with every day. Now this sort of holiness is not an aloof self-righteousness but rather a genuine humble piety that manifests itself as that which Christ did two millennia ago. He was truly gracious in all that He did, going about doing good. Colossians 3:12-15 is a beautiful description of a truly gracious person:

> 'Tender mercies, kindness, humility, meekness, longsuffering,
>
> bearing with one another, forgiving one another ... above all love
>
> which is the bond of perfection and let the peace of God rule in your hearts'.

The bearing of a truly gracious person instils restfulness, attraction and pleasure, as also does a salubrious natural environment at a physical level. Thus the next foundational stone here is an emerald, which is a rich translucent green. It portrays an impression of a deep, rich shining lustre that irradiates an inherent beauty, intimating a congenial harmony of soul by association with an idyllic natural scene, also giving the picture of testimony, the life of Christ shining out from His people as a living witness to the glory of His being.

In chapter 4 the judgement throne is surrounded, indeed enclosed, by a halo of green emerald, a glowing green lustre that is redolent of the glory and radiance of the graciousness of God. This is what is experienced subjectively and reflected by those that know Him.

> Jesus Christ is... made unto us... righteousness' 1 Corinthians 1:30.

5. Sardonyx - Righteousness

If Holiness is the very nature of God, something that we are also called to become, then Righteousness describes His state of mind in all His purposes in creation and with regards to mankind. God cannot do wrong, nor can He be tempted to, and it is this that we are also called to become, 1 Peter 2:21-24. In addition there are many scriptures encouraging us to be righteous, something that is quite alien to our human nature such that we cannot even conceive the perfection of God ourselves. A natural concept of righteousness is only relative to our culture or personal ideals; a Divine concept of righteousness however is a personal quality, the character of God Himself. It is therefore a righteousness, which we are given, appropriated through faith and assimilated into our own outlook and temperament as the Holy Spirit guides us into all truth.

Now this fifth foundation is said to be Sardonyx, being a stone of red and white layers, offering a dramatic contrast of colours, distinct and yet fully integrated together. Red, as in our language, alludes to what is fiery in scripture, indicating passion or belligerence according to the context. It can also suggest what is healthy or conspicuous. Here its interpretation is confined to a Divine attribute, so that would indicate only what is pure and gracious, for example fervour or ardour.

White in scripture, as well in our own language, would indicate something more personal and characteristic, a distinct and spiritual property, with the context giving the best application; unadulterated, unqualified, absolute, complete, unmodified, for example. White however as a description of God's people is more specific, inferring purity and righteousness; for example in Revelation 19:14 the saints are dressed in white linen, pure and clean, that is said to indicate the righteousness of the saints.

Jesus said in Matthew 5:6:

'Blessed are those who hunger and thirst for righteousness for they shall be filled.'

Being fervent in righteousness is an absolute, essential and fundamental characteristic of the mindset of those in the service of their Divine master, in this world and the next; the New Heaven and Earth. Sardonyx then as a blending of red and white layers would suggest just that, a blending of zeal and purity as a description of one's disposition and purpose, a hunger and thirsting after righteousness.

6. Sardius – Love

This righteousness, however, is not a sanctimonious denigration of those that do not aspire to or attain to certain codes of behaviour. This is the pure expression of holiness in action, something that emanates directly from that most fundamental aspect of God's nature. Neither is it a righteousness that is merely idealistic but one that extends to all the works of God in creation. It aspires to the very best that can be for all God's creatures, though we do not yet see that final goal arrived in this world, it is that same love that in us inspires and motivates us. This then is epitomised and expressed in another matchless quality of God that we are called to as being His children as explained in Ephesians1:3-4:

> 'The God and Father of our Lord Jesus Christ…
> chose us in Him before the foundation of the world,
> that we should be holy and without blame before
> Him in love.'

This is what the Love of God is, pure, selfless and all embracing. 1 Corinthians 13 is that well known description of that quality of divine love.

This sixth foundation stone is sardius, a red stone. We noted with the previous stone that red is a picture of fire, but more specifically it is a sardius stone that also describes the one on the throne in chapter 4:3. This was probably a bright red stone of slightly cloudy appearance, suggesting a private, passionate sentiment. Here again its interpretation is confined to the appearance of God, so it describes an attribute that we can perceive and know directly. God is Holy, Righteous and also, as the scriptures testify often, He is a God of Love, that very love that we have talked about. This is the love that He bestows freely on all that come to Him in humility and repentance. It is a love that He then infuses into us that we might know Him to the fullness of our being and then to become fully like Him ourselves. It is a love that unfolds to us all the graciousness of God that describe not only His personality that we can become acquainted with ourselves, but also it is this Divine personality that is revealed in us through His Spirit. Galatians 5:22-23 describes succinctly those characteristics that can and are generated within us day by day:

> '… Love, joy, peace, longsuffering, kindness, goodness,
> faithfulness, gentleness and self-control.'

7. Chrysolite – Faithfulness

If the Love of God then derives from His immaculate righteousness, then the next quality that forms the foundation of that heavenly City is a sequel to that love, something that again is a feature of that Divine character of the life that we receive in Christ. 1 Corinthians 4:2 tells us that 'It is required in stewards that one be found faithful'. Revelation 17:14 tells us that those with the Lamb (cp chapter 14) are those that 'are called, chosen and faithful'.

Now chrysolite is a golden stone, that is, having a golden lustre, conveying a sense of what is rich and glorious. As a conceptual symbol, what is golden represents what is imperishable or eternal; as a spiritual metaphor then it signifies faithfulness, steadfastness and truth. God alone is absolutely faithful, eternally dependable and true, never ever retracting what He has promised, Romans 11:29. It remains only for us to enter into those blessings as we continue our spiritual journey through life. Likewise as God's children, as presenting our part of the foundations of that glorious future state, He calls us to be of the same disposition and character, something that we cannot attain to except through His salvation.

8. Beryl - Authority

Divine Love and faithfulness are established directly on the righteousness of God, although they are separate and defining qualities of His; they must also be possessed by every servant of God. There is, however, another primary attribute that we must possess to be partakers of His purposes, another attribute that derives from the righteousness that is God's nature. This defining characteristic of God is His strength. We do need to understand, however, what is implied in the notion of Divine strength. It is not just a physical strength as we understand it but primarily a moral legitimacy and competence that can and does create all things good. It is an all-embracing efficacy and worth; it is virtuous and pre-eminent power. This also is a power that we are availed of when the life of Christ is effective in us. It is something that we know in small measure now in our personal experience in overcoming worldly influence and our natural weaknesses, something that becomes more fully developed as we progress in the faith.

The eighth foundation stone then is Beryl, what is sometime called Aquamarine, which hints at its aesthetic properties. As its alternative name suggests, the colour of Beryl is sea blue-green, a stone with a deep shining lustre, calling attention to its inherent properties. With the simple association of colour that we find in scripture to indicate an analogy of an ethical or spiritual nature, and calling to mind the sea, this would indicate what is massive, overwhelming, irresistible and powerful.

There are other uses of 'beryl' in scripture to describe the particular qualities of something in this way; in Song 5:14, the hands of the Shulamite's beloved are set with beryl. In Ezekiel 1:16 and 10:9, the wheels (wheels there perhaps intimating purpose or government) are like beryl and in Daniel 10:6 the body of the angel was like beryl. In each of these examples the use of the comparison with beryl evokes the concept of moral efficacy or authority. This virtuous power, something that is developed within us, will be in this life what gives us victory over all that is of this world and human nature.

> 'Jesus Christ is... made unto us wisdom'
> 1 Corinthians 1:30.

9. Topaz - Wisdom, That is Divine Insight

The ninth foundation of the Holy City is the precious stone topaz. Now this stone was most probably the Hebrew 'pitdah', a golden-coloured stone, as can be the modern topaz. We know from its context here that it represents a Divine characteristic residing within us, an exquisite beauty of personality that shines from within, to the extent that Christ is living within us. This connotation is also reinforced in other parts of the scripture, in the High Priest's breastplate of judgement; for example in Exodus 28:17 it is the second precious stone in the first row. The context here of the breastplate is similar in that the gems represent the special characteristics of the people of God, qualities that the High Priest carried into the presence of God once a year under the Old Covenant. This also is a picture of Christ as our great High Priest presenting these Divine qualities within the saints to God as the basis of our relationship with Him.

This does not tell us, however, what this particular quality of topaz represents, which it is the purpose of this study to delineate. There is another reference, however, in scripture to this gemstone, in the book of Job chapter 28:19. Here it says that wisdom does not equal the topaz of

Ethiopia, that is to say that it cannot be arrayed with it, it is not of the same class or standard. 'Topaz' must, however, necessarily share some feature with wisdom, in being compared specifically to the topaz of Ethiopia, to be able to compare its excellence. Wisdom itself, however, is not a quality but an aptitude. By way of illustration, in Amos 9:7-8 sinful Israel is likened to Ethiopia, suggesting that Ethiopia represents in scripture what is of a corrupt human nature in contrast to the pure Divine nature of God. Likewise the quality of topaz in Revelation is far above that which is natural in standard but something that qualitatively is intrinsically a feature of wisdom.

The answer to the question then as to what this quality is, is given by Job himself in verse 28 in his description of the true nature of wisdom; namely 'The fear of the Lord, that is wisdom'. It is a definition that is repeated in other scriptures; Psalm 111:10 and Proverbs 1:7 for example. Fear here means and entails reverence, honour, obedience and submission, also in this context, responsibility. This is an attitude of complete dependence and humility, depending on Him for every opportunity, ability and resource, a humility that displaces any sense of self-worth or assumed piety but is a true and sincere piety that is born of God alone, something that is of the very nature of God Himself. This is what topaz represents in our passage and indeed what defines the spiritual wisdom that we find in scripture.

The first great and fundamental Divine attribute that we considered, in the context of 1 Corinthians 1:30 in being the first foundation of the Holy City, was holiness. This very concept defines God Himself; or rather what God is defines what holiness is. Holiness is the whole character of being, as being apart from all else. The second fundamental attribute of our God was the fifth stone; that is righteousness, absolute, and again is defined by what God is in His nature; He is the source of everything that is pure and true. This describes moral character, however, rather than essence. However there is this third great and fundamental character of God that is inherent in the foundations of the Holy City and that is this Wisdom; a Divine wisdom that is far more than sound practical judgement as we might use the term in relation to the natural course of this life. Again it is a facet that is defined by who God is and all He does in creation and through creation. It infinitely exceeds our human concept of wisdom. It is something that as always in these verses can never be even imagined but only revealed to those that are humble enough to receive it. Wisdom in an every-day context is the 'quality of having experience, knowledge and good judgement' (Oxford Dictionary). In scripture, however, it has a deeper meaning, an essentially spiritual meaning:

'Wisdom... which the Holy Spirit teaches,
comparing spiritual things with spiritual': 1 Corinthians 2:13.

It is in fact a wisdom that supersedes human wisdom, see 1 Corinthians 3:19. It is a wisdom that comes from knowing God and in no other way. It is beyond the comprehension of anyone who does not know God and of those that do only by those that totally acknowledge and revere Him; see Proverbs 3:6. It was for this very reason to administer the wisdom of God in this age and in the next that the church was instituted by Him, Ephesians 3:10-11. It is a personal quality defining the way we are involved first with our God and Father Himself, then those of the household of faith in their various divisions and levels of spiritual maturity, our involvement with and witness in the world and also with our environment as a whole.

10. Chrysoprase - Godly order

Spiritual wisdom then is more than just experience, knowledge and good judgement relating to the things of this life. It is that of course, but primarily it is judgement based on our bearing towards the Almighty; it is spiritual quality, an orientation of the heart, an appreciable relationship with Him, something that characterises us rather than just something we possess. It is then a Divine relationship that informs every other relationship, with others, ourselves and with the world at large as it derives from this Divine quality of wisdom. From a practical perspective this relationship with God and the rest of creation implies order, a personal integrity of purpose that gives us a complete sense of unity and peace, peace and unity that enables us to see and rise above our personal circumstances and connect with all that is good. This in fact is what Paul refers to in in Colossians 2:5, (there in the context of our daily walk with Christ).

This personal harmony then is the very substance of the tenth foundation, chrysoprase. Literally the word means 'a golden leek'; it is a translucent, yellowish-green stone, which at first may seem rather enigmatic, but expressing an exquisite character of sincerity and charm. It gained its popular meaning in ancient times from a simple association with the leek, a popular delicacy at that time and also, by extension, a leek or any vegetable garden, a place with rows of leeks or other vegetables, alluding both to pleasure and order. The name itself, Strong's concordance tells us, in the original language would have signified this to contemporaries, chryso meaning gold and prasso meaning a leek, implying a garden patch, an arrangement. This would have been a common metaphor or analogy at the time this was written, meaning order and system. In the context here of spiritual characteristics therefore we may conclude that the image portrayed here then is a disposition of contentment, tranquillity, wholeness and harmony. Order here is a quiet and gentle spirit that exudes the nature of Christ. Specifically here maybe we can add that the spiritual analogy is the picture of 'order in the garden', that is, in the community of the apostles and by extension the church.

This does not mean that we will be naturally well organised and efficient however, even well-disciplined from a general point of view. Quite the opposite; this is the end of all that is natural, our own purposes and interests, ideas and ideals. As the word 'chryso', that is golden, implies, this is ordering according to incorruptible, eternal principles; it is the end of all our own agendas in every aspect of our mundane lives, only the New Order pertains now. Our lives are lived entirely according to God's own agenda for us as citizens of that realm. Our hearts in that Eternal City will be ruled by Divine objectives alone, a life of pure integrity, as even now as our hearts and lives are changed from day to day to be conformed more into the image of Christ to be suitable for that realm. It is His perfect life of complete submission and humility that is the order of that Heavenly City that will be its tenth foundation stone, godliness.

11. Jacinth – Sacrifice

Next there is another direct consequence of a life of godliness and obedience. In addition to a disposition of peace and harmony, there is a life of worship and sacrifice. In 2 Thessalonians 1:11-12 the apostle Paul prays for the Christians at Thessalonica that they might be worthy of this calling:

> '...that the name of our Lord Jesus Christ
> may be glorified in you and you in Him.'

It is a reason for our redemption that Christ should be glorified in us and through us. In us particularly as we are filled with His glory in spontaneous praise and worship; pictured as a well of water springing up into eternal life, as Christ promised to the woman of Samaria in John's gospel chapter 4:14. He is, however, also glorified through us as we live our lives according to His purpose for us: 'This is the will of God your sanctification' 1 Thessalonians 4:3. Also in 1 Peter 1:2, 'in sanctification of the Spirit for obedience and sprinkling of the blood of Jesus Christ.'

This means that more and more as we progress along the Christian pathway we are occupied and concerned with the work that God is doing in our lives rather than with our own or social objectives and agendas. This is the message in Romans 12:1, where Paul speaks about that response, pleading with us:

> 'That you present your bodies a living sacrifice, holy, acceptable to God, which is your reasonable service.'

This is the picture that we get vicariously in the burnt offerings and sacrifices in the Old Testament. It is the smoke that symbolises the consuming sacrifice, the sacrifice that is the consuming of our primary animal nature, ascending to God as a sweet smelling aroma, something that carries through the scripture into the New Testament where this imagery is employed. In Ephesians 5:2 we are exhorted to walk in love, as imitators of God, being like Christ who:

> 'Gave Himself for us, an offering and a sacrifice to God for a sweet smelling aroma.'

This then is the picture that is presented in the 11th foundation, Jacinth, a hyacinth; a blue stone, the colour of smoke, for example that of the burnt sacrifices in the tabernacle and temple from the time of Moses until the time of the coming of Christ. It is this colour of hyacinth blue, the colour of Jacinth, that is specifically identified as smoke in Revelation 9:17, where it is associated with the fire and sulphur in the breastplates of the 200 million horsemen. It is an image of that which has been consumed and then dispels into the air, signifying both personal sacrifice of our ideas and agendas and this leading directly to the worship of God in the beauty of holiness.

12. Amethyst - Reigning

This then brings us to the final foundation of that Holy City, something that all the other foundations underpin, qualities of Divine origin that precede this final attribute and all together form the basis of its status quo. Christ is our supreme and consummate example in every aspect of these Divine features, features that we cannot know intuitively but which are revealed to us and in us as we walk with Him in our pathway in this life. Christ Himself, we are told, increased daily in wisdom and favour; it is His peace and harmony that we can know as we grow in grace, it was His supreme sacrifice of affliction and death we are taught to identify with now. Above all these qualities, however, the thing that encapsulates them all is that He came to Earth for one purpose alone, a purpose in which every minute of His life was engaged, and that was to fulfil the will of His Father. This disposition of perfect obedience led Him to do only good, disseminating the truth of the Kingdom of God and making evident the persona of God Himself. As ambassadors of Christ that is what we are also called to do, in some small measure, even while we are still inhibited and tested by our natural being. In that future state, however:

> 'The wise shall shine like the brightness of the firmament and those who turn many to righteousness like the stars for ever and ever',
> Daniel 12:3.

This is what this final precious stone signifies; this is true sonship in its full scriptural meaning, a meaning that was inherent within the Hebrew culture. Pictured here is a life lived not only carrying out the purposes of God unhindered by self-interest or human weakness, but a life representing God Himself in all His majesty, nobility and power. Thus the final precious stone is amethyst, a purple gem that signals royalty and wealth. Its appearance is a deep rich purple, shining brightly as it reflects the light. In its spiritual context this defines that nobility of character, that Divine identification as God's children in pursuing God's Holy affairs for all eternity. This is what the scripture means when it refers to reigning with Christ, 2 Timothy 2:12, 'If we endure, we shall also reign with Him', and Revelation 5:10, 'You... have made us kings and priests to our God and we shall reign on the Earth.'

At this present time it is Christ that reigns in us as we put away sin and selfishness through His sacrifice, but always it is to this purpose that ultimately at His coming we will be qualified to reign as co-regents with our Lord and Master in His Kingdom and throughout eternity as His Divine nature will be all that inspires us. Christ then will reign not only in us but also through us, unhindered by anything of this natural order as at present.

Summary of the Foundational Character of the Holy City Together with Suggested Classifications of those Characteristics
Cp Mark 12:30

Classifications

	Character	Disposition	Purpose
Soul	Holiness	Righteousness	Wisdom
Heart	Spirituality	Love	Godliness
Mind	Priesthood	Faithfulness	Sacrifice
Will	Graciousness	Strength	Reigning

This little mnemonic may help in formulating and grasping the order and personal relevance of those spiritual qualities in the summary above that characterises the whole. of the glorified Church, those things that we collectively and individually aspire to now. This classification however is merely a help to memory, not an interpretation.

SECTION 4: PART 13

Paradise Restored

Revelation Chapters 21-22

The Earth Will be Filled with the Knowledge of the Glory of the Lord as Mankind is Restored to Its Special Place of Privilege and Responsibility

After all the momentous drama that must take place in the bringing in of His final plan for mankind and His creation, at the end of this whole vision God shows us in just one chapter a summary of how this paradise will function and in particular the effect that that should have on all of us now. This explains in part why God reveals all these things to us.

In Genesis the Garden of Eden was, or typified, the place where man in his innocence had unhindered spiritual communion with God. In Genesis 3:24 however, things had changed; man was now excluded from the Garden of Eden so that he could not have access to the tree of life, since he was disqualified through the sin of unbelief and disobedience. The way back to that tree of life, the tree that is the representation of what sustains our life in Christ, however, is now restored to 'him that overcomes', see Revelation 2:7. That life is something that we can never possess of ourselves, within ourselves, but will forever receive from that tree, maintaining our spiritual union with Christ. A parallel imagery from John 10:28 describes how that union takes effect:

> 'I give them eternal life and they shall never perish, neither shall anyone snatch them out of My hand.'

This chapter 22, however, is not concerned with the individual life, our private spiritual experience as we have in John 10, that is our personal confidential relationship with our Lord, the relationship that is painted for us in Revelation 2:17, for example. Instead this chapter is concerned with externals, the outward character of life, the communal order of associations, its outward manifestations and experiences. That intricate spiritual and intimate inner relationship has been delineated in detail in chapters 7 particularly and 21 for example and is the central theme of much of scripture. This is complementary to that, describing the public presentation of the world to come. It does not give us a physical picture here even so; whatever the substantial nature of that world might be we are not given any details here. What is described, however, is how this world will operate, according to spiritual principles and not material values. Perhaps for this reason we could not understand anything of that world beyond what the scriptures tell us here. To try and imagine ourselves some tangible concept of that heavenly realm, as children must inevitably do if they will understand anything, can only distort the purity of what is represented for us in the scriptures. Let us therefore consider what we are told about that place to see what it is that is of significance.

The Seven Features of 'the Paradise of God'

'And he showed me a pure river of water of life', that is one that is uncorrupted, unadulterated, complete and unmodified, something flowing, outpouring in abundance and provision. First we are told where and how that life emanates. It is described as a pure river of water of life, something that provides refreshment, something irresistible, overwhelming in giving vitality and happiness. It is clear as crystal, that is it has moral clarity, lucidity and holiness; it is genuine and unequivocal in its manifestation. It proceeds from the throne of God and of the Lamb. Now God is all in all; Christ as the lamb is also on His Father's throne. It is that enthroned disposition of a lamb that rules that realm, it can only be so, so that all these blessings can flow so fully and unmitigated to all who attain to that sphere. God is that life, He is all and in all. Christ as the meek and lowly lamb shows us that this is the way that the life from God will be imparted and manifested in all that dwell there.

In Ezekiel from chapter 40 to the end of the book there is a comprehensive description of a future temple that

Ezekiel foresaw. This was an account of how God would dwell with His people in the future, given in precise symbolic detail. In chapter 43, verses 6-7 is mentioned the nature of God's relationship with them:

> 'Then I heard Him speaking to me from the temple,
> while a man stood beside me. And He said to me,
> 'Son of man, this is the place of My throne and the place of the soles of My feet,
> where I will dwell in the midst of the children of Israel forever.'

Here then we also get the expression 'the place of the soles of My feet,' signifying that He is standing, in possession, of that blessed sanctuary, only what He decrees is sanctioned in that place.

Next we are told where we can find this life. Now in the middle of that city's street, that is in the centre of the focus of that civic life; the street, that is where all the associations and activity of the city take place, is where the tree of life is to be found. Also on either side of the river that flows out from the throne, enclosing the river, forming its boundary, the tree of life was to be found. This tells us that the life that is to be found in Christ exists nowhere but in communion with Him through the life that flows from His throne, that is from His absolute sovereignty, and also by extension through those that dwell in Him, those that walk in His way and keep His commandments.

Thirdly we are shown how the tree of life will provide life, how that life is mediated and how it is sustained. Firstly the tree bore twelve fruits, twelve signifying God working in and through mankind. Secondly it bore fruit, which speaks of what is continuously generated from growth to create more life and to give succour and comfort to other creatures. Each tree yielded its fruit every month, a month being a Divinely-ordered period of purpose. The picture here then is one of God supplying through His people the needs of all the nations according to whatever the need or situation may be.

This tree however also provided for the healing of the nations. Now that does not imply that in that perfect place there will be illness and disease, rather 'healing' here means 'service' or 'attendance' as might be provided for the members of a large household, as in Luke 12:42 for example.

What, however, we may ask, is this 'tree' that provides sustenance and nurture for all mankind? As always in scripture, what is being spoken of is not focusing on the primary physical object, though that may be present, we don't know, rather it is speaking of the quality of what is being provided, the quality of life that is mediated, in other words what is spiritual and therefore part of our immediate experience, not the thing that may act as agent in providing it.

There is a similar image in Ezekiel 47:1-12 where the river flows out from two sides of the temple, becoming deeper as it flows out, to water the land that provides food and healing for the nations. Trees generally signify in scripture fruitfulness or shelter, cp Job 40:21-22, Ecclesiastes 2:5.

The fourth feature of this paradise is that the blessings of that place will be unmitigated, not compromised or qualified in any way. There shall be no more curse, ie despising, hating, loathing or condemning. No one there will find themselves censured or rejected. Where evil cannot exist, there is no place for division or criticism. Rather it will be the throne of God and of the Lamb that shall be in it. That alone shall be sovereign; the glory of God will be the experience and measure for all and the ascendancy of that life will be the humility and gentleness of the Lamb; acceptance, gentleness and devotion will alone hold sway. It can only be those that are of this character, those that have the life of Christ that can ever occupy a place there, or even in this life to appreciate its reality.

The first four features then describe the quality of life in that heavenly country; the fifth feature of that scene now depicts how it will function. The whole principle on which that world operates is that it is God-centred. His servants shall serve Him, that is they specifically serve God; His will alone is fulfilled while His love and peace alone are unchallenged. They serve Him continuously in worship, praise, devotion and obedience, as Anna in Luke 2:37. It is this relationship with God that informs all their actions and service to the rest of mankind. As God Himself is a Holy, righteous and loving God, so are His servants, filled only with His Spirit, serving Him, not just in deed in a physical sense, but completely from the heart. There can be no duplicity in that scene; as a result of this they shall see His face, His disposition, that is they shall see Him plainly as He is without any obscurity or confusion, as we so often are subject to now on Earth. Also as a direct consequence of this relationship that they have with their God, His name shall be on their foreheads (cp Revelation 3:12). This is saying in a way that we can picture that they are owned by Him, supported and kept securely; but much more than that they have His Divine character embedded on their foreheads, suggesting both that this is now also their own 'face' or disposition and that their thinking is rooted in His nature. This then will be presented clearly for all to see.

The sixth feature then reveals how that world will be understood and comprehended. We shall not see it by any remote medium such as we see naturally by the reflected light from a physical object; rather our appreciation will be given directly from God Himself, by His Spirit. Again it is the spiritual quality of that world that we will experience directly that is being described, not just a detached understanding. Our understanding and appreciation of that world will be directly through our immediate association with the Almighty, just as even now to a lesser degree we understand the life that we have in Christ directly by His Spirit.

There shall be no night there, the night being the time of obscurity and gloom, the time of genesis, a time that gives birth to the new day, a time of anticipation of the daylight. Night is a time that is essential for us now as we are changed from glory into glory into the fullness of the likeness of Christ. However, when that which is perfect is come there will be no need for these times of change. Rather that day will be one continuous, never-ending day, a time of full understanding and contentment, something that is given directly by God to each of His creatures. They need no lamp or light of the sun, for the Lord God gives them light. An external light, natural or artificial is not needed because this is not a physical world that is being spoken of but rather how the world will function, how each of His creatures will function. The light here is full and continuous understanding; the Lord God gives of Himself, through His servants to all creatures, because He is light.

Finally we are told that His servants shall reign forever and ever. To reign, to be a king, to have dominion over, not physically as in this world, but in this scene it is how this world will remain. Their presence there as the servants of God, filled only with His Spirit and where no other human or competitive spirit abides, will guarantee that the benevolent purposes of God for all His creation will continue without contention. They shall reign first in the sense that Christ reigns in our hearts now when He has full sway over our minds and wills. Then there will be no competition from our natural desires; it will be His life that alone will govern. They shall also reign as His servants in serving His interests in the whole of that city, administering His will throughout all of that world.

Then he said to me, 'These words are faithful and true.' They are not some fantasy, wishful imagination or a vague idealism for which we must dream or strive. This is truly what will take place, a reiteration of Revelation 1:1. Not only are they true but also they are guaranteed because He who reveals these things is He who is absolutely faithful and will bring all to pass.

Postscript: the End of the Visual Imagery

This then is the end of the vision of the full revelation of Jesus Christ and all that God has and will yet achieve through Him. The rest of this chapter is a postscript conveying in plain words a final message from Christ, a message that is delivered by the Christ that reigns in our hearts:

> 'And the Lord God of the holy prophets sent His angel to show His servants the things which must shortly take place'.
> 'Behold, I am coming quickly!'

Seven times in this book Christ says that He is coming quickly, that is He is coming speedily. That was nearly two millennia ago, however, so what did He mean? The time of His coming is unknown, but when that time comes there will be no delay or deliberation. The scriptures, however, are quite clear what has to be fulfilled before that time can come. Christ did return at Pentecost when He sent His Holy Spirit to be our comforter and encourager here on Earth, but He also said that He would come again and take us to be with Himself, which is what is being referred to here, spoken by our Lord 60 years after Pentecost, behold, I am coming quickly. However the scriptures also say in Hebrews 10:36-37:

> 'You have need of endurance,
> so that after you have done the will of God,
> you may receive the promise,
> for yet a little while and He who is coming
> will come and will not tarry'.

So the will of God in salvation must be fulfilled first, in us both individually and also so that the salvation of all believers must come first;

> '...until the fullness of the Gentiles has come in,' Romans 11:25
> '...until the times of the Gentiles are fulfilled,' Luke 21:24

So that the end times will not come until the full number of believers has been 'brought in' to a full experience of salvation and that all those that are to be saved have come into full knowledge of that salvation. Speaking also of the end times; 2 Thessalonians 2:3, 'That Day will not come unless the falling away comes first'. The 'falling away' here could refer to a forsaking of the truth by believers, though this is something that has been ongoing throughout history and therefore too vague to be a specific sign and would in any case be entirely incidental to the context there. However it could refer to an actual falling away from, a specific separation of believers mentioned in verse 1, from their present troubles to be gathered to their Lord. This interpretation aligns better with chapter 1, where Paul refers to the believer's present sufferings and the two separate yet relative futures for the persecutors and the persecuted. It also means that the end cannot come until this separation has occurred. This point is discussed in more detail in the epilogue, 'The day of the Lord.'

So God has not revealed when Christ shall return for His people and will not until it happens, but He has left clear indications of why His coming has not yet occurred, indicating that His work is not yet complete and that includes His work in us and through us.

> 'Blessed is he who keeps the words of the prophecy
> of this book.'

That is to keep watch and observe, to take notice. This is a difficult book to understand, if not impossible, if we try to understand it with our natural minds, seeing it as a catalogue of dramatic or even mythical events. It is a book though that is concerned with what is spiritual, something that is much closer to 'home', involving not just our outward experience and existence but who we are and what we are, our characters, personalities and inner experience. It highlights the magnitude of that great watershed of mankind, if we have the life of God through faith in Christ or not. If we have, then the significance of this book is what difference these things will make to us and in us. They will be a blessing to all that believe, focusing our minds on God's purposes for us and His creation and so sanctifying our hearts to His Divine ideal.

> 'Now I, John, saw and heard these things.
> And when I heard and saw, I fell down to worship
> before the feet of the angel who showed me these things.
> Then he said to me, 'See that you do not do that.
> For I am your fellow servant, and of your brethren
> the prophets,
> and of those who keep the words of this book.
> Worship God.'

And he said to me, 'Do not seal the words of the prophecy of this book, for the time is at hand'. That is, the prophecy is relevant now, to the present time, it is about the times in which we are living now, how we should respond to its message during our time here and how this world is set for judgement as Christ returns as Lord and King of all. It is in this age that God is establishing His Kingdom, at present just in the hearts of those that know and love Christ; but the culmination of this age will bring about the complete revelation of Christ to all. It is a process that has been in preparation since the times of the patriarchs, as chapter 12 of the Book shows us, but it is something that should inform our mind-set and affections in this present time, so that our objectives and purposes in life become aligned to the Divine purpose of all history.

This message itself, however, will convince no one else; those that live apart from God, those that remain separated from Him; those that live according to the principles of this life will just continue to do so. However those that have been saved by grace, who know and follow Christ, residing in Him, are given encouragement to continue in that way, ever seeking to maintain His perfect standard:

'He who is unjust, let him be unjust still', that is to do wrong or hurt.

'He who is filthy, let him be filthy still.' Filthiness, that is dirt, that which fouls and pollutes, in a word, unholiness or ungodliness. But:

'He who is righteous, let him be righteous still'.
'He who is holy, let him be holy still'.
'And behold, I am coming quickly, and My reward is with Me, to give to every one according to his work. '

Again Christ reiterates the message that He will come

immediately that all is ready. Here it is in the context that every believer will be judged according to what he has done in this life. His sudden coming is for all that have lived for Christ, who have lived His risen life and who have shown in their lives the working of the Holy Spirit, they will receive a reward, the reward of Christ Himself, as a verse of the hymn, 'Jesus the very thought of Thee' puts it:

> 'Jesus, our only joy be Thou
> As Thou our prize will be
> Jesus, be Thou our glory now
> And through eternity'

This is guaranteed and given further emphasis by affirming that He is the fulfilment of all of history, the only thing in all of time of any consequence, anything that will last is only what God Himself has given and completed in Christ:

> 'I am the Alpha and the Omega,
> the Beginning and the End,
> the First and the Last.'

Therefore He goes on to say that the only thing in this life that is worth living for is to follow Him; this Book then is an exhortation to faithfulness and diligence and a persuasion not to be occupied with things now that are only passing.

> 'Blessed are those who do His commandments,
> that they may have the right to the tree of life,
> and may enter through the gates into the city.'

As he also said in John 14:15-21, 'If you love Me, keep

My commandments'. In other words, to summarise the message of the scriptures, our final outcome is all dependent on our relationship with Christ. If we keep His commandments, if we live according to the benchmark that He Himself lived, we will be given the right to that glorious dwelling place. Then if we love Him we will keep His commandments, no question, it is as simple as that. The first letter of John was written for that purpose to show that, that if we love Him then we are sure that we dwell in Him and if we dwell in Him we will keep His commandments.

For the second time after assuring His people that He will return for them though, after His words of encouragement and promise, He contrasts His words with a sombre caution; something that should cause us both hope for the future and restraint for the present.

> 'But outside are dogs and sorcerers
> and sexually immoral and murderers
> and idolaters, and whoever loves and practices a lie.'

In this coming God-filled world Christ no longer rules with a rod of iron, as in Psalm 2, for there is nothing there that is contrary to the will of God to repress. In the beginning God created everything in this physical world perfect, though it was not made to have any consequence in itself for itself, but made to serve God's ultimate purpose, see Romans 8:20.

> 'I, Jesus, have sent My angel to testify to you these things in the churches.'

This is to bear witness, cp verse 20, though here the witness is found in the churches - typically all seven – it is in the community of believers that we witness the truth of these things, it is in the community of those that sincerely love their Lord that an understanding and conviction of these things is to be found and the evidence of that quality of life.

'I am the Root,' that which provides stamina and continuity, that which provides identity and character, cp chapter 5:5.

'And the Offspring of David', a man after God's own heart in whom the promise of the continuity of His kingdom is fulfilled.

'The Bright and Morning Star' (meaning 'the early dawn'). In chapter 2:28 a different word is used in the original meaning just 'early' or 'former', the morning star that may arise in our hearts there is that which gives assurance and relevance of that coming dawn. Here though it is He Himself and His coming that will herald the coming of that Day of the Lord. The witness then of the Holy Spirit within us is to respond with longing, the whole of His church together respond in the same way.

> And the Spirit and the bride say, 'Come!'
> And let him who hears say, 'Come!'

That is whoever gives ear to, that is whoever is receptive to and aspires to His coming; 'And let him who thirsts come'. Anyone who just longs for what is revealed here, whoever they are: 'Whoever desires, let him take the water of life freely.'

There are no conditions or cost attached; the invitation is open to any that want it, which is the only condition, to want it. That must be, however, to accept it only as it has now been revealed in Jesus Christ.

If we are totally focused on our Lord, longing for Him to come, the more He is our cynosure, the centre of our attention, then are we the more 'Transformed into His image', from glory to glory 2 Corinthians 3:18:

> 'For I testify to everyone who hears
> the words of the prophecy of this book.'

'That is to hear' means to take heed, to accept and believe. The prophecy of this book is the public exposition of the whole, not just the prediction of future events as we take the word to mean generally today. This book is not about telling the future but about revealing Jesus Christ in all His glory to us now and describing how He will be revealed to the whole world at His coming, with the conditions that must prevail before that occurs. To attempt to add to or subtract from the word of God, to change the terms or the substance thereof, either to deceive oneself or another, for personal or political motive or to accept persuasion from any source, is to receive this stern warning from our Lord Himself. It is a sombre warning that divides between those that have true faith in the person of their Lord and those that just have faith in a system of belief that may include teaching from the scriptures.

> 'If anyone adds to these things,
>
> God will add to him the plagues that are written in this book;
>
> and if anyone takes away from the words of the book of this prophecy,
>
> God shall take away his part from the Book of Life,
>
> from the holy city, and from the things which are written in this book.'

With that final caveat declared, Christ then says for the third time, to confirm the absolute certainty and significance of His coming and Who it is that guarantees it:

> 'He who testifies to these things
> says, 'Surely I am coming quickly.'

In verse 20 it is now the Lord Himself that bears witness to our hearts, not an angel to the churches generally.

This time His people are now fully prepared and ready and respond wholeheartedly: 'Amen. Even so, come, Lord Jesus!'

'He whose glory fills the skies', will then also fill all our own horizons if we can truly echo those words with all our heart. Then will the blessings alluded to in Revelation chapter 7 and detailed in Ephesians Chapter 1 become our whole experience and quality of life; then will the precious stones of the heavenly city fully characterize our whole heart and being. Even so come, Lord Jesus.

The grace of our Lord Jesus Christ be with you all. Amen.

EPILOGUE

1

The Day of the Lord

The Day of the Lord and the Coming of Christ. How Are These Concepts Related?

He Preserves the Way of His Saints, Proverbs 2:8

Perhaps the scriptures have more to say about the Day of the Lord than any other subject, so it is something that we do well to take note of. It is not about a single event either but a day as the word is used metaphorically, meaning a specific time or era in the context of certain issues. The Day of the Lord in Scripture has different titles in various places, each one relevant to the significance that is being presented there. It also covers different episodes, of both physical and spiritual significance. From the point of view of its temporal manifestation it involves this schedule, probably in this order.

- The 'Time of Jacob's Trouble', as it is described in the Old Testament, a time of unprecedented turmoil and confusion on Earth, Joel 2:1-2, Jeremiah. 30:7 and

Daniel. 12:1 for example. It will begin with the arising of a singularly evil person, variously described as a terrible beast, a prince, the antichrist and the man of sin, depending on the significance to the context referred to.

- The return of Christ to Earth as:

Israel's Messiah and Deliverer and King.

The judge and ruler of all mankind.

The resurrection of the saints to reign with Christ on Earth.

The reign of Christ on Earth for a thousand years, until His authority is completely established without dissent. During this time He will reign without compromise, but in absolute righteousness and impartiality.

- The resurrection of the rest of mankind, all that have ever lived.

- The final judgement of all mankind when their eternal destiny is determined.

- The replacement of the existing Heaven and Earth with a whole new order, 2 Peter 3:10-13.

The new Heaven and Earth that will follow, however, will be unchanging, eternal and perfect, peace and righteousness will prevail without constraint. Only perfect love and goodness can and will flourish.

There is, however, another event that has already been alluded to in this study that is associated with the Day of the Lord. This is an event that has several facets to it, one that will happen physically but one that the scriptures are specifically silent as to when it will occur. The incident is of course the coming of Jesus Christ for His Church, those saints of His that have come to know Him since the time of Pentecost in the first century AD up until the time He returns. This we might assume will happen when Christ returns as mentioned in the schedule above. There are, however, serious problems with this assumption, not the least that Christ Himself said that we can have no idea when this will be, something that the writers of the New Testament reinforce consistently. The Book of the Revelation significantly makes no mention of it at all. Seeing that the book of the Revelation is all about the manifestation of Jesus Christ, we must infer that it will not necessarily be synonymous with it.

Another problem with the assumption that it will occur at the same time as His coming as King to Israel has already been mentioned in part one of section three of this study, that we are given a time scale in Matthew 24 between what is described in the above schedule, yet we are told that we can have no idea when Christ will return for His Church. It fact Christ went further, to say that it will be at a time when we think it won't be or on the other hand it will be at a time that we are not expecting. If we try to predict it at all then we will be wrong. Anyone therefore that even correlates it with a known event or projected time is lying, deceived or mistaken. The reason why this is completely hidden from us is so that we trust in God alone for everything and learn to live in simple obedience to Him, the fact of Christ's coming at any time informing our outlook and faithfulness now to our Lord. To be just occupied with coming events just make us preoccupied with sensational scenarios and temporal matters.

How then is this coming related to the Day of the Lord, what similarities does it have and how does it differ from it?

- It will be different in nature. Zechariah 14:4 tells us that Messiah will come and stand on the Mount of Olives and that there will be dramatic convulsions of the landscape as a result. 1 Thessalonians 4:17 however tells us that He will meet His saints in the air.

- It will be different in style. Matthew 24 vv27-30 tells us that His coming to reign will be a very public and awe-inspiring event. However John 14:1-3 says that His coming for His Church will be a personal event specifically to take His saints away to be with Himself.

- It will be two different experiences for the believer and the sceptic. 1 Thessalonians 5:3 describes it as an abrupt affair bringing sudden destruction on the unwary and nonchalant. 1 Thessalonians 4:18, however, anticipates Christ's coming as something to comfort believers in times of doubt and confusion.

- God will mete out His indignation on the godless and deceitful see Romans 1:18 and 2:5. However Romans 5:9 and Revelation 3:10 state that the just will not suffer His wrath.

- He did not say to His disciples that He would come back to Earth and be with them again here either, which is what we would expect given the account in

Matthew's gospel and so many Old Testament scriptures, but rather that He would come and take them back to be with Himself, where He was, in His Father's House, see John 14:1-3.

- Christ spoke of His coming as a coming to a wedding celebration, the millennium in Revelation 19 also speaking of Christ coming with His bride, as the wedding practice of the day would have been. This would mean that He would have His bride already with Him at His coming to the celebration. This may be 'reading' into the metaphor more than we are meant to, though the image of the wedding schedule would have been firmly imprinted in the minds of those to whom the picture was first presented.

This list of examples is probably not exhaustive, but is perhaps sufficient to show that Christ's coming has completely different implications for those that are expecting Him and those that are not. Luke 17:26 also illustrates this well if we consider that those that entered into the ark represent those that will be saved when the 'flood' comes. Those that spurn God will be carried away in judgement.

Does all this, however, tell us that Christ will come to take His saints away from this world before the catastrophic turmoil of the troubles come, even that it will be Christ's coming to meet His saints in the air that will usher in that time of conflict as some sincerely believe? Admittedly if that were to happen it would explain the dichotomy in Matthew 24 referred to earlier, that we can have no idea when it will be. However if that is to be so it raises another problem, if we can be confident that we will be spared even seeing the troubles, that encourages complacency and the nonchalance of the sceptics of 1 Thessalonians 5:3 and the Laodicean church in Revelation 3. We are inclined then to have the whole scenario catalogued and finalised in our minds. Christ's actual coming for His saints then becomes a side issue, even a distraction to our whole way and manner of life, when it should be absolutely central to every aspect of our spiritual growth. Christ Himself warned of this attitude particularly in Matthew 24:44-51 with the consequences of not staying vigilant. Other scriptures in the New Testament also warn us to be vigilant and to be ever looking forward to His coming.

What then are we to understand from the anomalies mentioned in items 1-5 above? As we have maintained already, the scriptures are about spiritual issues, not primarily about physical temporal issues. This was the mistake the Pharisees made in Jesus' time, that they interpreted the scriptures literally without understanding the spirit of the Law that they strived so earnestly and arrogantly to fulfil. All these differences and anomalies, if we consider them carefully, show us that they are not a matter of status but of a manner of life. If we are faithful, Christ will be faithful and protect us; if we are unfaithful, we will suffer for it as we implicitly persist in independence of Him. That is the principle that is being conveyed. We should be reassured and comforted if we love the Lord, live godly lives and are yearning for His return. If we live for the concerns of today or our own self-righteous ideals or are preoccupied with side issues, we should be warned of the dangers. Our Lord, however, doesn't expect perfection of us yet; it is just a matter of where our affections lie, on things above or on things below.

This, however, does not explain sufficiently another scripture that some Christians have difficulty with, 2 Thessalonians 2. Now it is of course the spiritual implications of His return that our Lord and the scriptures focus on mostly, but the fact that it will be also a physical event is clearly described in the Holy Word. It is important to establish the truth about the physical aspects of Christ's return as our understanding of this has a very significant bearing on the spiritual truths that relate to this subject.

Paul in his letter to the Romans 11:25 refers to Israel being at this present time in a state of partial blindness during this present time when the gentiles are coming into blessing. This time, however, he implies will have a cut-off point, when the full number is complete, then Israel's turn will come again. Christ also spoke of this period in Luke 21:24 from the perspective of Israel's imminent destruction saying that Jerusalem would be overrun by gentiles until the gentiles' time was fulfilled. Some Christian see this time, implicitly the time when the Holy Spirit is present here in the lives of individuals, as being what at present prevents the Man of Sin being revealed. It is a reasonable possibility, but the scriptures do not link this fact with the coming of Christ for His Church so we must be careful not to surreptitiously introduce ideas of our own without realising it.

2 Thessalonians 2 describes the manifestation of the 'man of sin', clearly portrayed there as the abomination of desolation of Matthew 24 and the beast of Revelation 13 and 17.

There he is speaking of something that is at present preventing the manifestation of this being and hence the

Day of the Lord. There it appears to be something of a different character, some object or corporate thing that is holding back the great day of reckoning that the Day of the Lord will be.

First, however, we must consider the context in which chapter 2 appears. The second letter was written about a year after Paul's first letter; the first letter had been in response to a worry that they had about what had happened to their loved ones who had died before Christ had returned. He had explained to them then in chapter 4 that when Christ appeared they would be resurrected and all the Church would then go together to be with Him. There, however, it does not state where the Church will be gathered, as in a place, simply that we will all be with Christ and that is all that matters; that is in perfect security and peace. John 14:2 does say that it will be 'in My Father's house', but that is in Heaven, not a physical location necessarily but a spiritual realm; the dwelling place of God, though He is everywhere.

The immediate context, however, of chapter 2 of the second letter is the previous chapter where Paul first commends the believers there for their godliness and spiritual maturity, explaining to them that the persecution they were suffering at that time was a time of testing for them, purifying their faith. He says that God will be faithful and recompense them for their faithfulness and judge those that persecute them. In the first verse then of chapter 2 he refers to both these matters, the gathering of the church to be with Christ and the troubles that they were then suffering. He says their present troubles, however, were not the Day of the Lord as they had supposed or had been told.

He then goes on to explain to them that the Day of the Lord could not begin until this 'man of sin' is revealed, profaning the temple etc. 2 Thessalonians 2:3, cp Matthew 24:15. However He could not appear yet because there was something that prevented him at present from appearing, this he seems to describe in this verse as 'the apostasy' as it is usually translated in most modern translations. Rather than that actually preventing his appearance, however, it just says that it had to come first and that would then remove the hindrance to the manifestation of this man.

What then is this 'apostasy'? The actual word in the original means to fall away, that is literally 'to have away from status', 'become at a distance'; not implying intent or having any moral meaning necessarily but merely stating a passive change in relative position of one thing to something else. This could of course mean in an abstract sense being removed from the truth, apostasy we might say. The only other place though in the New Testament where this word is used is Acts 21:21 where that meaning is implied, when Paul is accused of forsaking the doctrines of Moses. There, however, there is a distinct difference; there in the original the word is used with the conjunction 'from', implying an active moving away. The meaning then in Thessalonians could mean a falling away from the truth, but it does leave some doubt. The word, however, does not in itself imply a moral fall, it could simply mean a physical disengagement of two objects, the context defining the actual circumstance. In view of Paul's reference in verse one to our gathering to Christ, the 'falling away' could be the counterpart, implying the church falling away from an alien environment and being gathered to Christ as outlined in 1 Thessalonians chapter 4. This in fact is the alternative rendering given of this verse in the Amplified Bible. How and when that will transpire, however, we are not told, for reasons discussed. This, however, still does not explicitly define what it is that is preventing the beginning of the Day of the Lord; the passage seems ambivalent and uncertain, equivocal and enigmatic.

Paul, however, says in verse 6 that now you know what is restraining him, so that He will come at the time appointed for him, you can be confident of your situation. We might think, however, that the situation is far from explained; is it an event, an entity or a moral situation that is preventing the Day of the Lord getting under way? Are we left just to make a choice, none of which really fits the text unequivocally?

The problem in that case is perhaps our perception of what Paul is saying. As always, prophecy in scripture is not about predicting certain events for our curiosity or just to allay anxieties about the future, but to reveal to us something about the character or claims of God and encourage faith in Him. It is a spiritual principle that Paul is explaining here, and when we grasp that the whole issue becomes clearer, what is and what isn't being said. The principle is easiest to explain first as it is applicable to us personally now. It is the same principle we considered earlier, the principle of faithfulness. If we remain faithful to our Lord and to His truth, the spirit of the man of sin, that 'mystery of lawlessness' that Paul refers to in verse 7 is kept concealed, inoperative. If however we fall away from that position, whether by being misled, by negligence or deliberate choice, this mystery of lawlessness, that hidden principle of rebellion as the Amplified Bible renders it, can become manifest in our hearts. This in fact is an important application of the scripture here, though not necessarily its primary interpretation.

Paul here is applying that principle not to individuals but to a global situation. The same principle applies, however, because it is a spiritual principle decreed by God. The physical epitome of that spirit of lawless, this man of sin will not be revealed while the witness of Christ and the conduct of God's truth are present. If, or rather here when, the world falls away from that position, then can that evil person be revealed, so either of the above scenarios could pertain, a moral or physical 'apostasia', a falling away.

This could be the isolation of the church from having any effect on the world, by being physically removed from it, for example, or it could be the overwhelming apostasy of mankind generally or it could be both; the actual circumstances are not given. The point that Paul is making primarily is that if we stay faithful to our Lord and to the Truth then are we kept from sin and its consequences, personally and communally. How or when or in what order or sequence of events this will happen is not given to us to know. If we seek to try and work this out, then are we become 'fallen away' from the principle of simple faith of trusting that God will protect and care for us at all times, keeping out of danger if we stay close to Him. We are told in the scriptures what the Earth will be like during the period of Christ's reign on Earth, we are told what the future eternal state will be like, but we are not given details of any interim arrangements that may transpire. We have to ask if we are filling in those details ourselves or adopting others' ideas if we think we do know.

However there is another possibility that Paul is referring to here, something that has featured quite a lot in this study. The Amplified Bible gives us a fuller rendering of this 'falling away in 2 Thessalonians 2:3:

'Let no one deceive or beguile you in any way,
for that day will not come except the apostasy comes first
(Unless the predicted great falling away
of those who have professed to be Christians has come),
and the man of lawlessness (sin) is revealed,
who is the son of doom (of perdition).'

If this rendering of this passage is better and this apostasy is one that was generally expected by the faithful at that time, then the apostasy of Isaiah 28:14-17 is very probably what is being referred to here (applying to Israel, however, rather than Christians specifically). This prophecy was mentioned in more detail in section1 part 5.

Daniel 9:26 confirms that the troubles will be a Divinely-appointed time so Christians at that time of Paul would have known of and expected it. This particular apostasy of Isaiah had plainly not happened, as the Jews had not been reinstated to a position of being protected by any worldly power, they were still under a repressive rule, in fact nearing their time of annihilation as a nation.

This latter meaning then is perhaps the most likely event that Paul is referring to here, though it really doesn't change the point that Paul is making. He is reassuring the Christians at Thessalonica that the Day of the Lord with all its agonies could not have occurred, so they must not doubt that God had failed to fulfil His promises. He was also encouraging them to stay faithful themselves; God had a purpose for them in their own troubles that they were then facing.

In verses 10-15 Paul addresses their uncertainties and discusses the character of the man of sin in some detail. He also mentions their faithfulness and the glories they can expect if they stay faithful. He then goes on to illustrate the very point made above when he encourages the believers at Thessalonica to stand fast in the faith, because this is now the time when their salvation is being formed within them. Those that reject God and persecute His saints, however, will suffer great distress in the future as He persuades men to the very last to repent. God is absolutely faithful, however, and will care for and protect His children in His way at the time, whatever happens; His children are those that are faithful to Him, those that are sealed with His Spirit. God will save and protect us whatever happens, whenever it happens, but in His way, not according to our ideas.

There is however a seeming difficulty that hasn't been addressed here. It begs the question why the Christians at Thessalonica would be disturbed if the Day of the Lord had already started.

Was he saying that 'the coming of our Lord Jesus Christ' and 'our gathering together unto Him' were two different events or the same thing? Either construction is valid.

- If two different events, was he saying in verse 3 that the Day of the Lord couldn't happen until we had been gathered unto Him and that was the fear that the Christians had, that Christ had failed to come as promised?

- If the same thing though, the coming of the Day of Christ would imply the imminence of their being gathered to Him, so why were they worried?
- The fact that there might be some other factor preventing the coming of our Lord would not have concerned them if they were not aware of it.

The text then again would seem irreconcilably ambiguous if we look at it purely from a rational perspective. Is the scripture ambiguous and uncertain? Is the word of God open to interpretation? The problem is again the way we approach the scripture. If we consider it in respect of our natural concerns, then we bring an agenda with us when we think about it; we view it through tinted spectacles. 'Take no thought of tomorrow', our Lord said; we must read this passage through the enlightenment of the Holy Spirit, the Spirit guiding us, the spirit of humility and dependence upon God and the looking to know His mind and will. This is the tenor of Paul's writing always. He is throughout this letter, as in his other letters, concerned with the spiritual wellbeing of the Christians he is addressing. Paul is not concerned here with their confusion over events and the relationship those events may have to each other, rather he is concerned about their occupation with events at all. Like Peter when he walked on the water with his master, when he started looking at the waves he began to sink. The same thing was happening at Thessalonica; they were taking their eyes off the coming of the Lord and focusing on the events that were happening around them. Christ had first foretold that when the abomination of desolation desecrated the Holy Place in the temple that would be the beginning of the end. Paul in 2 Thessalonians 2 then refers to the same occasion, calling this abomination 'the man of sin'. This is something that appears several times throughout scripture as we have seen in this study and is a significant prophecy. To be looking out for that, however, rather than just being forewarned of its significance, is to become detached from our occupation with our Lord Himself and His coming. If we are looking for His coming, we stay faithful to Him and we will then one day be gathered to Him; the time in between then will be one of hope and expectation and growing in spiritual maturity. To be trying to second-guess when He will be coming is to take our eye of the ball, to lose the plot, to be distracted from our true focus and purpose.

2

The Purpose of History

God Explains to Daniel by His Angel what He is Preparing His People Israel for; To Be Ready for the Coming of Their Messiah.

'It is Not for You to Know Times and Seasons Which the Father has Put in His Own Authority.' Acts 1:7

Daniel 9, verses 1-2 and 24-27 in particular, should be read in perspective with the other visions described in Daniel. In chapter 2 Nebuchadnezzar has a dream of a spectacular image that is then interpreted as describing five empires that will be instrumental in forming the character of Israel until the coming of their Messiah. This is not an account of the course that history will take generally, but just non-consecutive periods that relate to Israel's moral training. Not a timeline of history, but what God will achieve in His people through history. The time relates just to the periods that God is actively working with them through the various epochs. These times are outlined in section 4 part 9, 'Seven Hills and Seven Kingdoms.'

The verses 24-27 of Daniel 9 particularly do not focus on the passage of time as we might be inclined to assume; the periods spoken of here are relevant particularly to their moral effect, and so the periods have particular spiritual symbolism. This fact is emphasised by the intricate expressions employed in the text to describe these periods. Even so they are specific periods of time with particular practical significance.

To just try and 'decipher' the time scale of this prophesy, however, to see how the world - as we see it – will end, is to miss completely the message of this passage and will probably mislead us, as all we will be left with is incomplete impressions and ideas that conflict with other parts of scripture. At best it will give us a superficial, temporal view of scripture, which is simply an instinctive understanding, not an enlightened one. We miss what this passage is really telling us about Israel primarily, but then also typically about ourselves and as regards the obligation of mankind generally.

The fact that the time given of 70 x 7 is literally years, 490, has been shown to be true; the time from the decree to rebuild Jerusalem to when Messiah would be rejected, cut off, would be 483 years (given as 7 + 62, x 7; verse 25). The exact dates involved are not known to history, though we do know approximately. Christ was born about 4 BC, it is now generally reckoned. The scripture says He was about 30 years of age when He began His ministry and that continued for about three years. We might calculate then that He was crucified in about 29 AD. That would mean that the original decree was made in 454 BC. The date calculated from the date given in Nehemiah chapter 2, with the dates that we have from general history, however, would be about 446 BC; eight years difference.

Given the uncertainty of the times and approximation of the dates after 2000 years though it is quite apparent that what we can calculate is close enough to be possibly exact and to show that the faithful at the time of Christ of those that knew their God and the scriptures, like Simeon and Anna in Luke chapter 2 verses 25-38 for example, were expecting their Messiah. The first coming of the Messiah then is perhaps the one event in all of scriptural prophecy where a date is signified.

The significance, however, of this extract is much greater than its superficial elements; first, however, we should consider the significance of whole chapter.

Daniel is first praying and fasting to know the will of God for His people; that is the only way that any of us can know what the will of God is for us, corporately and personally, waiting on Him in diligence, perseverance and dependence.

The first part of God's dealings with His people, their captivity in Babylon, was coming to an end, see verses 1-2, and Daniel was worried about what was to happen to them after that. See also Jeremiah 25:11.

The answer was then revealed to Daniel by the archangel sent from God, after Daniel had passed an appropriate length of his time in fasting and prayer. The angel then revealed not just what would happen next but what God's ultimate purpose was for Israel and how that would be achieved. It is an example to us that when we humbly and earnestly seek to know what God's will is for us, He will reveal that to us when we are ready to receive it. It is important to note that Daniel's attitude was one of repentance and dependence upon God first, for which he was commended by the angel. This is always paramount if we are ever to know what God's will is firstly in us and then for us.

Next we must look briefly at the symbolic significance of the epochs that are described here.

The background: Israel had been held captive in Babylon for nearly 70 years. This had been foretold by Jeremiah in his prophecy, chapters 25:11 and 29:10. This happened just as predicted as recorded in 2 Chronicles 36:21. This period coincided with the head of Nebuchadnezzar's image, referred to above, defined as the kingdom of Babylon up until the time of its overthrow by Persia.

This 70 years was the time that Israel had broken the law of God in not observing the sabbatical year, see Leviticus 25:4:

'But in the seventh year there shall be a Sabbath
of solemn rest for the land, a Sabbath to the Lord.
You shall neither sow your field nor prune your vineyard.'

During this year the poor were allowed to reap a harvest and animals to forage.

Now 70 in scripture signifies the call or request for reconciliation and forgiveness through humiliation and penitence; see -

- Judges 9:56 — The penalty for wickedness.
- Isaiah 23:15-17 — The time of humiliation on account of pride and idolatry.
- Jeremiah 25:11-12 — The time of humiliation and recompense for idolatry and disobedience.
- Zechariah 7:5 — A time of penitence and fasting.
- Luke 10:1 and 17 — The number for preparation for Christ's Kingdom.
- It is the ending of our own striving and trusting the mercy and peacefulness of God (though this may of course be entered into hypocritically).

However seven, sevenfold or seven times in scripture suggests completeness or the consummation of effect or function, for example:

- Genesis 4:15 — The fullness of revenge or penalty
- Psalm 12:6 — The completeness of purification
- Proverbs 6:31 — The full recompense for crime
- Isaiah 30:26 — The completeness of mercy and blessing
- Matthew 18:21 — Sufficiency of forgiveness or fulfilment of obligation
- Luke 17:4 — Totality of forgiveness

7 fold 7 - Leviticus 25:8, 'And you shall count seven sabbaths of years for yourself, seven times seven years; and the time

of the seven sabbaths of years shall be to you forty-nine years.' This was then followed by the year of jubilee celebration, see verse Leviticus 25:10.

With 7 fold 70, the two are compounded:

- Matthew 18:22   Completeness of forgiveness and reconciliation

The fundamental symbolic significance then of the 70 years' captivity then was a time of adversity and humiliation for God's purpose of bringing His people to penitence and reconciliation. Then this another epoch is established of 70 x 7; as it transpires this was also to be years, 70 sabbatical years, years are relevant by implication as being a complete cycle of time. Inferred here then is that this period of 7 fold 70 is a period of complete and final mortification and then reconciliation of Israel as a people so that God could dwell with them unhindered and without compromise, as is stated in verse 24 of Daniel 9.

What then is revealed is what is to be achieved during this time, by whom, in whom, how the time scale will be divided up and the effect that will be accomplished.

- The rebuilding of the temple was started under Cyrus the First in about 536 BC.

- It is the decree authorising the rebuilding of the city in about 446 BC though that the prophesy starts from and what is relevant to the objectives of verse 24, namely that it will take 7 x 7 (years), a time of complete re-establishment of the government of Jerusalem.

This of course establishes a spiritual principle that is relevant to ourselves; typically for us signifying the heavenly city, New Jerusalem, where we reside and by which we are governed, see Galatians 4:26 and Hebrews 11:10. This is the complete rule of God in our lives.

- To return to Daniel, 62 x 7 years then passes over the Greek period of domination when the temple was again destroyed by Antiochus IV and rebuilt later by Herod the Great. This period is not relevant, however, to what is being brought before us here, so it is not mentioned except to give Israel the timescale in which God is still working with His people, fulfilling His objectives of verse 24.

- Messiah then comes towards the end of this period but then is 'cut off', that is rejected and murdered. 'But not for Himself', His death vicariously achieved the objectives of verse 24 for His people. Other translations render 'but not for Himself' as 'and will have nothing', that is He did not receive His Kingdom openly at that time which is also true.

It is quite apparent that the Sabbath in the Old Testament was an important and broad institution. It was a day of each week, one year in seven, a jubilee every 50 years, and a period of 70 x 7 years. This was rest from effort, signifying a rest from effort to keep the law, restraint of self-will or the struggling to succeed or excel. It is apparent that the significance of the seven is that seven here means what is complete, what is Divinely accomplished; it is the end of all work and effort and in the last period of 'seven' the completeness of forgiveness and reconciliation.

This also is a fundamental principle of salvation under the new Covenant; in Hebrews chapter 4 we enter that rest through belief in Christ, trusting in Him wholly to bring us into that state of resting in Him. It is a wholly spiritual experience, a rest that encapsulates respite from all effort and obligation.

Verse 24 says that this time is allocated to complete the whole process of salvation, here nationally for Israel as it is also true individually for anyone.

- 'To finish the transgression;' that is to stop committing individual sins through repentance, turning from them to God in a state of humility and contrition.

- 'To make an end of sins;' this is more than just repentance, it is then to change one's propensity to sin. This is the deliverance from the power of sin by removing the very nature that causes us to sin. This is the process of mortification that continues throughout our lives.

- 'To make reconciliation for iniquity;' the price of reconciliation in the Old Testament was to restore seven fold for wrongdoing to establish forgiveness and reconciliation. Christ has paid that price of redemption for us now, though it is through the continuous regeneration of God throughout our lives that our fellowship with Him is maintained. This reconciliation is the counterpart to (b), 'making an end to sin.'

- 'To bring in everlasting righteousness;' this for Israel will be as it is for us now a Divinely orchestrated process, a change of life, an entirely spiritual process, it is the building up of a new nature within us to replace our innate nature, the nature of Christ Himself, put on as it were a garment day by day. This is the process of purification, as we are washed from all that is unholy, and sanctification, which is establishing what is holy within us.

- 'To seal up vision and prophecy;' that is that it must continue right up until full realization, there cannot be a partial completion of the expectation that is set before us, of all that is required of us. It is of course God's work in us but is appropriated by faith.

- 'And to anoint the Most Holy;' for Christ to become unequivocally Lord of All. This will be established one day globally, in the meantime it is something we look and long for now personally, His coming again for us when all will be revealed and realised.

Verse 26 though reveals something else that will happen during this whole period though right at the end, following Messiah being 'cut off', ie after the 483 years.

> 'The people of the prince who is to come
> shall destroy the city and the sanctuary.
> The end of it shall be with a flood,
> and till the end of the war desolations are determined.'

This occurred as predicted in AD 70, or perhaps it means it started then and continues to the present. The prophecy then continues:

> 'Then he shall confirm a covenant with many for
> one week;

> but in the middle of the week
> he shall bring an end to sacrifice and offering.
> And on the wing of abominations shall be one who makes desolate,
> even until the consummation, which is determined,
> is poured out on the desolate.' (or desolater)

Under the pretext of providing a 'wing' of protection by some Machiavellian means, creating a false peace, this evil protector reneges on his treaty and wreaks desolation on the nation. This continues until all that has been determined, that is decreed by God Himself, has been achieved.

It is constructive now to ask what Daniel would have made of this revelation. He would have noted that Messiah would come at some unknown time in the future but that He would at first be rejected before later being accepted and anointed as King. If he had considered the timing of all these things however, he would have been completely wrong as we can see from hindsight. He would no doubt have thought that Messiah would be anointed seven years after His rejection; the seven years being a time of great trouble. Daniel though was not occupied with that, he was concerned with the sin and reconciliation of His people and how that would be achieved. This is what God honoured and so He revealed His purposes to him. This was not about a time limit for the Jews to get themselves sorted out but about what God would achieve in them through their Messiah.

Nehemiah, however, would have realised that when the command to rebuild Jerusalem by Artaxerxes was given, the date was then known when the Messiah should come. This perhaps is the only incidence in scripture when a date for a significant event was foretold. This was so that faithful and spiritually-minded Jews would have expected Him and known who He was. Such saints from that time could also earnestly anticipate Him. That occasion, however, has now happened and we now look back to be reassured as to God's faithfulness to His people.

We may ask, however, what the disciples would have made of Daniel's prophecy. They now knew that Messiah had come, so were they now looking for Him to be crowned as King and their national deliverer within seven years? They may well have thought that and perhaps that is why they asked Jesus after His resurrection if He would then restore the Kingdom to Israel. They would have seen Daniel's prophecy almost fulfilled and were then looking for its complete fulfilment. Jesus simply replies:

'It is not for you to know times and seasons
which the Father has put in His own authority,' Acts 1:7.

They should simply do their duty as servants in the light of God's promises to be implemented at any time. To be preoccupied with times and events was just a distraction and disobedience.

Jesus, however, did have something to add to Daniel's prophecy. In Luke 21 Jesus foretells the destruction of Jerusalem and the temple and this was then fulfilled in AD 70, after Jerusalem was compassed about with armies, about 40 years after His death and resurrection.

Jesus' foretelling of the destruction of Jerusalem in what we know as the Olivet Discourse, reference to verse 27 of

Daniel 9, and the sinister events that will take place before the whole vision is consummated, is not mentioned in Luke's account. This later part is recorded, however, in Matthew's gospel, where Jesus tells about the 'Abomination of Desolation spoken of by the prophet Daniel' desecrating the Holy Place. Here, however, He links it with His coming again as King. This then is the consummation of Daniel's prophecy when Christ is then anointed as the Most Holy. The treaty foretold in verse 27 of the text purports to be one of protection for Israel by this evil prince, though he will in fact renege on it half way through the period of the treaty and seeks to wipe out the nation. The prophecy will, however, be consummated; will be sealed up in the words of verse 24 and judgement dispensed on the desolater when Christ returns.

It has become apparent as centuries have unfolded that the events described in Luke 11 of the destruction of the city and the second coming of Christ would not be concurrent; they would be linked as far as the prophecy and purposes of God were concerned, but this was not to be linked chronologically. Jesus' prophecy allowed for that eventuality so that future generations would see how God was continuing to work, though only by continuing to trust in God and His programme in time, a timeknown only to Himself.

At about the same time that the gospels of St. Matthew and St. Luke were being written, the apostle Paul wrote a letter to the Thessalonians, referred to in the previous epilogue, where he talks about the 'falling away' or apostasy that would precede the coming of the 'man of sin', this prince, as Daniel describes him. This apostasy will be something dramatic and already prophesied, it would seem, in the prophecy of Isaiah 28, made roughly 200 years before Daniel's prophecy. This was discussed in parts 3-4 of this study. This is something that has not yet been fulfilled, although it does have meaning typically for us now. How those events will actually unfold we cannot know and are foolish to enquire about or speculate, just as Daniel and Nehemiah would have got it wrong had they made assumptions, then so will we.

All these examples reflect the fact that scripture is not concerned with the course of history but about what God is achieving during the course of history. They are ever an encouragement for us to examine what God is doing through past events, in our own lives and in the ancient and more recent history of His people.

The conclusion then must be that we cannot and must not project into the future what God will do, when He will fulfil what He has told us will happen or even to propose how things will happen. We are called to live by faith. When these things materialise we will recognise them, but not as we might previously have imagined. The more spiritually-minded we are however, the closer we are likely to be to the truth. To become occupied with events distracts our attention away from eternal issues that God is calling us to consider and act upon.

> To be carnally minded is death
> but to be spiritually minded is life and peace
> Romans 8:6

3

Moral Responsibility

Moral Responsibility Implies an Inherent Incompatibility Between Self-Determination and Accountability

'The Tree That is in the Middle of the Garden You Shall Not Eat Thereof, Neither Shall You Touch it Lest You Die.' Genesis 3:3

Mankind, though made a physical being, was also created as a morally-intelligent being and more than that a spiritual being too, a creature that could love and commune with God through faith, that is through obedience and dependence upon Him, which is what the word 'faith' implies. This was so that he should have a specific purpose, the purpose of caring for and moral governance of God's creation, see Genesis 1:26, and as such to be accountable to God in what he did. The fall, however, was inevitable as such love and obedience can only be self-motivated or it is merely compulsion or conditioning. This, however, begs the question as to why God created mankind as morally intelligent creatures to be able to perform His created purpose and yet He told them not to 'eat of the tree of good and evil' from where they could gain that understanding.

Does that mean effectively that he was to remain morally naive but that the onus was on him to remain morally responsible? Whether we take the story as literally true or as a metaphor, was that in effect creating a trap for mankind that he would inevitably fall into? By no means.

What God was saying here is not that they should not have any understanding of what was good and what was evil but that they should not assume the knowledge of it for themselves, to make moral decisions independently of God. Only God Himself was wise and knowledgeable enough to do that and man must accept God's own judgment if they were not to go astray. Mankind must depend upon God in faith if they were and are to remain in communion with Him in simplicity and righteousness. By assuming in pride the choice for themselves mankind died, they lost that true life that is in God alone and maintained through communion with Him: Paradise lost.

However, God in His wisdom provided before even the world was formed for the eventuality, indeed one would say the inevitability, that man would fail, by making a plan of salvation; see Revelation 13:8. This entailed not only His Son being made in our likeness, but also for us to be then re-made in His likeness, so that we could share in the fellowship of the Godhead. The world of sin and corruption that had come into being as man lived apart from God then formed that very environment of adversity in which faith can be built and strengthened and moral insight developed.

Faith is tested and confirmed by being in an environment that is alien to it, proving that faith is real by living in dependence upon the Almighty, by living in His Spirit.

Sometimes we need to go our own way, perhaps unwittingly, until we are shown that it is the wrong way, as did Adam and Eve; see Isaiah 30:21. In this way we learn intelligently to choose what is right according to God's understanding; that way we learn and choose His way, proving for ourselves what is 'The good and acceptable and perfect will of God,' Roman's 12:2. This is the way that we come to know and love God truly and live in the glory of that relationship. That is something that God could only create through time, through the process of revealing Himself to us and in us through that process called sanctification.

What then was God's original intention for His creation when He formed it, and how does that differ from the world we see around us now? Romans 8:19-23 sets that out in a nutshell; here is part of the quote:

'The earnest expectation of the creation
eagerly waits for the revealing of the sons of God...'

'Because the creation itself will be delivered from the bondage of corruption into the glorious liberty of the children of God... we also ... eagerly awaiting the adoption, that is the redemption of our body.'

If the implication here is that it will be the resurrection and glorification of the saints that will be the means or the catalyst for establishing peace and harmony throughout all of creation, it then also explains and confirms why God created mankind and what His original purpose was for him. Although we might say 'but the Church is a heavenly people,' Paul does not say in Romans here that he is referring to the Church of Christ exclusively but he is saying effectively that the Church may have a heavenly character and indeed heavenly purpose on Earth, but it will eventually also have an earthly function, as all of mankind in that Kingdom will have.

Appendices

APPENDIX 1
An Outline of the Consecutive and Recurrent Themes

Consecutive Themes

1. God's Purposes for Mankind
2. The character of the settings or arenas for there implementation
3. The removal of the old Natural Order
4. The Kingdom of God on earth; the new state of Divine Order

In Sections 1-4
The Recurrent Themes

1. The temporal or physical perspective
2. The heavenly or spiritual perspective
3. The moral or ethical perspective
4. The judicial perspective, manifesting all that is evil and separating us from God, yet calling for repentance while offering forgiveness and protection
5. The full realisation of God's purposes

1. Matthew 21-22, Revelation chapters 1-3, 8, 12 and 19a
   - Parable of the vineyard etc
   - Christ as head of the Church
   - Silence in heaven
   - The woman clothed with the sun etc
   - The bride made ready

APPENDICES

2. Matthew 24a, Revelation chapters 4-5, trumpets and 10, 13 and 19b
   - The nature of the end times leading to Christ's second coming
   - The taking of the scroll
   - The 6 trumpets
   - The Beast and 666
   - The coming of Christ with the armies of heaven

3. Matthew 24b, Revelation chapters 6a, 11, 15-16 and 20
   - The tribulation period on earth
   - The opening of the seals
   - The measuring of the temple
   - The bowls of wrath
   - The millennium; Christ's absolute reign in righteousness

4. Matthew 25, Revelation chapters 6b, 11.17-18 and 21-22
   - The setting up of the kingdom on earth
   - The character of the kingdom as defined by the names of the 12 tribes
   - The 7th trumpet and the establishment of God's law on earth
   - The end of the 7 kingdoms and the whore
   - The new heavens and earth

APPENDIX 2

How the Sequence of Themes Intersects

	The temporal perspective	The Heavenly perspective	The moral perspective	The eschatological perspective	The Divine Objective
God's Purposes for Mankind, revealed in the person of Jesus Christ	Matthew 21-22 Part 1 – The Right Character	Revelation 1-3 Part 2 The Right Pedigree Part 3 The Calling to Account	Revelation 8:1-6 Part 4 A Deafening Silence	Revelation 12 Part 5 A Spectacular Phenomenon	Revelation19:1-10 Part 6 The Imminent Marriage Part 7 The Perfect Marriage
The character of the settings, or the arenas of implementation of those purposes. The Context in which God's Objectives are Realised:	Matthew 24:1-14 Part 1 The Age of Duplicity and Doubt	Revelation 4-5 Part 2 The Four Living Creatures within the Throne Part 3 The Supremacy of the Lamb	Revelation 8:7-10 Part 4 A Fanfare of Trumpets Part 5 The majesty of God and His Mission	Revelation 13 Part6 The Sinister Beast Part 7 '666'	Revelation19:11-21 Part8 The Return of the King
The removal of everything of the old Natural Order that prevents the Reign of Christ at present	Matthew 24-15-51 Part 1 The End of an Era	Revelation 6:1-7 Part 2 Where are we all Going?	Revelation 11:1-12 Part 3 The Irresistible Presence Part 4 Broken Promises	Revelation 15-16 Part 5 Mankind's Last Chance	Revelation20 Part 6 The Die is Cast
The Kingdom of God on earth: the new state of Divine Order The Earth Shall be Filled With knowledge of the Glory of God	Matthew 25 Part 1 Parables of the Kingdom	Revelation 7 Part 2 The Kingdom of God Within Us: Part 3 The Heavenly Life Within us: Part4 Christ in us the Hope of Glory Part 5 If Anyone is in Christ He is a New Creature Part 6 Spiritual Maturity	Revelation 11:13-19 Part 7 The Kingdom of our Lord	Revelation 17-18 Part 8 Spiritual Adultery Part 9 Seven Hills and Seven Kingdoms Part 10 Seven Hills: a Spiritual Allegory	Revelation 21-22 Part 11 The New Heavens and Earth Part 12 The Holy City Part 13 Paradise Restored

APPENDIX 3

A Summary of the Gospel Discourse and the Four Main Sections of the Revelation

The Recurrent Themes through the Revelation and the Gospel Discourse	The Gospel Discourse — The Temporal Perspective	Revelation chapters One to Seven — The Heavenly Perspective	Revelation Chapters Eight to Eleven — The Moral Perspective	Revelation Chapters Twelve to Eighteen — The Judicial Perspective	Revelation Chapters Nineteen to Twenty-Two — The Divine Consummation
The Significant Principles on which God's Kingdom is set up. God reveals to mankind what His Purposes are for us and how they will be instigated	The parable of the Misappropriated Vineyard; the rejected corner stone and the spurned marriage feast. Woe to the Pharisees etc: 'Behold your house is left unto you desolate.	Christ as the First and the Last. Christ's right as Lord and redeemer, as head of his Church. The divine Christ amongst the candlesticks. The Letters to the seven churches	7th seal The golden censer thrown to earth. The prayers of saints	The woman with a crown of twelve stars; The Dragon. Christ called up to Heaven; Israel dispersed. The overcoming of the brethren (saints). Satan cast out of heaven and his onslaught against Israel	Christ as the Bridegroom, Judge, King, Light and Eternal God. The call to the Marriage supper Christ and His saints as His Bride
The spiritually significant background in achieving this. The Significant issues and affairs that give warning of the end of all that prevents the realization of God's objectives	The Temple will be destroyed False Christs, wars, famines, earthquakes then persecution, martyrs, treachery, false prophets, apostasy. The Gospel preached worldwide, The End Signs and wonders, False Christs and prophets, His coming as the lightening	The scene... in Heaven of things hereafter, 24 Elders: Creatures give glory honour etc Elders worship before the throne The Lamb takes scroll amidst the Elders and Creatures Elders, Creatures angels worship Every creature blesses God	Seven Trumpets, to earth 's inhabitants The scene... on earth The Angel declaring the imminent end The little scroll The Gospel is sweet But repentance is bitter	The Beast with seven heads blaspheming God His tabernacle and warring with saints Second beast and 666. The Lamb, The 144000 sealed, Angels preach judgement, The reapers, Armageddon Nations sing the song of Moses.	The Scene – The 2nd Coming of Christ as King of Kings With the armies of Heaven The Beast and false prophet cast into the lake of fire
God's scheme in the implementation of His Purposes: God promises a new kingdom of only love and righteousness, but warns that all that is contrary to that must go first	The Abomination of Desolation in the Holy Place, Judea must flee, Great tribulation, Immediately after the sun and moon darkened, The Son of Man appears, Angels gather elect from the 4 winds	The action...the seals of the scroll of authority given to Christ as Lord of all – revealing to mankind their depravity The sixth seal, imminence of The Great tribulation, such as was not since the beginning of the world: see Mat. 24: 21	The action... measuring of the Temple The two witnesses in sackcloth; killed then raised	The action: the quality of life turns foul) The Bowls of Wrath, Babylon divided into three ch.16: 19	The action – The first judgement, of the faithful, The millennium The second judgement
The fulfilment of God's Plans in salvation and the establishment of Perfection. Even the 'Kingdom of God' on earth is a transition to a perfect world where only righteousness dwells	The Parables: Of the Ten Virgins, The servants and the talents, The sheep and the goats Each illustrating the Kingdom of Heaven at Christ's second coming	The outcome... 144000 of Israel sealed The very great multitude saved Angels worship before the throne, elders and creatures	The outcome...7th trumpet: Christ's reign and judgement foreseen. Elders only worship, intelligently	The outcome: The great whore and Babylon as oppressors and instrument of Israel's salvation is destroyed. The end of Satan's rule – 'The Lord God Omnipotent' reigns.	The outcome – The new heaven and earth The city new Jerusalem, a State of perfection and the light to the nations

APPENDIX 4

Symbolic Meanings

When considering the symbolic meaning of words in scripture the meaning can often convey an idea intuitively but this can be misleading or limited. Careful consideration of the use of the word elsewhere in scripture will give a better understanding, especially where it is used poetically, in the poetic and apocalyptic books and also sometimes in the prophets and parables of our Lord, for example. The meaning gleaned however should always be consistent with all scripture; bearing in mind that context can vary an applied meaning. Poetic meaning is not the same as rational meaning, being broader and conveying character or experience rather than overt description. It takes a lot of mental effort and should be done prayerfully and meditatively. Never assume a symbolic meaning deduced from one verse of scripture alone, a meaning will be consistent with all references, bearing in mind that some words used symbolically may have more than one meaning, depending on the context. As with all scripture its significance is spiritual and symbolic meaning is directly so, as a rule at least. Such study is a minefield for the unwary and non-spiritually minded, but a source of profound wisdom and blessing for the diligent, meek and sincere.

There is considerable difference in ideas expressed by different people as to the meaning of scriptural symbolism. These ideas presented here are from a careful consideration of the usual poetic use of words in scripture. References given are a guide only as a start and it is recommended that anyone reading the scripture should do so carefully, studying to see what the scriptures are really saying, ready to criticise, qualify or amend received and preconceived ideas from any quarter. These definitions suggested here are meant as a help to getting to understand the full meaning and application of scripture. Each definition attempts to summarise a broad, central idea or concept as a starting point for personal study, but even there does not claim to be authoritative, the meaning is inevitably subjective and therefore limited to some degree, though the application of all scripture is not for any private interpretation only, cp 2 Peter 1: 20-21.

APPENDICES

Numerical

<u>Represents inherent effect or significance, emphasising calibre or value</u>

1. Identity or unity, Gen. 1: 9, Ps. 14: 3, Prov. 1: 14
2. Witness, confirmation:
   >Reliability, emphasis,
   >Contrast or doubling.
   >Ex. 31: 18, Deut. 17: 6.
3. Solid, real, substantial, a complete set,

   a. John 2: 19, the full course
   b. Luke 13: 32, to fulfilment, also Genesis 40: 12,13,18,19

4. Universality, Full earthly representation or material completeness Isaiah 11: 12
5. Full provision, more than sufficient or is merited – hence sometimes implying grace 1 Samuel 17: 40, Matthew 14: 19
6. Creativity, effort, labour: - human or divine. Exodus 20: 9 and 11, 21: 2, 23: 10.
7. Completeness, the consummation of effect or function: - Psalm 12: 6, Proverbs 6: 31, Matthew 18: 21 (thus perfection in relation to what is moral) Rest after work is completed
8. Dedication, renewal, circumcision Exodus 22: 30, John 20: 26, Luke 2: 21
10. Comprehensive in effect, fully or doubly sufficient Job 19: 3, Eccl. 7: 19
12. Divine administration or effectiveness, full and devoted service. Matthew 10: 1, 14: 20, 19: 28 and 26: 53
20. Full strength or development, Lev. 27: 3,5.
30. Age of maturity, Numbers 4: 3, typically days in a month – see below
40. All-inclusive or replete *Administration* Psalm 95: 10, Deuteronomy 25: 3 Luke 4: 2
50. Jubilee, deliverance, a time of consummation Leviticus 25: 11, Esther 5: 14
60. Length of man's working life; full maturity, 1 Timothy 5: 9

70.	The call or request for reconciliation and forgiveness through humiliation and penitence; Judges 9: 56, Isaiah 23: 15-17, Jeremiah 25: 11-12, Zechariah 7: 5 and Matthew 18: 22
100.	Full Sufficiency Full provision of strength Proverbs 17: 10, Ecclesiastes 6: 3
600.	Full provision of work cp Genesis 7: 6
666.	Full intensity, duration and limit of effort cp 1 Kings 10: 14 In respect of the 'Beast' of Rev.13, 'It is the number [calibre] of a man,' so he is the embodiment of all that man can achieve or is capable of.
1,000	Full Representation of all, or everyone of a group, totality Psalm 50: 10, 90: 4
10,000	Myriads, an innumerable amount, all inclusive 1 Samuel 18: 7, Jude 14

Multiple numbers usually signify the addition of the meaning of each part of the number, such as 666 above [= 6 x 100 plus 60 plus 6]

Fractions:

A half	the dividing of, partial, inadequate 1 Kings 10: 7
A third part	The complete or final part, that part which gives meaning or certainty. 1 Samuel 3: 8
A fourth part	Perhaps a representative part of what is universal

Seasonal Features - Emphasise Function

1. A 'month' is an allocated period of purpose with focus on its mission or duty, cp 1 Kings 4: 7
2. A 'day' suggests a specific occasion or era with focus on [with regards to] its effect, for example the 'Day of the Lord; cp Psalm 2: 7, 50: 15, Matthew 24: 50
3. An Hour, a specific incident or occasion Matthew 24: 42-44, 27: 45
4. A 'time' signifies a specifically appointed time with a focus on [with regards to] an event and its significance, Daniel 3: 5
5. Weeks – Seven days from Sabbath to Sabbath – A period of completeness – Jeremiah 5: 24
6. Year – A repetition; a cycle of Time Hebrews 9: 25, 10: 1
7. Season - A Fixed Time or appointed period, an occasion Psalm 1: 3
8. Age – an epoch, maturity, a lifetime – Hebrews 5: 14

Scenic Features - Emphasise Character of Environment

1. Trees – Fruitfulness and shelter Job 40: 21-22, Ecclesiastes 2: 5
2. Green grass – Flourishing, life giving, health and succour Psalm 23: 2, 72: 16 and Psalm 92: 7
3. Sea – Great expanse Job 11: 9, trouble Psalm 89: 9, or threat Psalm 65: 7)
4. Mountains – Position of security and confidence or authority, Psalm 125: 2, obstacle Isaiah 40: 4

Human Features - Emphasise Quality of Life

1. Blood – The life, Leviticus 17: 11 hence shed blood, death Psalm 30: 9
2. Voices – Giving witness to or asserting, Luke 23: 23, Acts 13: 27
3. 13 tribes – Typical of the Life we can possess in Christ. In Deuteronomy 32 less Simeon, Revelation less Dan and Ephraim, but including Manasseh
4. Face of a Man –, Mindful expression, human qualities or approval Job 41: 14 Psalm 5: 8, cp Daniel 5: 9

Animal Features - Emphasise Character of Natural Spirit

1. Lion – Bold and aggressive, Proverbs 28: 1+15
2. Calf– innocence, Isaiah 11: 6; gaiety, spontaneity Psalm 29: 6, 68: 30
3. Flying Eagle – Facility, exhilaration Isaiah 40: 31 mystery Proverbs 30: 19, expeditious, proud Jeremiah 49: 16
4. Horse – Military might, a spirit of assertion or belligerence, Proverbs 21: 31
5. A wing – usually a provision of protection as a chicken protects her chicks, Psalm 91: 4. It can also be a covering of modesty or of flight, depending on the context, Isaiah 6: 2.

Mineral Features - Emphasise Consequence

1. Gold – What is inherently valuable, everlasting and will not tarnish, divine features in mankind where relevant, Job 23: 10
2. Pure Gold - What is of God Himself where relevant, 1 Kings 6: 21
3. Silver –Value or preciousness Job 28: 15
4. Brass or copper - Strength, Job 41: 27 Judges 16: 21
5. Iron – what is hard, inflexible and dogmatic

Aesthetic Features - Emphasise Experiential and Personal Qualities

1. White – Unadulterated, unqualified, pure, Isaiah 1: 18 Daniel 11: 35, Lamentations 4: 7
2. Red – full of life Canticles 5: 10, anger or fieriness Isaiah 63: 2
3. Black – Burned Canticles 1: 6, consumed Job 30: 30, darkness Revelation 6: 12
4. Pale [green] – fear Jeremiah 30: 6, humiliation Isaiah 29: 22
5. Rainbow – Faithfulness, the sign of covenant, Genesis 9: 13

Effectual Features - Emphasise Attributed Qualities

1. Bow- Strength; Psalm 7: 12, Readiness Habakkuk 3: 9
   Might; Jeremiah 49: 35, Power; Jeremiah 51: 56, Threat; Lamentations 2: 4
2. Throne – Judgement and administration, Psalm 9: 4, Hebrews 4: 16
3. Crown – Bestowed identity, reward, excellence, achievement, satisfaction Psalm 21: 3, Revelation 2: 10
4. Elder – Leaders, experience, maturity 1 Timothy 5: 17
5. Lightening – Arrows of (divine) offensive, conquest, Subjection 2 Samuel 22: 15
6. Thunder – Voice of divine censure, 1 Samuel 12: 17, Psalm 104: 7

Cosmic Features - Emphasise Environmental and Pesonal Status Quo

1. Earthquake – The disruption of all that is secure and established in daily life Matthew 24: 7
2. Hail – Divine censure and destruction rained down Psalm 78: 47-48
3. Fire – Passion, Canticles 8: 6, Psalm 79: 5, Psalm 89: 46
4. Sun darkened – Understanding, insight and comfort curtailed, Micah 3: 6-7
5. The moon - constancy and hope Psalm 72: 7; therefore when turned to blood it is the death of, that is the end of well-being; despair
6. The heavens depart, rolled up – anarchy, Isaiah 34: 4
7. The stars: minor authority Psalm 136: 9, or guide Jude verses 4+13. Fall from heaven; the downfall of such institutions or individuals
8. Mountains moved – Secure institutions become unstable, 1 Corinthians 13: 2
9. Islands moved –communities disrupted, Psalm 72: 10

Roles Featured in Revelaion Chapter 18

1. Kings - leaders and civil servants
2. Merchants of luxury goods - manufactures and retailers
3. Sailors and captains - those extending the culture around the world
4. Celebration and happy times - of all those that are absorbed by its seductions

Fabricated Articles - Symbolise

1. Door – The way in, opportunity, imminence, John 10: 9
2. Trumpet – The voice of authority calling for attention, Numbers 10: 10

APPENDIX 5

A Comparison of the Themes in The Seven Letters to the Churches In Revelation Chapters 2 and 3

This is the words of scripture only, but analysed into its component sections

Spiritual Experience	Christ's authority Presented	Spiritual Status and Progress	Strengths and Weakness	Admonition and Exhortation	Warnings and Encouragement	Reward to Overcomers
Ephesus Ch2: 1-7 The Loveless Church	These things says He who holds the seven stars in His right hand, who walks in the midst of the seven golden lampstands.	I know your works, your labour, your patience, and that you cannot bear those who are evil. And you have tested those who say they are apostles and are not, and have found them liars.	Thou hast borne and hast patience and for my name sake hast laboured and hast not fainted. Against thee; thou hast left thy first love and you have persevered and have patience, and have laboured for My name's sake and have not become weary.	Nevertheless I have this against you, that you have left your first love. Remember therefore from where you have fallen; repent and do the first works, or else I will come to you quickly and remove your lampstand from its place unless you repent.	But this you have, that you hate the deeds of the Nicolaitans, which I also hate.	He who has an ear, let him hear what the Spirit says to the churches. To him who overcomes I will give to eat from the tree of life, which is in the midst of the Paradise of God.
Smyrna Ch2: 8-11 The Persecuted Church	These things says the First and the Last, who was dead, and came to life.	I know your works, tribulation, and poverty (but you are rich)	I know the blasphemy of those who say they are Jews and are not, but are a synagogue of Satan.		Do not fear any of those things which you are about to suffer. Indeed, the devil is about to throw some of you into prison, that you may be tested, and you will have tribulation ten days Be faithful until death, and I will give you the crown of life.	He who has an ear, let him hear what the Spirit says to the churches. He who overcomes shall not be hurt by the second death.
Pergamum Ch2: 12-17 The Compromising Church	These things says He who has the sharp two-edged sword.	I know your works, and where you dwell, where Satan's throne is.	You hold fast to My name, and did not deny My faith even in the days in which Antipas was My faithful martyr, who was killed among you, where Satan dwells.	But I have a few things against you, because you have there those who hold the doctrine of Balaam, who taught Balak to put a stumbling block before the children of Israel, to eat things sacrificed to idols, and to commit sexual immorality. Thus you also have those who hold the doctrine of the Nicolaitans, which thing I hate.	Repent, or else I will come to you quickly and will fight against them with the sword of My mouth.	To him who overcomes I will give some of the hidden manna to eat. And I will give him a white stone, and on the stone a new name written which no one knows except him who receives it.
Thyatira Ch2: 12-17 The Compromising Church	These things says the Son of God, who has eyes like a flame of fire, and His feet like fine brass.	I know your works, love, service, faith, and your patience; and as for your works, the last are more than the first	Nevertheless I have a few things against you, because you allow that woman Jezebel, who calls herself a prophetess, to teach and seduce My servants to commit sexual immorality and eat things sacrificed to idols.	And I gave her time to repent of her sexual immorality, and she did not repent. Indeed I will cast her into a sickbed, and those who commit adultery with her into great tribulation, unless they repent of their deeds. I will kill her children with death, and all the churches shall know that I am He who searches the minds and hearts. And I will give to each one of you according to your works.	Now to you I say, and to the rest in Thyatira, as many as do not have this doctrine, who have not known the depths of Satan, as they say, I will put on you no other burden. But hold fast what you have till I come.	And he who overcomes, and keeps My works until the end, to him I will give power over the nations— He shall rule them with a rod of iron; They shall be dashed to pieces like the potter's vessels—as I also have received from My Father; and I will give him the morning star.
Sardis Ch3: 1-6 The Dead Church	These things says He who has the seven Spirits of God and the seven stars.	I know your works, that you have a name that you are alive, but you are dead.	Be watchful, and strengthen the things which remain, that are ready to die, for I have not found your works perfect before God.	Remember therefore how you have received and heard; hold fast and repent. Therefore if you will not watch, I will come upon you as a thief, and you will not know what hour I will come upon you.	You have a few names even in Sardis who have not defiled their garments; and they shall walk with Me in white, for they are worthy.	He who overcomes shall be clothed in white garments, and I will not blot out his name from the Book of Life; but I will confess his name before My Father and before His angels.
Philadelphia Ch3: 7-13 **The Faithful Church**	These things says He who is holy, He who is true, "He who has the key of David, He who opens and no one shuts, and shuts and no one opens.	I know your works. See, I have set before you an open door, and no one can shut it.	For you have a little strength, have kept My word, and have not denied My name.	Indeed I will make those of the synagogue of Satan, who say they are Jews and are not, but lie—indeed I will make them come and worship before your feet, and to know that I have loved you.	Because you have kept My command to persevere, I also will keep you from the hour of trial which shall come upon the whole world, to test those who dwell on the earth. 11 Behold, I am coming quickly! Hold fast what you have, that no one may take your crown.	He who overcomes, I will make him a pillar in the temple of My God, and he shall go out no more. I will write on him the name of My God and the name of the city of My God, the New Jerusalem, which comes down out of heaven from My God. And I will write on him My new name.
Laodicea Ch3: 7-13 **The Lukewarm Church**	These things says the Amen, the Faithful and True Witness, the Beginning of the creation of God:	I know your works, that you are neither cold nor hot. I could wish you were cold or hot. So then, because you are lukewarm, and neither cold nor hot, I will vomit you out of My mouth.	Because you say, 'I am rich, have become wealthy, and have need of nothing'—and do not know that you are wretched, miserable, poor, blind, and naked.	I counsel you to buy from Me gold refined in the fire, that you may be rich; and white garments, that you may be clothed, that the shame of your nakedness may not be revealed; and anoint your eyes with eye salve, that you may see.	As many as I love, I rebuke and chasten. Therefore be zealous and repent. Behold, I stand at the door and knock. If anyone hears My voice and opens the door, I will come in to him and dine with him, and he with Me.	To him who overcomes I will grant to sit with Me on My throne, as I also overcame and sat down with My Father on His throne.

APPENDIX 6

The Seals, Trumpets and Bowls of Wrath Compared.
The Scroll - Christ's Authority, Delegated by God, to Reign on Earth.
The Lamb Opening the Seals - Exposes That which Prevents Christ's Reign on Earth

	Seals of the Scrolls Social Events The effect of Man's evil and independence from God which seal the scroll and 'prevent' the reign of Christ until they are revealed for what they are.	Trumpets of the 7th Seal and Censor Spiritual Effects The divine warnings that follow – The break-up of the collective and the individual quality of life	The Bowls of Wrath God moves in Judgement The Break-up of all resistance to Christ's reign as life becomes too painful, foul and hopeless
1	The White Horse – bow and crown - Man's Conquering and dominating nature	Hail, fire and blood cast to earth– 1/3 trees and all green grass burnt up	Sores on those with the mark of the Beast
2	The Red Horse – taking peace from the Earth and making war - Man's assertive nature and propensity to make war	Mountain, as it were, (as having the character of) on fire, cast into the sea 1/3 became blood, 1/3 creatures died, 1/3 ships destroyed	Sea becomes as a dead man's blood- all creatures die
3	The Black Horse – the balances - Famine that follows, Man's vulnerability to his own exploitive predisposition	Great star, as a lamp, falls on rivers and fountains, 1/3 became wormwood – many die	All the rivers and fountains became as blood- 'men are given blood to drink for shedding the blood of saints etc'.
4	The Pale Horse – Death and Hades. 1/4 of earth killed with sword, hunger, death (disease?) and beasts	Sun and 1/3 of the moon and stars smitten, 1/3 of day and night curtailed.	The Sun scorches with great heat – Still no repentance
5	The Martyrs: For testimony to the Word; Their blood calling for judgement and justice, (white robes given: their numbers are incomplete as yet)	The star descends, opens the Pit – smoke and locusts emanate giving a scorpion sting for 5 months on those without God's seal. Apolyon and his figurative army. Men seek death in vain	The seat – residence - of the beast is in darkness, men gnaw their tongues in pain and blaspheme- Still no repentance
6	Anarchy – social chaos and fear. Earthquake, sun blackened, moon turned to blood, stars fall, heaven rolled away, mountains and islands moved. Kings, great, rich, captains, mighty, bond and free hid in caves etc.; being aware of but not recognizing the lamb.	Figurative army of 200 thousand released from Euphrates to kill 1/3 of mankind by fire smoke and brimstone for hour, day, month and year– still no repentance of idol and devil worship	The river Euphrates is dried up to prepare for the Kings of the East – gathered by 3 unclean spirits from the dragon, beast and false prophet to Armageddon
7	Silence in Heaven and trumpets get ready, the incense with prayers of the saints. Censor cast to earth, voices thunder lightening, earthquake	Christ is announced as King of Kings - by an angel in midst of heaven -	Voices from the Temple, the Throne – thunder, massive earthquake, Jerusalem divided in 3, cities fall, Babylon's cup of wrath, islands and mountains disappear, great hail

APPENDIX 7

Summary of the Historical Significance of the Seven Heads of the 'Beast' to Israel

Period of Adversity	Daniel's Image	The 'Head', mind or dominion	The 'Kings' in power	Dates	The 'Hill' or Period of Adversity	The 'Hill' or Anguish Suffered
1st	Head	Babylon	Nebuchadnezzar to Belchazzar	606 - 536 BC	Captivity	Subjection to alien control
2nd	Chest	Persia	Cyrus 1	536 - 486 BC	Rebuilding temple	Worldly interference in rebuilding the Temple
		Medes	Artaxerxes	486 - 332 BC	Rebuilding the city	Frustration with rebuilding of the City
3rd	Thighs	Greece	Alexander to Antiochus 3	323 - 175 BC	4 smaller horns	North/South Conflict – Insecurity?
4th		Little horn	Antiochus 4th Epiphanies	175 - 164 BC	Persecution	Affliction and misery
5th	Legs	Rome	Pompey to Tiberius	63 BC- 70 AD	Cruelty – threat of extinction	Menace, fear of annihilation
6th		The whole nation now scattered	Islamic control of the Land	7th C. - 1948 AD	Dispersion of the Jews	Disorientation: loss of identity Anti-Semitism
7th with the 8th	Feet	An oligarchy of 10 kings co-rules with the Prince that shall Come' - the 'Beast'	The 'King' for a 'Short Space'	Future	The 'Covenant with death;	Disillusionment
			The 'Beast' -still future		Tribulation	Terror and conflict

See 'Seven Hills and Seven Kingdoms' part 9 of section 4
For an explanation of the significance of these times of adversity
And the deeper spiritual significance to ourselves

APPENDIX 8

General Index of Bible References

This does not include references to the verses within the chapters being discussed but only those cross references with the rest of scripture

Introductions

1. A Disconnected World
2. A Kaleidoscope of Images
3. Why was the Revelation Written?
4. Tis Jesus the First and the Last
5. The Testimony of Jesus is the Spirit of Prophecy

Section One:

God is Working His Purpose Out

Preface to Section One

Romans 14: 17
Matthew 21: 28
Matthew 23: 39
Revelation 1 – 3 Revelation 8,
Revelation 12
Revelation 19
Romans 12:2
Matthew 25

The Right Character
Psalm 118:22
Part
Preface to Section One
Romans 14: 17
Matthew 21: 28
Matthew 23: 39
Revelation 1 – 3 Revelation 8,
Revelation 12
Revelation 19
Romans 12:2
Matthew 25

1. The Right Character

Psalm 118:22
Philippians 2: 5-11
Matthew 28:18
2 Corinthians 2:15
Ephesians 5:2
Acts 4:11
1 Peter 2:7
Ephesians 2: 19-22
Psalm 81:9-12
Revelation 19: 7-8
Luke 15:22
Matthew 24
Psalm 23
Hosea 2: 19-20

2. The Right Pedigree
Daniel 12:31
Corinthians 15:41
Psalm 104:1-4
Hebrews 1:14
2 Corinthians 11:14
2 Corinthians 12:7
Revelation 22:9
Luke 17: 21
Isaiah 49:3
Revelation 21-22
Revelation chapter 12: 11

3. A Calling to Account
Luke 8: 16
Luke 11: 33
Matthew 6: 20-23
Hebrews 4: 12
2 Peter 2: 10-15
Numbers 22-24
1 Kings 18-21
2 Kings 9
Isaiah 11: 2-3
2 Peter 1: 19
Matthew 24: 42-48
Romans 8: 8-9
1 Corinthians 3: 12-15
2 Timothy 4:7
John 16: 8

4. A Deafening Silence
Matthew 25: 13
Matthew 26: 40
Acts 19: 8 +10
Revelation 14: 7
Luke chapter 15
Genesis 1:28
Romans 8: 29
John 14: 13
John 14: 13
John 15: 16
Philippians 2: 5

1Peter 2: 5-9
Philippians 2:8
Exodus 30: 1+3
Hebrews 1:14
Isaiah 6: 1-4
Matthew 4:11
Hebrews 2:10-17
Numbers 16:39
Leviticus 10:1-2
Acts 2:3-4
Numbers 16:18 –38
Revelation 3: 10
Revelation 7: 9+14
Leviticus 4
Revelation 11

5. A Spectacular Phenomenon
Psalm 89: 37
Job31: 26
Psalm 72: 7
Genesis 37: 9
Psalm 2
Genesis 26: 4
Galatians 3: 16
Micah 4: 6-8
Jeremiah 32: 36-41
Romans 11: 23
Amos 9: 9
Micah 5: 2-3
Romans 11: 26-27
Micah 5: 3
Joel 3:1
Jeremiah 30-33
Genesis 15: 5,
Genesis 22: 17,
Genesis 26: 4,
Exodus 32: 13
Genesis 1: 16
Genesis 22: 18
Genesis 37: 9
Luke 10: 18
Isaiah 14: 12-15

APPENDICES

Ezekiel 28: 12-15
Hebrews 2: 14-15
Romans 11
Luke 21: 24
Ephesians 3: 9
Colossians 1: 24 + 26
Ephesians 3: 91
John 5: 4-51
Thessalonians 1: 10
Hebrews 2: 14
Isaiah 28: 14-18
Daniel 9: 27
Daniel 7: 25
Jeremiah 30: 7
Daniel 12: 11
Corinthians 10:13
Joel 2: 28-29
Galatians 3: 7
1 John 5: 4-5

6. The Imminent Marriage
Matthew 22
Ephesians 1: 4
Luke 17: 21
Ephesians 5: 22-32
Isaiah 62: 5
Matthew 9: 15
John 3: 29, 2
Corinthians 11: 2
Colossians 1: 18
Philippians 2: 12-13,
Matthew 25
Revelation 6: 10

7. The Perfect Marriage
1 Corinthians 11
1 Timothy 2,
Colossians 2,
Ephesians 5
Ephesians 5: 28
1 Peter 3: 4+6
Corinthians 14.
Romans 12: 2
Ephesians 5: 27
Philippians 3: 14
2 Timothy 2: 15
Matthew 5: 48
Galatians 5: 22
1 Peter 3: 1
Matthew 5: 16
Proverbs 3: 5-6
Philippians 2: 5-8
Matthew 12: 43-45
Matthew 11: 291
Corinthians 13: 4-8
Revelation 3: 16
Genesis 2
Romans 8

Section Two:
The Spiritually Significant Setting in Achieving This

Preface to Section Two
Genesis 6: 3
Matthew 24: 1-14
Revelation 4,
Revelation 9-11
Revelation 13
Revelation 19
Matthew
21-23
Revelation1-3

1. The Age of Duplicity and Doubt
Deuteronomy 7: 8
Genesis 22: 16
Jeremiah 31: 3 + 10
Psalm 77: 8.
2 Chronicles 36: 21
Romans 11: 25
John 16: 33

2. The Four Living Creatures within the Throne
Revelation 12
Revelation 9
Revelation 5
Revelation 14
Revelation 7
Revelation 6
Revelation 15
Habakkuk 2: 14
Genesis 9
Ezekiel 1

3. The Supremacy of the Lamb
Revelation 1
Revelation 2
Revelation 3
Revelation 5:6
Revelation 5: 9-10
1 Chronicles 24
Genesis, 3: 21
Exodus chapter 12: 2
Luke 22: 151
Corinthians 5: 7
Ephesians 1: 3
Romans 8: 19
Job 19: 23
Isaiah 30: 8
Revelation 4: 6
Matthew 9: 20
Revelation 4: 8
Mark 7: 21
Revelation 11: 15
1 Corinthians 1: 18
Matthew 28: 18
Revelation 4: 5.
Revelation 5: 6
Isaiah 11:2
Revelation 3: 21
Zechariah 12: 10
Galatians 5: 22
Romans 8: 4
Romans 1: 4
John 14: 16
Romans 8: 15
1 Peter 4: 14
Revelation 19: 10
John 16: 13
Isaiah 5: 30,

APPENDICES

2 Corinthians 11: 26,
James 1: 6,
Jude 13
Psalm 24: 1-2
Job 28: 17
Revelation 21: 11,
Revelation 22: 1
Revelation 4: 6
Revelation15: 2
Revelation 15: 2
2 Chronicles 4: 1-5

4. A Fanfare of Trumpets
Revelation 16,
Revelation 13
Revelation 7
Revelation 13
Revelation 8: 3
Revelation 19: 19
Revelation 16
Matthew 6: 19-20
Ephesians 2: 2
Lamentations 3: 6
Proverbs10: 26
Jeremiah 48: 9
Matthew 7: 13
Romans 12: 2
Luke 21: 26
Exodus 30:1
Genesis 15: 18
Daniel 7: 10
Revelation 16: 16
Isaiah 9: 14-16
Matthew 5: 21-22
Matthew27-28
Mark 12: 30-31

5. The Majesty of God and His Mission
Revelation 11
Revelation 2:6
Revelation 5

Revelation 1
Revelation 9
1 Corinthians 2: 16
Romans 8; 6
Hebrews 1:14
Genesis 2: 21
Samuel 12: 17
Samuel 12: 20
2 Corinthians 12: 4,
Daniel 8: 26,
Daniel 12: 4-9,
Mark 13: 32
Matthew 24: 44
2 Corinthians 12: 4
Psalm 119: 97

6. The Sinister Beast
Samuel 12:
Daniel. 1
Daniel 12: 1
Matthew 24: 15
Ezekiel 6: 8
Genesis 3: 15
Isaiah 13
Ecclesiastes 1: 92
2 John 7
1 John 2: 18
1 John 4: 3

7. '666'
Revelation 16
Revelation 19
Revelation 13: 11 – 17,
Revelation16: 14
Revelation 19: 20
Revelation 7: 3-4.
Revelation 11: 3
Revelation 14: 9-11
Revelation 15
Psalm 111: 10
2 Thessalonians 2: 4
Matthew 24

Daniel 7:25
1 Kings 10: 14
2 Chronicles 9: 13
Exodus 29: 9,
Job 5: 19,
Proverbs 6: 16
Isaiah 6:2
Ezekiel 41: 1-8
Luke 17: 26
Revelation 16: 14
Revelation 19: 20
John 3: 12;
James 3: 15
2 Corinthians 4:7
Daniel 8: 20
Matthew 24
Daniel 9: 27
Matthew 7: 15
Matthew 24: 11
Mark 13: 22
Matthew 24: 11
1 John 2: 181
 John 2: 22

1 John 4: 3
2 John 7
Deuteronomy 18: 15-19
Psalm 110:4
2 Samuel 7: 12-13.
1 John 2: 18
Psalm 2: 6

8. The Return of the King

Hebrews 13: 8
Ephesians 5: 27
Revelation 1: 14
Revelation 2: 18
Hebrews 4: 12
Matthew 11: 27
Nahum 1: 7
John 10: 14,
Revelation 2: 17
John 1: 1
Philippians 2: 6-9
Hebrews 4: 12
Genesis 40:17 –19
John 16: 8

APPENDICES

Section Three:
God's Scheme in the implementation of His Purposes

Preface to Section Three
Acts 14: 22
Matthew 24: 1-14
Revelation 6
Revelation 11
Revelation 15-16
Revelation 20
Matthew 21-23
Daniel 12: 1
Revelation 12
Revelation 13
1 Corinthians 15: 25

1. The End of an Era
John 14: 26.
Romans 11
John 15: 15
John 14: 22
John 17: 20
Acts 1:6-7
Luke 21: 20-24
Daniel 9: 27
Romans 11: 25
Zechariah 9: 9-10
2 Thessalonians 2: 4
Zechariah 14: 1-9
Matthew 25
Luke 4:18
Isaiah 61: 1-2
Luke 17: 21
Romans 14: 17
Philippians 2: 12-13

2. Where are We all Going?
Matthew 28: 18
Revelation 11: 15
Revelation 4
Revelation 5
Revelation 8
Revelation 9
Revelation 12: 14
1 Corinthians 11: 31
Zechariah 6: 1-8
Job 39: 19-25
Psalm 33: 17
James 3: 3
Genesis 1: 28
1Kings 18: 45
Hebrews 12: 18
Job 3: 5
Job 6: 16,
Isaiah 29: 22,
Psalm 31: 17
1 John 4: 7
Matthew 5: 13
Galatians 5: 22
Romans 8: 7
Romans 7: 23
Revelation. 19: 8
Matthew 24
Joel 2: 10
Joel 2: 31,
Joel 3: 15
Matthew 24: 21
Matthew 24: 29
Isaiah 29: 6
Psalm 72: 5
Acts 7: 49

3. The Irresistible Presence

1 Kings 8:13
2 Corinthians 6:16
Hebrews 13:13-15
John 4:23
Matthew 15:8-9.
Ezekiel 40 – 47
Acts 21: 28-29
Luke 21
Revelation 12: 14
1 Kings 4: 7
Daniel 7: 25
Daniel 9: 27
Hebrews 3
Hebrews 4
Matthew 24
Exodus 7
1 Kings 17:11 Kings 16: 29-34
Jeremiah 23:29
Revelation. 12:6
Deuteronomy 14: 2
Galatians 3: 7
Romans 8:28
Matthew 18:16
Luke 12:47
Psalm 119:105
2 Peter 1:19

4. Broken Promises

Daniel 9
Revelation 12: 14
Revelation 13: 7
Isaiah 28: 14 –15
Jeremiah 25: 11
Jeremiah 29: 10
Daniel 9: 27
Daniel 7: 25
Daniel 12: 1
Daniel 12: 7
Revelation 12: 14
Revelation13: 7
Isaiah 28: 16-18

5. Mankind's Last Chance

Revelation 11: 19
Revelation 12: 14
Revelation 12
Revelation 19: 15
Revelation 13
Revelation 7: 9
Revelation 14
Revelation 7: 10
Revelation 14-17
Revelation 15: 3-4
Revelation 13: 7
Revelation 2
Revelation 3
Revelation 21: 7
Revelation <u>12: 11</u>
Revelation 13: 17
Revelation 11: 1
Deuteronomy 30: 16
Hebrews 8: 10.
Revelation 13: 5
1 John 2: 18
Ephesians 2: 2
Ezekiel 1: 24,
Ezekiel 3: 13
Ezekiel 10: 5
Job 37: 2+42
Samuel 22: 15
Acts 1: 8
Matthew 22: 11
Revelation. 1:13
Isaiah 6: 4
Psalm 68: 2
Psalm 102: 3
Revelation 8: 8
1 John 2: 17
Isaiah 28: 17
Galatians 6: 7-8
Genesis 15:18
Revelation 9: 13
Psalm 78: 45

APPENDICES

6. The Die is Cast
Revelation 20
Daniel 7
Revelation 12.
Revelation 5.
Revelation 12.
Revelation 4.
Revelation 6: 9.
Revelation 2: 11
Ezekiel 38

Genesis 10
Matthew 25
Revelation 20
1 Corinthians 15
Romans 8: 20
Psalm 2: 9
Romans 8: 38-39.
Hebrews 11: 10
Matthew 25

Section Four:
The Consummation of All History

Preface to Section Four
Habakkuk. 2: 14
Matthew 25
Revelation
Revelation 7
Revelation 11
Revelation 17-18
Revelation 21-22
Matthew 24
Revelation 7
Revelation 11
1 Corinthians 15: 24-26
Revelation 20
Hebrews 11: 10

1. Parables of the Kingdom
Matthew 22
Matthew 24
Matthew 5
Ephesians 6
2 Thessalonians 1: 10
Genesis 28: 18
Matthew 5: 14+16
Acts 1: 8
Galatians 5: 22
John 15: 5
Matthew 22: 14
Luke 19
Romans 8: 17
James 2: 5
Luke 17: 21
1 Corinthians 4: 20
Romans 14: 17
Ephesians. 4: 13
Luke 19
Philippians 2: 12-13
Matthew 12: 50

2. The Kingdom of God within Us
Revelation 6
Revelation 8
Romans 9
Matthew 25
Revelation 9: 4
Ezekiel 9: 4-6
Revelation 14: 1
Psalm 50: 10
Revelation 17: 8
Revelation 14
John 1: 47
Revelation 17
Revelation 14: 4
Genesis 12: 3
Galatians 3: 16
John 4: 14
Philippians. 2: 12-13
Revelation 4
Revelation 5: 9
Acts 14: 22
Revelation 7
Ephesians 1: 3

3. The Heavenly Life Within Us
Hebrews 8: 4–5
Matthew 25
Galatians 5: 16
1 Corinthians 5: 7
1 Corinthians 10: 2
Exodus 25: 8
Heb. 11: 30
Ephesians 1
John 15
Ruth 4: 11

APPENDICES

Genesis 29
Matthew 11: 28
Matthew chapter 5
Song of Songs 5: 13
Revelation 7: 5-8
Genesis 30
Genesis. 41: 51
Genesis 30: 6

4. Christ in us the Hope of Glory

Colossians 1: 27
Ephesians 4: 1
Philippians 2: 13
Corinthians 9: 27
Ephesians 6: 12
Romans 8: 37
Ephesians 1: 11
Ephesians 1: 22
Philippians 3: 13.

5. If anyone is in Christ He is a new Creation

Philippians; 2: 13
Ephesians 1: 17
John 3: 3
Ephesians 4: 13
Galatians 5: 22
Galatians 5: 23
1 Peter 2: 9
Philippians 2: 9
Philippians 2: 11
2 Peter 1: 11
Luke 17: 21
Luke 12: 32
John 6: 29
Jeremiah 31: 33:

6. Spiritual maturity

John 15: 4
Colossians 1: 27
2 Corinthians 5: 17
Galatians 2: 20
John 15: 5
John 15
Song of Songs 3: 1-3
Ephesians 2: 6
Philippians 2: 5-8
2 Corinthians 5: 17
Genesis 30
Philippians 2: 12-13
Philippians 2
Romans 12: 11
Corinthians 9: 27
Roman's 12: 1-22
Timothy 2: 21
John 6: 38

7. The Kingdoms of our Lord

Matthew 25
Revelation 22
Ephesians 1
Luke 17: 21
Revelation 10: 7
Matthew 5-7
1 Corinthians 15: 25
Revelation 2 and 3
2 Peter 3: 9
Psalm 2
James 1
 Revelation 20: 12
Revelation 22
1 Corinthians 15: 25
Genesis 1:28
Revelation 4: 5,
Revelation 8: 5
Revelation 16: 18
Matthew 13: 11

8. Spiritual Adultery

Revelation 2
Revelation 3
Revelation 3: 1
Jeremiah 3:9
Ezekiel 16: 31-32

Ephesians 5: 5
Colossians 3: 5
Exodus 20: 17
Luke 12: 15
Psalm 10: 3
Matthew 6: 19-20
Daniel 2
Revelation 18
Jeremiah 51
Revelation 18:41
John 2: 15
Isaiah 10: 10-11
Isaiah 19: 1-22
Corinthians 11: 2
Revelation 18: 41
Corinthians 2: 14
2 Timothy 2: 15
2 Timothy 3: 16-17
Luke 6: 41-42
Revelaltion16: 19
Revelation 17: 42
Revelation 19
Thessalonians 2: 7
Matthew 23: 35
Luke 11: 51
Hebrews 11: 4
Genesis 4: 5-8
Deuteronomy 32: 42
Psalm 23: 5
Matthew 26: 39
Jeremiah 51: 7
Jeremiah 51: 13
Nahum 3: 4-7
1 John 2: 16
1 John 2: 21
1 John 2: 21] 1 John 2:.24
1 John 2: 3: 1
Matthew 5
James 1: 27

9. Seven Hills and Seven Kingdom

Romans 11: 25
Daniel 3
Daniel 11
Daniel 8
Daniel nine
Revelation 13
Daniel 2
Amos 9: 11
Deuteronomy 28: 15-68,
Deuteronomy 28: 36
Deuteronomy 28: 63
Ezekiel 12: 15
Jeremiah 25: 11,
Daniel 9: 2
Ezra 9: 2
Ezra 4: 4
Nehemiah 4: 8
Daniel 11: 21
Daniel 7: 22
Daniel 7: 26,
Daniel 8: 25
Daniel 11: 36-45
Matthew 24
Psalm 111: 10
Matthew 5: 14
Psalm 2: 6
Daniel 2: 35
John 4: 20
Psalm 76: 4
Luke 3: 5
1 Corinthians 13: 2

10. Seven Hills: A Spiritual Allegory

John 11
Romans 10
Romans 11.
Daniel 9: 27
Hosea 14: 5-6
John 16: 33
Daniel 12: 10
Revelation 3
Philippians 3: 19-21
Philippians 2: 12-13
Ephesians 2: 22.
Daniel 9
John 15: 18-19
1 Corinthians 3: 11-17
Romans 8:35-39
1 Corinthians 10: 13
Luke 21: 12-18
Daniel 3
Daniel 2: 40
Luke 3: 1
Luke 6: 29
Matthew 5: 41
Matthew 5: 41
Matthew 5: 44
Daniel 9: 26
Zechariah 9: 9
Daniel 9: 26
Matthew 23: 38
Matthew 23: 39
Matthew 21: 9
Matthew 23
Matthew 24: 30
Romans 11: 11
John 15
Amos 9: 8-9
Revelation 7
Revelation 14
Daniel 2.
Daniel 7: 24
Revelation 14: 7
Revelation 18.
Daniel 7: 7
Isaiah 28: 15
Isaiah 18

11. The New Heaven and Earth

Romans 8: 20
John 4: 14
Revelation 12: 11
Revelation 2
Revelation 31
John 5: 10
2 Corinthians 11: 2
Matthew 22
Matthew 25
1 Corinthians 2: 14
Revelation 4
Ephesians 1
1 John 3: 2
Ephesians 4: 13-16.
Revelation 7
Psalm 102: 19
Ephesians 3: 18
Revelation 4: 3
John 8: 12

12. The Foundations of the Holy City

Revelation 4: 3
Ephesians 5: 27
Proverbs 10: 25
Psalm 87: 1
Isaiah 28: 16
1 Corinthians 3: 11
Ephesians 2: 20
1 Corinthians 1: 30
Matthew. 16: 18
Matthew. 13: 46
Hebrews 11
2 Timothy 1: 9
Hebrews 3: 1

Ephesians 1: 5
Romans 8: 29
1 Corinthians 1: 30.
 Romans 1: 7
1 Corinthians 1: 2
1 Peter 1: 16
Philippians 2: 5
Romans 8: 5-6
1 Corinthians 2: 16
Ezekiel. 1: 26
Ezekiel 10: 1
Exodus. 24: 10.
Romans 8: 6
1 Peter 2: 9
Numbers 4
Colossians 3: 12-15
1 Peter 2: 21-24
Revelation 19: 14
Matthew 5: 6
Ephesians1: 3-4
Galatians 5: 22-23
1 Corinthians 4: 2
Revelation 17: 14
1 Corinthians 4: 2
Revelation 14
Romans 11: 29
Song 5: 14
Ezekiel 1:16
Ezekiel 10: 9
Daniel 10: 6
Exodus 28: 17
Job chapter 28: 19
Amos 9: 7-8
Psalm 111: 10
Proverbs 1: 7
1 Corinthians 2: 13
1 Corinthians 3: 19
Proverbs 3: 6

Ephesians 3: 10-11
Colossians 3: 15
2 Thessalonians 1: 11-12
John 4: 14
1 Thessalonians 4: 3
1 Peter 1: 2
Romans 12: 1
Ephesians 5: 2
Revelation 9: 17
Daniel 12: 3
2 Timothy 2: 12
Revelation 5: 10

13. Paradise Restored
In Genesis 3: 24
Revelation 2: 7
John 10: 28
Revelation 2: 17
Revelation 7
Ezekiel 40 -43,
Ezekiel 43: 6-7
Luke 12: 42
Ezekiel 47: 1-12
Job 40: 21-22
Ecclesiastes 2: 5
Luke 2: 37
Revelation 3: 12
Revelation 1: 1
Hebrews 10: 36-37
Romans 11: 25
Luke 21: 24
2 Thessalonians 2: 3
John 14: 15-21
Romans 8: 20
Revelation 5: 5
Revelation 12
Revelation 2: 28

Epilogue

1. The Day of the Lord

Proverbs 2: 8
Joel 2: 1-2,
Jeremiah. 30: 7
Daniel. 12: 1
2 Peter 3: 10-13.
Matthew 24
Zechariah 14: 41
Thessalonians 4: 17
Matthew 24 vv27-30
John 14: 1-31
Thessalonians 5: 31
Thessalonians 4: 18
Romans 1: 18
Romans 2: 5.
Romans 5: 9
Revelation 3: 10

John 14: 1-3
Luke 17: 26
1 Thessalonians 5: 3
Revelation 3
Matthew 24: 44-51
2 Thessalonians 2
Revelation 13 and 17.
John 14: 22
Thessalonians 2: 3
Matthew 24: 15
1 Thessalonians 4: 6
2 Thessalonians 2: 3
Isaiah 28: 14-17
Daniel 9: 26
2 Thessalonians 2: 10-15

2. The Purpose of History

Acts 1: 7
Daniel 9: 1-2
Daniel 9: 24-27
Luke 2: 25-38
Jeremiah 25: 11
Jeremiah 25: 11
Jeremiah 29: 10
2 Chronicles 36: 21
Leviticus 25: 4
Judges 9: 56
Isaiah 23: 15-17
Jeremiah 25: 11-12
Zechariah 7: 5
Luke 10: 1
Luke 10: 17

Genesis 4: 15
Psalm 12: 6
Proverbs 6: 31
Isaiah 30: 26
Matthew 18: 21
Luke 17: 4
Leviticus 25: 8
Matthew 18: 22
Galatians 4: 26
Hebrews 11: 10
Acts 1: 7
Luke 21: 27
Daniel 9
Matthew 24
Isaiah 28

3. Moral Responsibility

Genesis 1: 26
Revelation 13: 8
Isaiah 30: 21

Roman's 12: 2
Romans 8: 19-23

APPENDIX 9

General Index of themes

This does not include the themes expressed in each text, but those that are ancillary to each.

The themes contained in the scriptures themselves are summarised in the appendix 1, particularly 'The Recurrent and Consecutive Themes'

Introductions

1. A Disconnected World
The natural spirit
Universal peace
Darwin and philosophy
Superstition
Rational thinking
Pontifex Maximus
Humanism and relativism
The Kingdom of Heaven

2. Why was the Revelation Written?
Who the 'revelation' is addressed to
Who are the elders?
The Nature of Priesthood
Six hundred, sixty and six.
The Promised Blessings
The many lessons

3. Tis Jesus the First and the Last
What this Book is about
Symbolic meaning
What the world is

4. The Testimony of Jesus is the Spirit of Prophecy
What prophecy is

Section One:
God is Working His Purpose Out

Preface to Section One

1. **The Right Character**
   Roman tyranny
   Jewish Elitism
   Israel Rejected
   The New Jerusalem

2. **The Right Pedigree**
   Man has exploited not governed creation.
   Jewish Elitism
   Angel messengers
   Failings of the churches,

3. **A Calling to Account**
   Promised rewards
   The error of Balaam
   Idolatry and adultery

4. **A Deafening Silence**
   The breaking of the 7 seals
   The priesthood of the Aaronic order
   Gethsemane
   The disobedience of Nadab and Abihu

5. **A Spectacular Phenomenon**
   Israel blessed
   Israel captive
   Israel dispersed
   Israel restored
   Satan – a red dragon,
   Satan cast out of Heaven
   The time of the Gentiles
   The sabbatical year
   Anti-Semitism

6. **The Imminent Marriage**
   Marriage established by God
   Israel's married to God
   Marriage to Christ
   Marriage an eternal principle
   Marriage a divine principle
   Post-modernist idealism
   Individualism
   Church etiquette
   Marriage a sanctifying influence
   Marriage a witness
   The emancipation of women
   Church constitution

APPENDICES

Section Two:

The spiritually significant Setting in achieving this

Preface to Section Two

1. **The Age of Duplicity and Doubt**
   Israel's rejection of their Messiah
   The Faithfulness of God
   Israel's captivity BC 483
   Israel's dispersion

2. **The Four Living Creatures within the Throne**
   The great multitude
   The elders
   The 144,000
   The bowls of wrath

3. **The Supremacy of the Lamb**
   The sacrifice of Christ
   The elders
   The twenty-four courses of the Aaronic priesthood
   The authority of the Scroll
   Boaz and the redemptive price

4. **A Fanfare of Trumpets**
   A trumpet calls attention
   144000 of Revelation 7
   The 'Beast' from the bottomless pit
   The altar of incense in the tabernacle
   The people that waited on the Ancient of Days
   Armageddon
   The contemporary view of morality

5. **The Majesty of God and His Mission**
   The Lamb as slain
   Sea as a mass of something
   Angels are messengers
   The covenants of God
   The Garden of Eden
   Significance of prophecy
   Prophetic demonstration
   The seven churches

6. **The Sinister Beast**
   Isaiah's foretelling of the fall of Babylon
   Jews in 600BC
   The last days
   Seven heads and seven hills
   The Jews dispersed
   Messiah, the woman's seed
   Anti-Semitism
   Whatever the world promises
   Beguiling philosophy
   Antichrist

7. **'666'**
   The second beast
   Antichrist
   The 144,000
   Armageddon
   Eternal torment

8. **The Return of the King**
   Flesh implies all that is foreign to God's nature
   The lake of fire

Section Three:
God's Scheme in the implementation of His Purposes

Preface to Section Three

1. **The End of an Era**
   The church age
   Israel in Matthew 24
   Daniel chapter 9, the present age
   The Time of the Gentiles
   The Day of The Lord
   Israel's cutting off

2. **Where are We all Going?**
   The warning trumpets
   The bowls of anger
   Fruit of the Spirit
   Day of the Lord
   Exploitation of the vulnerable

3. **The Irresistible Presence**
   The Old Testament temple
   Herod's temple
   Ezekiel temple
   Time, times and half a time
   Sabbatical years
   Moses
   Elijah and Ahab
   Ancient Egypt
   The beast
   Origins of Babylon
   Sodom and Egypt
   World
   Antichrist

4. **Broken Promises**
   Apostasy
   The captivity of Israel 760 BC
   The captivity of Judah 600BC for 70 years
   Time, times and half a time

5. **Mankind's Last Chance**
   The breaking of the seals
   The trumpets
   Those on the sea of glass
   Those repented and gained victory
   The Beast and his name
   The new covenant
   Global warming
   The sacrifice of Christ
   The sixth trumpet
   The weight of a talent
   The new life in Christ

6. **The Die is Cast**
   The resurrection
   Sermon on the Mount
   Babylon
   The world has no inherent purpose
   Democracy
   Death in scripture
   The lake of fire
   The millennium
   God is in Himself Love
   Redeeming
   The age of grace
   Moral responsibility
   Gog and Magog

APPENDICES

Section Four:

The consummation of all History

Preface to Section Four

1. **Parables of the Kingdom**
   A Jewish wedding
   Jacob had a dream
   Temple worship
   Shepherds separating the sheep and the goats
   Christ's natural human family

2. **The Kingdom of God within Us**
   The breaking of the seals
   The 144,000 sealed
   The evil beast and his mark
   The great multitude
   Pilgrim's Progress

3. **The Heavenly Life Within Us**
   The old covenant
   The Holy Spirit
   The Promised Land
   The Passover in Egypt
   The tabernacle
   The crossing of the Jordan
   The Ark of the Covenant
   Spiritual battles
   Jacob or Israel
   Leah and Rachel
   Spiritual inheritance

4. **Christ in us the Hope of Glory**
   Conquering of the land
   Joseph's life of slavery

5. **If anyone is in Christ He is a new Creation**
   Ben-oni, Son of my sorrow
   Spiritual dying
   Baptism

6. **Spiritual maturity**
   Relationships
   Jacob and Laban
   Solomon and the Shulamite
   Reuben and the mandrakes

8. **Spiritual Adultery Babylon**
   The twenty-four elders
   The Day of the Lord
   The Ark of the Covenant

9. **Seven Hills and Seven Kingdom**
   Babylon
   The great prostitute
   Religious art
   Spiritual discernment
   Hypocrisy
   Materialism
   The Beast
   Martyrs
   Nineveh

10. **Seven Hills: A Spiritual Allegory**
    Nebuchadnezzar's dream
    Israel's captivity circa 606 BC
    Alexander the Great
    The four Greek generals
    King Ptolemy
    Antiochus IV, Epiphanies
    The Maccabean uprising
    Caesar Augustus
    Jerusalem razed AD 70
    Israel scattered
    Daniel's beast
    The 2nd beast
    The great prostitute
    1947 the Jewish state

11. Seven Hills: A Spiritual Allegory
Babylonian captivity
The rebuilding of the Temple
The rebuild the city of Jerusalem
Antiochus Epiphanies
Romans cruelty
The Messiah's death
The dissolution of Israel
Israel re-established
The beast
The confederation of ten kingdoms
Worldly promises of security

11. The New Heaven and Earth
Christ as King
Foundation of our faith
Aesthetic beauty
The judgement throne
High Priest's breastplate
200 million horsemen

12. The Foundation of the Holy City

13. Paradise Restored
The Garden of Eden
A personal relationship with our Lord
Ezekiel's future temple
The river flowing from Ezekiel's temple
Night, the time of obscurity and gloom
Christ reigning in our hearts
The fullness of the Gentiles
The falling away

APPENDICES

Epilogue

1. **Parables of the Kingdom**
   Time of Jacob's Trouble
   The return of Christ
   The resurrection of the saints
   The reign of Christ on earth
   The final judgement
   The new Heaven and Earth
   The coming of Jesus Christ for His Church
   The literal interpretation of the scriptures
   Status or manner of life
   The man of sin
   Heaven a spiritual realm
   The great apostasy
   The mystery of lawlessness
   The abomination of desolation
   The beast

2. **Parables of the Kingdom**
   Nebuchadnezzar's dream
   Instinctive and enlightened understanding
   The captivity in Babylon
   The sabbatical year
   The rebuilding of the temple
   The Sabbath: a broad institution
   70 x 7 years: the whole process of salvation
   The desolations of AD 70
   Jesus and Daniel's prophecy
   The falling away or apostasy

3. **Parables of the Kingdom**
   Mankind: a morally intelligent and spiritual being
   The Garden of Eden
   Good and evil
   Paradise lost
   The plan of salvation
   Faith in an environment of adversity
   God's original intention for His creation

Credits

Quotations are from the New Kings James version of the Bible unless otherwise stated.

There is little or no reference to outside sources for the interpretation of this book other than all the other books of the Bible itself. Reference is acknowledged in the text where other sources have been used.

It is suggested that a good concordance, preferably an analytical concordance is used when studying the Book of the Revelation, or any other scripture, and in this study to identify and compare when the characters and images reappear elsewhere in the Book and elsewhere in the scriptures. Also a good concordance helps considerably in understanding the symbolic and spiritual meaning of scripture generally.

www.ingramcontent.com/pod-product-compliance
Lightning Source LLC
Chambersburg PA
CBHW031128160426
43193CB00008B/68